AF522218

FORCES LAW REVIEW

Volume I, 2025

Honorary Chief Editors

Franklin Rosenblatt
Shruti Bedi
Navdeep Singh

Title: Forces Law Review Vol I, 2025
Editor: Franklin Rosenblatt, Shruti Bedi, and Navdeep Singh

ISBN: 978-93-49042-72-8

Published by:
JGS Enterprises Pvt Ltd
Imprint: The Browser

Publisher's Address:
SCO 14-15, FF, Sector 8-C, Chandigarh 160 009

Website: thebrowser.org
Email: service@thebrowser.org

Printed in India

© Layout and Cover Design by 99 beagles
99beagles.com

Publishers & Booksellers | Oral History & Military Publishing

About *Forces Law Review*

Forces Law Review (FLR) is the first-ever international journal on law featuring matters of the Defence Services and other uniformed forces, such as the Police, the Paramilitary, and the Armed Police Forces.

The National Institute of Military Justice (NIMJ), Washington DC, USA, and the Centre for Constitution & Public Policy (CCPP), University Institute of Legal Studies, Panjab University, Chandigarh, India, have joined hands to produce the journal as part of a unique global academic cooperative effort.

This volume contains an opening section of contributed opinion pieces approved by the editors, followed by the summary/gist, headnotes and text of important judgments from all over the world, principally from constitutional/appellate courts with precedential value, and ending with a section on briefs of recent important developments on the subject.

In addition to the editorial oversight undertaken by three nominated Honorary Chief Editors, the Editorial Advisory Board comprising reputed personalities from the fields of law, judiciary, and academia has guided the effort.

The summaries have been prepared by six Student Editors selected from the USA and India.

www.forceslawreview.com | flr@thebrowser.in

Justice Augustine George Masih

Supreme Court of India
Tilak Marg,
New Delhi - 110 001.
Ph.: 2321 0069

March 22, 2025

MESSAGE

I am delighted to extend my best wishes on the launch of the *Forces Law Review* (FLR), a significant initiative dedicated to advancing the study and understanding of military law and law relating to other uniformed forces. By compiling key judgments, legal analyses, and expert opinions, this journal will serve as a valuable resource for legal practitioners, scholars, and policymakers working in this specialized field.

The legal framework governing the armed forces and other uniformed services presents unique challenges that demand careful scrutiny and informed deliberation. By fostering scholarly engagement, *Forces Law Review* will contribute to a deeper understanding of these critical issues and support the evolution of legal thought in this domain.

I commend the Chief Editors and the entire editorial team for their dedication to this initiative and have no doubt that FLR will play a pivotal role in shaping discourse in military law inspiring meaningful legal advancements.

(AUGUSTINE GEORGE MASIH)

Flat No.7A, Tower - A1, Supreme Court Guest House, Deendayal Upadhyaya Marg, New Delhi - 110 001.

Justice Rajendra Menon
(Former Chief Justice, Delhi High Court)
Chairperson

Armed Forces Tribunal
West Block-8, Sector-1,
R.K. Puram, New Delhi-110066
Tel. : 011-26105363
Fax : 011-26105123

04th April, 2025

Message

It is with immense pride that I introduce the inaugural volume of *Forces Law Review*—the first global, collaborative publication dedicated to military law.

The launch of *Forces Law Review* marks a significant milestone in the evolution of military legal scholarship and I am honored to witness this pioneering effort come to life, bridging gaps in military legal thought and practice across jurisdictions.

This inaugural volume seeks to address the pressing legal challenges and opportunities arising from contemporary military operations. From the intersection of technology and warfare to the complexities of international humanitarian law, we face an unprecedented need for legal frameworks that evolve alongside the rapidly changing landscape of military engagement. Through this journal, we aspire to foster a forward-thinking dialogue on the future of military law—ensuring justice, accountability, and compliance in an era of constant transformation.

The collaborative nature of this endeavor is especially noteworthy. By bringing together voices from diverse legal traditions and perspectives, *Forces Law Review* exemplifies the power of global cooperation. It reaffirms that, despite our differences, the rule of law must remain the foundation of military conduct worldwide.

I encourage readers and contributors alike to look beyond the boundaries of conventional military law and consider the long-term implications of the legal principles we uphold today. *Forces Law Review* is not merely a reflection of where we stand—it is a vision for where we must go.

Congratulations to the National Institute of Military Justice, Washington DC and the Centre for Constitution & Public Policy, University of Legal Studies and Punjab University, Chandigarh and all who have contributed to this landmark achievement. I look forward to seeing how this journal will continue to shape the future of military law.

(Justice Rajendra Menon)

Res. : 99, New Moti Bagh, New Delhi-110021

Professor Renu Vig
Vice-Chancellor

PANJAB UNIVERSITY
CHANDIGARH, *India* 160 014

MESSAGE

It is a matter of great pride that the inaugural edition of the *Forces Law Review* (FLR) is being launched as a collaborative effort between the National Institute of Military Justice (NIMJ), Washington DC, and the Centre for Constitution & Public Policy (CCPP), University Institute of Legal Studies, Panjab University, Chandigarh. This pioneering initiative marks a significant step toward advancing scholarship in the domain of military law at a global level.

The *Forces Law Review* fills a crucial gap by providing a dedicated platform for legal discourse on issues pertaining to military and uniformed forces, including matters of discipline, service conditions, and constitutional principles that govern their functioning. By bringing together significant judgments from around the world, expert analyses, and thought-provoking opinion pieces, this journal will serve as a valuable resource for academics, practitioners, policymakers, and members of the armed forces.

Panjab University has always been committed to fostering academic excellence and encouraging meaningful legal research. The launch of *Forces Law Review* is a testament to this commitment and to the dedication of the editorial team in creating a journal of high scholarly value. I congratulate the Chief Editors, Editorial Advisory Board, Student Editors, and all contributors for their efforts in bringing this initiative to fruition.

I extend my best wishes for the success of *Forces Law Review* and hope that it will grow to become a leading publication in the field of military law, contributing to informed legal discussions and policy developments across jurisdictions.

(Renu Vig)

Telephones : 0091-172-2541945 (Office), Fax : 0091-172-2541022, E-mail : vc@pu.ac.in
Website : www.pu.ac.in

Message

I am very honoured to be invited to join such a distinguished group of experts in military justice on the editorial board of the Forces Law Review. It is a little surprising that a journal on military justice has not been published before now at a global level, but better late than never.

This publication will provide judges, practitioners and commentators with an invaluable resource. My experience as a judge advocate over the last fifteen years has taught me that there is much to learn from other jurisdictions. As Judge Advocate General in the United Kingdom, I regularly look beyond our shores for guidance on how legal issues have been resolved. In a world where the role of the armed forces is under considerable focus, the Forces Law Review will be a valuable resource to those who practise, study and advise on military justice.

It is particularly fitting that Eugene Fidell, who has made such an important contribution to global military justice, should write the very first article.

His Honour Judge Alan Large

Judge Advocate General, United Kingdom

Honorary Chief Editors

Franklin Rosenblatt

The current President of the *National Institute of Military Justice,* Washington DC, USA. he teaches Law at Mississippi College School of Law in Jackson, Mississippi, USA where his scholarship focuses on criminal law. He is a retired Judge Advocate from the United States Army where he served for 20 years and attained the rank of Lieutenant Colonel. After his military service, he joined the litigation department at a major law firm where he headed the firm's Military & National Security Law practice group. He participated in numerous military operations around the globe, including in the Balkans, Southwest Asia, and Southeast Asia. He frequently speaks and writes on military law topics and has co-authored multiple military justice books. He was also a part of the historic "Yale Draft" (Principles) on Military Justice, an improvement of the existing United Nations document on the same subject, at a *Yale Law School* conference attended by global jurists and representatives of the United Nations. Franklin also serves as a Court of Appeals judge with the Mississippi Army National Guard. He is also associated with the *International Society of Military Law* and *the Law of War,* Brussels. Belgium.

Professor Shruti Bedi

Currently Professor of Law and Director of the *University Institute of Legal Studies,* Panjab University, Chandigarh, India. An internationally recognized legal scholar, she is the first International Fellow at the *National Institute of Military Justice,* Washington DC, USA with Navdeep Singh, and a Visiting Professor at *Universitas Airlangga,* Indonesia. She also serves as the Director of the *Centre for Constitution and Public Policy.* With ten books and over 90 publications to her credit, her work also explores constitutional law, counterterrorism, and AI law. A TEDx speaker and recipient of The Phenomenal She, 2022 award by the Indian National Bar Association, she has been honoured by the British High Commission for her contributions to India-UK legal heritage.

Navdeep Singh

Former Major and practicing lawyer at the Punjab & Haryana High Court, India on the constitutional side, he is a globally recognised expert and practitioner of constitutional law, military-related law and reform in administration of justice, including military justice. He was also the founder President of the Armed Forces Tribunal Bar Association, Chandigarh, India. Along with Franklin Rosenblatt, he too was a Member-Participant of the "Yale Draft" at the *Yale Law School*. He is a former Member of a high-level Committee of Experts constituted by the Indian Ministry of Defence on directions of the Prime Minister to reduce litigation and initiate reform in redressal of grievances in the Armed Forces. He is Member of *International Society for Military Law and the Law of War* at Brussels, Belgium, the first International Fellow of the *National Institute of Military Justice* at Washington DC, USA and one of the five appointed members of the military justice advisory committee of the *Commonwealth Secretariat* at London.

Part I: Opinion Pieces

Part II: Reported Judgments

Part III: Notable Events

PART I

Opinion Pieces

A Military Justice Agenda

Eugene R. Fidell[1]

When a ship is launched, the custom is to smash a bottle of champagne against her bow, after which the crowd cheers as the vessel slides into the water. Without in any way suggesting that the Forces Law Review will, like any seaworthy craft, remain dry, it does seem unfortunate that there is no comparable ceremony for the launch of a legal periodical. Perhaps the best we can do in preparation for its maiden voyage is to consult the tides and currents before getting underway. What do we learn? What sea conditions await? What rocks and shoals lurk? In a nutshell, those about to embark can expect an exciting voyage, and not necessarily in a bad sense.

There will be challenges as well as opportunities. For starters, *Forces Law Review*'s creators have chosen to commence this voyage in an era of significant shooting wars in Europe, the Middle East, and Africa, as well as more localized simmering conflicts elsewhere. Wars test the rule of law as contending state and non-state actors vie for the upper hand. The prospect of gaining ground, or preventing the opposing force from doing so, offers a strong incentive to bend or ignore the rules. War crimes must be prevented, investigated, and punished, typically through national military justice systems. As the dust settles from the current array of devastating wars, those systems, backed up by the machinery of the International Criminal Court, will be put to the test, not only with regard to familiar kinds of misconduct, but also taking account of the breathtaking changes that continue to emerge as the technology of warfare

---

1. Visiting Lecturer in Law and Senior Research Scholar, Yale Law School; Of Counsel, Feldesman Leifer LLP, Washington, DC.

evolves, thinking here of drones, booby-trapped personal communications equipment, the weaponization of artificial intelligence, and other "advances" that we cannot even begin to predict.

Experience also teaches that nation states are not typically aggressive when it comes to punishing their own military forces for violations of the law of armed conflict, and when they do, the impulse of political leaders may be to grant unwarranted pardons or other clemency (raising further questions as to whether clemency in war crimes matters is itself a war crime). Additionally, urgent operational needs may stand in the way of prompt investigation and prosecution. I hope this new journal will report on developments in this core area, through rigorous scholarly contributions as well as dissemination of key decisions of national and international tribunals. If it does nothing more, that will justify the editors' and publisher's efforts.

Shooting wars and their high-tech equivalents aside, what does the future hold in store? Here there is some good news. Specifically, with the benefit of experience since the end of the Second World War and the development of human rights as a (more or less) universal value, it does seem that there is broad recognition of military justice reform as an enduring rather than merely episodic optional exercise. Country after country has found it important to take critical stock of their military justice and disciplinary systems with a view to keeping them at least roughly in sync with evolving national values and choices about the administration of justice writ large. When a state's criminal justice system changes, sooner or later the light will go on that some corresponding change may be called for in the code of military justice. At times, these two platoons – civilian and military justice – may not be quite in step, but when one gets too far out of step, it is only a matter of time before corrective action comes up for discussion. The same is true, I will optimistically suggest, when a state – especially one that is committed to democratic values – finds that human rights norms have evolved in ways that suggest a need for a fresh look at longstanding national institutions of military justice.

Unfortunately, some states will be deaf to that foghorn's insistent but far-off call. Whether they are may reflect the health or frailty of democracy, or whether the state's armed forces have grown used to wielding political power, regardless of democratic norms much less international values. A glance at the list of states that insist on using military courts to try civilians shows that military institutional interests may dominate, or present a persistent threat either to civilian legal institutions or to whatever modicum of independence their military justice apparatus has been able to develop.

There is little that is amusing in this process, but occasionally there is reason to muster a smile. In the United States, for example, the armed forces bitterly opposed recent and ultimately successful legislative efforts to transfer to lawyers outside the chain of command the commander's traditional power to decide who should be prosecuted for what offenses and at what level of gravity. Within a short time after Congress enacted this historic reform, and the new system of "special trial counsels" was stood up, the armed forces were touting the importance of the change. Somewhat in the same vein, I can recall when the U.S. military decorated judge advocates who had been involved in the move to afford military judges the modest protection of short fixed terms of office – a basic reform the government had fought tooth and nail in the courts for years.

But reform is here to stay. The evidence is everywhere. In the United States, the National Institute of Military Justice and its affiliated (but editorially-independent) blogs – CAAFlog and Global Military Justice Reform – are thriving. NIMJ itself is well into its fourth decade and has attracted a new generation of gifted scholars and practitioners. The reform impulse is also apparent in the Commonwealth Military Justice Transformation Project undertaken under the auspices of the Commonwealth Law Ministers, the International Society for Military Law and the Law of War, the Geneva Centre for Democratic Control of Armed Forces, as well as the International Military Justice Forums that have been organized by Saint-Cyr Coëtquidan. There is more to be done. While the UN's Office of the High Commissioner for Human Rights made a historic contribution to military justice with the Draft Principles Governing the Administration of Justice Through Military Tribunals (also known as the Decaux Principles, after Prof. Emmanuel Decaux of the University of Paris), the 2006 draft never achieved final approval by the General Assembly. An updated version was crafted at a Yale Law School workshop in 2018, and has kept the original project alive, albeit on life-support. It is to be hoped that the OHCHR will revive its excellent initiative. Until that happens, it will remain for the Special Rapporteurs on the Independence of Judges and

Lawyers to monitor this field as part of their portfolio. Given the broad scope of that important mandate, however, perhaps the time has come for a new mandate that will address military justice in all its aspects. Considering the frequency with which human rights issues arise in the context of military courts, a focused mandate would be a wise use of UN resources.

Among the reefs with which the navigators of *Forces Law Review* will want to concern themselves, three stand out: judicial independence, jurisdiction, and transparency. Each has proven to be a hazard from the standpoint of public policy, human rights, and public confidence in the administration of justice. A few words are in order on each.

It seems amazing, but judicial independence is a fiction, or close to it, in numerous military justice systems. Some tradition-bound national systems continue to conduct trials without a legally-qualified judge at the helm. And if there is such a judge, they may lack the power to deliver final rulings on issues of law. Some states rely on judges who serve at will, or afford terms of office that are too brief or have too many escape hatches to guarantee either the reality or the appearance of independence. Can a uniformed judge ever be independent? That question was raised in *R. vs Edwards* in the Supreme Court of Canada in 2024. It merits further scrutiny. Major judicial independence issues were addressed in 2024 by the Constitutional Court of South Africa in *O'Brien vs Minister of Defence & Military Veterans*. The Constitutional Court of Uganda has broadly suggested that military courts cannot be independent.

Independence extends to the prosecution function as well. Should lay commanders be making charging decisions or negotiating plea bargains? This has been a concern in the United States not only in connection with the Gillibrand reform referred to above, but more recently in the effort of outgoing Secretary of Defense Lloyd J. Austin III to rescind plea bargains that had been negotiated by prosecutors and approved by his appointed subordinate in three of the military commission cases being tried at Guantánamo Bay, Cuba. That contentious matter is in litigation, but it is not without irony, since General Austin (a nonlawyer) had personally approved shifting commanders' power to dispose of court-martial charges to lawyers outside the chain of command.

The on-again, off-again Guantánamo plea bargains also point to a severe problem of transparency. Despite extraordinary media and public interest in the controversy, it took months for the government to release the pretrial agreement documents and related legal pleadings to the public. The military commission system already had engendered little to no public confidence, but this delay was nothing short of preposterous. Access to case documents in courts-martial also remains a low priority in many countries. There is no reason for this in an era in which timely access to official documents is easily achieved and so obviously critical to public confidence.

Jurisdictional issues lurk everywhere in the sea of military justice. A handful of countries, such as Uganda, Lebanon, and Pakistan, make a regular practice of trying civilians in military courts. To what end? If the civilian courts are dysfunctional, as is surely the case in some places, then fix those courts. Similarly, even states that should know better (the United States is one) insist on trying military retirees.

Another fault line concerns the trial by military courts of offenses that lack any significant connection to military service other than the accused's status as a member of the armed forces. Otherwise solidly democratic countries have found it impossible to jettison this abusive policy either through legislative action or constitutional adjudication. Military justice reformers should make service-nexus a high priority requirement in national legislation or decisional law. As the Guantánamo cases lingered beyond all reason, I concluded that if any such case could be tried in a civilian court, that is where it ought to be tried. I have come to believe that a similar approach is right where courts-martial and civilian courts have concurrent jurisdiction over an offense by a member of the armed forces: except when an offense occurs outside the country, if it can be tried "downtown," that it where it should be tried. This will not happen tomorrow, but I believe that is where the matter will in time come to rest.

These are big issues. There are others, of course. For example, disciplinary proceedings for minor military offenses far outnumber courts-martial, yet they are little studied. In 2019, another Yale workshop generated basic principles for these proceedings. Victims' rights have been a fertile field for litigation in some military justice systems. In legal systems that do not ordinarily permit civil parties in criminal litigation, this may be problematic. I encourage scholars and practitioners to keep a weather eye on this. Finally, in recent years, a surprising number of flag and general officers have found themselves at the wrong end of the military justice system, often for offenses of a sexual nature. Enlisted personnel and junior officers may look on this with *schadenfreude*, but evenhanded justice is essential to public confidence, not only belowdecks but to those watching attentively from the shore.

Bon voyage, Forces Law Review and shipmates.

The Independence and Impartiality of Military Judges in Canada

Alison Duxbury[1]

Introduction

In 2024 the highest courts of two countries delivered judgments dealing with the independence and impartiality of military judges. In *R v Edwards,* a majority of the Supreme Court of Canada in a decision delivered by Kasirer J, upheld the constitutionality of the dual role of military judges as both judges and military officers.[2] In a unanimous judgment, the Constitutional Court of South Africa in *Lieutenant Colonel K. O'Brien N.O v Minister of Defence and Military Affairs* found that provisions of South African defence legislation violated the Constitution of the Republic of South Africa on the basis that they undermined the independence of military judges.[3] While this note will focus on the decision in *Edwards,* handed down in April 2024, the December 2024 judgment in *O'Brien* is a reminder that issues regarding the

1. Professor, Melbourne Law School, University of Melbourne, Australia; Former Visiting Fellow, All Souls College (2023-2024). Her areas of research are human rights law, international humanitarian law, the law of international organisations and military justice. This note draws on an earlier article, Alison Duxbury, 'Military Justice in the Spotlight (Again): R v Edwards in the Supreme Court of Canada' (*Oxford Human Rights Hub,* 14 May 2024) <https://ohrh.law.ox.ac.uk/military-justice-in-the-spotlight-again-r-v-edwards-in-the-supreme-court-of-canada/> accessed 1 February 2025.

2. *R v Edwards* [2024] SCC 15 *(Edwards).*

3. *Lieutenant Colonel K. O'Brien N.O v Minister of Defence and Military Affairs (and others)* Case CCT 14/23 (20 December 2024) *(O'Brien).*

application of fair trial rights in military courts or tribunals around the world are by no means settled. Together, the two cases add to the jurisprudence of national and regional courts and commissions, including the European Court of Human Rights,[4] on the factors that impact the application of the right to fair trial in military justice hearings.

The Challenge in *R v Edwards*

The appellants, members of the Canadian Armed Forces (CAF), challenged provisions of the National Defence Act[5] ('the Act') requiring military judges in Canada to have a dual status as judges and military officers. The CAF members had been charged with serious violations of the Code of Service Discipline (CSD) contained in the Act. These violations included disobeying a lawful command, trafficking and possession of illegal drugs, and sexual assault.[6] Their cases were heard before courts martial, with appeals to the Court Martial Appeal Court of Canada.

Section 165.21 (1) of the Act establishes two preconditions for appointment as a military judge:

> The Governor in Council may appoint any officer who is a barrister or advocate of at least 10 years standing at the bar of a province and who has been an officer for at least 10 years to be a military judge.[7]

The appellants objected to the requirement that military judges must be officers, thereby making military judges subject to the chain of command and military discipline. It was argued that these factors exposed military judges 'to real and perceived pressure in the exercise of their judicial duties'.[8] In the

4. For example, European Court of Human Rights cases involving the United Kingdom military justice system include: *Findlay v United Kingdom* (1977) 24 EHRR 221; *Grieves v United Kingdom* (2004) 39 EHRR 2; and *Cooper v United Kingdom* (2004) 39 EHRR 8. See Alison Duxbury, 'The Curious Case of the Australian Military Court' (2010) 10 Oxford University Commonwealth Law Journal 155, 165-169.

5. RSC 1985, c C-46.

6. See *Edwards* (n 1) [16-26] for the offences.

7. The relevant provisions of the Act are included in *Edwards* (n 1) [62].

8. *ibid* [51].

appellants' view, this violated s 11(d) of the Canadian Charter of Rights and Freedoms, which states that a person charged with an offence 'has the right ... to be presumed innocent until proven guilty according to the law in a fair and public hearing by an independent and impartial tribunal.'

This was not the first time that the Canadian military justice system had been the subject of a constitutional challenge. In 1992, the Supreme Court case of *R v Généreux*[9] held that some features of Canada's military justice system, including insufficient security of tenure for military judges, were contrary to s 11(d) of the Charter. In the following years, there were several reforms aimed at increasing the independence and impartiality of military justice.[10] However, fundamentally, the Supreme Court in *Généreux* and again in *R v Stillman*, affirmed '[t]he existence of a parallel system of military law and tribunals, for the purpose of enforcing discipline in the military.'[11] While the military justice system was subject to the Charter, it was not 'by its very nature' inconsistent with s 11(d).[12]

Arguments and Decision

Although developments in Canada's military justice system had increased its independence and impartiality since the decision in *Généreux*', underlying the appellants' argument in *Edwards* was the belief that these changes had not gone far enough. For the appellants, 'social changes affecting military justice' meant that, to be 'truly independent' for the purpose of the constitutional standard, military judges should be civilians.[13] This argument is part of a larger debate regarding the 'civilianisation' of military law and the reform of military justice

---

9. *R v Généreux* [1992] 1 SCR 259 (*Généreux*).

10. For a discussion of these reforms see *R v Stillman* [2019] 3 SCR 144, 173-8 (*Stillman*); *Edwards* (n 1) [101-102]. Subsequent amendments to the CSD, in 2022, are outlined in Afton David and Rory Fowler, 'Independence of the Canadian Military Judiciary: Much to be Desired?', (Canadian Global Affairs Institute, November 2024) <https://www.cgai.ca/independence_of_the_canadian_military_judiciary_much_to_be_desired> accessed 25 January 2025.

11. *Généreux* (n 8) 295; *Stillman* (n 9) 159.

12. *Stillman* (n 9) 133 (summarising the decision of Lamer CJ in *Généreux*).

13. *Edwards* (n 1) [6, 50]

systems throughout the world. Civilianisation in this context means 'the incorporation of the norms of the institutions and norms of the civilian legal system into military law.'[14] In terms of military justice, civilianisation includes closer alignment of military justice with civilian justice and can involve the inclusion of civilians in military justice hearings. The appellants referred to the experience of other countries (for example, the United Kingdom and New Zealand) to demonstrate that civilians, particularly former members of the military, would have the 'necessary understanding of military life' to be military judges.[15]

The Crown referred to a range of safeguards for military judges, including security of tenure, financial security and administrative independence.[16] These 'essential conditions' for judicial independence were established by Supreme Court of Canada in *Valente v The Queen.17* With respect to security of tenure, the majority in *Edwards* highlighted reforms since *Généreux* that had eliminated fixed, renewable terms. They also dismissed the appellants' claim that military judges could be removed from their roles via the 'back door' given that they were subject to the CSD.[18] Section 165.21(3) of the Act, which provides that a military judge can only be removed by the Governor General in Council following a recommendation from the Military Judges Inquiry Committee, was considered sufficient protection to ensure security of tenure.[19] Similarly, the majority dismissed the appellants' arguments regarding administrative independence by highlighting the responsibility of military judges 'for decisions that must be left to judges', including establishing their own procedural rules.[20] Although the appellants did not contest the *Valente* requirement of financial security, the majority set out the

---

14. Matthew Groves, 'The Civilianisation of Australian Military Law' (2005) 28 UNSW Law Journal 364-395, 366-7. See also GR Rubin, 'United Kingdom Military Law: Autonomy, Civilianisation, Juridification' (2002) 65 Modern Law Review 36.

15. *Edwards* (n 1) [65, 6].

16. *ibid* [52].

17. *Valente v The Queen* [1985] 2 SCR 673.

18. *Edwards* (n 1) [107-108].

19. *ibid* [109].

20. *ibid* [117].

remuneration scheme in the Act, including the role of the Miliary Judges Compensation Committee, and remarked on its similarity to the scheme for civilian judges.[21]

The appellants further argued that the dual status of military judges as judges and officers gave rise to a 'reasonable perception that they are not impartial.'[22] This argument focussed on the perceived conflict between military judges' executive and judicial roles and the hierarchical structure of the military.[23] This argument also failed with the majority stating that 'military judges can lay aside their duties and allegiances as officers when they exercise their judicial duties.'[24] Ultimately, the majority found that the appellants had not demonstrated that 'a reasonable and informed person would be concerned that the independence or impartiality of military judges' was undermined by their status as officers.[25]

Karakatsanis J, in her dissenting judgment, agreed with the majority's position that officer status 'did not necessarily contravene' s 11(1)(d) of the Charter.[26] She also pointed to reforms since *Généreux* designed to address the three hallmarks of judicial independence in *Valente*.[27] However, for Karakatsanis J these safeguards were insufficient to address the risk of interference by the chain of command.[28] In coming to this conclusion, she focussed on the 'constitutional imperative' of judicial independence – an imperative that 'cannot be sacrificed' for military objectives.[29] While she accepted military judges' dual status if 'properly designed and protected'[30], her concern lay with the fact that military judges not only faced the possibility of civilian prosecution and review through a judicial conduct committee (as

21. *ibid* [114].

22. *ibid* [118].

23. *ibid* [125].

24. *ibid* [128]

25. *ibid* [148].

26. *ibid* 150].

27. *ibid* [151].

28. *ibid* [153].

29. *ibid* [154].

30. *ibid* [161].

with other judges), but also military discipline.[31] Karakatsanis J referred to the oft-cited purpose of military justice – 'discipline, efficiency and morale' – as creating 'a posture of deference towards hierarchy which can conflict with a judge's duty of independence and impartiality.'[32] In Karakatsanis J's view, subjecting military judges to the broader range of offences under the CSD, administered by the executive, gave rise to an apprehension that military judges 'would be influenced by their loyalty to rank ... to the detriment of the rights of accused members before them.'[33]

The Relevance of Policy Recommendations and International Developments

While both judgments in *Edwards* referred to recommendations in external reviews of Canada's miliary justice system, developments in other jurisdictions and at the international level received little attention. Both judgments cited the *Report of the Third Independent Review Authority to the Minister of National Defence* (2021) (the 'Fish Report'), which recommended the appointment of 'civilianised' judges – that is, judges who have experience of military life, but are no longer CAF members.[34] The Supreme Court also referred to the *Report of the Independent External Comprehensive Review of the Department of National Defence and the Canadian Armed Forces* (2022) (the 'Arbour Report'), which focussed on the handling of sexual misconduct cases and cited concerns regarding the independence of military tribunals.[35] For the majority, these policy recommendations were matters more suitable for the legislature rather than being determinative of the question whether the constitutional standard had been infringed.[36] Karakatsanis J appeared to give more weight to the findings of these reviews as highlighting the longer

---

31. *ibid* [184].
32. *ibid* [186].
33. *ibid* [209].
34. E.g. *ibid* [73, 188].
35. E.g. *ibid* [78, 185].
36. *ibid* [75].

history of concerns relating to independence of Canada's military justice system.[37]

In *Edwards* the two judgments referred sparingly to developments in other jurisdictions and to international instruments.[38] The appellants' comparisons with the United Kingdom and New Zealand did not move the majority, who were concerned with the question whether the officer status of military judges violated the Charter, rather than whether the system could 'practically function with civilian judges.'[39] The majority emphasised that it is not for the Court to examine models in other countries to determine their appropriateness in the Canadian context.[40] This approach may be contrasted to *O'Brien*, where the imperative in the South African Constitution to consider international law in interpreting the Bill of Rights and South African legislation[41] led the Constitutional Court of South Africa to examine the principles of judicial independence and impartiality and their application to military tribunals in treaties and other international documents, as well as developments in other countries.[42] The Constitutional Court also discussed case law in similar jurisdictions, including *Edwards*, although it did not express agreement (or otherwise) with the Canadian decision.[43] Given that the challenge in *O'Brien* concerned matters that had been resolved in Canada, including the appointment of military judges for short renewable terms and the possibility of executive removal without independent oversight, the Constitutional Court cited with approval legislative reforms in Canada, as well as the United Kingdom and New Zealand.[44]

---

37. E.g. *ibid* [185].

38. *ibid* [6, 72, 170].

39. *ibid* [72].

40. *ibid* [14]. For a critical discussion of the utility of comparative law in analysing military justice reforms see Mike Madden, 'Keeping up with the Common Law O'Sullivans? The Limits of Comparative Law in the Context of Military Justice Reforms' (2013) 51 Alberta Law Review 125.

41. Constitution of the Republic of South Africa, ss 39(1); 233.

42. *O'Brien* (n 2) [86-104].

43. *ibid* [75].

44. *ibid* [114, 121].

Conclusion

The majority in *Edwards* affirmed the 'similar but different' status of Canada's military justice system posited in *Généreux*: civilian and military judges must meet the requirements of independence and impartiality, but there may be 'different modalities for ensuring that military judges have a degree of independence that meets the constitutional minimum.'[45] By concentrating on 'the constitutional minimum', the Court did not need to consider whether removing military judges from the jurisdiction of the CSD would increase their independence or whether Canadian military judges should properly be considered members of the executive or the judiciary.[46] It also meant that the Court's focus was on substance (the constitutional standards) rather than form (military or civilian). This approach aligns with discussions at the international level.

Experts convened by the United Nations and the Commonwealth Secretariat have drafted principles designed to ensure that military justice systems comply with certain standards, including human rights law. Both the Decaux Principles Governing the Administration of Justice through Military Tribunals and the draft Commonwealth Military Justice Principles have a particular emphasis on the independence and impartiality of the personnel involved, notably military judges.[47] Like the Supreme Court of Canada and the Constitutional Court of South Africa, the international principles do not mandate civilian judges, but the desire to remove military justice from the influence of the 'military hierarchy'[48] or 'command interference'[49] suggests an increasing push to civilianisation. Such a push will be questioned where it is

45. *Edwards* (n 1) [82]. See also [57].

46. See discussion in David and Fowler (n 9).

47. Draft Principles Governing the Administration of Justice through Military Tribunals, UN Doc E/CN.4/2006/58 (13 January 2006) (Decaux Principles); 'Commonwealth Military Justice Principles – Stellenbosch Draft', (Stellenbosch, South Africa, 7 November 2023) (Draft Commonwealth Principles) <https://thecommonwealth.org/news/transformative-military-justice-principles-envisioned-experts-across-commonwealth> accessed 27 January 2025.

48. Decaux Principles, (n 46) Principle 13.

49. Draft Commonwealth Principles (n 46) Principle 2.

perceived that the impact of additional legal regulation on the armed forces could adversely affect their combat function or operational effectiveness.[50] However, the potential for conflict between the application of human rights law and military effectiveness should not be overstated: '[e]nsuring that the human rights of armed forces personnel are respected is also a matter of effectiveness.'[51] While the appellants in *Edwards* were ultimately unsuccessful, given the reports of independent reviews cited in the judgments and developments in military justice systems elsewhere, it is unlikely that calls to civilianise military justice will cease, either in Canada or elsewhere.

50. Matthew Groves and Alison Duxbury, 'The Reform of Military Justice', in Alison Duxbury and Matthew Groves (eds), *Military Justice in the Modern Age* (Cambridge University Press, 2016) 4.

51. DCAF/OSCE, *Human Rights of Armed Forces Personnel: Compendium of Standards, Good Practices and Recommendations* (2021) 16.

Contemporary Conflicts: Challenges to Peacekeeping and International Humanitarian Law

Lt Gen Harinder Singh (Retd)[1]

The war in Middle East continues to garner headlines. Elsewhere, in Ukraine, Syria and Sudan, conflicts continue to linger. Tigray, Sahel, and Myanmar are other emerging hotspots. *While wars are inevitable, the moral persuasion to prevent conflicts is on the wane for two principal reasons. First, the international order is fraying on who will intervene and act and second,* the laws of armed conflict are proving to be increasingly ineffective and fragile. What can be legally targeted, and whether targeting critical public infrastructure such as hospitals, schools, humanitarian camps, etc is lawful military action, is becoming a matter of serious international concern.

Following the end of the Cold War, the international response to prevent conflicts was to use peace keeping as a tool to contain escalation. Far from being a perfect tool, the international effort was concentrated on preventing conflicts, and if these did break out, to minimise collateral damage. However, this paradigm is now breaking down. With fewer tools to prevent ongoing inter or intra-state conflicts, the warring sides are becoming more inclined to use of force and unilateral action. What explains this change in global approach towards conflict management and its timely resolution is first, the

1. The writer is a former commander of UN Multi-National Peacekeeping Brigade (MONUSCO) in Democratic Republic of Congo (DRC) and with military components from India, South Africa, Nepal, Uruguay, Ukraine, Egypt, Jordan and Guatemala handled the M23 rebellion in Eastern Congo, in 2013. The officer earlier served as a UN Staff Officer with UNAVEM-III (1997-98) in the Republic of Angola.

UN Security Council seems more circumspect and less enthusiastic now. And second, why any global or regional attempts to re-think peace or peacekeeping operations continue to struggle, including poorly-led or resourced missions.

The question then is, when peace efforts are floundering, the laws of armed conflict must work. But when these too become tools of political malaise and rhetoric, the issue becomes more complicated This essay attempts to analyse this contradiction of declining global interest in peacekeeping efforts and the growing propensity among state and non-State actors to blatantly defy the laws of armed conflict. A moral reset is necessary, lest ongoing wars continue to set a bad precedence for wrongful conduct by States and non-State actors in combat operations.

Preventing Conflict

Since the 1940s, UN peacekeeping has been an important tool for preventing and limiting armed conflict. UN peacekeepers have helped calm conflicts, protect civilians, steer security sector reforms, and strengthen rule of law in conflict prone regions. Till date, the UN has deployed over 120 peace operations in more than 50 countries.[2] On an average, five to six missions remained deployed each year until the late 1980s. Post the Cold War, the deployments grew to a figure of 34 missions, which is now down to 28. The UN funding has also increased over the years, with peak expenditure reported in 2008. As regards the number of active peacekeepers, the figure touched a high of 100,000 personnel, in 2014, which is now down to 70,000 personnel.

Functionally speaking, these 120-odd missions have tackled a broad range of threats and challenges, from benign to robust, resulting in over 1000 overlapping mandates.[3] All together, these 1000-odd peace mandates can be placed in broad categories to include military observer missions, peace enforcement missions, electoral assistance, security sector reforms (SSR)

2. El-Ghassim Wane, Professor Paul D. Williams, Professor Ai Kihara-Hunt, 'The Future of Peacekeeping, New Models, and Related Capabilities' (*United Nations*, October 2024) <https://peacekeeping.un.org/sites/default/files/the_future_of_peacekeeping_new_models_and_related_capabilities_-_nov1.pdf>

3. *ibid.*

and demobilisation, disarmament and rehabilitation (DDR) mandates and climate security mandates, among others. While the principal task of these mandates has been to provide strategic direction, they have burdened with additional tasks, sometimes quite dissimilar and fragmented, without a commensurate increase in resources. Overburdened missions have lost focus, resulting in weak peace outcomes. Evidently, these mandates have to be anchored in sound political strategy, yet remain flexible to evolve in keeping with the changes in the local context.

However, in recent years, the intensification of global competition have complicated peacekeeping endeavours. With over 130 ongoing conflicts, the UN confronts an increasingly contested and difficult environment. Struck by UNSC's hesitancy to intervene, these conflicts have proliferated, making them more protracted and peace making more difficult. The pressure to scale down peacekeeping budgets, a largely dysfunctional UN Security Council and the growing belief that there is little or no peace to keep, are other contributory factors.[4] Moreover, armed conflicts have not only become lethal but unmanageable too, with a growing recurrence of earlier resolved conflicts.[5] Mass atrocities and utter disregard to laws of conflict in Ukraine and Gaza have led to record levels of fatalities, forced displacement and destruction.

A few aspects merit attention. First, broader geopolitical tensions and ensuing geo-strategic competition are impacting the international consensus on managing armed conflicts. Finding consensus on casting new mandates or even amending existing mandates have proved difficult. Next, the host governments continue to pose a major hurdle to effective peace interventions and fielding of large peacekeeping missions, as there is a growing discontentment over their reduced effectiveness in protection of civilians, or enforcing peace under Chapter VII of the UN Charter. And third, the

---

4. Edith M. Lederer, 'UN peacekeeping on 75th anniversary: successes, failures and challenges ahead in a divided world' (*The Associated Press*, 26 May 2023) <https://apnews.com/article/un-peacekeeping-75-anniversary-successes-failures-challenges-5a18ab63c9d54104c6863b71aed552cb#:~:text=Lacroix%20pointed%20to%20other%20challenges,of%20conflict%20%E2%80%94%20including%20transnational%20criminal> accessed 8 February 2025.

5. Dennis C. Jett, *Why Peacekeeping Fails* (20th Anniversary edn, Springer Nature 2019).

traditional troop-contributing countries (TCCs) are increasingly shy on using force and reluctant to commit personnel in difficult environments.[6]

Regional Interventions

Since armed conflicts are on the rise and peacekeeping requirements are not fructifying, there is a marked shift from UN-led peacekeeping operations towards an increase in the number of peace operations deployed by regional organizations.[7] A majority of these are in Africa, with troops from the African continent. These regional missions largely concentrate on anti-terror operations. One such example is the AU-mandated Multinational Joint Task Force (MNJTF) comprising five African countries deployed in Sahel region, to combat the Boko Haram.[8] Mali is yet another example, where several actors are involved.[9] What began in 2003 as a small anti-terrorist mission has now evolved. Two EU-mandated missions EUCAP and EUTM, and the G5 Sahel Joint Force are deployed in Mali. EUCAP endorses security sector reform in Mali, while EUTM constitutes the military component.

Mutual solidarity is their greatest asset, but then these interventions face several challenges.[10] First, African-led missions tend to focus on security-related tasks, limited to a part of the strife-torn country. Next, these regional

6. Chiara Ruffa, *Military Cultures in Peace and Stability Operations* (University of Pennsylvania Press June 2018).

7. Paul D. Williams, The African Union's Conflict Management Capabilities (Council on Foreign Relations, October 2011) <https://www.cfr.org/report/african-unions-conflict-management-capabilities> accessed 9 February 2025.

8. Report No 291, 'What Role for the Multinational Joint Task Force in Fighting Boko Haram?' (International Crisis Group, 7 July 2020) <https://www.crisisgroup.org/africa/west-africa/291-what-role-multinational-joint-task-force-fighting-boko-haram> accessed 9 February 2025.

9. Peacekeeping, 'Emerging Lessons from MINUSMA's Experience in Mali' (Stimson, 31 July 2024) <https://www.stimson.org/2024/emerging-lessons-from-minusmas-experience-in-mali/#:~:text=MINUSMA's%20experience%20in%20Mali%20offers,actors%2C%20and%20the%20impact%20of> accessed 9 February 2025.

10. Benjamin Petrini, 'Peacekeeping in Africa: from UN to regional Peace Support Operations' (International Institute for Strategic Studies (IISS), 18 March 2024) <https://www.iiss.org/online-analysis/online-analysis/2024/03/peacekeeping-in-africa-from-un-to-regional-peace-support-operations/> accessed 9 February 2025.

missions are poorly resourced. They have less manpower, less equipment, and are frugally provisioned. Consequentially, they need funding and support from other international organizations to meet developmental challenges in the target country.

On the other hand, African-led missions also have several advantages. First, they have better insights into regional issues, better access to the warring parties, and greater ability to mobilize consensus between them. Second, they are quicker to deploy, and much cheaper to support. Third, they are not risk-averse and willingly undertake tasks that other troop-contributing countries would avoid. Today, AU-led missions are actively engaged against Islamist insurgents in Somalia and the Lake Chad Basin that would have been difficult for the UN.

Minimalistic Interventions

While regional peacekeeping remains an option, minimalist interventions[11] offer a more cost-effective approach to achieving peace and stability. Short and strategic operations, often supported by private military security companies, have played a role in peacekeeping by providing personnel, logistics, intelligence, and risk assessment. Quasi-state entities like the Wagner Group have operated in conflict zones, offering advisory support during peace agreements, often without official acknowledgment from the states responsible for their deployment. However, in complex environments, large-scale and prolonged military interventions are often necessary to secure lasting peace. Minimalist efforts, though effective in addressing immediate threats, rarely tackle the root causes of conflict or fully dismantle rebel groups.

Understanding the limitations of minimalist interventions is crucial. They are most effective when armed groups are already weak and when host governments are willing to accept the short-term human costs of such missions. However, their success remains contingent on complementary measures that cut off insurgent resources and sustain long-term stability.

---

11. Jake Sherman, Agathe Sarfati, & Ilhan Dahir, 'The Future of UN Peacekeeping and Parallel Operations' (International Peace Institute, 2021) <https://www.ipinst.org/wp-content/uploads/2021/01/Future-of-Peace-Operations-and-Parallel-Forces-js.pdf>

Some Concerns

Beyond the regional and minimalistic interventions, the current trends in peacekeeping point towards four directions. First, the polarization in the UNSC and the regional security forums would continue to result in inaction in preventing or containing future conflict. Second, the lack of decision making and consensus seems to be moving towards de-institutionalisation of UN peace efforts, implying that they will increasingly take place outside existing institutional frameworks and forums. Third, the increasing use of private military security companies, as an alternative to peacekeeping operations, suggests that international conflict management frameworks are becoming fragmented. Fourth, the resulting political stasis on conflict management has the potential to significantly alter the future of multilateral peace forums and interventions.[12]

Future peacekeeping efforts must therefore reflect on both the possibilities and the limitations.[13] It is therefore incumbent on international actors to strengthen tools of peace intervention. Few aspects standout. First, given the surge in armed conflicts, the UN force generation capacities are far too thin to prevent or contain conflicts. Second, the growth in urban violence limits the thresholds to which UN components can be gainfully employed. Third, the emergence of new technologies such as drones and improvised explosive devices restrict the ability of blue helmets to keep pace in lethal war-fighting environment. Suffice to say that there are limits to the employment of UN components as a useful peacekeeping tool. If future missions have to act robust, then they need to prepare themselves for it, or choose to prune their mandates for low-risk tasks.

Mitigating Human Cost

Preventing the human cost of war is a key purpose of international humanitarian law (IHL). While the relevant clauses under the UN Charter seeks peaceful

12. Todd Sandler, 'International Peacekeeping Operations: Burden Sharing and Effectiveness' (2017) 61(9) J Conflict Res 1875-1897.

13. Sarah-Myriam Martin- Brûlé, *Evaluating Peacekeeping Missions: A Typology of Success and Failure in International Interventions* (Routledge 2018).

resolution of armed conflict, the Hague and Geneva Conventions take effect, when everything else fails. To that end, the Hague Convention lays out the rules of conduct in armed conflict, the Geneva Convention addresses the rights of civilians and prisoners in war and the Rome Statue lists out the war crimes as internationally accepted. These Conventions are at the heart of the law of armed conflict; a set of moral norms that constrain the behaviour of warring parties in conflict, no matter who started the war or how it might have started.[14] While all States are not party to all these laws, the provisions are binding, and as such are regarded as IHL.

Purpose

The purpose of humanitarian law is to protect the people in conflict. The IHL works on a premise that the warring sides will invariably kill, maim, or hold hostages. These conventions try to make wars less inhumane by balancing the use of force by protecting innocent civilians. A vast set of rules bind these into rules of permissible targeting, detention and interrogation, caring for the sick and wounded, and the treatment of the population when placed under the adversary's control.

In a way, IHL sets limits of acceptable behaviour, stepping beyond which, acts like torture, rape, targeting of civilians and the wounded, cannot be justified. It provides a safety net that allows use of force, while mitigating the worst consequences of war.[15] For instance, it emphasises that incidental civilian casualties must be avoided, or at least minimized. It aspires to seek a modicum of guarantee in combat situations, where humanitarian concerns have been compromised or are likely to be compromised.

But then, IHL can be undermined through lenient or irresponsible interpretation by the warring sides or legitimate governments in any armed conflict. And, if lackadaisical application proliferates, the balance tips towards IHL becoming a tool for repressive military action, rather than assuring

---

14. Adil Ahmad Haque, 'Whose armed conflict? Which law of armed conflict?' (*Just Security*, 4 October 2016) <https://www.justsecurity.org/33362/armed-conflict-law-armed-conflict/> accessed 10 February 2025.

15. Cordula Droege, 'War and What We Make of the Law' (Just Security, 10 July 2024) <https://www.justsecurity.org/97582/war-law/> accessed 10 February 2025.

protection to affected communities or parties in conflict prone regions. This is more important, when international actors care about some victims more than others, like the case of absolute silence of certain Western powers over the Israeli interventions in Gaza and Lebanon.

The Case of Gaza

Israel's offensive in Gaza raises two questions about the laws of war.16 First, is Israel intentionally targeting civilians, as Hamas did in its attack? Under the laws of war, one must not mean or look to harm the civilians, which is demonstrated by the choice of targets and methods of attack.[17] Second, if these are not intentional, then are the strikes proportionate to the military objectives a State wishes to achieve?[18] Israel's actions have raised a doubt on its indiscriminate use of force and rather unrestrained methods of attack while prosecuting military operations against Hamas and its affiliates in Lebanon. Even if the civilian fatalities are proportionate, how does the IHL explain this immense human suffering in the Middle East?

These rules on immunity to target civilians in armed conflict are paradoxical. First, the rules of war require belligerents to exercise moral and tactical diligence to minimize civilian casualties, by outlawing wilful targeting of the civilian population, schools, hospitals and humanitarian relief camps. The only exception being, if civic infrastructure is being used by belligerents in combat. And second, by providing clear and useable avenues for civilians to move out of harm's way. Whether Israel's military offensive in Gaza has been in conformity with these rules of war, is the question that seeks an answer.

16. John B. Bellinger, Geoffery S. Corn, Janina Dill, & Patrick Hamilton,'The Laws of Armed Conflict and Ethics in the Israel-Hamas War' (Council on Foreign Relations, 19 December 2023)<https://www.cfr.org/event/laws-armed-conflict-and-ethics-israel-hamas-war> accessed 10 February 2025.

17. Ryan Goodman, Michael W. Meier and Tess Bridgeman, 'Expert Guidance: Law of Armed Conflict in the Israel-Hamas War' (*Just Security*, 17 October 2023) <https://www.justsecurity.org/89489/expert-guidance-law-of-armed-conflict-in-the-israel-hamas-war/> accessed 11 February 2025.

18. Michael W. Meier, 'The principle of proportionality in the DoD Law of War Manual' (*Just Security*, 18 January 2024) <https://www.justsecurity.org/91319/the-principle-of-proportionality-in-the-dod-law-of-war-manual/> accessed 12 February 2025.

The Israeli military has justified these attacks on hospitals, schools, and humanitarian shelters on the basis that terrorists are located and based in sensitive sites. Several states have justified their support for Israel in the war against Hamas on grounds that it is fighting known terrorist organisations. But the legitimacy of the international system and rule of law depends on its commitment to IHL, without invoking counterterrorism as a carte blanche for military misconduct or repression.[19] Since Israel has failed to do so, it is now up to the international community to hold Israel accountable for its blatant misuse and abuse of its counterterrorism policy in violation of international law.

Rules and Reality

The gap between rules and reality presents a serious challenge to the laws of armed conflict. While IHL acknowledges the inevitability of war's destruction, it lacks clear standards for military conduct and is often misused to justify repressive actions rather than provide protection to civilians. Violations occur openly and frequently, leading to widespread disillusionment with the effectiveness of these laws. To bridge this gap, States and international institutions must take decisive action to curb impunity in the use of force.

The ambiguity of IHL allows for contradictory interpretations[20], affecting its ability to safeguard human life and dignity. Its true impact depends on good-faith application that prioritizes civilian protection, recognizing the intrinsic value of all human life regardless of faith or creed. While IHL does not explicitly prohibit civilian casualties, it mandates due diligence and prohibits disproportionate harm. Addressing this moral gap requires signatory States to lead by example, ensuring that violators are held accountable and that all parties adhere to the same standards.

---

19. David J. Scheffer, 'What International Law Has to Say About the Israel-Hamas War' (Council on Foreign Relations, 19 October 2023) <https://www.cfr.org/article/what-international-law-has-say-about-israel-hamas-war> accessed 12 February 2025.

20. Clive Balwin, 'How Does International Humanitarian Law Apply in Israel and Gaza?' (Human Rights Watch, 27 October 2023) <https://www.hrw.org/news/2023/10/27/how-does-international-humanitarian-law-apply-israel-and-gaza> accessed 13 February 2025.

Making Laws Work

Governments must not only uphold the laws of war but also respect the humanitarian principles that underpin them. If these laws are manipulated for political ends, they risk losing legitimacy and effectiveness as a public good. A culture of genuine legal compliance, rather than mere rhetoric, is necessary to ensure that States adhere to human rights obligations and hold their forces to the highest standards. The laws of armed conflict must intervene where and when humanitarian concerns are most pressing, serving as a means of mediation and enforcement.

For these laws to be truly effective, warring States must be held accountable for their actions, and mechanisms of international justice must be directed at those who violate them. The international community must also ensure that these laws are not exploited to justify the killing of innocent civilians. It is not too late for conflict-ridden nations to reverse their course, as seen in recent ceasefires and more precise military operations aligning with international law.

Reversing the Course

The intersection of peacekeeping and the human cost of war is complex - encompassing direct killings, injuries, and displacement, as well as indirect deaths from disease and malnutrition. The destruction of infrastructure, economic instability, and the breakdown of social structures further deepen the devastation. Loss of cultural heritage and community cohesion adds to the long-term impact. Acknowledging these complexities is crucial to developing effective strategies that mitigate suffering and promote sustainable peace.

Promoting sustainable peace requires applying peacekeeping strategies, tools, and technology to enhance security in conflict zones. Reducing the human cost of war involves preventive measures, adherence to IHL, and post-conflict rehabilitation. Key recommendations include:

- **Prevention through Diplomacy and Peacebuilding:** Engage in diplomacy, mediation, and arbitration to resolve conflicts early. Develop early warning systems to detect tensions and invest in peacebuilding efforts addressing economic and political disparities.

- **Adherence to IHL:** Ensure compliance with IHL principles—distinction, proportionality, and necessity—to protect civilians. Train military personnel and establish accountability mechanisms for violations.

- **Technological and Tactical Adjustments:** Use precision weaponry to minimize collateral damage, designate safe zones for civilians, and apply intelligence-driven strategies.

- **Humanitarian Access and Aid:** Guarantee aid organizations unimpeded access to conflict zones for essential services like food, medical care, and shelter. Deploy rapid-response teams for immediate relief.

- **Post-Conflict Recovery:** Rebuild infrastructure, education, healthcare, and economic opportunities to prevent conflict relapse. Provide psychological support for trauma survivors, including veterans.

- **Innovative Approaches:** Apply harm reduction strategies to conflicts, such as valuing human life in decision-making, utilizing economic sanctions over military action, and adopting non-lethal conflict resolution methods.

- **Community and Local Involvement:** Empower grassroots movements, including women and youth, to participate in peace processes where international efforts may struggle.

- **Global Governance and Advocacy:** Strengthen institutions like the UN in peacekeeping and conflict mediation while raising public awareness about the human cost of war.

These strategies require international cooperation, a commitment to human rights, and a shift from short-term solutions to holistic approaches focused on long-term stability. Their effectiveness is evident in past multilateral peace agreements and post-conflict recovery programs when implemented with sincerity and sustained effort.

Sealed Cover Procedure: An Antithesis to Wednesbury Principles

Dhiraj Chawla[1]

Introduction

The recent judgment of the Hon'ble Supreme Court of India passed in *Amit Kumar Sharma vs Union of India*[2] decided on 20th October 2022, has deprecated and flagged a significant issue of fairness in the procedure having been adopted by the Principal Bench of the Armed Forces Tribunal where it adjudicated on the validity of the selection proceedings when relevant material was disclosed only to it and that too in a sealed cover. This practice, which effectively precluded the affected party from accessing the material relied upon for adjudication, raises fundamental questions about transparency, natural justice, and due process.

Understanding the Sealed Cover Procedure

Before delving into the implications of the judgment, it is pertinent to analyse the concept of the 'Sealed Cover Procedure.' This legal practice involves the submission of confidential or sensitive information to a court or tribunal in a sealed envelope, which is only accessible to the adjudicating authority. While no statutory provision explicitly defines the procedure, the Supreme Court

---

1. Advocate, Punjab & Haryana High Court, Chandigarh. Email: dhiraj_attorney@yahoo.com

2. 2022 SCC OnLine SC 1570.

derives its authority to employ it from Rule 7 of Order XIII of the Supreme Court Rules, 2013 and Section 123 of the Indian Evidence Act, 1872 (now Section 129 of the Bharatiya Sakshya Adhiniyam, 2023). The sealed cover procedure is typically invoked in situations involving ongoing investigations, cases where disclosure may violate privacy rights, or matters concerning national security.

Historical Evolution of the Sealed Cover Procedure in India

The origins of the sealed cover procedure can be traced back to colonial-era legal practices, though its scope and application have significantly evolved in post-independence India. A historical analysis reveals the following developments:

- **British Colonial Era (Pre-1947)**

  The British administration maintained a high degree of secrecy in judicial and administrative proceedings, particularly in matters concerning state security, espionage, and political dissidence.

  The practice of submitting confidential reports to the judiciary, while not widespread, was primarily restricted to intelligence and defence-related matters.

- **Post-Independence Period (1950s–1970s)**

  In the early years following independence, Indian courts emphasized greater transparency; however, the executive retained its prerogative to withhold classified documents in cases involving national security and foreign relations.

  Courts frequently relied on government affidavits and reports submitted in sealed envelopes, particularly in cases concerning defence, foreign policy, and internal security.

  The Indian Evidence Act, 1872 (Sections 123 and 124) permitted the government to withhold documents if their disclosure was deemed detrimental to state security.

Contemporary Application of the Sealed Cover Procedure

While originally conceived as an exceptional measure, the sealed cover procedure has increasingly permeated various domains of judicial proceedings. Broadly, its application can be categorized into the following areas:

- **National Security and Public Interest:** Courts frequently resort to sealed cover submissions in cases concerning intelligence operations, defence strategies, and classified government documents.
- **Ongoing Investigations:** To safeguard the integrity of probes conducted by investigative agencies such as the Central Bureau of Investigation (CBI) and the Enforcement Directorate (ED), courts may accept confidential reports in sealed envelopes.
- **Service and Appointment Matters:** In disputes concerning government appointments, promotions, or disciplinary proceedings, sealed covers are often used to present confidential assessments or reports.
- **Whistleblower and Witness Protection:** Courts employ sealed cover mechanisms to protect the identities of whistleblowers or witnesses in sensitive cases involving corruption, national security, or organized crime.
- **Election and Reservation Disputes:** Sealed cover submissions are sometimes used in electoral disputes or cases involving reservations where confidential reports from constitutional authorities, such as the Election Commission of India, are required.

Factual Matrix

Coming back to the case in question which relates to adjudication of claims of the Short Service Commissioned Officers in the Indian Navy for Permanent Commission by the Principal Bench of the Armed Forces Tribunal. During the course of hearing, the Indian Navy filed its written submissions wherein it was submitted that "minute details of vacancy calculation cannot be put in the open domain for the obvious reasons and the Tribunal will be provided with a detailed note with respect to vacancy calculation in a sealed envelope (as and when sought)."[3] It was also submitted that the fairness of the selection process "would be amply clear from the selection Board Proceedings which would be provided for perusal in the sealed cover, if need for the same arises."[4] Accordingly, the selection proceedings were indeed supplied only to the Tribunal as recorded in the judicial orders and eventually the claims of the applicants came to be rejected by the impugned orders by concluding that the selection process was fair and based on objective criteria such as ACR (Annual Confidential Report) merit, seniority, war performance, peer review, and recommendations for PC which was on account of the fact that the Tribunal relied exhaustively upon material given to it in sealed cover including the files connected with the Selection Board convened in December 2020, the record of previous Selection Boards held for the grant of PC, the management of SSC Officers and the dossiers containing the confidential reports of 32 applicants before the Tribunal. On an examination of the Board proceedings which was supplied in sealed cover, the Tribunal observed that there were no mala fides in the parameters which were prescribed or the procedure adopted. It was also observed that the officers were not granted PC because of their comparative merit against limited vacancies and, in certain cases, the officers were not found suitable.

Aggrieved, the Short Service Commissioned Officers approached the Hon'ble Supreme Court of India where the question of law for adjudication was, Whether the Armed Forces Tribunal (AFT) could adjudicate on the validity of the selection proceedings for PC "when relevant material was disclosed only to the AFT in a sealed cover?"[5] The question arose whether this process was transparent and fair. The Hon'ble Supreme Court observed that while the sealed cover procedure was used, the AFT thoroughly perused the records, including the selection criteria and processes adopted by the Indian Navy. The sealed cover procedure, while not ideal for transparency, was deemed acceptable by the Tribunal which was given full access to the relevant materials. The AFT's validation of the process indicates that it did not find any procedural unfairness or bias.

3. *ibid* [8].

4. *ibid*.

5. *ibid* [3].

It is evident that significant prejudice has resulted from the process of disclosing vacancy information and Board proceedings exclusively to the Tribunal in a sealed cover. In *Khudiram Das vs State of West Bengal,*[6] the Hon'ble Supreme Court emphasized that the test for determining whether material should be disclosed is whether, in "reasonable probability," the material would influence the authority's decision.[7] The human mind does not function in isolation; it integrates impressions from various sources, and it is impossible to dissect or exclude certain impressions from the decision-making process once they have been received.

Similarly, in *T. Takano vs Securities and Exchange Board of India,*[8] the Hon'ble Supreme Court held that all relevant information must be disclosed. The Court outlined three key purposes served by disclosure: (i) *Reliability,* ensuring that shared information aids the court in evaluating the truth of the parties' contentions; (ii) *Fair Trial,* enabling parties to effectively participate in the proceedings by having access to pertinent information; and (iii) *Transparency and Accountability,* ensuring that adjudication processes remain open and subject to scrutiny, thereby fostering trust in judicial outcomes.[9]

Impact of Withholding Information on Judicial Transparency

Denying a party access to information influencing an adjudicatory decision undermines the transparency of the judicial process. It prevents effective scrutiny by the concerned party and the public at large, creating an information asymmetry. The purpose of disclosure extends beyond preventing errors in verdicts; it serves the larger institutional goals of ensuring fairness and transparency. Disclosure must address both the reliability of the outcome and the integrity of the process. A disclosure rule limited to material explicitly relied upon fails to address the broader institutional purpose, making it essential that all relevant material is disclosed, except in cases involving sensitive information or national security.

---

6. (1975) 2 SCC 81.
7. *ibid* [15].
8. (2022) 8 SCC 162.
9. *ibid* [28].

The Perils of Sealed Cover Procedure in Adjudication

A fundamental legal principle mandates the disclosure of all material relied upon in judicial proceedings. Even if not explicitly relied upon, any information that could reasonably influence the outcome must be shared. A one-sided submission of adjudicatory material violates natural justice and prejudices affected parties, as evidenced in this case, where officers' careers suffered due to undisclosed material.

The practice of presenting relevant material exclusively to the adjudicating authority (here, the Armed Forces Tribunal) in a sealed cover sets a concerning precedent, fostering opacity and unfairness. This raises two key issues: (i) It denies the aggrieved party the ability to challenge the decision effectively, as the adjudication rests on undisclosed material, undermining meaningful scrutiny; (ii) It cultivates secrecy, concentrating power in the adjudicating authority and often favouring the state, which controls the information. Judicial orders must provide stated reasons, but the sealed cover procedure obscures this process, eroding justice at both individual and institutional levels.

Balancing Confidentiality with Transparency in Adjudication

Not all information warrants unconditional disclosure, and exceptions for sensitive matters should be proportionate and exceptional rather than routine. While sealed cover submissions may protect confidential information, particularly in national security matters, their overuse compromises transparency. In this case, officers denied permanent commission (PC) lacked access to the materials evaluating their candidacy, raising serious concerns about fairness and due process. Restricting affected parties from understanding the rationale behind decisions undermines justice and accountability.

Judicial Precedents on the Sealed Cover Procedure

Indian courts, including the Supreme Court, have adjudicated on multiple occasions regarding the use of the sealed cover procedure. While this practice inherently limits transparency, it has been deemed justifiable in circumstances where the disclosure of sensitive information could compromise judicial proceedings or national security. However, courts have consistently underscored that the use of sealed cover must not impede the fundamental principles of natural justice and procedural fairness.

In *Karnataka Public Service Commission vs B.M. Vijaya Shankar*[10], the Supreme Court acknowledged that while the sealed cover mechanism serves to maintain confidentiality, it must not hinder the ability of the court to dispense justice effectively. The Court emphasized that the adoption of this procedure must be balanced against the overarching principles of transparency and accountability. It reiterated that while sealed cover submissions could be necessary in certain exceptional cases, the judiciary must scrutinize the material thoroughly to ensure that it does not lead to an unfair trial or biased adjudication.

Over the years, the sealed cover procedure has been utilized in various significant cases. In *S.P. Gupta vs Union of India*[11], the Supreme Court ruled that the government could not withhold documents arbitrarily and must establish a tangible risk to public interest to justify non-disclosure, curbing the indiscriminate use of sealed covers. Similarly, in *K. Veeraswami vs Union of India*[12], sealed cover submissions were used to protect whistleblower identities in judicial corruption cases, ensuring their safety from retaliatory measures. The *BCCI Reforms Case*[13] saw the Court permitting sealed cover submissions to maintain the confidentiality of cricketers accused of match-fixing, reflecting a balancing act between privacy and public interest. In the *Rafale Deal Case*[14], the Supreme Court required the government to submit sensitive defence procurement details in a sealed cover, sparking debates on judicial transparency and state accountability. The *Bhima Koregaon Case*[15] raised significant concerns regarding the accused's right to a fair trial, as Maharashtra Police submitted evidence in a sealed cover, limiting the defence's ability to contest the allegations effectively.

---

10. AIR 1992 SC 952.

11. AIR 1982 SC 149.

12. 1991 SCC (3) 655.

13. *Board of Control for Cricket in India vs Cricket Association of Bihar,* 2015 3 SCC 251.

14. *Manohar Lal Sharma vs Narendra Damodardas Modi,* (2019) 3 SCC 25.

15. *Romila Thapar vs Union of India,* (2018) 10 SCC 753.

More recently, in *Madhyamam Broadcasting Ltd vs Union of India*[16], the Supreme Court reaffirmed that the principles of natural justice require the disclosure of relevant material to the affected party. The judgment observed that reliance on undisclosed documents by the opposing party, typically the State, compromises the affected party's ability to present a defence. Even in matters concerning national security, the State bears the burden of justifying any deviation from procedural fairness. On 3 January 2024, the Supreme Court rejected the Government's proposal to submit the names of committee members in a sealed cover in the *Adani-Hindenburg* matter, underscoring the necessity of maintaining transparency in judicial proceedings, particularly in cases of significant public interest.[17] The Court's decision was pivotal in affirming regulatory accountability, particularly in response to allegations by Hindenburg Research that the Adani Group engaged in stock manipulation and financial misconduct.

While the sealed cover procedure remains an established judicial tool, its application must be carefully circumscribed to prevent undue secrecy from eroding the foundational tenets of justice and due process.

Threat to Fairness and Transparency in Legal Proceedings

In a democratic society governed by the rule of law, fairness and transparency are fundamental to a just legal system. Accepting closed-envelope documents in court undermines these principles, leading to procedural unfairness, potential bias, and diminished public trust. Courts should reject such submissions to maintain balance in legal proceedings, ensuring both parties have equal access to evidence and the opportunity to challenge it. Closed-envelope documents create an asymmetry that contradicts the adversarial system's core principle of a level playing field.

Transparency is essential for maintaining public confidence in the judiciary. When courts accept undisclosed documents, proceedings become

---

16. (2023) 13 SCC 401.

17. Krishanadas Rajagopal,'Hindenburg-Adani case | Supreme Court says no to sealed cover suggestions' (*The Hindu,* 17 February 2023) <https://www.thehindu.com/news/national/adani-issue-sc-pils-over-setting-up-experts-panel-to-strengthen-regulatory-mechanisms/article66520027.ece> accessed 11 February 2025.

opaque, fostering suspicions of hidden bias or undue influence. By rejecting closed-envelope submissions, courts reaffirm their commitment to justice and prevent reputational harm to the legal system. Moreover, allowing undisclosed documents, especially from powerful institutions like the government, risks perceptions of favouritism, even where none exists. Upholding impartiality requires courts to ensure all parties have equal access to critical information.

Safeguarding the Right to a Fair and Transparent Hearing

The right to a fair hearing, enshrined in constitutional and human rights frameworks, includes access to all relevant evidence. Closed-envelope submissions risk depriving parties of this right by concealing key information that could impact case outcomes. Courts must protect litigants' fundamental rights by ensuring open and equal access to all evidence, reinforcing due process and confidence in judicial proceedings.

Upholding Judicial Integrity Through Open Evidence Practices

Rejecting closed-envelope submissions aligns with fairness, transparency, and equal treatment—principles crucial to judicial legitimacy. Courts must ensure all evidence considered is fully accessible to all parties, safeguarding procedural fairness and public trust. By adopting a strict policy against undisclosed documents, the judiciary strengthens its commitment to impartiality and justice.

To 'State' the Obvious...

Challenges to Revitalizing Litigation

Anu Pal[1]

Introduction

STATE...the guarantor of our rights; follows the rule of law; committed to justice, equality and liberty for its people. Amidst all these lofty ideals, Gopal Bijawat, a part-time labourer had to wait 22 years to reap benefits awarded to him by the Labour Court.[2]

The courts are replete with such like instances; so be it a citizen fighting against the state in the High Court over medical reimbursement despite having won from two lower courts;[3] an ex-army employee having to fight it out for his legitimate claim over pension;[4] the widow of an ex-army man engaged in a legal battle with the Union over her legitimate right on Liberalised Family Pension;[5] an ex-employee grappling with a charge sheet slapped on him 4 years after his

---

1. Advocate, Punjab and Haryana High Court, Chandigarh.

2. *State of Rajasthan vs Gopal Bijawat*, SLP (C) No. 3398/2024, decided on 16.02.2024

3. *The Financial Commissioner and Secretary to Government of Haryana vs Jagdish Chand Garg*, CM No. 4311-C of 2017 in/and RSA No. 1780 of 2017, decided on 11.05.2017

4. *Union of India vs Karan Singh*, LPA(SW) No. 41 of 2007; LPA(SW) No. 127 of 2007 and LPA(SW) No. 209 of 2006 (Jammu and Kashmir High Court (DB)), decided on 20.11.2013

5. *Union of India vs Saroj Devi*, Civil Appeal No. 13730 of 2024, decided on 03.12.2024

voluntary retirement for an offence allegedly committed 6 years prior!;[6] two departments of the Government entangled in a title dispute over land which was protracted at different levels for 37 years before the Supreme Court finally declared the same to be that of private individuals![7]; a war widow having to knock the doors of court twice to finally get land allotted to her for exhibition of gallantry by her husband;[8] the son of an army man having suffered 90% disability being forced to resort to litigation, having been denied his claim as a dependent of an ex-serviceman (disabled);[9] a sailor of the Indian Navy being left with no choice but to challenge cryptic orders denying his claim for disability, aggravated by naval service before the AFT and then having to face Union of India in the High Court after having being given his rightful claim by the tribunal;[10] all these instances highlighting that we still have a long way to go in securing rights for all citizens. No wonder, Justice Krishna Iyer was compelled to observe the callous and cantankerous approach of the government, expecting instead, a "*finer sense and sensibility in its litigation policy.*"[11]

Courts in India, the watchdogs of the Constitution, having recognised Rule of Law as an aspect of the basic structure of our Constitution, which even the plenary power of Parliament cannot reach to amend,[12] have since long expected the state to be a 'virtuous litigant.'[13]

It is no secret that courts across the nation today are inundated with heavy work load. It is not just the sheer volume but the variety and complexity

---

6. *Punjab State Power Corporation Ltd. Patiala vs Atma Singh Grewal,* SLP (Civil) No. 29589 of 2009, decided on 17.09.2013

7. *Chief Conservator of Forests Govt. of A.P. vs Collectors,* AIR 2003 SC 1805, decided on 18.02.2003

8. *Balwant Kaur vs State of Punjab,* CWP No. 25871 of 2022 P&H (DB), decided on 04.05.2023

9. *Rahul vs State of Haryana,* CWP No. 23346 of 2021 d/d 13.9.2024 P&H, decided on 13.09.2024

10. *Union of India vs CDR AK Srivastava (Retd.),* W.P.(C) 15493/2024 Delhi HC (DB), decided on 12.11.2024

11. *Dilbagh Rai Jarry vs Union of India,* AIR 1974 SC 130.

12. *Kesavananda Bharati vs State of Kerala,* (1973) 4 SCC 225.

13. *Balwant Kaur* (n 7).

involved thereof which contributes greatly to the pendency. With new legislations being enacted,[14] the onus is upon the Constitutional Courts to interpret, ensure effective implementation in the spirit in which they were enacted apart from of course determining their legality, if need so arises. Given the important and often convoluted questions of law that need to be adjudicated upon, it comes as no surprise that the already overburdened courts, working with a dismal judge per case ratio come down heavily on the state in matters which could have easily been resolved outside of court. Particularly when the courts have also held that public administration is responsible for effective implementation of rule of law and constitutional commands which effectuate fairly the objective standards laid down by law.[15] Every public servant after all has been held to be a trustee of the society and is accountable for due effectuation of constitutional goals.[16]

And the spirit of fair assistance to the Court is not unique to India, but is universal. As Justice Robert H. Jackson of the Supreme Court of the United States famously said in 1940, "although the government technically loses its case, it has really won if justice has been done." The Supreme Court of Canada in 1955,[17] underlined that the duty by counsel representing the government "should be done firmly and pressed to its legitimate strength but it must also be done fairly," adding further that it "excludes any notion 'of winning or losing', rather is a matter of public duty."

Litigation Policy as a Possible Solution

The Law Commission in its 126th report culled out numerous case law observing the 'sordid picture of utter indifference and callousness...'[18], in order

14. In a press release posted on January 3, 2024, the Ministry of Parliamentary Affairs stated that during January-December 2023, a total of 49 Bills were passed by both Houses of Parliament and assented to by the President. Ministry of Parliamentary Affairs, 'Year End Review 2023' <https://pib.govsin/PressReleasePage.aspx?PRID=1992755> accessed 9 January 2025.

15. *State of Punjab vs G.S. Gill*, (1997) 6 SCC 129.

16. *Superintending Engineer vs Kuldeep Singh*, (1997) 9 SCC 199.

17. Boucher vs The Queen [1955] SCR 16.

18. Law Commission of India, '126th Report on Government and Public Sector Undertaking Litigation Policy and Strategies' (1988) <https://cdnbbsr.s3waas.gov.in/

to highlight the reckless litigious culture adopted by the government and its agencies. The Government formulated the National Litigation Policy in 2010 with an aim to transform itself into an 'efficient' and 'responsible' litigant. Status note on the same[19] revealed that since the same could not be implemented, formulation of a new policy of 2015 is under consideration. The latest draft formulated in 2024 is pending approval of the Cabinet. Several states had formulated and have recently revised their respective policies.

The starting point of all policies is the recognition that the government and its entities are a party in majority of the matters pending before the courts and quasi-judicial authorities and the state, by transforming itself into an efficient and responsible litigant, would help curb future and ongoing litigation. And though it would be a near impossible task to get the exact number of matters where state or its entity is a party, an online hunt would seem to peg it down at 73%. This statistic alone would be enough for anyone to believe that the State is a chronic litigator but a word of caution here would be important. State is necessarily a party in all criminal matters so if my neighbour wants to be free on bail after committing murder, statistics against the State will drastically come down if such like matters are taken out from the reckoning. There are also innumerable civil matters where state is not a contesting party, adding unnecessarily to the statistical count. That having said, one cannot overlook the somewhat lackadaisical approach of the state functionaries. The Bihar High Court was rightly irked when the ground situation had not improved despite repeated reassurances to rectify the position and the Chief Secretary along with other officers had to be called to court. The court highlighted innumerable petitions which were being filed; either to direct the quasi functional authorities to decide matters since the officers were not holding their court regularly; or to issue certified copies of orders; or where incomplete, unsatisfactory affidavits were being filed as a matter of routine by the government; where unreliable, irresponsible, and false statements were being made in these affidavits; or where there was non-implementation of orders; where frivolous appeals in matters of land acquisition and other cases were being filed where the valuation ranged from rupees five hundred to a few

s3ca0daec69b5adc880fb464895726dbdf/uploads/2022/08/2022080866-1.pdf>

19. Department of Legal Affairs, 'Status Note on National Litigation Policy' <https://legalaffairs.gov.in/sites/default/files/status%20note%20on%20nlp_0_0.pdf>

thousand rupees. It also observed that 95% of the matters which pertained to pension were essentially clerical in nature where though the government had admitted the dues yet sanction orders had not been issued; and that innumerable and needless contempt petitions due to non-execution of the orders passed were pending.[20] The court summarised the majority of the problems due to which the dockets of the courts remain clogged.

Working of the Policies

The revised policy of most of the States lays down certain key features like encouraging alternate dispute resolution system, to train officers to pass well-reasoned and speaking orders, to avoid litigation where matters are already covered by judgements that have obtained finality or where no further or useful purpose would be served in continuing the matter; to abstain from appealing against *ex-parte* interim orders, or in trivial matters or where the decision pertains to pensionary or retirement benefits etc., with of course a caveat... to go ahead where a substantial question of law is involved or a precedent wrongful precedent is set. Punjab is probably one of the only states having a financial criterion as well... no appeal if financial implication is below a particular amount with of course, a similar caveat. Apart from this, an institutional framework has been set up with an aim to affix accountability.

A perusal of the policies would leave almost anyone impressed. On paper, the states have seemingly covered all bases, including measures of affixing accountability but a question that naturally comes to mind after reading the policies is, have the states not reduced in writing, in one single document, what everyone is supposed to be doing in the first place? Why, then, has the government been unable to do this seemingly simple and normal task in practical terms? The answer may not be far to seek. If a government employee can be slapped with a show cause notice simply because the legal opinion, she gave was incorrect in the opinion of higher authorities and even though the same was not acted upon, no employee, who is already neck deep in work, would be ready to withstand the possible repercussions. No wonder the attitude of, 'let the courts decide' is

20. *Rakesh Kumar vs State of Bihar*, CWJC No. 13843 of 2003 Patna High Court, decided on 08.09.2004.

rampant. Policies may also allude to mediation or alternate dispute resolution but who, in the hierarchical set up would have the authority to concede or meet the other party mid-way to arrive at an amicable settlement? This is again in the context of having to possibly face unwarranted proceedings at a later stage in one's career.

Another factor in the nonchalant manner in dealing with matters could be the impersonal nature of everyone involved, coupled with of course the inherent fear of having to bear the brunt in case something was to go wrong, even for no fault of the government employee. This brings us to another aspect... does the state need to have a separate litigation policy when it comes to the armed forces? And even though it seems just and fair at first glance, the answer may not lie there. Just as the answer may not lie in having litigation policies, to begin with.

Responsibility of Private Litigants

Before I come to discussing the non-requirement of a policy in the first place, I must delve into another aspect. That of the entirely vexatious petitions preferred by private litigants. Petitions where high courts are approached directly without invoking available alternate remedies and so on. It seems fashionable to put the blame on the government for everything. And even though the government has earned this reputation of its own doing, one should not loose objectivity. A classic example is where a Public Interest Litigation was filed challenging before the High Court, the appointment of the Advocate General of Uttaranchal (now Uttarakhand) on the ground that he was more than 62 years of age.[21] On the state filing appeal, the Supreme Court came down heavily on the respondent in light of the fact that not only had this controversy been settled by a catena of earlier judgements but also that the respondent was himself a lawyer. Similarly, the Supreme Court held that it was the bounden duty of the court to not have reopened the controversy once settled by an authoritative judgement. Discourage litigation, said Abraham Lincoln, "*...persuade your neighbours to compromise whenever*

21. *State of Uttaranchal vs Balwant Singh Chaufal*, Civil Appeals Nos. 1134-1135 of 2002, decided on 18.1.2010.

you can. Point out to them how the nominal winner is often a real loser in fees and expenses." It is time that all lawyers start giving wise, fair and just counsel in order that the likes of Addison Mizner are no longer able to say, "*Where there is a will, there is a lawsuit.*"

Conclusion

Coming back to the relevance of litigation policies, would one not be living in a fairyland if one were to believe that a litigation policy would magically bring down the pendency in courts? Can the government alone be blamed for something that is so inextricably entwined across the pillars of our democratic set up?

The need of the hour is for an overall improvement of work ethos; be it the state or its entities, the various functionaries of the state at all levels, litigants from all sections of society, lawyers representing the state or private parties and the judiciary; to increasing the number of officials and judges; for all branches to work in tandem; to have a more pragmatic approach towards dealing with issues involved, resulting in increased productivity and efficiency, naturally decreasing the work load, instead of formulating policies with the fundamental aim of decreasing work.

The state functionaries need to be trained to acquaint themselves with the relevant laws depending on which branch they work in, listen to the grievances and then arrive at reasoned decisions, recording the same in writing in order that when the same is subject to judicial review, the courts should know that the decision was not taken mindlessly or due to lack of knowledge of the authoritative judgments but because the official genuinely believed the claim to be not maintainable. To review the matters already pending in light of the latest rulings and directions of courts. To effectively implement those rulings and avoid future litigation. To stop filing appeals mindlessly. To ensure efficient inter departmental communication and information sharing and conveyance of the same with equal promptitude to the state counsel in order to ensure that the justified stand is put before the court effectively and on time. To not to shy away from accepting mistakes and rectifying the same. To be bold enough to take decisions based on law and equity. To be just enough to protect one's own officers when such like decisions are taken. In short, to simply do one's job sincerely.

And once everyone starts doing simply what they are supposed to be, the vexed questions pertaining to the need of having new policies, a different stance of the government towards armed forces or other categories would simply fade away since we already have adequate laws, rules and regulations sufficiently protecting everyone's interest. And even though the onus lies on us all, the state will need to lead and show the way because after all, apart from being the paramount champion of all our rights, the state also is, as Justice Krishna Iyer puts it, '*a virtuous litigant.*'

PART II

Reported Judgments

(2025) I FLR 46 (United States of America)

United States Court of Military Commission Review

Case Number CMCR 24-001

In Re Khalid Shaikh Mohammad, Walid Muhammad Salih Mubarak bin 'Attash, and Mustafa Ahmed Adam al Hawasawi

Composition of Court: Schenck, Richardson, and Kirkby, JJ

Date of Decision: 30 December 2024

Counsel for the Petitioner: Michael J. O'Sullivan; Haridimos V. Thravalos; Bryce G. Poole; Clay Trivett; and Rear Admiral Aaron C. Rugh, JAGC, U.S. Navy.

Counsel for the Respondents and Intervenor: Gary D. Sowards; Nicholas W. McCue; Gabriela M. McQuade; Melanie T. Partow; and Major Michael P. Leahy, JA, U.S. Air Force; Walter B. Ruiz; Suzanne M. Lachelier; Sean M. Gleason; Major Kerry A. Mawn, JA, U.S. Air Force; and Major Patrick C. Tipton, JA, U.S. Air Force; James G. Connell, III; Alka Pradhan; Rita J. Radostitz; Defne Ozgediz; Major Jessica Casciola, JA, U.S. Army; and Lieutenant Jennifer Joseph, JAGC, U.S. Navy.

Summary

Mohammad, Hawasawi, and Ali, accused of the 9/11 attacks, made pre-trial agreements (PTAs) with the petitioner, agreeing to plead guilty, stipulate facts, and forgo legal challenges. The convening authority approved the PTAs on July 31, 2024, and the respondents began fulfilling their obligations. However, on August 2, 2024, the Secretary of Defense revoked the convening authority's power to enter these agreements, claiming the authority for himself and withdrawing the existing PTAs.

The court addressed two issues: the validity of the PTA withdrawals and the Secretary's authority. The petitioner argued for the Secretary's right to limit subordinate authority. The respondents contended that the revocations breached the agreements, especially after performance had begun.

The court held that while the Secretary can limit a subordinate's PTA authority, he cannot revoke PTAs once performance has commenced, as per Rule for Military Commissions 705(d)(4). This rule permits withdrawal only before performance or if the agreement itself allows it. Therefore, the Secretary retains the power to delegate convening authority for future PTAs as he sees fit.

Headnotes

Facts: Respondents Mohammad and Hawasawi and intervenor Ali Abdul Aziz Ali were accused of planning the terror attacks against the United States on September 11, 2001. Respondents and intervenors entered into pre-trial agreements (PTAs) with petitioner. In the PTAs, respondents agreed, among other things, to plead guilty, sign a stipulation of facts, accept admissibility of Letterhead Memoranda summarizing statements made by each to the FBI, not litigate or contest motions in respondents' case, and not cross-examine petitioner's witnesses. Respondents signed the PTAs on July 29 and 30, 2024. The convening authority signed both PTAs on July 31, 2024. Respondents then began performance of their PTA. On August 2, 2024, the Secretary of Defense withdrew the convening authority's authority to enter into PTAs with respondents, reserved such authority to himself, and withdrew the PTAs.

Issue: Under the Rules for Military Commissions whether 1) whether a convening authority may withdraw the PTAs after respondents had begun performance; and 2) whether a superior convening authority may reserve authority to him or herself for future PTAs.

Contentions of the Parties: Petitioner argued that there was "ample precedent" for a superior convening authority limiting the authority of a subordinate convening authority. The military judge erred when he ruled that the Secretary of Defense lacked the authority to withdraw the subordinate convening authority's ability to enter into PTAs and withdraw consent to the existing PTAs. Respondents argued that revocation of the PTAs would be a breach of that agreement. Moreover, the PTAs could not be revoked because at least one respondent had begun performing.

Held: 1) Though the Secretary of Defense does have authority to limit a subordinate's authority to enter into a PTA, the military judge correctly held that the Secretary, or any other convening authority, did not have the authority to revoke the PTAs. Rule of Military Commissions 705(d)(4) only allows a convening authority to withdraw a PTA before the accused begins performance of the PTA or if the PTA provides for such a withdrawal. 2) Because of this holding, the Secretary may choose how to delegate his convening authority for future PTAs. However, the Secretary took no action in regard to future PTAs.

Case Law Cited

In re Ali, 558 F. Supp. 3d 1167 (CMCR 2021)

United States vs Mohammad, 280 F. Supp. 3d 1305 (CMCR 2017)

Cheney vs U.S. District Court, 542 U.S. 367 (2004)

United States vs Khadr, 717 F. Supp. 2d 1212 (CMCR 2007)

Al Bahlul vs United States (Al Bahlul IV), 967 F.3d 858 (D.C. Cir. 2020)

Mabry vs Johnson, 467 U.S. 504 (1984)

United States vs Acevedo, 50 M.J. 169 (C.A.A.F. 1999)

Cooper vs United States, 594 F.2d 12 (4th Cir. 1979)

United States vs Moreno-Membache, 995 F.3d 249 (D.C. Cir. 2021)

United States vs Fleming, 2 A.B.R. 359 (1931)

Hayes vs Maksym, No. NMCCA 200301982, 2004 CCA LEXIS 35 (N-M. Ct. Crim. App. Feb. 11, 2004)

United States vs Hardy, 4 M.J. 20 (C.M.A. 1977)

United States vs Blaylock, 15 M.J. 190 (C.M.A. 1983)

United States vs Leahr, 73 M.J. 364 (C.A.A.F. 2014)

United States vs Dean, 67 M.J. 224 (C.A.A.F. 2009)

United States vs Hunter, 65 M.J. 399 (C.A.A.F. 2008)

United States vs Williams, 60 M.J. 360 (C.A.A.F. 2004)

United States vs Allen, 31 M.J. 572 (N-M.C.M.R. 1990)

United States vs Kroetz, No. ACM 40301, 2023 CCA LEXIS 450 (A.F. Ct. Crim. App. Oct. 27, 2023)

United States vs Saulter, 23 M.J. 626 (A.F.C.M.R. 1986)

United States vs Finch, 79 M.J. 389 (C.A.A.F. 2020)

In re Al-Nashiri (Al-Nashiri I), 791 F.3d 71 (D.C. Cir. 2015)

In re Kellogg Brown & Root, Inc., 756 F.3d 754 (D.C. Cir. 2014)

Nat. Res. Def. Council vs EPA, 777 F.3d 456 (D.C. Cir. 2014)

Nat'l Ass'n of Criminal Def. Lawyers, Inc. vs DOJ, 182 F.3d 981 (D.C. Cir. 1999)

Quaker Action Grp. vs Hickel, 429 F.2d 185 (D.C. Cir. 1970)

Schick vs Reed, 419 U.S. 256 (1974)

Biddle vs Perovich, 274 U.S. 480 (1927)

Andrews vs Warden, 958 F.3d 1072 (11th Cir. 2020)

O'Connell vs Shalala, 79 F.3d 170 (1st Cir. 1996)

United States vs O'Neil, 11 F.3d 292 (1st Cir. 1993)

Al-Nashiri III, 921 F.3d 224 (D.C. Cir. 2019)

In re United States, 32 F.4th 584 (6th Cir. 2022)

Opinion for the court
Schenck, Judge:

Respondents Khalid Shaikh Mohammad (KSM or Mohammad), Walid Muhammad Salih Mubarak Bin 'Attash (WBA or Bin 'Attash), and Mustafa Ahmed Adam al Hawsawi (MAH or Hawsawi) are three of four co-accused being tried by military commission at Guantanamo Bay, Cuba, in *Khalid Shaikh Mohammad et al.* The other co-accused, Ali Abdul Aziz Ali, also known as Ammar al Baluchi, moved to join as an intervenor in the writ petition that was filed in this court by petitioner, the United States Government. Ali Mot. to Intervene (Dec. 6, 2024). In September 2023, the military commission severed from *Mohammad et al.*, the fifth defendant, Ramzi Binalshibh, because he lacked capacity to stand trial. Pet'r's App. 628 (Nov. 26, 2024).

Petitioner seeks a writ of mandamus and prohibition and asks our court to vacate the military judge's rulings in AE 955J (KSM), AE 956J (WBA), and AE 957I (MAH). Pet'r's Br. 1–2 (Nov. 26, 2024). The military judge ruled that the Secretary of Defense (Secretary) did not have authority to "withdraw" Brigadier General (BG) (Retired) [hereinafter (Ret.)] Susan Escallier's authority to enter into pretrial agreements (PTA)[1]and retroactively replace the convening authority with himself as the convening authority authorized to make PTAs in the case of *Mohammad et al.*, and to vacate existing PTAs[2] between these accused and the convening authority.

1. In military commissions, the term "pretrial agreement" refers to "terms or conditions requested by the accused, within the power of the convening authority, and not otherwise prohibited," which the convening authority may agree to as a step in the disposition of offenses. Rule for Military Commissions (R.M.C.) 705(b), Manual for Military Commissions, United States (MMC) (2019 ed.). In courts-martial, the term "plea agreement" is the same as pretrial agreement (PTA). See Rule for Courts-Martial (R.C.M.) 705(b), Manual for Courts-Martial, United States (MCM) (2024).

2. The pretrial agreements are filed under and remain under seal except as indicated in this decision. Pet'r's App. 912–14 (Nov. 26, 2024).

We deny the writ of mandamus and prohibition for two reasons. First, we conclude that although the Secretary had authority to replace BG (Ret.) Escallier with himself as the convening authority for *future* PTAs, the Secretary has not taken any actions on future PTAs. Advisory decisions on writs of mandamus and prohibition are not permitted. And second, we agree with the military judge that the Secretary did not have authority to revoke respondents' existing PTAs because the respondents had started performance of the PTAs.

Respondents are charged with multiple violations of the law of war under the Military Commissions Act of 2009 (M.C.A.), 10 U.S.C. §§ 948a–950t, for their alleged roles in the planning and execution of the September 11, 2001, attacks on the United States. *See In re Ali*, 558 F. Supp. 3d 1167, 1170 (CMCR 2021). The charges allege that respondents aided, abetted, and conspired with 19 al Qaeda hijackers to commit attacks, which resulted in the deaths of 2,976 people. Pet'r's Br. 1 (citing Pet'r's App. 774 (charge sheet, referred April 4, 2012)); see *United States vs Mohammad*, 280 F. Supp. 3d 1305, 1308 (CMCR 2017) (listing charges). Their capital charges were referred to trial by military commission, pursuant to the 2009 MCA. Pet'r's App. 775; see 10 U.S.C. § 948b. Our court has resolved twelve writs or government appeals in this case. See Ali, 558 F. Supp. 3d at 1170–71 (detailing writ and appellate history).

I. Statement of facts

On August 21, 2023, the Secretary appointed BG (Ret.) Escallier as the convening authority for respondents' military commission effective on October 8, 2023. Pet'r's App. 670. The appointment memorandum stated that "Ms. Escallier shall exercise her independent legal discretion with regard to judicial acts and other duties of the Convening Authority." *Id.* at 401. On July 29 and 30, 2024, petitioner and respondents signed stipulations of fact and respondents signed PTAs. *Id.* at 29, 149, 280, 298; *see also id.* at 402–03. The resulting three PTAs contained numerous requirements, including that the respondents enter into stipulations of fact, accept admissibility of Letterhead Memoranda (LHM) summarizing statements made by each accused to the Federal Bureau of Investigation (FBI) in 2007, and also in 2008 for Bin 'Attash, and not litigate or contest motions in respondents' case. *Id.* at 12–13, 15, 20 (KSM PTA);

133–36, 140 (WBA PTA), 281–83, 289 (MAH PTA); *see also id.* at 403, 404 n.41. The PTAs included stipulations of fact and partially redacted LHM statements as Attachments A and B. *See, e.g., id.* at 680–81 (WBA PTA) (citing AE 956 (GOV), Attach. B, at 53–148). Petitioner and each respondent signed that respondent's stipulation of fact on July 29 or 30, 2024. Id. at 58, 174, 328. "Paragraph 56 of the PTA provides that 'the Convening Authority's acceptance of this Offer, including Attachments A and B[,] will transform this Offer into an Agreement binding upon the Accused and the Government.'" Id. at 681 (WBA PTA) (alteration in original). On July 31, 2024, the convening authority signed each PTA. Id. at 30, 50, 298, 403 & n.30

The next day, on August 1, 2024, petitioner notified the military judge at a hearing that "the convening authority has reached pretrial agreements in this case" with respondents. Id. at 912; *see id. at* 404. That same day, during a discussion with the judge about severing Mohammad, Bin 'Attash, and Hawsawi (the individuals who had PTAs) from the trial of Ali (who did not have a PTA), trial counsel stated: "But at this point, with the waiver of all motions from three of the four accused, they can't actively continue to participate in any of the contested litigation based on [their] pretrial agreement[s]." Id. at 917–18. An FBI special agent testified later that same day. *Id.* at 926. Ali's counsel cross-examined the witness; counsel for the three respondents did not ask any questions. *Id.* at 404; see id. at 926.

On August 2, 2024, the Secretary issued a memorandum to the convening authority, Subject: Authority to Enter into Pre-Trial Agreements in *United States vs Khalid Shaikh Mohammad et al. (United States vs Khalid Shaikh Mohammad; United States vs Walid Muhammad Salih Mubarak Bin 'Attash; United States vs Mustafa Ahmed Adam al Hawsawi; United States vs Ramzi Binalshibh; and United States vs Ali Abdul Aziz Ali)*, which states:

> I have determined that, in light of the significance of the decision to enter into pre-trial agreements with the accused in the above-referenced case, responsibility for such a decision should rest with me as the superior convening authority under the Military Commissions Act of 2009. Effective immediately, I hereby withdraw your authority in the above-referenced case to enter into a pre-trial agreement and reserve such authority to myself.

> Effective immediately, in the exercise of my authority, I hereby withdraw from the three pre-trial agreements that you signed on July 31, 2024 in the above-referenced case.

Id. at 405, 636. Prior to issuing his memorandum, the Secretary did not issue or place any limitations on BG (Ret.) Escallier's authority to enter into PTAs that are relevant to the mandamus petition before the court. *Id.* at 401, 411.

Counsel for Hawsawi noted on the record that if Hawsawi's PTA was "to be somehow revoked or removed, that [] would be a breach of [the] agreement" because specific performance on Hawsawi's agreement had already begun because he had abstained from examining witnesses. Id. at 684 (citation omitted). The parties briefed the issues. *See id.* at 644.

After the PTAs were signed, respondents did not file motions (other than for scheduling matters), request discovery, examine witnesses, or argue motions. *Id.* at 405. The military judge found that BG (Ret.) Escallier had continued to act as the convening authority in this case. Id. at 406. She did not, however, take any actions with respect to the three PTAs in respondents' case—there is no evidence of changes to those PTAs. Nor is there any evidence of a PTA between Intervenor Ali and the convening authority, BG (Ret.) Escallier.

On November 6, 2024, the military judge ruled in AE 955J (KSM), AE 956J (WBA), and AE 957I (MAH) that the Secretary's memorandum was *void ab initio*. *Id.* at 424 n.122. He further determined that the Secretary could not withhold ex post facto the authority already given and exercised to make PTAs. *See id.* at 419–20. Regarding *withdrawal* from the PTAs, the military judge stated:

> R.M.C. [Rule for Military Commissions] 705(a)[, Manual for Military Commissions, United States (MMC),] grants authority to prescribe limitations regarding the entering of PTAs. R.M.C. 705(d)(4)(B), which discusses withdrawal from PTAs, has no comparable provision. Under that Rule, withdrawal authority belongs to the convening authority alone and is not subject to a limitation as the Secretary may prescribe. The Secretary did not purport to make himself the Convening Authority for this case. Thus, even if he possessed legal authority to enter into a PTA, the Rules reserved withdrawal authority to the Convening Authority,

> Ms. Escallier. This asymmetrical result that would ensue if the SECDEF Memo is given effect is further evidence that the roles of the convening authority cannot be so spliced as the Prosecution urges; the fair-handed, even administration of justice requires a singular entity with oversight over the case at large to be able to act on matters before him or her.

Id. at 421 (footnotes omitted). The military judge also cited practical difficulties involved in parsing responsibilities between two convening authorities, and the absence of legal precedent for two convening authorities on the same case. Id. at 417–21.

Petitioner said in its petition that there is ample precedent for superior convening authorities granting or limiting the authority of subordinate convening authorities.[3]

Additionally, the military judge suggested that the Secretary could not appoint himself as the convening authority for future PTAs, and determined he could not withdraw from the PTAs because respondents' performance had begun. *Id.* at 417–20. The military judge stated:

> Performance began in a number of ways. All three Accused signed lengthy confessional stipulations of fact, which could be used to establish their guilt and for the Panel Members to determine an appropriate sentence. All three Accused negotiated an acceptable version of their respective LHMs which can be offered against them in presentencing proceedings without certain objections. All three Accused refrained from examining the witness(es) for pretrial motions while the Prosecution and Defense Counsel for Mr. Ali questioned those same witnesses. The Trial Counsel himself insisted upon that

3. Petitioner quotes from The Judge Advocate General's Legal Center & School, U.S. Army, Criminal Law Deskbook, at 1-6 (Jan. 2019), noting it states, "[b]y policy, the Secretary of Defense has withheld the disposition authority for all sexual offenses." Pet'r's Br. 22 (Nov. 26, 2024) (alteration in original) (quoting Pet'r's App. 1115). Petitioner quotes from The Judge Advocate General's Legal Center & School, U.S. Army, Commander's Legal Handbook, Misc. Pub. No. 27-8, at 18 (2019), noting it states that a superior commander may "[w]ithhold authority over types of offenses, types of offenders, or certain commanders." Id. (alteration in original) (quoting Pet'r's App. 1102). Petitioner also compares Rule for Military Commissions 401(a) with Rule for Courts-Martial 306(a)(2), and 10 U.S.C. § 837(d)(1), and cites to paragraph 12-1 of the Regulation for Trial by Military Commission. ¶ 12-1. Id.

> course of action so that the Defense teams did not violate a material term of their agreements.

Id. at 422 (footnotes omitted). The military judge noted: "That these three Accused agreed to not lodge certain objections to versions of the LHMs is a dramatic change of litigation posture. . . ." Id. at 422 n.113.

II. Law and analysis

This court has jurisdiction over mandamus petitions for extraordinary relief under the All Writs Act, 28 U.S.C. § 1651(a) (2024). *See In re Al-Nashiri (Al-Nashiri III)*, 921 F.3d 224, 227, 233 (D.C. Cir. 2019). A writ of mandamus may only be granted when a petitioner demonstrates

> that [his] right to issuance of the writ is clear and indisputable, the party seeking issuance of the writ [must] have no other adequate means to attain the relief he desires, and the issuing court, in the exercise of its discretion, must be satisfied that the writ is appropriate under the circumstances.

Id. at 233 (alterations in original) (internal quotation marks omitted) (quoting *Cheney vs U.S. District Court*, 542 U.S. 367, 380–81 (2004)).

A. The Secretary's decision to appoint himself as the convening authority for future PTAs

The parties and intervenor do not cite any authority explicitly authorizing a superior convening authority to withdraw authority from a subordinate convening authority to make PTAs or explicitly prohibiting a superior convening authority from withdrawing the authority of a subordinate convening authority to enter into PTAs, without withdrawing all convening authority responsibilities. See Resp'ts Mohammad & Hawsawi's Br. 24–26 (Dec. 11, 2024); Resp't 'Attash's Br. 9–19 (Dec. 11, 2024); Intervenor Ali's Br. 7–25 (Dec. 11, 2024). The Secretary's action results in two convening authorities in respondents' case with different responsibilities, which may potentially overlap or conflict.

The military judge ruled that, in these circumstances, the Secretary lacked authority to reserve for himself the authority to enter into PTAs.

Pet'r's App. 421. The judge provided three reasons for his ruling that the Secretary could not be the convening authority for PTAs with respondents. First, the Secretary did not "reserve" to himself the authority to *withdraw* from PTAs or to withhold BG (Ret.) Escallier's authority to withdraw. Id. at 411–12 (quoting R.M.C. 705(d)(4)(B)), 421.[4] Second, respondents had already begun their performance, and third, the Secretary was not specifically authorized under the PTAs or Rule for Military Commissions 705 to be the convening authority for PTAs. Id. at 414–15, 422–23; *see* sealed AEs (Pet'r's App. vols. 1–3). We agree with the military judge's observations about the absence of authority in the PTAs and Rule for Military Commissions 705 for the Secretary's actions, and that respondents had already begun performance under the PTAs.

We agree with petitioner that powerful "interlocking authorities" give the Secretary of Defense supervisory authority to replace BG (Ret.) Escallier as convening authority for PTAs without taking all convening authority responsibilities from her. Pet'r's Br. 15. The Secretary "is the principal assistant to the President in all matters relating to the Department of Defense." 10 U.S.C. § 113(b). "[H]e has authority, direction, and control over the Department of Defense." *Id.* "Unless specifically prohibited by law, the Secretary [of Defense] may, without being relieved of his responsibility, perform any of his functions or duties or exercise any of his powers through, or with the aid of, such persons in, or organizations of, the Department of Defense as he may designate." 10 U.S.C. § 113(d). In *United States vs Khadr,* 717 F. Supp. 2d 1212, 1213 (CMCR 2007), the court stated, "The plain language of 10 U.S.C. § 113(d) provides the Secretary broad authority to delegate his powers as he sees fit, subject only to the limitation that he may not do so when it is *"specifically prohibited by law."* In *Khadr,* we "appl[ied] the ordinary meaning of the terms 'specific' and 'prohibit' in analyzing this provision and [found] no 'explicit or definite' provision of law" that prohibited the action taken by the Secretary of Defense in Khadr; we denied the challenge to the Secretary's authority

4. Unless stated otherwise, all references to the Manual for Military Commissions refer to the 2019 version; all references to the Regulation for Trial by Military Commission refer to the 2011 version; all references to the Manual for Courts-Martial refer to the 2024 version; all references to the Military Commissions Act, 10 U.S.C. §§ 948a–950t, refer to the 2009 version, and all other citations to the United States Code refer to the 2024 version.

to "delegat[e]" his "authority to appoint appellate judges to this court." *Id.* at 1213–14.

The Secretary has authority under the Military Commissions Act to prescribe "[p]retrial, trial, and post-trial procedures, including elements and modes of proof, for cases triable by military commission under this chapter." 10 U.S.C. § 949a(a). He also has authority to convene trials by military commissions or to appoint "any officer or official of the United States" to be a convening authority. 10 U.S.C. § 948h; *see Al Bahlul vs United States* (*Al Bahlul IV*), 967 F.3d 858, 868–69 (D.C. Cir. 2020) (discussing Secretary's designation authority under 2006 MCA).

Based on 10 U.S.C. § 949a, the Secretary of Defense issued the Manual for Military Commissions, which was adapted from the Manual for Courts-Martial, United States (MCM). MMC, at Foreword (2019 ed). The Manual for Military Commissions contains the Rules for Military Commission. The Secretary also issued the Regulation for Trial by Military Commission (2011 ed.) (RTMC). Under this regulation, "The Secretary of Defense is responsible for the overall supervision and administration of military commissions within the DoD [Department of Defense]." RTMC, ¶ 1-3(a).

Rule for Military Commission 401 provides the procedures and authorities for disposition of charges. That rule provides:

> Rule 401. Forwarding and disposition of charges in general
>
> (a) Who may dispose of charges. Only the Secretary or an officer or official of the United States designated by the Secretary for the purpose to convene military commissions may dispose of charges. A superior competent authority may withhold the authority of a subordinate to dispose of charges in individual cases, types of case, or generally.
>
> (b) How charges may be disposed of. Unless the authority to do so has been limited or withheld by a superior competent authority, an authority may dispose of charges by dismissing any or all of them, forwarding any or all of them to another authority for disposition, or referring any or all of them to a military commission.

One tool in the disposition of charged offenses is through a PTA. "[P]lea agreements [must be] consistent with the requirements of voluntariness and intelligence -- because each side may obtain advantages when a guilty plea is exchanged for sentencing concessions, the agreement is no less voluntary than any other bargained-for exchange." *Mabry vs Johnson,* 467 U.S. 504, 508 (1984). In military commissions, PTAs are "created through the process of bargaining, similar to that used in creating any commercial contract. As a result, we look to the basic principles of contract law when interpreting pretrial agreements." *United States vs Acevedo,* 50 M.J. 169, 172 (C.A.A.F. 1999) (citing *Cooper vs United States,* 594 F.2d 12, 16 (4th Cir. 1979)); see also *United States vs Moreno-Membache,* 995 F.3d 249, 256 (D.C. Cir. 2021) ("Because a plea agreement is a contract, it must be read as a whole.").

The procedures, limitations, and requirements for PTAs in trials by military commission are detailed in Rule for Military Commissions 705(a). That rule states, "(a) *In general.* Subject to such limitations as the Secretary may prescribe, an accused and the convening authority may enter into a pretrial agreement in accordance with this rule." This provision is repeated in paragraph 12-1 of the Regulation for Trial by Military Commission. Petitioner has not cited any defects in the negotiation process or in the three PTAs.

The Secretary of Defense is a "superior competent authority," and as such, he "may withhold the authority of [his] subordinate," BG (Ret.) Escallier, "to dispose of charges." R.M.C. 401(a). Rule for Courts-Martial 401(a) (R.C.M.), MCM, and Rule for Military Commissions 401(a) have the same language. For at least ninety years, higher-level military commanders have had authority to withhold the authority of lower-level military commanders to serve as convening authorities in specific cases, and higher-level commanders also have occupied that role. However, the role of a superior convening authority is not to tell a subordinate convening authority what action he or she should take in a particular case. The following two cases address when a superior convening authority's intervention in the disposition of charges has been upheld.

In *United States vs Fleming,* 2 A.B.R. 359, 372 (1931), the United States Army Board of Review considered a court-martial in which the department commander withheld authority of subordinate commanders to dispose of charges against Captain Fleming. Pet'r's App. 985. The Fleming Board of Review said, "It is believed that the right of a superior commanding officer to order his military inferiors not to dispose of a given case, thus reserving disposition thereof to himself, is a necessary attribute of command without which he might become powerless to maintain discipline." *Id.*

More recently, in *Hayes vs Maksym,* No. NMCCA 200301982, 2004 CCA LEXIS 35 (N-M. Ct. Crim. App. Feb. 11, 2004) (unpub.), Hayes filed a petition for a writ of mandamus to overturn the decision of a superior convening authority to withdraw and refer his case to a higher-level court-martial. After arraignment for a special court-martial, Hayes submitted a PTA offer; the special court-martial convening authority agreed to refer his case to a lower-level summary court-martial in return for a guilty plea in a summary court-martial. Id. at *3. The maximum possible confinement was less at a summary court-martial than at a higher-level special court-martial. Later, based upon Rule for Courts-Martial 401(a), a superior convening authority withheld the authority of a special court-martial convening authority to dispose of Hayes' charges at a summary court-martial. *Id.* at *4. The superior convening authority then referred to a special court-martial the same charge and specifications upon which Hayes had previously been arraigned. Id. The United States Navy-Marine Corps Court of Criminal Appeals noted that Hayes "can point to no provision in the Uniform Code of Military Justice, the Manual for Courts-Martial, or case precedent that prohibits what happened in this case." Id. at *7. The Court of Criminal Appeals denied Hayes' petition for a mandamus writ. Id. (citing R.C.M. 401(a)).

The Secretary, as a superior convening authority, has an important role in referral of charges to trial by military commission. He "may cause charges, whether or not referred, to be transmitted to the authority for further consideration, including, if appropriate, referral." R.M.C. 601(f); *see* R.M.C. 601(b) ("A convening authority may refer charges to a military commission convened by that convening authority, or a predecessor, unless the power to do so has been withheld by superior competent authority."). The Secretary also "may for any reason cause any charges or specifications to be withdrawn . . . at any time before findings are announced." R.M.C. 604(a); *see also* R.C.M 604(a) (stating same), quoted in *United States vs Leahr,* 73 M.J. 364, 369 (C.A.A.F. 2014). However, the charges may not be re-referred if the withdrawal was "for an improper reason." *Leahr,* at 369 (quoting R.C.M. 604(b)); see R.M.C. 604(a), Discussion ("Charges should not be withdrawn from a court-martial arbitrarily or unfairly to an accused." (quoting R.C.M. 604(b)).

The Secretary of Defense's intervention in respondents' existing PTAs is without precedent. Service secretaries, nonetheless, occasionally intervene in the disposition of individual cases. *See, e.g.*, Message from Stanley R. Resor, Sec'y of the Army, to Maj. Gen. George L. Mabry, Jr., Commanding General, The Support Troops, USARV, Subject: Charges Against Colonel Rheault et al (Sept. 29, 1969)[5] (Pet'r's App. 1080) ("Acting as a superior convening authority under the provisions of Article 22, UCMJ, I hereby assume jurisdiction over and hereby dismiss the court-martial charges . . . alleging conspiracy to murder and the murder of [an individual] on or about 20 June 1969."); see also Pet'r's Br. 18 n.83 (citing and discussing same message). We note that this precedent petitioner provides is for a superior convening authority to intervene by taking complete jurisdiction over disposition of a case—not partial control by being the convening authority for PTAs, while leaving the remainder of control to a subordinate convening authority.

Next, we consider concerns about the Secretary exercising improper influence over BG (Ret.) Escallier in his new role as convening authority for PTAs in respondents' case. The military judge stated in his ruling that respondents' motions seeking enforcement of their existing PTAs "are not being resolved on unlawful influence grounds, but [on] the idea that each of the Convening Authority's actions and decisions are immediately reversible if the Secretary disagrees[, which] potentially raises the specter of unlawful influence." Pet'r's App. 417. The military judge acknowledged that the Secretary could impose limits on BG (Ret.) Escallier's authority, see id., yet concluded that "any prescribed 'limitations' must be in effect before the convening authority acts. Otherwise, the convening authority enjoys no real discretion to act in any circumstance without the fear of reversal, let alone with the 'sole discretion' the Secretary had previously bestowed upon Ms. Escallier." *Id.* at 418–19.

The military judge expressed additional concern about the independence of BG (Ret.) Escallier because of the Secretary acting as convening authority for PTAs and BG (Ret.) Escallier acting as convening authority for all other matters in respondents' cases. The military judge noted that "[i]t is difficult to

5. (Message No. DA OUT 925536) (File No. OSA 250.1 VIETNAM), in NARA-RG 335 (UD-UP Entry 35), Security Classification: UNCLAS EFTO.

foresee the functionality of a system of co-convening authorities over different aspects of the same case where one is the boss of the other, yet remain faithful to statutory, regulatory, and case law prohibitions against unlawful influence." Id. at 418; see Resp'ts' Br. 23, 31–32.[6]

Intervenor Ali relies on *United States vs Hardy*, 4 M.J. 20 (C.M.A. 1977), abrogated on other grounds by *United States vs Blaylock*, 15 M.J. 190, 192–93 (C.M.A. 1983), to support his argument "that a superior convening authority may either take over a case in its entirety, or allow the lawfully designated subordinate to exercise its authority over the case without interfering with the subordinate's exercise of discretion." Intervenor Ali's Br. 13; see id. at 14. In Hardy, the case was referred to a special court-martial, and a superior convening authority ordered the subordinate convening authority who referred the case to withdraw the charges from the special court-martial. Hardy, 4 M.J. at 21.

The United States Court of Military Appeals in Hardy stated:

> Where, as here, the superior commander seeks to affect a *particular* case by *countermanding* discretionary judicial decision of a subordinate commander which the latter made pursuant to his then existing powers under the Uniform Code of Military Justice, the superior has injected the spectre of unlawful command control over the judicial act of the subordinate. This contravenes the intent of Article 37(a), UCMJ.[7]

---

6. Petitioner argues that unlawful influence is not ripe for consideration because the military judge's ruling was decided on other grounds. Pet'r's Reply Br. 18 n.101 (Dec. 16, 2024) (citing App. 406 n.46; Resp'ts 'Attash & Hawsawi's Opp. to Ali's Mot. to Intervene 1–3 (Dec. 12, 2024)).

7. The version of 10 U.S.C. § 837(a) in effect when Hardy was decided stated:

> No authority convening a general, special, or summary court-martial, nor any other commanding officer, may censure, reprimand, or admonish the court or any member, military judge, or counsel thereof, with respect to the findings or sentence adjudged by the court, or with respect to any other exercise of its or his functions in the conduct of the proceeding. No person subject to this chapter may attempt to coerce or, by any unauthorized means, influence the action of a court-martial or any other military tribunal or any member thereof, in reaching the findings or sentence in any case, or the action of any convening, approving, or reviewing authority with respect to his judicial acts. . . .

Id. at 24. The court further observed that the order of the superior convening authority was improper because the subordinate convening authority's withdrawal of charges from the special court-martial "must result from his own decision . . . . His action in withdrawing a specific case from a court to which it already properly had been referred must not be the result of a superior's order to do so pursuant to the *superior's* decision." Id. at 23. The court in *Hardy* added, "to tolerate otherwise would permit that superior commander, in a specific case and after-the-fact, to influence directly the action of the subordinate convening authority with respect to the latter's judicial acts *already properly taken* in that case." Id. (footnote citation omitted; emphasis added).

We find that Hardy stands for the proposition that the Secretary of Defense cannot order BG (Ret.) Escallier to withdraw from respondents' PTAs, which were already approved. Hardy, however, does not prevent the Secretary of Defense from withdrawing BG (Ret.) Escallier's authority to approve *future* PTAs in respondents' case.

Unlawful influence of convening authorities for military commissions is prohibited in 10 U.S.C. § 949b(a)(2), which states, "No person may attempt to coerce or, by any unauthorized means, influence . . . (B) the action of any convening, approving, or reviewing authority with respect to their judicial acts[.]" This language is similar to the language in the version of 10 U.S.C. § 837(a) that the Court of Military Appeals applied in *Hardy*. *See supra* note 7.

Title 10, section 837(d) of the United States Code, which applies to courts-martial, not military commissions, states:

> (1) A superior convening authority or commanding officer may withhold the authority of a subordinate convening authority or officer to dispose of offenses in individual cases, types of cases, or generally.
>
> (2) Except as provided in paragraph (1) or as otherwise authorized by this chapter, a superior convening authority or commanding officer may not limit the discretion of a subordinate convening authority or officer to act with respect to a case for which the subordinate convening authority or officer has authority to dispose of the offenses.

Act of Oct. 24, 1968, Pub. L. No. 90-632, § 2(13), 82 Stat. 1335, 1338.

See also R.C.M. 104(d) (same). Section 837(d)(1) is repeated in Rule for Military Commissions 401, supra, but section 837(d)(2), prohibiting limitations on a convening authority's discretion, is not reflected in Rule for Military Commissions 401. Moreover, the Uniform Code of Military Justice provision prohibiting unlawful influence of superior convening authorities (R.C.M. 104(d)) is broader than what is provided for in the Military Commissions Act (R.M.C. 401(b)). In any event, the issue of unlawful influence was not fully litigated before respondents' military commission, and this issue therefore is not ripe for our consideration. See Pet'r's Reply Br. 18 n.101 (Dec. 16, 2024).

Nevertheless, neither of the litigants cited caselaw nor Rule for Military Commissions 401 to support prohibiting the Secretary from withdrawing BG (Ret.) Escallier's authority to approve future PTAs by withholding that authority now.

We agree with Intervenor Ali that the Secretary is prohibited "from telling the Convening Authority how to accomplish her judicial functions, including the negotiation of pretrial agreements." Intervenor Ali Br. 20 (citing 10 U.S.C. § 949b(a)(2)).[8] Section 949b(a)(2) provides: "No person may attempt to coerce or, by any unauthorized means, influence . . . (B) the action of any convening, approving, or reviewing authority with respect to their judicial acts . . . ." Paragraph 12-1 of the Regulation for Trial by Military Commission, entitled "Authority to Conclude Agreement" (emphasis omitted), provides additional guidance, as follows:

> Unless such authority is withheld by a superior competent authority, the Convening Authority is authorized to enter into or reject offers to enter into Pretrial Agreements (PTAs) with the accused. The decision to accept or reject a PTA offer submitted by an accused is within the sole discretion of the Convening Authority who referred the case to trial. See R.M.C. 705.

The Secretary has vast authority in the Department of Defense, and in military commissions. Logically, this vast authority includes the authority to act as convening authority to approve or disapprove PTAs without taking

---

8. Intervenor Ali's brief cites to 10 U.S.C. § 949(a)(2). We corrected the section number to read § 949b(a)(2).

all of the responsibilities of the convening authority. A review of the First Circuit decision in *United States vs O'Neil,* 11 F.3d 292 (1st Cir. 1993), is helpful in explaining our analysis. That case discussed the principles of "the greater includes the lesser" and "avoiding illogical results" in the interpretation of statutes. The First Circuit stated:

> The principle that the grant of a greater power includes the grant of a lesser power is a bit of common sense that has been recognized in virtually every legal code from time immemorial. It has found modern expression primarily in the realm of constitutional law.
>
> While this principle has nested less frequently in the criminal law context, it is fully applicable in that milieu. . . .
>
> . . . .
>
> . . . It is also an established canon of statutory construction that a legislature's words should never be given a meaning that produces a stunningly counterintuitive result -- at least if those words, read without undue straining, will bear another, less jarring meaning.

Id. at 296–97 (citations omitted); see *Andrews vs Warden*, 958 F.3d 1072, 1076 (11th Cir. 2020) ("Because the greater power ordinarily includes the lesser power, the President's pardon power includes the authority to commute a sentence to a lesser punishment." (emphasis added) (citing *Schick vs Reed,* 419 U.S. 256, 265–66 (1974); Biddle vs Perovich, 274 U.S. 480, 486–87 (1927))); *O'Connell vs Shalala,* 79 F.3d 170, 177 (1st Cir. 1996) ("[T]he statutory grant of a greater power typically includes the grant of a lesser power . . . ."). The United States Court of Appeal for the District of Columbia Circuit (D.C. Circuit) also has proclaimed that "[t]he greater power includes the lesser." Quaker Action *Grp. vs Hickel,* 429 F.2d 185, 192 (D.C. Cir. 1970) (per curiam). The D.C. Circuit, however, has noted that the scope of the "greater-includes-the-lesser-power argument" is limited when a "statute disallows the agency" from taking action to eliminate part of the requirements without eliminating all of them. See Nat. Res. Def. Council vs EPA, 777 F.3d 456, 471 (D.C. Cir. 2014). There are no such statutory limitations on the Secretary of Defense's authority relating to PTAs in the 2009 Military

Commissions Act, the Manual for Military Commissions, or the Regulation for Trial by Military Commission.

Essentially, the Secretary has the power to withhold the authority of BG (Ret.) Escallier to dispose of charges in respondents' case under Rule for Military Commissions 401(a), and Regulation for Trial by Military Commission, paragraph 12-1. Accordingly, he has the lesser authority to withhold BG (Ret.) Escallier's power to approve PTAs in respondents' case, which is used in the process of disposing of charges. When BG (Ret.) Escallier signed the PTAs, she had authority to do so. Once those PTAs were signed, withdrawal could only occur if there was authority within the pretrial agreement itself, or there was statutory or rule authority to do so. Brigadier General (Ret.) Escallier's authority to withdraw from the PTAs in this case, however, is unavailable in any event because respondents began performance under these PTAs.[9]

The authority that the Secretary of Defense exercised in this case is located in Rule for Military Commissions 705(a), which authorized him to prescribe limitations on convening authorities to enter into PTAs. See *United States vs Allen*, 31 M.J. 572, 594 (N-M.C.M.R. 1990) (en banc) (stating Rule for Courts-Martial 705(a) "authorized the Secretary of the Navy to prescribe limitations on convening authorities to enter into pretrial agreements and that is exactly the authority that the Secretary exercised via § 0129c, JAGMAN," which "specifically prohibits a convening authority from entering into a pretrial agreement in a national security case without first obtaining the approval of the Secretary of the Navy"); Sec'y of Navy Instr. 5800.7D, Manual of the Judge Advocate General (JAGMAN) § 0137c (Mar. 15, 2004) [hereinafter JAGMAN Instr.] (Pet'r's Suppl. App. 32) ("No official of the [Department of the Navy] is authorized to enter into a pretrial agreement in any national security case . . . without first obtaining permission to do so from the Secretary of the Navy."); JAGMAN Instr. 5800.7E at § 0137c (June 20, 2007) (Pet'r's Suppl. App. 35) (same); see also *United States vs Kroetz*, No.

9. Brigadier General (Retired) Escallier retains authority to take any necessary actions on the existing PTAs in the case at bar. See, e.g., *United States vs Hunter*, 65 M.J. 399, 400 (C.A.A.F. 2008) (involving whether convening authority had authority to withdraw from sentence limitation in PTA); United States vs Williams, 60 M.J. 360, 363 (C.A.A.F. 2004) (involving whether trial counsel had authority to withdraw from PTA due to untimely restitution

ACM 40301, 2023 CCA LEXIS 450, at *11–12 (A.F. Ct. Crim. App. Oct. 27, 2023) (noting applicability of an Air Force instruction prohibiting "plea agreements involving an exact term of confinement," but noting absence of prohibition limiting agreements "to a particular punitive discharge"), petition for rev. denied, 84 M.J. 417 (C.A.A.F. Apr. 25, 2024); *United States vs Saulter,* 23 M.J. 626, 627 (A.F.C.M.R. 1986) (stating differences in "service-level restrictions" on PTAs may result in different outcomes among the services).

Statutory and regulatory authorities permit the Secretary to appoint himself as convening authority in full in respondents' case and to remove a subordinate convening authority in full. 10 U.S.C. § 948h. The Secretary of Defense also has authority to prescribe pretrial, trial, and post-trial procedures for military commission cases. 10 U.S.C. § 949a(a); Al-Bahlul IV, 967 F.3d at 872 (citing § 949a(a)); 10 U.S.C. § 948h. More specifically, the Secretary may prescribe limitations on the content of PTAs. R.M.C. 705(a); R.C.M. 705(a) (same). That secretarial authority is evident in another military commission rule, which provides: "A superior competent authority may withhold the authority of a subordinate to dispose of charges in individual cases, types of cases, or generally." R.M.C. 401(a); R.C.M. 401(a) (same); see *Blaylock,* 15 M.J. at 194 (stating a superior convening authority "may intervene to cause the withdrawal and rereferral of charges which in his view should be tried by a different kind of court-martial").

These broad authorities—including the specific authorities supporting the Secretary's appointment of convening authorities and withdrawal and re-referral of charges to a higher-level court (so long as those charges are not for improper reasons)—encompass the authority to withhold BG (Ret.) Escallier's authority to enter into PTAs with respondents. See RTMC, ¶ 12-1. Accordingly, we find a lack of evidence that the Secretary of Defense attempted to coerce or improperly influence BG (Ret.) Escallier with issuance of his August 2024 memorandum.

B. Vacation of respondents' existing pretrial agreements (PTAs)

The military judge determined the Secretary's withdrawal from the three PTAs was void because respondents had begun performance under the PTAs before that withdrawal. Pet'r's App. 411–13, 421–25. He concluded that performance of the PTAs began when respondents: (i) signed stipulations of fact; (ii) negotiated and agreed to their respective LHMs; (iii) did not cross-examine "witness[es] for pretrial motions while the Prosecution and Defense Counsel for Mr. Ali questioned those same witnesses"; and (iv) did not file motions. Id. at 421–23.

The military judge based his decision primarily on Rule for Military Commissions 705(d)(4)(B) and he concluded that *United States vs Dean,* 67 M.J. 224, 227–28 (C.A.A.F. 2009), was "controlling." Id. at 424 n.120; see id. at 411–13, 422–24. Our court is not bound by *Dean's* ruling regarding when an accused begins performance of a PTA because decisions of the United States Court of Appeals for the Armed Forces are not binding on our court. See 10 U.S.C. § 948b(c) ("The judicial construction and application of chapter 47 of this title, while instructive, is therefore not of its own force binding on military commissions established under this chapter."). Similarly, appellate court decisions discussing the Rules for Courts-Martial that are worded the same as Rules for Military Commissions are instructive but not binding on our court. See generally *United States vs Finch,* 79 M.J. 389, 395 (C.A.A.F. 2020) (finding interpretation of a word in federal appellate courts to be instructive when language of military rule "is identical to the corresponding federal rule").

In *Dean,* the following series of events occurred: "Contemporaneous with the Offer to Plead Guilty, Dean submitted a stipulation of fact to the convening authority which had been executed by Dean, his defense counsel and the trial counsel. The convening authority accepted and signed the Offer to Plead Guilty on [the same date]." 67 M.J. at 226. On the eve of Dean's trial, the trial counsel sought to amend the stipulation of fact to add additional misconduct, the defense counsel objected, and the convening authority withdrew the PTA. Id. The military judge permitted the withdrawal of the PTA, and after a contested trial, Dean received, and the convening authority approved, a sentence exceeding the limit in the PTA. *Id.*

The Dean Court cited Rule for Courts-Martial 705(d)(4)(B), and stated:

> In this case, Dean either performed or began to perform several of the promises listed in the agreement before the convening authority announced his withdrawal . . . : Dean elected trial by military judge alone . . . ; he

> entered into a stipulation of fact with trial counsel as to the circumstances of the offense . . . ; and . . . he filed an amended witness list which complied with two separate promises he made regarding the production of witnesses. The convening authority's right to withdraw "any time before the accused begins performance of promises contained in the agreement" therefore terminated before he announced his withdrawal from the agreement.

Id. at 228. Dean's election of forum and entering into a stipulation of fact with trial counsel both occurred before the convening authority signed the PTA; the amended witness list was filed after the convening authority approved the PTA. Id. at 226, 228.

In the case at bar, the military judge said, "Just as in Dean, where entering into a confessional stipulation of fact and electing a military judge alone forum was sufficient to qualify as beginning performance, here all three co-Accused have begun performance simply by entering into a Stipulation of Fact as was required by each of the three PTAs." Pet'r's App. 423.

Setting the stage for our continuing analysis, we discuss Rule for Military Commissions 705(d)(4), concerning withdrawal from a PTA, which states:

Withdrawal.

> (A) *By accused.* The accused may withdraw from a pretrial agreement at any time; however, the accused may withdraw a plea of guilty or a confessional stipulation entered pursuant to a pretrial agreement only as provided in R.M.C. 910(h) or 811(d), respectively.
>
> (B) *By convening authority.* The convening authority may withdraw from a pretrial agreement at any time *before the accused begins performance of promises contained in the agreement,* upon the failure by the accused to fulfill any material promise or condition in the agreement, when inquiry by the military judge discloses a disagreement as to a material term in the agreement, or if findings are set aside because a plea of guilty entered pursuant to the agreement is held improvident on appellate review.

(Third emphasis added.) This provision is repeated in paragraph 12-3(a) of the Regulation for Trial by Military Commission. Until 2018, Rule for Military Commissions 705(d)(4)(B) and Rule for Courts-Martial 705(d)(4)(B) were the same.

On August 1, 2024, the day before the Secretary withdrew the PTAs in respondents' case, an FBI special agent testified on a pretrial motion. Pet'r's App. 906, 923, 926. Petitioner objected to respondents' "participat[ion] in any of the contested litigation based on the [PTAs]," reminding the respondents of their obligation under the PTAs. *Id.* at 917–18. Accordingly, respondents' counsel did not ask any questions of the witness. *Id.* at 404, 917–19. Respondents clearly began performance of a promise contained in the PTA—not to make or participate in motions—and Rule for Military Commissions 705(d)(4)(B) precluded the convening authority's withdrawal unless one of the circumstances in Rule 705(d)(4)(B) applied. See infra Part III.A. None of those circumstances apply at this point in the litigation.

III. Application of Cheney tests

Petitioner's writ of mandamus and prohibition must meet all three of the *Cheney* tests, 542 U.S. at 380–81, otherwise we cannot grant relief. Extraordinary relief is available to enforce a PTA; yet, the right to relief must be "clear and indisputable." *See In re United States,* 32 F.4th 584, 597–98 (6th Cir. 2022) (concluding that government's writ of mandamus seeking to require reconsideration of improperly rejected plea agreement provided a "clear and indisputable right to mandamus").

A. Right to issuance of the writ must be clear and indisputable

Our analysis on the right to issuance of the writ involves two matters, (i) the military judge's vacatur of the Secretary's memorandum withdrawing from respondents' PTAs, and (ii) the military judge's order vacating the Secretary's memorandum pertaining to future PTAs. Petitioner has not established a clear and indisputable right regarding the first matter but has established a clear and indisputable right regarding the second matter.

Respondents began to perform a promise contained in their PTAs when they refrained from cross-examining an FBI special agent on August 1, 2024. Therefore, neither BG (Ret.) Escallier nor the Secretary could withdraw from the PTAs unless one of the other conditions in Rule for Military Commissions 705(d)(4)(B) applies; however, there is no evidence that any of those circumstances currently apply. Petitioner has not clearly established their right to a writ reversing the military judge's decision to vacate the Secretary's memorandum withdrawing the PTAs. The issue of the Secretary's withdrawal of the existing PTAs is resolved against petitioner.

We note, the authority of the convening authority to withdraw from a PTA is different under the Manual for Military Commissions than under the Manual for Courts-Martial. Under the Manual for Courts-Martial, the performance in this case would not have foreclosed the convening authority's withdrawal from the PTAs. In the 2018 amendment of Rule for Courts-Martial 705(e)(4)(B)(i),[10] the President authorized the convening authority's withdrawal from a plea agreement "(i) before substantial performance by the accused of promises contained in the agreement." (Emphasis added.)

"Pursuant to 10 U.S.C. § 949a, the Manual for Military Commissions is adapted from the Manual for Courts-Martial." MMC, Foreword. Consistency between Rule for Military Commissions 705(d)(4)(B) in the Manual for Military Commissions and Rule for Courts-Martial 705(e)(4)(B)(i) in the Manual for Courts-Martial should be maintained. *See generally In re Al-Nashiri (Al-Nashiri I)*, 791 F.3d 71, 86 (D.C. Cir. 2015)

---

10. Rule for Courts-Martial 705(e)(4)(B) (2024) now states:

(B) *By convening authority or special trial counsel.* The convening authority or special trial counsel, as applicable, may withdraw from a plea agreement at any time:

(i) *before substantial performance by the accused of promises contained in the agreement;*

(ii) upon the failure by the accused to fulfill any

material promise or condition in the agreement;

(iii) when inquiry by the military judge discloses a disagreement as to a material term in the agreement; or

(iv) if findings are set aside because a plea of guilty entered pursuant to the agreement is held improvident on appellate review.

(Second emphasis added.) The "substantial performance" standard was added to Rule 705 in the Manual for Courts-Martial by Executive Order 13825, 83 Fed. Reg. 9889, 9967 (Mar. 8, 2018), effective January 1, 2019. Rule for Military Commissions 705(d)(4)(B), however, has not been amended.

(recommending change to appointment process of CMCR judges to avoid constitutional issues).

We agree with the military judge that the Military Commissions Act and the Manual for Military Commissions do not use the plural of the word convening authority, and practical and legal difficulties with overlapping responsibilities are possible with two convening authorities on the same case. Pet'r's App. 418 & n.100. The Secretary nonetheless clearly has the authority to withdraw or withhold BG (Ret.) Escallier's authority in respondents' case to enter into future PTAs and reserve for himself such authority without requiring the Secretary to withdraw all convening authority responsibilities from BG (Ret.) Escallier. *See, e.g., In re Kellogg Brown & Root, Inc.*, 756 F.3d 754, 762 (D.C. Cir. 2014).

Here we find a clear abuse of discretion to the extent the military judge's order vacated the Secretary's memorandum pertaining to future PTAs. Thus, the first *Cheney* test is met with regard to potential future PTAs. Petitioner has satisfied the conditions in the first test. We next consider the second *Cheney* test.

B. No other adequate means to attain the relief desired

In *Al-Nashiri* I, 791 F.3d 75, Al-Nashiri "alleged that military judges are assigned to the CMCR in violation of the Appointments Clause, U.S. Const. art. II, § 2, cl. 2." The Court denied a writ of mandamus and prohibition seeking to recuse the military judges because the issue could be resolved on direct appeal, and it would constitute an advisory opinion to grant the writ of mandamus and prohibition. Id. at 80–81. In respondents' case, even though we find the military judge committed error when he vacated the Secretary's decision to withdraw BG (Ret.) Escallier's authority to enter into future PTAs and reserved such authority to himself, Pet'r's App. 405, this finding does not support the issuance of a writ of mandamus because the error "could be corrected on appeal without irreparable harm." See *Nat'l Ass'n of Criminal Def. Lawyers, Inc. vs DOJ*, 182 F.3d 981, 987 (D.C. Cir. 1999).

Petitioner essentially urges us to act in an advisory capacity, as the Secretary has not entered into any PTAs in this case. "Even if we were willing, we are unable to use advisory mandamus here because it would circumvent the no-other-adequate-means requirement." *Al-Nashiri* I, 791 F.3d at 80.

IV. Conclusion

Having found that petitioner failed to meet at least one of the first two *Cheney* tests—because petitioner has "other adequate means to obtain desired relief"—it is unnecessary to address the third test concerning appropriateness of the writ under the circumstances. *Id.* at 80–82 (dismissing writ of mandamus and prohibition without addressing third *Cheney* test).

Accordingly, it is hereby

ORDERED that petitioner's motions to admit appendix and supplemental appendix are GRANTED. It is

FURTHER ORDERED that respondents Mohammad and Hawsawi's appendix is **ADMITTED.** [11]It is

FURTHER ORDERED that respondent Bin 'Attash's motion to admit appendix is **GRANTED.** It is

FURTHER ORDERED that petitioner's motions for leave to file an outsized brief and reply brief are **GRANTED.** It is

FURTHER ORDERED that respondent Bin 'Attash's motion to file an outsized brief is **GRANTED.** It is

FURTHER ORDERED that the motion for leave to file an *amicus curiae* brief in support of respondents is **GRANTED.** It is

FURTHER ORDERED that respondents Bin 'Attash and Hawsawi's motion for leave to file out of time an opposition to Ali's motion to intervene is **GRANTED.** It is

FURTHER ORDERED that intervenor Ali's motion to dismiss is **DENIED** and motion to intervene is **GRANTED.** It is

FURTHER ORDERED that petitioner's writ of mandamus and prohibition is **DENIED.**

11. Respondents failed to move for admission of their appendix.

(2025) I FLR 73 (South Africa)

Constitutional Court of South Africa

Case Number CCT 14/23

Lieutenant Colonel K.B. O'Brien N.O. vs Minister of Defence and Military Veterans and Anr

Composition of Court: Chief Justice Zondo, Acting Deputy Chief Justice Madlanga, Justice Kollapen, Justice Majiedt, Justice Mathopo, Justice Mhlantla, Justice Rogers, Justice Theron, Acting Justice Tolmay and Justice Tshiqi (Ten Judge Bench)

Date of Decision: 20 December 2024

Counsel for the Applicant: G. Marcus SC, C. McConnachie, M. Marongo and M. Kritzinger
Counsel for the Respondent: E. Tsatsi SC and C. Kwinda
Counsel for Amicus Curiae: E. Webber and E. Van Heerden

Summary

The Constitutional Court of South Africa addressed the constitutionality of provisions in the Defence Act (42 of 2002) and the Military Discipline Supplementary Measures Act (16 of 1999) (MDSMA) concerning the independence of military courts. Lieutenant Colonel Kevin O'Brien challenged sections 101 and 102 of the Defence Act and sections 15 and 17 of the MDSMA, arguing that they violated judicial independence by allowing executive interference in military judges' appointments, terms, and removals. The respondents (the government) contended that the provisions were constitutional, arguing that military judges are not strictly judicial officers and already enjoy security of tenure. The Court ruled that military courts qualify as courts under section 166(e) of the Constitution and that structural independence, including non-renewable terms and protection from executive interference, is essential. It declared the impugned provisions unconstitutional, suspended the invalidity for two years for legislative correction, and prescribed interim remedies. The Court upheld the appeal and granted the leave to appeal. While the applicant achieved partial success, the Court awarded him half of the costs in the High Court and Supreme Court of Appeal and full costs in the Constitutional Court, highlighting the significance of judicial independence in ensuring fair trials and compliance with constitutional and international standards.

Headnotes

Facts: The applicant, a Lieutenant-Colonel in the South African National Defence Force (SANDF) and a former military judge during 2013, 2014 and 2016, challenged, in a counter-application before the High Court, Gauteng Division, Pretoria (High Court), the constitutionality of Sections 101 and 102 of the Defence Act (42 of 2002) and Sections 15 and 17 of the MDSMA (the impugned provisions). The applicant is currently employed as an instructor at the School of Military Justice, Pretoria. The main application was a review application by the first respondent, the Minister of Defence and Military Veterans, against certain orders made by the applicant in proceedings where he had presided as a military judge, concerning his apprehension about the unconstitutionality of the impugned provisions. The High Court upheld the review relief and dismissed the applicant's counter-application on the basis that the impugned provisions were constitutionally compliant. The Supreme Court of Appeal dismissed the applicant's appeal on the basis of mootness. The applicant now seeks leave to appeal in this Court. The application for leave to appeal is confined to the applicant's counter-application; the applicant has no issues with the Supreme Court of Appeal's judgment and order pertaining to the review application brought by the respondents.

Issue(s): (i.) Whether, in respect of Sections 101 and 102 of the Defence Act, it is constitutionally permissible for members of the Executive to have the power to initiate and control boards of inquiry to investigate judicial officers' fitness and the conduct of their cases?

(ii.) Whether the power under Section 15 of the MDSMA, permitting the Minister and the Adjutant General to make renewable assignments of military judges, for short periods, at their sole discretion, and without any objective criteria, passes constitutional muster?

(iii.) Whether the Executive's authority under section 17 of the MDSMA to remove military judges without independent oversight infringed the principles of judicial independence?

(iv.) Whether the constitutional challenge was moot, or whether it raised live and justiciable constitutional issues?

Contentions of the Parties: The applicant contended that the matter was a constitutional issue as it concerned the constitutionality of national legislation and the judicial independence of military courts and military judges. It was further submitted that a constitutional challenge to legislation that is in operation is a live issue and that therefore the matter was not moot. In respect of Section 15 of the MDSMA, the applicant submitted that this power is inconsistent with the principle of judicial independence and is out of step with trends observed in foreign jurisdictions. On the power to remove a military judge upon the recommendation of the Adjutant General according to Section 17 of the MDSMA, it was contended that it is impermissible for members of the Executive to hold the power to exercise discipline over judicial officers without any independent assessment of cause. Lastly, on the power to appoint boards of inquiry in terms of Sections 101 and 102 of the Defence Act, the applicant submitted that this power interferes with a military judge's freedom to hear and decide cases without interference from government, pressure groups, or individuals. On the contrary, the respondents contended the jurisdiction and asserted that the matter was moot as it was not in the interests of justice to entertain the application. The respondents argued that Section 15 does not solely pertain to the assignment of military judges but applies to various categories of military personnel. It was contended that if Section 15 were deemed unconstitutional, it would impact the deployment of all types of military personnel. The respondents emphasised on the military judges' security of tenure. Lastly, the respondents asserted that section 17 does not specifically address the removal of "*a military judge*" but rather the removal of "*a person*", indicating that military judges are not strictly categorised as judicial officers but as members of the SANDF.

Amicus Curiae's Contention: The ICJ (full form?) was admitted as *amicus curiae* and was permitted to present written and oral arguments. The ICJ made submissions on South Africa's obligations under international law to ensure that courts and tribunals, including military courts, are competent, independent, impartial, and afford litigants a fair and public hearing. In addition, with reference to the Ministerial Task Team Report, the ICJ emphasised the necessity for military courts to exhibit independence and impartiality in handling cases involving sexual offences committed by members of the SANDF.

<ins>Held:</ins> With regard to the jurisdiction, the Court held that the matter engages both the constitutional and general jurisdiction of the Court as it concerned a challenge to the constitutionality of the impugned provisions, the constitutionally guaranteed judicial independence of military courts under the Constitution and raised arguable points of law. The Court also considered the legal status and independence of military courts in South Africa and found that military courts undoubtedly qualify as courts under Section 166(e) of the Constitution by virtue of their criminal jurisdiction. On the mootness aspect, the Court found that the Supreme Court of Appeal was plainly wrong in its findings and agreed with the applicant's contention that a constitutional challenge to existing and fully operational statutory provisions can never be considered moot. The Court reiterated that South Africa's international law obligations, alongside domestic requirements, mandate adherence to established standards of judicial independence. In respect of Sections 101 and 102 of the Defence Act, the Court held that the involvement of members of the Executive

in making decisions relating to boards of inquiry, insofar as they pertain to military courts and military judges, plainly offends the principle of separation of powers and subverts the independence of military courts. The Court thus held it invalid and unconstitutional to that extent. With regard to Section 15 of the MDSMA, the Court held that non-renewable terms for judges is an essential prerequisite of structural independence, and that it is constitutionally unpalatable that military judges are the only full-time judicial officers who are appointed for short, renewable terms, notwithstanding their significant geographical and penal jurisdiction. Hence, it is unconstitutional and invalid to the extent that it empowers the Minister of Defence and Military Veterans, acting on the recommendation of the Adjutant General, to assign judges for renewable periods. As far as Section 17 of the MDSMA is concerned, the Court held that it is unconstitutional for the Executive to have the power to remove military judges without independent oversight or control. Hence, the Court upheld the appeal and granted the leave to appeal. The order of the Supreme Court of Appeal is set aside to the extent that that Court dismissed the applicant's appeal against the High Court's refusal to grant the declarations of statutory invalidity sought by the applicant in his counter-application in the High Court. The Court awarded the applicant half of the costs in the High Court and Supreme Court of Appeal and full costs in the Constitutional Court.

Case Laws Cited

Freedom of Expression Institute v President, Ordinary Court Martial 1999 (2) SA 471 (C); Minister of Defence v Potsane; Legal Soldier (Pty) Ltd v Minister of Defence [2001] ZACC 12; Van Rooyen v S (General Council of the Bar of South Africa intervening) [2002] ZACC 8; Ex parte Chairperson of the Constitutional Assembly: In re Certification of the Constitution of the Republic of South Africa [1996] ZACC 26; De Lange v Smuts N.O. [1998] ZACC 6; Glenister v President of the Republic of South Africa (Glenister II) [2011] ZACC 6; Justice Alliance of South Africa v President of the Republic of South Africa [2011] ZACC 23; Mbambo v Minister of Defence 2005 (2) SA 226 (T); Council of Review South African Defence Force v Monnig [1992] ZASCA 64; Makana People's Centre v Minister of Health [2023] ZACC 15; Sonke Gender Justice NPC v President of the Republic of South

Africa [2020] ZACC 26; McBride v Minister of Police (Helen Suzman Foundation as amicus curiae) [2016] ZACC 30; The Queen in Right of Canada v Beauregard [1986] 2 SCR 56; Valente v The Queen [1985] 2 SCR 673; R v Généreux [1992] 1 SCR 259; Leblanc v The Queen 2011 CMAC 2

ORDER

On appeal from the Supreme Court of Appeal, hearing an appeal from the High Court of South Africa, Gauteng Division, Pretoria (High Court):

(1.) Leave to appeal is granted.

(2.) The appeal is upheld.

(3.) The order of the Supreme Court of Appeal is set aside to the extent that that Court dismissed the Applicant's appeal against the High Court's refusal to grant the declarations of statutory invalidity sought by the Applicant in his counter-application in the High Court.

(4.) The costs orders made in the Supreme Court of Appeal in relation to costs in that Court and in the High Court are set aside.

(5.) It is declared that:

(a.) Sections 101 and 102 of the Defence Act 42 of 2002 are unconstitutional and invalid to the extent that they permit members of the Executive to convene boards of inquiry to investigate military Judges and the content and merits of their judgments and rulings. Pending the coming into operation of remedial legislation, the phrases 'any matter', 'any member or employee' and the 'affairs of any institution' in Section 101 and 102 of the Defence Act and Section 136 of the Military Disciplinary Code, read with Rule 79 of the Military Discipline Supplementary Measures Act's Rules, must be read as excluding military Judges.

(b.) Section 15 of the Military Discipline Supplementary Measures Act 16 of 1999 is unconstitutional and invalid to the extent that it empowers the Minister of Defence and Military Veterans (Minister), acting on the recommendation of the adjutant general, to assign Judges for renewable periods.

(c.) The existing practice of assigning Judges for renewable periods of one to two years is unconstitutional and unlawful. Pending the coming into operation of remedial legislation, the assignment of a military Judge may not be renewed until the lapse of at least two years since that person's last assignment.

(d.) Section 17 of the Military Discipline Supplementary Measures Act 16 of 1999 is unconstitutional and invalid to the extent that it empowers the Minister, acting on the recommendation of the Adjutant General, to remove a military judge and that the Minister may do so without any independent inquiry into the fitness of the military judge to hold office.

(e.) Pending the coming into operation of remedial legislation, the Minister may devise processes for an inquiry into the fitness of a military judge and the composition of the inquiry body, provided that:

(i.) it is an independent inquiry; and

(ii.) a military judge may not be removed except on the recommendation of the independent inquiry.

(f.) The declarations of constitutional invalidity above are suspended for a period of 24 months to allow remedial legislation to be enacted and brought into operation.

(6.) The first Respondent is ordered to pay half of the costs of the Applicant in the Supreme Court of Appeal and the High Court, including the costs of two counsel where so employed.

(7.) The first Respondent is ordered to pay the costs of the Applicant in this Court, including the costs of two counsel where so employed.

JUDGMENT

MAJIEDT J (Zondo CJ, Madlanga ADCJ, Kollapen J, Mathopo J, Mhlantla J, Rogers J, Theron J, Tolmay AJ and Tshiqi J concurring):

Introduction

(1.) Military justice was previously dispensed in this country by way of ad hoc (for a particular purpose) courts-martial, but that system was declared unconstitutional by the Full Court of the Cape Provincial Division of the High Court in *Freedom of Expression Institute*.[1] The courts-martial system was abolished when Parliament enacted the Military Discipline Supplementary Measures Act[2] (MDSMA). In place of that system, the MDSMA established what this Court referred to as a system which 'shifted sharply from an essentially military system with forensic trappings to a system far closer to the ordinary criminal justice process.'[3]

(2.) This case concerns the independence of military courts, in particular two military courts of first instance established under the MDSMA, the Court of a Military Judge and the Court of a Senior Military Judge. The Applicant, a Lieutenant-Colonel in the South African National Defence Force (SANDF) and a former military judge, challenged, in a counter-application before the High Court, Gauteng Division, Pretoria (High Court), the constitutionality of Sections 101 and 102 of the Defence Act[4] and Sections 15 and 17 of the MDSMA (the impugned provisions). The Applicant is currently employed as an instructor at the School of Military Justice, Pretoria. The main application was a review application by the first Respondent, the Minister of Defence and Military Veterans (Minister), against certain orders made by the Applicant in proceedings where he had presided as a military judge, concerning his

---

1. *Freedom of Expression Institute v President, Ordinary Court Martial 1999 (2) SA 471 (C); 1999 (3) BCLR 261 (C) at para 19: 'The law as it stands invites arbitrariness as it allows executive interference into judicial process.'*

2. 16 of 1999.

3. *Minister of Defence vs Potsane; Legal Soldier (Pty) Ltd vs Minister of Defence [2001] ZACC 12; 2002 (1) SA 1 (CC); 2001 (11) BCLR 1137 (CC) (Potsane) at para 10.*

4. 42 of 2002.

apprehension about the unconstitutionality of the impugned provisions. The High Court upheld the review relief and dismissed the Applicant's counter-application on the basis that the impugned provisions were constitutionally compliant.[5] The Supreme Court of Appeal dismissed the Applicant's appeal on the basis of mootness.[6]

(3.) The Applicant now seeks leave to appeal in this Court. The application for leave to appeal is confined to the applicant's counter-application; the Applicant has no issues with the Supreme Court of Appeal's judgment and order pertaining to the review application brought by the Respondents.

(4.) There are three constitutional challenges against the impugned provisions:

(a.) first, in respect of Sections 101 and 102 of the Defence Act, whether it is constitutionally permissible for members of the Executive to have the power to initiate and control boards of inquiry to investigate judicial officers' fitness and the conduct of their cases, as occurred in the Applicant's case;

(b.) second, whether the power under Section 15 of the MDSMA, permitting the Minister and the Adjutant General to make renewable assignments of military judges, for short periods, at their sole discretion, and without any objective criteria, passes constitutional muster;

(c.) third, relating to the constitutionality of Section 17 of the MDSMA, which empowers members of the Executive – the Minister and the Adjutant General – to remove military judges for alleged misconduct or incapacity, without the involvement or oversight of any independent body.

---

5. *Minister of Defence and Military Veterans vs O'Brien NO, unreported judgment of the High Court of South Africa, Gauteng Division, Pretoria, Case No 76995/18 (2 August 2021); [2021] ZAGPPHC 520 (High Court judgment).*

6. *O'Brien NO vs Minister of Defence and Military Veterans [2022] ZASCA 178; [2023] 1 All SA 341 (SCA) (Supreme Court of Appeal judgment).*

Parties

(5.) The Applicant and first Respondent have already been described. The second Respondent is the Chief of the SANDF; the third Respondent is the Secretary of Defence and Military Veterans; and the fourth Respondent is the SANDF. All four Respondents oppose the application for leave to appeal. They are represented by one legal team. The International Commission of Jurists (ICJ) was admitted as an amicus curiae and was permitted to present written and oral arguments. The ICJ was also given leave to adduce as evidence the Ministerial Task Team Report on Sexual Harassment, Sexual Exploitation, Sexual Abuse and Sexual Offences within the Department of Defence (Ministerial Task Team Report). The Applicant did not oppose the ICJ's admission. However, the Respondents objected thereto on the basis that they have dealt with foreign and international law in their submissions, and that the introduction of information about sexual crimes in the military constitutes the introduction of fresh evidence which is inappropriate for amicus curiae to raise.

The Legislative Framework

(6.) It is useful, for a better understanding of the factual backdrop and the legal issues, to set out first the relevant legislative framework. Subsections 165(2) to (4) of the Constitution guarantee the independence of all courts:

> '(2.) The courts are independent and subject only to the Constitution and the law, which they must apply impartially and without fear, favour or prejudice.
>
> (3.) No person or organ of state may interfere with the functioning of the courts.
>
> (4.) Organs of state, through legislative and other measures, must assist and protect the courts to ensure the independence, impartiality, dignity, accessibility and effectiveness of the courts.'

(7.) As will be explained later, military courts fall within the definition of '"courts' in Section 166 of the Constitution, since they are 'any other court established or recognised in terms of an Act of Parliament' envisaged in Section 166(e). Section 174(7) of the Constitution further requires that all judicial officers 'must be appointed in terms of an Act of Parliament which must ensure that the appointment, promotion, transfer or dismissal of, or disciplinary steps against, these judicial officers take place without favour or prejudice.'

(8.) Section 175 of the Constitution, headed 'Appointment of acting Judges', provides:

> '(1.) The President may appoint a woman or man to serve as an acting Deputy Chief Justice or judge of the Constitutional Court if there is a vacancy in any of those offices, or if the person holding such an office is absent. The appointment must be made on the recommendation of the Cabinet member responsible for the administration of justice acting with the concurrence of the Chief Justice, and an appointment as acting Deputy Chief Justice must be made from the ranks of the judges who had been appointed to the Constitutional Court in terms of Section 174(4).
>
> (2.) The Cabinet member responsible for the administration of justice must appoint acting judges to other courts after consulting the senior judge of the court on which the acting judge will serve.'

(9.) The assignment of military judges occurs under Sections 13 and 14 of the MDSMA and the duration of such assignments is regulated under Section 15 of that Act. Section 13, headed 'Assignment of functions', reads:

> '(1.) Only an appropriately qualified officer holding a degree in law and of a rank not below that of colonel or its equivalent, with not less than five years' appropriate experience as a practising advocate or attorney of the High Court of South Africa, or five years' experience in the administration of criminal justice or military justice, may be assigned to the function of—
>
> (a.) Director: Military Judges;
>
> (b.) Director: Military Prosecutions;
>
> (c.) Director: Military Defence Counsel; or
>
> (d.) Director: Military Judicial Reviews.

(2.) Only an appropriately qualified officer holding a degree in law may be assigned to the function of—

(a.) senior military judge or military judge;

(b.) review counsel;

(c.) senior defence counsel or defence counsel; or

(d.) senior prosecution counsel.

(3.) Only an appropriately qualified officer or other member who holds a degree in law or who has otherwise been trained in law may be assigned to the function of prosecution counsel.'

(10.) Section 14, headed 'Minister's powers in respect of assignment', provides:

'(1.) The Minister shall assign officers to the functions—

(a.) at the level of Director referred to in Section 13(1); and

(b.) of senior military judge or military judge referred to in Section 13(2)(a), on the recommendation of the Adjutant General: Provided that the Director: Military Judges shall be deemed to have been assigned the function of senior military judge.

(2.) The Adjutant General shall not recommend any officer for assignment to any function referred to in subsection (1) unless, upon due and diligent enquiry, the Adjutant General is convinced that the officer is a fit and proper person of sound character who meets the requirements prescribed in this Act for such assignment.

(3.) Subject to Section 16 and the control of the Minister, the Adjutant General may assign any officer or member to any function—

(a.) referred to in Section 13(2)(b), (c) and (d) or (3); or

(b.) attached to any approved military legal services post other than those referred to in this Act.

(4.) Officers and members assigned to functions in terms of this Section shall perform those functions in a manner which is consistent with properly given policy directives, but which is otherwise free from Executive or command interference.'

(11.) Section 15 of the MDSMA, headed 'Period of assignment', reads:

'An assignment in terms of this Chapter shall be for a fixed period or coupled to a specific deployment, operation or exercise.'

(12.) Section 17, with the heading 'Removal from assignment', reads:

'The Minister, acting upon the recommendation of the Adjutant General, may remove a person from the function assigned to him or her for the reason of that assignee's incapacity, incompetence or misconduct, or at his or her own written request.'

(13.) Section 19 of the MDSMA is an important provision in the context of the central question of the independence of military Courts. It provides in relevant part:

'Every military judge and every senior military judge shall in the exercise of his or her judicial authority under this Act—

(a) be independent and subject only to the Constitution and the law;

(b) apply the Constitution and the law impartially and without fear, favour or prejudice;

(c) conduct every trial and proceedings in a manner befitting a Court of justice.'

(14.) In summary, Sections 101 and 102 of the Defence Act are concerned with the convening of boards of inquiry and the attendance of persons at boards of enquiry and witnesses respectively. Subsections 101(1) and (2) provide:

'(1.) The Minister, the Secretary for the Defence or the Chief of the Defence Force may, at any time or place, convene a board of inquiry to inquire into any matter concerning the Department, any employee thereof or any member of the Defence Force or any auxiliary service, any public property or the property or affairs of any institution or any regimental or sports funds of the said Force, and to report thereon or to make a recommendation.

(2.) Despite subsection (1), a Chief of a Service or Division may at any time and place convene a board of inquiry to investigate any matter concerning the Service or Division .... or any member or employee .... and the affairs of any institution of the said Service or Division, and to report or to make a recommendation thereon.'

(15.) Importantly, Section 102 sets out the procedure before a board of inquiry which is similar to that of a civilian criminal court.[7] Section 104(21) makes

---

7. Section 102 of the Defence Act headed 'Attendance of persons at board of enquiry, and witnesses' reads:

'(1) The President of any board of inquiry may summon any person in the Republic to attend such board of inquiry and to give evidence thereat.

(2) The President of any board of inquiry may administer the prescribed oath or affirmation to witnesses, interpreters and stenographers at such inquiry.

(3) (a) Any person giving evidence before a board of inquiry may be compelled to answer any question or to produce any article if the President of the board of inquiry so orders.

(b) No incriminating answer or information obtained or incriminating evidence directly or indirectly derived from a question in terms of paragraph (a) is admissible as evidence against the person concerned in criminal proceedings in a Court of law or before any body or institution established by or under any law, except in criminal proceedings where the person is arraigned on a charge of perjury or a charge contemplated in Section 104(21).

(4) Subject to subsection (5), the evidence of every witness called by a board of inquiry must be given orally and on oath or affirmation and must be recorded by or under the supervision of the President.

(5) A board of enquiry may admit a sworn statement by a witness as evidence where, with due regard to the exigencies of the service—

(a) by reason of his or her illness, the witness cannot attend;

(b) undue expense would be incurred by the attendance of the witness; or

(c) the evidence of the witness is of a purely formal nature.

non-compliance with a summons or warning to appear in terms of Section 102(1) an offence, punishable with the sanction of a fine or imprisonment.[8]

---

(6) Where the evidence is of such a nature that it is likely that the findings or recommendations would seriously affect the professional reputation of a person who is subject to the Code or a person who is in the employ of the Department, or that any disciplinary or other legal steps might be taken against such a person—

(a) the witness concerned must, despite subsection (5), be called to give evidence orally if the person who is likely to be affected, so requests;

(b) the person who is likely to be affected may be present at every meeting of the Board where such evidence is led, to cross-examine any witness giving such evidence, to give evidence himself or herself, even if otherwise called as a witness by the Board, and to call witnesses.

(7) The President of the Board must timeously notify a person contemplated in subsection (6) of the time and place of every such meeting and advise that person of the rights conferred upon him or her by that subsection.

(8) Any person contemplated in subsection (6) may at any stage of the proceedings determined by the board, address the board on the evidence referred to in that subsection and may—

(a) in the exercise of his or her rights under that subsection be represented by a legal representative of his or her own choice at his or her own expense; or

(b) if the person so requests, be assigned military defence counsel at State expense.

(9) Before the record of proceedings is submitted to the person who convened the Board, the relevant findings and recommendations of a board of inquiry must be communicated to each person who is adversely affected by such findings and recommendations and that person has the right to make written representations to the person who convened the board of inquiry within 14 days of receipt of the relevant findings and recommendations.

(10) Subsections (6) and (7) do not apply in relation to any board of inquiry convened under section 103.'

8. Section 104(21) of the Defence Act reads:

'(a) A person is guilty of an offence if he or she—

(i) having been duly summoned or warned to attend as a witness before a board of inquiry, fails to attend or to remain in attendance until authorised to leave;

(ii) being present at a board of inquiry after having been duly summoned or

Factual matrix

(16.) I confine the factual narrative to the bare minimum, that is, the facts necessary to understand how the central issues arose. The Applicant was assigned as a military judge for fixed periods during 2013, 2014, and 2016. During his time of service, the Applicant started to reflect on the constitutionality of consecutive fixed-term appointments of military judges. He formed the view that consecutive fixed appointments might impact on the independence of the Judiciary. The Applicant subsequently, of his own accord, began placing on record, at the commencement of matters in which he presided, his concerns regarding the constitutionality of the appointment of military Judges. He also made brief obiter (in passing) remarks, expressing concerns about renewable terms and their impact on the structural independence of the military Courts. The Applicant claimed that his views were based on this Court's case law, and he stated thus in these obiter remarks.

(17.) In 2014, the Applicant's superiors requested that he cease this practice, on the basis that he was bringing the credibility of the military legal system into disrepute. The Applicant relented and undertook not to raise his views in this manner in future cases before him.

(18.) In 2015, the Minister did not assign military judges, except for one or two reserve force military judges. In 2016, after he was again assigned to the Bench, the Applicant presided in the two matters that ultimately resulted in the current litigation (the Mokoena and Mabula cases). The Applicant once again reiterated his view regarding the constitutionality of the appointment of military judges and enquired from the parties whether they accepted the

---

warned to attend as a witness, fails or refuses to be sworn or to affirm;

(iii) uses threatening or insulting language at a board of inquiry or wilfully causes a disturbance or interruption thereat or wilfully commits any other act likely to bring the board of inquiry into contempt, ridicule or disrepute; or

(iv) having been duly notified of his or her call-up for service by way of a call-up order issued in terms of Section 53(3A), fails to present himself or herself at the time and place specified in the call-up order.

(b) Any person convicted of an offence contemplated in paragraph (a) is liable to a fine or imprisonment for a period not exceeding three months.'

Military Court's jurisdiction. The Applicant was concerned in both matters that the accused's trials were unduly delayed to the point that it might have impacted their right to a fair trial. He requested the legal representatives to address him on whether he could conduct an investigation as provided for in Section 342A of the Criminal Procedure Act[9]. That Section deals with unreasonable delays in criminal trials. Both legal representatives argued that he (the military Judge) was entitled to have regard to and implement the provisions of Section 342A of the Criminal Procedure Act.

(19.) Without the knowledge of and participation in the proceedings by the Minister, the Applicant, relying on what he considered to be 'public knowledge' and information in the public domain, concluded that the undue delay in prosecuting the respective matters was in part attributable to the Minister's failure to appoint military judges for the period 2015–2016, and in part to the prosecuting authority. He subsequently ordered that 'a copy of the written court ruling, a copy of the "Military Judges Concerns in respect of the Constitutionality of the Assignment of Military Judges",[10] and a copy

---

9. 51 of 1977.

10. In relevant part, that document reads:

> '8. Court is of the view that Section 14(1)(b) MDSMA might be unconstitutional based on the following:
>
> a. Fixed term from 19 May 2014 – 31 March 2015, does not meet the requirement that the military Judge shall have security of tenure of office.
>
> b. There may have been Executive interference in the functioning of the military Courts and/or the assignment of the military Judges for 2014/15:
>
> i. During February/March 2014, all military Judges were required to provide their Court hours for the previous three years to the adjutant general who in turn provided this information to C SANDF, who in turn provided this information to the minister. The amount of Court hours of each military Judge could have played a pivotal role in the assignment of the military Judges for 2014/15.
>
> ii. This was confirmed by the minister's assignment in mid-April 2014 of military Judges with satisfactory Court hours. Unfortunately, I was only assigned on 19 May 2014, after I had had to provide an explanation for my unsatisfactory amount of Court hours for 2013/14 i.e. 103 Court hours. My explanation being I had only sat as a military Judge for two weeks in June 2013 and from 15 January – 28

of Prosecution Counsel's and Defence Counsel's Heads of Argument' be served respectively on the Director, Military Prosecutions (Director) and the President of the Republic of South Africa (President) in his capacity as Commander-in-Chief of the SANDF. The Applicant regarded the Director and the President as the appropriate authorities to conduct an administrative investigation and consider possible disciplinary action against the prosecutorial staff and the minister, respectively, for their part in causing the delay.

(20.) The Applicant postponed the finalisation of the Mokoena and Mabula cases after holding that the delays incurred were more prejudicial to the prosecution than to the defence. Both the Director and the President were ordered by the Applicant to provide written reports to the Military Court, by 31 October 2016, setting out what actions, if any, had been taken against any of their staff members and the Minister, respectively.

(21.) The Applicant's superiors were, to put it mildly, startled by this development. The concerns were expressed in a letter by then Review Counsel, Lieutenant Colonel Kriek, on 6 November 2014 to the Director: Military Judicial Reviews. Those concerns were that the constitutional issue raised by the Applicant 'does not fall within the ambit of the procedural course of a Court case constituted under the [MDSMA]'. The upshot of the concerns was that the Applicant as a presiding military judge was in effect

---

February 2014 due to the fact that I had attended the SAMHS Junior Command and Staff Course from July – December 2013.

9. This Court has addressed its concerns in respect of the assignment of military Judges to both the director military Judges and to the Officer in Charge Operations Support Legsato.

10. Court is well aware of the provisions of Section 170 [of the] Constitution which states that: "Court of a status lower than the High Court may not rule on the constitutionality of any legislation."

11. Purposes of this trial Court is bound to accept that the provisions of Section 14(1)(b) of the MDSMA are constitutional and that we may then proceed.

12. Court wishes to give both counsel an opportunity to place on record whether they are willing to proceed and if so, whether defence counsel has any other objections in respect of the jurisdiction of the Court or in respect of the charges that they do not disclose an offence?'

challenging his appointment in open court, thus challenging the credibility of the military legal system. In that letter the question was also raised as to why a military judge who believes his appointment to preside in a military court is unconstitutional would continue with the matters before him even though the trials would then be invalid and null and void.

(22.) On 5 December 2015, the then Director: Military Judges, Brigadier General Slabbert, held a meeting with the Applicant to express his concern that, in having once again raised the constitutionality of assignments of military judges in open court, the Applicant had breached a previous undertaking. In the course of that meeting, the Applicant was instructed not to use his Military Court as a forum for his 'awareness campaigns and constructive criticism'. He was advised to use the proper channels of command and that, if he were to persist in his conduct, it may impact on his future assignment as a military judge.

(23.) A board of inquiry (Board) was then constituted (presumably in terms of Sections 101 and 102 of the Defence Act) to investigate whether his conduct brought the military legal system into disrepute. The Applicant was informed that no new cases would be assigned to him pending the finalisation of the matter by the Board. The Applicant objected to not being assigned new cases, and he was again assigned matters within the borders of South Africa pending the investigation by the Board.

(24.) Subsequent to the commencement of that investigation, the Applicant was informed that the mandate of the Board was extended to investigate all matters previously heard by him. The Applicant convened a court in October 2016 and summoned the accused, the prosecutor, and defence counsel in the Mokoena and Mabula matters to appear before him. After explaining what had transpired since the matters were postponed, he recused himself from hearing both matters because, in his view, the interference in his judicial functions gave rise to a reasonable apprehension of bias. Without any of his superiors or the officers involved in the Board having been notified of the procedure, he ordered that a copy of the record of the proceedings be served on the Minister to consider whether the officers named in the order had complied with the provisions of

Section 54(2)(g) of the Defence Act,[11] and to make recommendations to the Commander-in-Chief, the President, in this regard.

(25.) The Mokoena and Mabula cases were assigned to new military judges, and both matters have since been finalised. The Applicant was not subsequently assigned as a military judge after his fixed-term appointment lapsed. He was the only military judge who did not receive a consecutive assignment as a military judge. Litigation ensued, culminating in this application.

Litigation History

High Court

(26.) In 2018, the present Respondents instituted review proceedings in the High Court to review and set aside the judgments and orders handed down by the Applicant in his capacity as a military judge on 25 and 29 August 2016 and 14 October 2016. The Applicant, in turn, instituted a counter-application challenging the constitutionality of Sections 101 and 102 of the Defence Act, and Sections 15 and 17 of the MDSMA. The Respondents decided to suspend the Board pending the finalisation of the review proceedings and counter-application.

(27.) As stated, the Applicant's counter-application raised three principal issues concerning the constitutionality of Sections 15 and 17 of the MDSMSA and Sections 101 and 102 of the Defence Act. The High Court considered the three challenges in the following sequence. The first issue was the Section 15 of the MDSMA challenge: whether the Minister's power to reassign military judges for consecutive fixed periods of service is consistent with the principle of judicial independence.

---

11. Section 54(2)(g) of the Defence Act, headed 'Commissioned officers in Defence Force', provides:

> '(2) In order to qualify for a permanent commissioned appointment in the Defence Force, a person must—
>
> ...
>
> (g) be a fit and proper person to serve and must have a trustworthy and exemplary character.'

(28.) The second issue the High Court had to determine was whether Section 17 of the MDSMA, to the extent that the provision empowers the Minister, on the recommendation of the Adjutant General, without any independent inquiry into the fitness of the military judge to hold office, to remove military judges for alleged misconduct, is consistent with the principle of judicial independence and thus constitutional. Lastly, the third issue for determination was whether Sections 101 and 102 of the Defence Act empower the Executive (Minister and Adjutant General) to appoint boards of inquiry, staffed with non-judicial officers, to investigate military judges, their judgments, and the conduct of their cases. If they do, the High Court had to enquire into whether the provisions are consistent with the principle of judicial independence and thus into whether they are constitutional.

(29.) In respect of the first issue, the Section 15 challenge, the High Court pointed out that a military judge's term of office and reassignment relates to security of tenure. The High Court held that an assignment as a military judge does not affect a person's employment in the SANDF. A military judge's security of tenure as a military officer of a specific rank, and their financial position, are not dependent on their assignment as a military judge. The Court held further that military courts enjoy limited jurisdiction and their decisions are subject to appeal and review. In light of all of these findings, the Court held that there are sufficient safeguards in the MDSMA, and related statutes, to render the risk posed to judicial independence, by the power to make reassignments, negligible. Consequently, the Court dismissed this constitutional challenge.

(30.) On the second issue, the power to remove a military judge upon the recommendation of the Adjutant General found in Section 17 of the MDSMA, the High Court accepted that the MDSMA does not explicitly provide for a procedure in terms of which a preliminary, or any, investigation must be conducted or that a charge be brought against the military judge concerned. But, said the High Court, a proper interpretation of Section 17 in the context of the MDSMA, read with the Military Discipline Code (Code), the MDSMA Rules and the rules of natural justice, implies that the Adjutant General has an obligation to convene a board of inquiry to investigate alleged misconduct, incapacity or incompetence before recommending a military judge's removal from the function assigned to them. The investigation by a board of inquiry serves to ensure that the Adjutant General's recommendation is an informed recommendation as opposed to one based on their own whim. The High Court thus held that, if Section 17 is read within the legal matrix created by the MDSMA, MDSMA Rules and the Code, this constitutional challenge must fail.

(31.) On the third and last issue, that is the issue of whether, properly interpreted, Sections 101 and 102 of the Defence Act empower the Minister and/or the Adjutant General to appoint boards of inquiry to investigate military judges and the related issue of whether such a power is consistent with the principle of judicial independence, the Court held thus: The substance of Sections 101 and 102 of the Defence Act are repeated in the Code and the MDSMA Rules. A board of inquiry can thus be convened without reliance on the Defence Act. According to the Court, military judges should not be removed from their assignment unless their incapacity, misconduct, or incompetence has objectively been determined. Such a determination cannot be made without an investigation, and a board of inquiry is the appropriate mechanism to conduct such an inquiry.

(32.) The High Court held that to grant the order sought by the Applicant would be to incapacitate the Minister from removing a military judge in accordance with Section 17. To prevent a board of inquiry from convening before a military Judge's fixed appointment lapses will defeat the purpose of Section 17. In the premises, the Court held that Sections 101 and 102, properly interpreted, empower the Minister and/or the Adjutant General to appoint boards of inquiry to investigate military judges and that this power is consistent with the principles of judicial independence and is therefore constitutional.

(33.) In light of the above, the High Court dismissed the Applicant's counter-application with costs. With the leave of that Court, the Applicant appealed to the Supreme Court of Appeal.

Supreme Court of Appeal

(34.) The Supreme Court of Appeal dismissed all three constitutional challenges on the basis of mootness. The first challenge – directed at Section

15 of the MDSMA, (the power to renew term of office) – was moot, according to that Court, on account of the absence of a real and live dispute. The Court held that 'the case advanced in support of the Section 15 challenge is a purely conjectural one'. The Court held further that the Applicant sought to—

> 'have [it] express a view on legal issues that he hope[d] to have decided, which would not in any way affect his position relative to the Defence Force.[and that the Applicant, in effect, was seeking] legal advice from [the Court] in respect of legal disputes that may or may not arise in the future.'[12]

(35.) The second challenge aimed at Section 17 of the MDSMA, the power to remove military judges, had become moot, according to the Supreme Court of Appeal, because the Applicant was not facing, nor had he ever faced, removal from the position of military judge. The Court held that there was not the faintest hint that the Adjutant General had ever contemplated a recommendation to the Minister that the applicant be removed from office, nor was there a hint that the Minister herself had ever contemplated doing so.

(36.) And lastly, the Supreme Court of Appeal held that the third challenge concerning Sections 101 and 102 of the Defence Act, the power to appoint boards of inquiry, had become moot by reason that the SANDF had decided to collapse the Board established to investigate the Applicant's conduct, which had been held in abeyance pending the finalisation of the review application in the High Court. The Supreme Court of Appeal held further that, given the reservations expressed by the new Adjutant General as to the appropriateness of invoking those provisions in a case involving a military judge, and the unlikelihood of a recurrence of the question in the future, there was no live issue between the present parties that the Court needed to resolve.

(37.) In light of the above, the Supreme Court of Appeal dismissed the Applicant's appeal against the dismissal of his counter-application in the High Court. As stated, this application for leave to appeal is directed at that order.

12. Supreme Court of Appeal judgment above n 6 at paras 58-9.

In this Court

Applicant's Submissions

(38.) With regard to jurisdiction, the Applicant submits that the matter is a constitutional issue as it concerns the constitutionality of national legislation and the judicial independence of military courts and military judges. The Applicant submits that the matter is not moot and it is in the interests of justice to grant leave to appeal. That is so because, according to the Applicant, 'a constitutional challenge to legislation that is in operation is a live issue and the orders of this Court would have practical effect'. In the event that the Court finds that the matter is moot, the Applicant submits that it is nevertheless in the interests of justice to hear the appeal, because this case raises important, complex legal questions about the independence of military courts and military judges. The Applicant further submits that it would be in the interests of justice to hear the matter notwithstanding it being moot because of the broader practical impact that the order of invalidity would have. In addition, the Applicant submits that this Court has the benefit of the High Court judgment on these issues.

(39.) In respect of the merits, on the first issue, the power to renew terms of office in terms of Section 15 of the MDSMA, the Applicant submits that this power is inconsistent with the principle of judicial independence for two main reasons. First, because 'non-renewable terms are a core requirement of structur[al] independence' and renewable terms of office are inconsistent with the core guarantee of security of tenure. Second, renewable terms leave Judges open to threats and inducements or, at the very least, a reasonable apprehension of that. In further support of his argument, the Applicant submits that Section 15 is out of step with the trend observed in foreign jurisdictions such as Canada, New Zealand and the United Kingdom.

(40.) On the second issue, the power to remove a military judge upon the recommendation of the Adjutant General according to Section 17 of the MDSMA, the crux of the Applicant's submissions is this: it is impermissible for members of the Executive to hold the power to exercise discipline over judicial officers without any independent assessment of cause. According to the Applicant, this includes the unfettered power to remove judicial officers for misconduct or incapacity.

(41.) As to the third and last challenge, the power to appoint boards of inquiry in terms of Sections 101 and 102 of the Defence Act, the Applicant submits that this power interferes with a military judge's freedom to hear and decide cases without interference from government, pressure groups, or individuals. The Applicant submits that this power compromises military judges and judicial independence as it places judicial officers in a subordinate position in relation to the Executive.

(42.) The Applicant further submits that the composition of boards of inquiry is also inconsistent with the principle of judicial independence. According to the Applicant, the boards are often composed of individuals who are not judicial officers, and this is inconsistent with the principle of judicial independence. Lastly, the Applicant submits that the members of boards obey the Adjutant General and Minister's orders and are not independent. Consequently, they cannot be considered to be an independent check on the exercise of the powers of the Minister and Adjutant General.

Respondents' Submissions

(43.) The Respondents submit, without motivation, that this Court does not have jurisdiction to entertain the matter. They submit that the matter is moot and it is not in the interests of justice to entertain the application. That submission is primarily based on the Supreme Court of Appeal's reasoning. On the merits, the crux of their case is that this Court should not declare the impugned provisions unconstitutional, because those provisions apply to a number of groups in the SANDF and not just military judges and, as a result, a declaration of constitutional invalidity will affect the 'entire [SANDF]' and 'the Country'.

(44.) The Respondents argue that military judges do not fall within the definition of 'judicial officers' as outlined in Section 174(7) of the Constitution. They point out that the MDSMA does not categorise military judges as 'judicial officers'. While military courts hold jurisdiction over criminal matters, this jurisdiction does not extend to civilians. The Respondents make the point that only a Senior Military Judge can preside over cases involving serious offenses such as murder, treason, rape, or culpable homicide, and, even then, only if such crimes occur outside the country's borders. Moreover, the Respondents assert that military courts already possess sufficient judicial independence. They refer to *Potsane,*[13] which, they contend, suggests that the MDSMA was established to align the country's military justice system with the principles of constitutionalism.

(45.) Regarding the first challenge, the Respondents contend that the legislation does not explicitly state that a board of inquiry is authorised to investigate military judges, their rulings, or the handling of their cases. They assert that no constitutional arrangement can achieve a total separation of powers. They cite *Van Rooyen,*[14] where the inclusion of members of Parliament and the Executive on the Magistrates' Commission was held to be acceptable.

(46.) In respect of the second challenge, the Respondents argue that Section 15 does not solely pertain to the assignment of military judges but applies to various categories of military personnel. They assert that if Section 15 were deemed unconstitutional, it would impact the deployment of all types of military personnel. With reference to Van Rooyen the Respondents cite this Court's decision in the First Certification judgment,[15] that the appointment of Judges by the Executive, or in collaboration with Parliament, does not undermine the impartiality and independence of the Judiciary. They emphasise that military judges already have security of tenure. Additionally, they point out that there are relatively few cases for military judges to handle, and permanent appointments might hinder efforts towards transformation.

(47.) Regarding the third challenge, the Respondents assert that Section 17 does not specifically address the removal of 'a military judge' but rather the removal of 'a person', indicating that military Judges are not strictly categorised as judicial officers but as members of the SANDF. They point out that countries like New Zealand, Australia, and Canada have removal provisions

---

13. *Potsane above n 3.*

14. *Van Rooyen vs S (General Council of the Bar of South Africa intervening) [2002] ZACC 8; 2002 (5) SA 246 (CC); 2002 (8) BCLR 810 (CC) (Van Rooyen).*

15. *Ex parte Chairperson of the Constitutional Assembly: In re Certification of the Constitution of the Republic of South Africa [1996] ZACC 26; 1996 (4) SA 744 (CC); 1996 (10) BCLR 1253 (CC).*

involving both the Legislature and Executive. In contrast, in South Africa it is ultimately the President and the National Assembly who remove a judge upon the recommendation of the Judicial Service Commission, which is a composite body.

ICJ's Submissions

(48.) The ICJ makes submissions on our country's obligations under international law to ensure that courts and tribunals, including military courts, are competent, independent, impartial, and afford litigants a fair and public hearing. Concerning the importance of the country's international obligations, the ICJ refers to Sections 39(1) and 233 of the Constitution.

(49.) In addition, with reference to the Ministerial Task Team Report, the ICJ emphasises the necessity for military courts to exhibit independence and impartiality in handling cases involving sexual offences committed by members of the SANDF. The ICJ points out that military courts have jurisdiction over all domestic sexual offences, except rape, and also have jurisdiction over cases of rape committed extraterritorially. According to the ICJ, given that SANDF members are engaged in peacekeeping operations outside South Africa, notably in the Democratic Republic of Congo and Mozambique, this underscores the significance of ensuring the independence and impartiality of military courts.

Analysis

The Ministerial Task Team Report

(50.) It is convenient to commence with brief reasons why the ICJ was permitted to introduce the Ministerial Task Team Report. In directions issued by this Court, the ICJ was authorised to adduce that report in the following terms:

> 'The ICJ is granted leave to file the [Ministerial Task Team Report] of December 2020. . . . as evidence, provided that, in regard to complaints of sexual offences or other sexual misconduct recorded in the report,

> the report is admissible not as evidence of the truth of the complaints but only as evidence that such complaints were made and that they were investigated, addressed and resolved (where applicable) in the way summarised in the report.'

(51.) Thus, at a procedural level, we cannot now reject that report as inadmissible. In any event, it is of significant relevance and assistance in determining the central issue: the independence of military courts. In essence, the ICJ is placing reliance on the report to show that complaints of sexual offences are widespread in the SANDF and that the scourge of gender-based violence in the SANDF makes it all the more important that military courts should be truly independent. Plainly, the ICJ's contentions provide important context in the sense of the urgent and crucial need for military courts to be truly independent, against the backdrop of sexual offences and sexual misconduct that are said to go largely unreported in the military out of fear of retaliation of not being promoted to the next rank in their military career. It must also be said that the ICJ effectively relates the report to the impugned sections.

(52.) Furthermore, the ICJ makes useful submissions on international law and jurisprudence. The ICJ correctly makes the important point that international law and standards – both binding and non-binding – are important interpretative tools in constitutional South Africa.[16] It is well-established that, when interpreting the constitutional guarantee of judicial independence and the impugned provisions in this matter, interpretation must happen within the context of the Constitution and its values as a whole, to which international law is relevant.[17] The ICJ submissions in relation to international law and jurisprudence were based on what appeared in the report. For these reasons, that report was allowed as evidence.

---

16. *Glenister vs President of the Republic of South Africa [2011] ZACC 6; 2011 (3) SA 347 (CC); 2011 (7) BCLR 651 (CC) (Glenister II) at para 96.*

17. *Justice Alliance of South Africa v President of the Republic of South Africa [2011] ZACC 23; 2011 (5) SA 388 (CC); 2011 (10) BCLR 1017 (CC) (Justice Alliance) at para 37.*

Jurisdiction and Leave to Appeal

(53.) This matter engages both this Court's constitutional and general jurisdiction. The first constitutional issue is the challenge to the constitutionality of the impugned provisions. The second constitutional issue concerns the judicial independence of military courts, which is constitutionally guaranteed under Section 165(2) to (4) and Section 174(7), read with Sections 1(c) and 35(3) of the Constitution. The matter also engages this Court's general jurisdiction, raising, as it does, arguable points of law (the role of military courts and military judges) of general public importance which affect not only all SANDF members, specifically military judges who must exercise their authority independently and subject only to the Constitution and the law, but also the general public whom the SANDF is constitutionally enjoined to protect.

(54.) Regarding the interests of justice, it is plainly desirable that this Court should hear this case to resolve the complex, important legal questions raised here. The issues are novel, since this Court has not as yet considered and decided the question of the independence of military courts and military judges. Lastly, and importantly, we are dealing here with questions of law only and, inasmuch as factual considerations may arise, they are mostly common cause on material aspects. There is also the mootness aspect which loomed large in the Supreme Court of Appeal, to the extent that it was central to that Court's dismissal of all three constitutional challenges.

(55.) Leave to appeal must therefore be granted. It is convenient to deal first with mootness.

Mootness

(56.) The Supreme Court of Appeal was plainly wrong in its mootness findings. I agree with the Applicant that a constitutional challenge to existing and fully operational statutory provisions can never be considered moot. Constitutional validity enquiries are always objective.18 Here, moreover, the

---

18. *Secretary of the Judicial Commission of Inquiry into Allegations of State Capture, Corruption and Fraud in the Public Sector including Organs of State vs Zuma [2021] ZACC 18; 2021 (5)*

specific facts relating to the case fortify the Applicant's constitutional challenge in the sense that they bear out his constitutional invalidity complaints. The challenges brought by the Applicant plainly raise an existing or live controversy between the parties over the constitutionality of the impugned provisions and their proper interpretation. Any orders declaring the legislation to be constitutionally invalid would also have an immediate practical effect or result not only for the Applicant, but also for all members of the SANDF and the broader public.

Military Courts and Judicial Independence

(57.) This discussion commences with a consideration of the question whether military courts are "'courts' within the meaning of Section 166(e) of the Constitution. At the outset it must be said that the Respondents' submissions are, regrettably, not very helpful. The Respondents seek to persuade us that military courts are not "'courts'. I disagree – there can be little doubt that military courts fall within Section 166(e).[19] First, regard must be had to what these courts do – they deal with criminal matters, follow the procedures for criminal matters in Magistrates' Courts and High Courts, impose sentence after conviction, and they operate under their own rules of court.[20]

SA 327 (CC); 2021 (9) BCLR 992 (CC) at para 156 and Gory vs Kolver NO [2006] ZACC 20; 2007 (3) BCLR 249 (CC); 2007 (4) SA 97 (CC) at para 39.

19. In *Mbambo vs Minister of Defence 2005 (2) SA 226 (T) at 230A-C the Court held that military Courts are inferior Courts with a similar status as Magistrate Courts.*

20. Although the United States of America has a Constitution and Court system that differs from ours in several important respects, it is noteworthy that there, in *Ortiz vs United States 585 US 427 (Ortiz), the majority in the Supreme Court opined that the courts-martial system 'closely resembles civilian structures of justice' and that 'the judicial character and constitutional pedigree of the court-martial system enable that Court, in exercising appellate jurisdiction, to review the decisions of the Court sitting at its apex' (referring to the CAAF, the United States Court of Appeals for the Armed Forces). The majority opinion defended the judicial nature of the military Courts by citing examples where the military system is similar to civilian justice, that is, due process protections, an appellate review system, a stable body of case law and the res judicata (a matter judged) effects of its decisions. Ortiz is useful insofar as it acknowledges that even in the United States, there is a recent tendency towards harmonisation between the standards that apply to military and civilian Courts rather than an attempt to preserve their sui generis (of their own kind) nature.*

(58.) Secondly, and importantly, one must consider Section 19 of the MDSMA, read with Section 165(2) to (4) of the Constitution, which afford these courts independence guaranteed by the Constitution and the statute. Thirdly, when persons appear in these courts charged with offences under the Defence Act, the Code, or the MDSMA, they must plainly fall within the category of 'accused persons' with all the rights and protections afforded to them in Section 35(3) of the Constitution. Lastly, it is of some significance that even in pre-constitutional times a court-martial, the predecessor of a military court, was regarded as a court.[21] All these factors and considerations lead to the ineluctable conclusion that military courts are courts as envisaged by Section 166(e).[22]

(59.) The Respondents contend that military judges are not 'judicial officers' within the meaning of Section 174(7) of the Constitution. They are wrong – military judges deal with criminal matters with wide territorial jurisdiction (even beyond our borders) and substantial sentencing competence: up to two years' imprisonment in the case of a court of a military judge, and anything up to life imprisonment in the case of the court of the senior military judge.[23] When one examines how the military courts operate, their rules and powers, and the ultimate effect of their orders, the inescapable conclusion is that military judges are indeed judicial officers. Furthermore, as required by Section 174(7) of the Constitution, military judges are appointed in terms

---

21. *Council of Review South African Defence Force vs Monnig [1992] ZASCA 64; [1992] 4 All SA 691 (A). See also Freedom of Expression Institute above n 1.*

22. Recently, at their meeting during November 2022, Commonwealth Law Ministers mandated the Commonwealth Secretariat to produce Commonwealth Military Justice Principles. These principles record, amongst others, that there is a need to 'ensure that military Courts, when they exist, are part of a state's general judicial system under the authority of the Constitution or statute, respecting the principle of separation of powers and reflecting the rule of law and the obligations of international law' (Article 1(a)).

23. The Court of a senior military Judge may try a member of the SANDF for any offence committed in South Africa other than murder, treason, rape or compelled rape (as contemplated in Section 3 or 4 of the Criminal Law (Sexual Offences and Related Matters) Amendment Act 32 of 2007) or culpable homicide. Such a Court may try a member for the latter serious crimes if they were committed extraterritorially. The effect of Section 12(1) of the MDSMA is that the Court of a senior military Judge may impose any competent sentence that an ordinary Court could impose for the same crime.

of an Act of Parliament, namely, the MDSMA. There can therefore be little doubt that military judges qualify as 'judicial officers' under Section 174(7).

(60.) Flowing from these conclusions that military courts fall within the ambit of Section 166(e), and that military judges are judicial officers, the requirement of independence is stark. It bears repetition that the court of a military judge and the court of a senior military judge have wide criminal jurisdiction to try members of the SANDF for serious offences committed under the Code, the common law, and statute.[24] They also have the power to impose substantial sentences of imprisonment for these offences.[25] They wield exceptional, extraterritorial powers that are not available to ordinary criminal courts. Military courts are the only criminal courts in South Africa that have jurisdiction over serious crimes – including murder, rape, and other sexual offences – committed by members of the SANDF beyond South Africa's borders. They may also sit anywhere in the world.[26]

(61.) Reference has already been made to Sections 166(e), 165(2) to (4), and 174(7) of the Constitution.[27] These provisions guarantee the independence of military courts. Furthermore, judicial independence is an essential component of the right to a fair trial.[28] Members of the SANDF who are on trial in military courts are accused persons under Section 35(3) of the Constitution with all the rights that flow from that, including the right to a fair, public trial in an ordinary court.[29] This Court held in Potsane that without essential safeguards of independence, military courts cannot qualify as 'ordinary courts'.[30] Judicial independence is foundational to, and indispensable for, the rule of law as

---

24. Sections 9 and 10 of the MDSMA.

25. Sections 9 and 10 of the MDSMA. The Court of a Senior Military Judge may impose any unlimited sentence of imprisonment. The Court of a Military Judge may impose imprisonment for up to two years.

26. Id read with Section 5 of the MDSMA.

27. Above, in [6] and [7].

28. *Van Rooyen above n 14 at para 35.*

29. Section 35(3)(c) of the Constitution.

30. *Postsane above n 3 at para 10.*

guaranteed under Section 1(c) of the Constitution.[31] The principle of judicial independence is fundamental to the ethos of the Constitution, and it is not subject to any limitation.[32]

(62.) The principle of the independence of military courts enunciated in Section 19 of the MDSMA has been highlighted.[33] All military judges are required to swear an oath or affirmation in terms of Section 18 of the MDSMA, read with Rule 83 of the MDSMA Rules.[34] There are thus intended to be guarantees of the independence of military courts, both in the Constitution and statute. What bears consideration is whether these guarantees in the legislation do in fact exist in relation to military courts.

(63.) Notionally, independence consists of both subjective and institutional (or structural) independence. As was pointed out in Sonke, 'this distinction has been most clearly expressed in relation to the independence of individual judges and the independence of the Courts as institutions'.[35] In that regard, this Court cited Van Rooyen, *where it had highlighted the distinction between*

---

31. *De Lange vs Smuts NO [1998] ZACC 6; 1998 (3) SA 785 (CC); 1998 (7) BCLR 779 (CC) (De Lange) at para 59.*

32. *Van Rooyen above n 14 at para 10:*

> '[I]t must be kept in mind that judicial impartiality and the application without fear, favour or prejudice by the Courts of the Constitution and all law, as postulated by Section 165(2) of the Constitution, are inherent in an accused's right to a fair trial under Section 35(3) of the Constitution. One of the main goals of institutional judicial independence is to safeguard such rights. However, institutional judicial independence itself is a constitutional principle and norm that goes beyond and lies outside the Bill of Rights. The provisions of Section 36 of the Constitution dealing with the limitation to rights entrenched in the Bill of Rights are accordingly not applicable to it. Judicial independence is not subject to limitation.'

33. Above in [13].

34. The oath or affirmation reads:

> 'I will be faithful to the Republic of South Africa, will uphold and protect the Constitution and the human rights entrenched in it, and will administer justice to all persons alike without fear, favour or prejudice, in accordance with the Constitution and the law of the Republic of South Africa, and will perform my duties to the best of my ability. So help me God.'

35. *Sonke Gender Justice NPC vs President of the Republic of South Africa [2020] ZACC 26; 2021 (3) BCLR 269 (CC) (Sonke) at para 72.*

individual and institutional independence.[36] It was described thus in *Van Rooyen:*

> 'This requires judicial officers to act independently and impartially in dealing with cases that come before them, and at an institutional level it requires structures to protect courts and judicial officers against external interference.'[37]

(64.) In *Van Rooyen* this Court relied on the minority judgment of O'Regan J in *De Lange,* who cited the following passage from *Valente*[38] with approval:

'It is generally agreed that judicial independence involves both individual and institutional relationships: the individual independence of a judge, as reflected in such matters as security of tenure, and the institutional independence of the court or tribunal over which he or she presides, as reflected in its institutional or administrative relationships to the Executive and Legislative branches of government. . . .The relationship between these two aspects of judicial independence is that an individual judge may enjoy the essential conditions of judicial independence but if the court or tribunal over which he or she presides is not independent of the other branches of government, in what is essential to its function, he or she cannot be said to be an independent tribunal.'[39]

(65.) This Court in McBride acknowledged the challenge of 'attempt[ing] to define the precise contours of a concept as elastic as [independence]'.[40] Subjective independence is generally understood to entail an impartial state of mind.[41] In this matter, we are primarily concerned with institutional independence. The test for institutional independence is objective – whether

---

36. *Van Rooyen above n 14.*

37. Id at para 19.

38. *Valente vs The Queen [1985] 2 SCR 673; (1986) 24 DLR (4*'h) 161 (SCC) (*Valente).*

39. Id at para 171 as cited in the minority judgment of O'Regan J in *De Lange above n 31 at para 159.*

40. *McBride vs Minister of Police (Helen Suzman Foundation as amicus curiae) [2016] ZACC 30; 2016 (2) SACR 585 (CC); 2016 (11) BCLR 1398 (CC) (McBride) at para 31.*

41. *De Lange above n 31 at para 71 citing Le Dain J in Valente above n 38 at 169-170.685(g).*

a court 'from the objective standpoint of a reasonable and informed person, will be perceived as enjoying the essential conditions of independence'.[42]

(66.) Institutional independence has to do with the way in which the institution is structured. This Court has pointed out that institutional and operational independence are often discussed alongside each other as they are closely linked.[43] In Glenister II, this Court noted that the question is not whether an institution has 'absolute or complete independence', but whether it enjoys 'sufficient structural and operational autonomy so as to shield it from undue political influence'.[44] Testing the independence of a structure does not require actual evidence of violations or undue influence – the real possibility of it occurring is sufficient.[45]

(67.) There are core requirements (referred to in *Van Rooyen* as 'essential *conditions*'[46]) for institutional independence. These include: freedom from any outside interference (especially from the Executive), security of tenure, and non-renewable terms.47 In De Lange, this Court cited three seminal Canadian cases – *Beauregard*,[48] *Valente*,[49] and *Généreux*[50] – regarding what constitutes an independent and impartial court. Reliance was placed in particular on Beauregard, where Dickson CJ stated:

> 'Historically, the generally accepted core of the principle of judicial independence has been the complete liberty of individual judges to hear and decide the cases that come before them; no outsider, be it government,

---

42. *Van Rooyen above n 14 at para 32 citing R vs Généreux [1992] 1 SCR 259; (1992) 88 DLR (4th) 110 (SCC) (Généreux) at 433E–G.*

43. *Sonke above n 35 at para 76.*

44. *Glenister II above n 16 at paras 121 and 125. See also McBride above n 42 at paras 32-3.*

45. *Sonke above n 35 at para 76.*

46. *Van Rooyen above n 14 at paras 32-5.*

47. Id at para 29 and *Justice Alliance above n 17 at para 73.*

48. *The Queen in Right of Canada vs Beauregard [1986] 2 SCR 56; (1986) 30 DLR (4th) 481 (SCC) (Beauregard).*

49. *Valente above n 38.*

50. *Généreux above n 42.*

> pressure group, individual or even another judge: should interfere in fact, or attempt to interfere, with the way in which a judge conducts his or her case and makes his or her decision. This core continues to be central to the principle of judicial independence.'[51]

(68.) In *Généreux* the Canadian Supreme Court held that the military status of military judges does not violate the provisions of Section 11(d) of the Canadian Charter of Rights and Freedoms (Canadian Charter).[52] It was acknowledged in *Généreux* that the place of military judges in the military hierarchy detracts from absolute judicial independence, but it also confirmed that Section 11(d) does not require absolute judicial independence, or a sort of truly independent military judiciary that could only be assured by civilian judges. Absolute independence is not the constitutional standard endorsed in the Canadian Supreme Court's jurisprudence. *Généreux* is authority for the proposition that, whatever concerns might arise as a result of Parliament's choice to require that military judges be military officers, that model is not inherently unconstitutional under Section 11(d).

(69.) An assessment of whether a particular court has the institutional protection that it requires to function independently and impartially will consider the core protection given to all courts by our Constitution, to the particular functions that such court performs, and to its place in the court hierarchy.[53] Recently in *Makana* this Court confirmed that '[e]ven within the judicial hierarchy, there are degrees of independence'.[54]

(70.) Crucially important in an assessment whether independence in fact exists is the perception of independence as adumbrated by this Court in Van Rooyen where reliance was placed on the following dictum (pronouncement) of Le Dain J in *Valente*:

---

51. *Beauregard above n 48 at 491.*

52. *Canadian Charter of Rights and Freedoms, Section 11, Part I of the Constitution Act 1982, being Schedule B to the Canada Act 1982.*

53. *Van Rooyen above n 14 at para 23.*

54. *Makana People's Centre vs Minister of Health [2023] ZACC 15; 2023 (5) SA 1 (CC); 2023 (8) BCLR 963 (CC) at para 169.*

> 'Both independence and impartiality are fundamental not only to the capacity to do justice in a particular case but also to individual and public confidence in the administration of justice. Without that confidence the system cannot command the respect and acceptance that are essential to its effective operation. It is, therefore, important that a tribunal should be perceived as independent, as well as impartial, and that the test for independence should include that perception.'[55]

(71.) In *Glenister II*, this Court said:

> '[I]f Parliament fails to create an institution that appears from the reasonable standpoint of the public to be independent, it has failed to meet one of the objective benchmarks for independence. This is because public confidence that an institution is independent is a component of, or is constitutive of, its independence. . . .Whether a reasonably informed and reasonable member of the public will have confidence in an entity's autonomy-protecting features is important to determining whether it has the requisite degree of independence.'[56]
>
> (Emphasis added)

(72.) Before considering South Africa's international obligations, it is instructive to have regard to the position in Canada, New Zealand and the United Kingdom. In 2011, following *Leblanc,*[57] the Canadian Parliament amended Canada's National Defence Act[58] to provide that military judges are now appointed until a maximum retirement age of 60, or until their release from the Canadian Forces, and may only be removed for cause. These amendments were introduced by the Security of Tenure of Military Judges Act 2011.

(73.) In *Leblanc,* the Appellant had been tried and convicted of having negligently performed a military duty. The Appellant then challenged the

55. *Van Rooyen above n 14 at para 32 citing Valente above n 38 at 172.*

56. *Glenister II above n 16 at para 207.*

57. *Leblanc vs The Queen 2011 CMAC 2 (Le Blanc).*

58. R.S.C. 1985.

legality of the guilty verdict and the constitutionality of the relevant statutory provisions. The Canadian Military Appeal Court upheld the challenge to the renewable appointment of military judges. That Court held that the appointment of military judges on five-year renewable terms was in breach of Section 11(d) of the Canadian Charter, which gives an accused the right to a hearing before an independent and impartial tribunal.

(74.) The following passages in *Leblanc* bear directly on the central issues in this case as far as renewable terms of military Judges are concerned:

> '*It seems inconceivable to me, and I say this with all due respect for the contrary view, that military judges, who exercise the same functions and have essentially the same powers as superior and provincial courts of criminal jurisdiction, should be subject to the whims, the unknowns, the uncertainty and anxiety of having their positions come up for renewal every five years. In fact, they are the only judges with such jurisdiction to be subject to short, renewable terms of employment.*
>
> ...
>
> Judicial independence is 'for the benefit of the judged'. . . .*It is important for the accused person that the judge not be, and not appear to be, beholden to these five members of the chain of command, that his or her security of tenure is not subject to reappointment and that his or her institutional independence provides the accused with the assurance of a fair and equitable trial.*'[59]
>
> (Emphasis added)

(75.) Recently, the Canadian Supreme Court in *Edwards*[60] had to consider an appeal from the Court Martial Appeal Court of Canada. The central issue in the case was whether the military status of military judges violates the constitutional guarantee of judicial independence and impartiality to which persons tried before courts-martial are entitled. The nine accused were members of the Canadian Armed Forces who were charged with service offences under Canada's Code of Service Discipline (CSD), which forms Part III of their National Defence

---

59. Id *at paras 47 and 52.*

60. *R vs Edwards 2024 SCC 15 (Edwards).*

Act, and were brought before courts-martial. Under the CSD, members of the Canadian Armed Forces may be charged with service offences, which are serious and encompass offences specific to military personnel, and offences under Canada's Criminal Code or other Acts of Parliament. Service offences are tried before a court martial, which is a military court that has the same powers, rights, and privileges as a superior court of criminal jurisdiction. Courts-martial are presided over by military judges.

(76.) The nine accused challenged the statutory requirement that the military judges presiding over their courts-martial be military officers, alleging that it violates their right to a hearing by an independent and impartial tribunal under Section 11(d) of the Canadian Charter. In the courts-martial, which were held separately, some of the military judges held that they lacked judicial independence by reason of their dual status of judge and officer, and therefore that the respective accused's Section 11(d) rights were infringed. On appeal to it, the Court-Martial Appeal Court held that an informed person, viewing the matter realistically and practically and having thought the matter through, would conclude that military judges meet the minimum constitutional norms of impartiality and independence even though they are military officers, and therefore that the accused's Section 11(d) rights were not infringed.

(77.) The majority in the Canadian Supreme Court upheld the decision of the Court-Martial Appeal Court. The Supreme Court held that the status of military judges as officers under the National Defence Act is not incompatible with their judicial functions for the purposes of Section 11(d) of the Canadian Charter. Accused members of the Canadian Armed Forces who appear before military judges are entitled to the same guarantee of judicial independence and impartiality under Section 11(d) as accused persons who appear before civilian criminal courts, but this does not require that the two systems be identical in every respect.

(78.) The Court held further that, as presently configured in the National Defence Act, Canada's system of military justice fully ensures judicial independence for military judges in a way that takes account of the military context, and specifically of the legislative policies of maintaining discipline, efficiency and morale in the Armed Forces and public trust in a disciplined military. Accordingly, the requirement that military judges be officers pursuant to Sections 165.21 and 165.24(2) of the National Defence Act does not infringe Section 11(d) of the Canadian Charter.

(79.) The majority in the Supreme Court confirmed its earlier decision in *Généreux* where the Court had held that the military status of military judges does not violate the provisions of Section 11(d). The Court held that there was no reason to depart from the settled precedent enunciated in *Généreux*. The Court also referred to the three essential requirements for judicial independence enunciated in the leading decision of *Valente*.[61] It held that those 'three essential conditions of judicial independence for military judges are met through the provisions of the [National Defence Act]'.[62] In respect of security of tenure, the Court held that the National Defence Act provides that military judges are appointed by the Governor in Council and that, unless they are removed for cause, they hold office until they are voluntarily released from the military or resign from the position of military judge, or until they reach the age of 60. Military judges can only be removed from office by the Governor in Council, for cause, upon a recommendation of their judicial peers properly convened as the Military Judges Inquiry Committee (MJIC).

(80.) Regarding the second requirement of financial security, the Canadian Supreme Court held that it is amply met, as military judges have their own remuneration scheme and their compensation is fixed through a process that centres on an independent committee. In respect of the third requirement, military judges, including the Chief Military Judge, are responsible for the decisions that must be left to military judges in order for there to be sufficient administrative independence, such as assigning military judges to preside at courts-martial and establishing procedural rules. These matters are insulated from non-judicial interference by the chain of command. The majority thus concluded that the Court-Martial Appeal Court was correct in holding that the Appellants' Section 11(d) rights were not infringed.

---

61. *Edwards above n 60 at paras 27, 40 and 47 citing Valente above n 38 at 673.*

62. *Edwards above n 60 citing Généreux above n 42 at 259.*

(81.) In New Zealand, the Court-Martial Act of 2007, particularly Sections 16 and 19, introduced sweeping reforms, abolishing ad hoc courts and creating a permanent court-martial, comprising judges with secure, non-renewable tenure. Judges are now appointed until reaching the age of 70 and may only be removed for cause or by resignation. Renewable terms have been abolished.

(82.) Under the United Kingdom Armed Forces Act, both the Judge Advocate General and judge advocates are appointed on non-renewable terms, until retirement. That Act provides that judge advocates (the equivalent of military judges) including the Judge Advocate General, temporary assistants to the Judge Advocate General, and puisne judges (ordinary or lower ranking judges) of the High Court in England and Wales, following a request by the Judge Advocate General, are nominated by or on behalf of the Lord Chief Justice of England and Wales to sit as judge advocates.[63] Both the Judge Advocate General and judge advocates are drawn from the general Judiciary. They have security of tenure and are appointed on non-renewable terms, until retirement.

(83.) The Respondents' reliance on the renewability of terms of military Judges in Australia and the United States of America is misplaced. In Australia, courts-martial are not considered to be "'courts' and are excluded from constitutional guarantees of judicial independence.[64] This peculiarity of Australian constitutional law led to legislative reforms to the Australian military justice system, introduced in 2006,[65] being struck down by the High Court of Australia on the grounds that military courts could not be given 'judicial powers of the Commonwealth.'[66]

(84.) In the United States, the Supreme Court in Weiss[67] upheld the renewable appointment of military judges due to historical peculiarities of the constitutional text and context. Article 1, Section 8, Clause 14 of the US Constitution grants

63. Section 362 of the United Kingdom's Armed Forces Act of 2006.

64. *Re Tracey; Ex parte Ryan [1989] HCA 12; (1989) 166 CLR 518.*

65. Defence Legislation Amendment Act 2006 (Cth).

66. *Lane vs Morrison [2009] HCA 29; (2009) 239 CLR 230.*

67. *Weiss vs United States 510 US 163 (1994).*

to Congress the power to '*make rules for the Government and Regulation of the land and naval Forces*'. Exercising this authority, Congress enacted the Uniform Code of Military Justice (Uniform Code). In Weiss, the US Supreme Court reasoned that because of these wide constitutional powers, judicial deference is 'at its apogee when reviewing congressional decision making in this area'[68] and that only 'extraordinarily weighty'[69] considerations would overcome the balance struck by Congress, which, in enacting the Uniform Code, had not specified fixed terms. It would be fallacious to apply this sort of reasoning to the South African context. Here, we have strong constitutionally entrenched guarantees of judicial independence for all courts, without exception. The United States is therefore an improper comparator.

International Obligations

(85.) International law imposes obligations on South Africa in the international sphere.[70] This Court stated in Law Society that international law 'enjoy[s] well-deserved prominence in the architecture of [South Africa's] constitutional order'.[71] Our Constitution requires that we must have regard to international law. Section 39(1)(b) enjoins a Court when interpreting the Bill of Rights to consider international law.[72] Section 231 sets out the status of international agreements.[73] And Section 233 states that, when interpreting

---

68. Id at 177 citing *Rostker vs Goldberg 453 US 57, 67 (1981) at 70.*

69. Id at 179.

70. *Glenister II above n 16 paras 90-1.*

71. *Law Society of South Africa vs President of the Republic of South Africa [2018] ZACC 51; 2019 (3) SA 30 (CC); 2019 (3) BCLR 329 (CC)* at *para 4.*

72. Section 39(1)(b) provides:

> '(1) When interpreting the Bill of Rights, a Court, tribunal or forum—
>
> ...
>
> (b) must consider international law.'

73. Section 231 headed 'International agreements' reads:

> '(1) The negotiating and signing of all international agreements is the responsibility of the national executive.
>
> (2) An international agreement binds the Republic only after it has been approved

legislation, a Court must prefer any reasonable interpretation of legislation that is consistent with international law over an alternative, inconsistent, interpretation.[74]

(86.) The interpretation of the constitutional guarantee of independence and the impugned provisions in this matter must be considered within the context of the Constitution and its values as a whole, to which 'international law is relevant'.[75] In *Justice Alliance*, this Court recognised the importance of international law in relation to judicial independence, noting that judicial independence in democracies is recognised internationally and that 'the international community [including South Africa] has subscribed to basic principles of judicial independence through a number of international legal instruments'.[76]

(87.) Our international law obligations inform the internationally accepted standard of judicial independence. That is the standard by which we ought to assess the guarantee of judicial independence provided for in the Constitution, which includes that such a guarantee must be afforded to military courts. Judicial independence in Section 165 of the Constitution must be contextually interpreted in light of the rights in the Bill of Rights, including

---

by resolution in both the National Assembly and the National Council of Provinces, unless it is an agreement referred to in subsection (3).

(3) An international agreement of a technical, administrative or Executive nature, or an agreement which does not require either ratification or accession, entered into by the national executive, binds the Republic without approval by the National Assembly and the National Council of Provinces, but must be tabled in the Assembly and the Council within a reasonable time.

(4) Any international agreement becomes law in the Republic when it is enacted into law by national legislation; but a self-executing provision of an agreement that has been approved by Parliament is law in the Republic unless it is inconsistent with the Constitution or an Act of Parliament.

(5) The Republic is bound by international agreements which were binding on the Republic when this Constitution took effect.'

74. *Glenister II above n 16 at para 179.*

75. *Justice Alliance above n 17 at para 37.*

76. Id at para 38.

the fair trial rights under Section 35(3), of which judicial independence is an essential component; the rule of law in Section 1(c) of the Constitution; and the obligation on the State in Section 7(2) to promote, protect, fulfil and respect the rights in the Bill of Rights, which obliges the State to ensure that the military courts which hear, amongst others, cases of sexual violence, including assault and rape, are adequately independent.[77] Furthermore, our international law obligations must inform this Court's interpretation of the impugned provisions.[78]

(88.) International and regional instruments recognise that these core protections for independence must extend to all courts, including military courts.[79] According to the African Commission on Human and People's Rights (African Commission), 'military tribunals must be subject to the same requirements of fairness, openness, and justice, independence, and due process as any other process.'[80] This is echoed in the 'Decaux Principles'[81] on the administration of justice in military courts, which have been cited with approval by the European Court of Human Rights. Principle 13, headed 'Right to a competent, independent and impartial tribunal', specifically emphasises that the 'independence of judges vis-à-vis the military hierarchy must be strictly protected, avoiding any direct or indirect subordination, whether in the organisation and operation of the system of justice itself or in terms of career development for military judges'.

(88.) South Africa's binding primary international treaty obligations pertaining to judicial independence are set out in the International Covenant

---

77. In this regard, the Ministerial Task Team Report provides useful insight. See [50] above.

78. Section 233 of the Constitution requires a Court to prefer an interpretation that aligns with international law standards, rather than that which is inconsistent with such standards. See also *Glenister II above n 16 at para 179.*

79. See, among others, Tshivhase 'Military Courts in a Democratic South Africa: In Search of their Judicial Independence' (PhD Thesis, UCT 2012) chapter 5.

80. *Civil Liberties Organisation vs Nigeria (Communication 218/98) [2001] ACHPR 30; (2001) AHRLR 75 (ACHPR 2001) at para 44.*

81. Draft Principles Governing the Administration of Justice Through Military Tribunals (2006) (Decaux Principles), UN Doc. E/CN.4/2006/58 at 4.

on Civil and Political Rights[82] (ICCPR) and the African Charter on Human and People's Rights[83] (African Charter), both of which contain guarantees of judicial independence and impartiality. Furthermore, there are the UN Basic Principles[84] and the Bangalore Principles of Judicial Conduct (Bangalore Principles) that bear consideration.[85]

The ICCPR

(90.) Article 26 of the ICCPR guarantees equality before the law and equal protection of the law. Article 14(1) requires that, in the determination of any criminal charge or of rights and obligations in a suit of law, every person shall 'be entitled to a fair and public hearing by a competent, independent and impartial tribunal established by law'. That Article has been interpreted by the UN Human Rights Committee in General Comment No.32.[86] The

---

82. International Covenant on Civil and Political Rights, 16 December 1966. South Africa signed the ICCPR on 3 October 1994 and ratified it on 10 December 1998.

83. African Charter on Human and Peoples' Rights, 27 June 1981. South Africa acceded to the African Charter on 9 July 1996.

84. Basic Principles on the Independence of the Judiciary (1985) (UN Basic Principles), endorsed by United Nations General Assembly resolutions 40/32 of 29 November 1985 and 40/146 of 13 December 1985.

85. Bangalore Principles of Judicial Conduct (2002) (Bangalore Principles), endorsed by the Economic and Social Council in resolution ECOSOC 2006/23. Although non-binding, it bears reference that the Commonwealth Military Justice Principles (see above n 23) in Article 2 seek to—

> '[e]nsure that proceedings in military Courts are presided over by independent, impartial and legally qualified Judges who have security of tenure and are free from:
>
> (a) command interference;
>
> (b) executive or political influence or interference;
>
> (c) improper career consequences;
>
> (d) perceived or actual bias; and
>
> (e) personal interest in the proceeding.'

86. United Nations Human Rights Committee, General Comment No.32 on Article 14: Right to equality before Courts and tribunals and to fair trial, UN Doc CCPR/C/GC/32, 23 August 2007 (General Comment No.32).

Committee's conclusions were: first, the provisions of Article 14 apply to all courts and tribunals within the scope of the Article, whether ordinary or specialised, civilian or military. Trials conducted in military courts must be 'in full conformity with the requirements of Article 14 and its guarantees cannot be limited or modified because of the military or special character of the court concerned.'[87]

(91.) Second, the requirement of competence, independence and impartiality of a tribunal is absolute and not subject to any exception.[88] Independence refers, amongst others, to 'guarantees relating to security of tenure' and 'the actual independence of the judiciary from political interference by the Executive branch and Legislature.'[89] States should take specific measures to guarantee independence, including the adoption of laws establishing clear and objective criteria for the 'appointment, remuneration, tenure, promotion, suspension and dismissal of the members of the judiciary and disciplinary sanctions taken against them.'[90] A situation where the Executive is able to control or direct judicial functions is not compatible with the notion of an independent tribunal.[91]

(92.) Third, Article 14(1) in relation to a fair hearing by a tribunal refers to a hearing by a 'body, regardless of its denomination, that is established by law, is independent of the Executive and Legislative branches of Government or enjoys in specific cases judicial independence in deciding legal matters in proceedings that are judicial in nature.'[92]

(93.) Fourth, to ensure independence, judges may only be dismissed on serious grounds of misconduct or incompetence. The 'dismissal of judges by the Executive, without any specific reasons given to them and without effective judicial protection being available to contest the dismissal, is incompatible with

87. Id at para 22.

88. Id at para 19.

89. Id.

90. Id.

91. Id.

92. Id at para 18.

the independence of the judiciary'.[93] Finally, the requirement of impartiality is twofold: the first is subjective – the judges themselves must not allow their judgements to be influenced – and the second is objective – 'the tribunal must appear to a reasonable observer to be impartial'.[94] This requirement is the individual (subjective) and institutional (or structural) independence alluded to earlier.

The African Charter

(94.) Article 7 of the African Charter provides that every person shall have the right to have his cause heard. This consists, amongst others, of the right to be tried 'by an impartial court or tribunal',[95] which encompasses the principle of independence. The requirement of an independent and impartial tribunal in Article 7 extends to military tribunals.[96]

(95.) Article 26 of the African Charter provides that State parties shall have the duty to guarantee the independence of the courts. This requires states to guarantee the independence of the courts and national institutions established for the promotion of African Charter rights.[97]

---

93. Id at para 20. See Pastukhov v Belarus (Communication 814/1998) UN Doc CCPR/C/78/D/814/1998 (UN Human Rights Committee 2003) at para 7.3, where the dismissal of a Judge prior to the expiry of the term for which he had been appointed, and in circumstances where no effective judicial protections were available to him to contest his dismissal by the Executive, was said to constitute 'an attack on the independence of the Judiciary'.

94. General Comment No.32 above n 86 at para 21.

95. Article 7(1)(d) of the African Charter above n 83.

96. See *Civil Liberties Organisation vs Nigeria above n 80 at para 44 where the African Commission emphasised that 'a military tribunal per se is not offensive to the rights in the Charter. We make the point that military tribunals must be subject to the same requirements of fairness, openness, justice, independence, and due process as any other process'. See also: Wetsh'Okonda Koso vs Democratic Republic of the Congo [2008] ACHPR 94; (2008) AHRLR 93 (ACHPR 2008) (Koso) at para 77.*

97. *Civil Liberties Organisation vs Nigeria* (Communication 129/94) *(2000) AHRLR 188 (ACHPR 1995) where the Commission held that this provision 'speaks of the institutions which are essential to give meaning and content to the right'. It held further that this 'clearly envisions the protection of the Courts'.*

(96.) In *Constitutional Rights Project vs Nigeria,*[98] the African Commission held that where a military tribunal is composed of persons belonging largely to the Executive branch of government, it cannot be said to be impartial. Regardless of the character of the individual members, 'its composition alone creates the appearance, if not actual, of lack of impartiality. It thus violates Article 7(1)(d).'[99] The right to an impartial tribunal, therefore, requires the absence of bias, actual or perceived.[100]

(97.) The African Commission has, in the Principles and Guidelines on the Right to a Fair Trial and Legal Assistance in Africa[101] (African Principles), set out relevant principles to give content to Articles 7 and 26 of the African Charter. Principle 1 of the African Principles reiterates that '[i]n the determination of any criminal charge against a person, or of a person's rights and obligations, everyone shall be entitled to a fair and public hearing by a legally constituted competent, independent and impartial judicial body'. Principle 4 gives content to the concept of an independent tribunal.[102]

---

98. *Constitutional Rights Project in re: Lekwot and Others vs Nigeria (Communication 87/93) [1995] ACHPR 6 (22 March 1995); (2000) AHRLR 183 (ACHPR 1995) (Lekwot).*

99. Id at para 14.

100. Naluwairo 'Improving the administration of justice by military Courts in Africa: An appraisal of the jurisprudence of the African Commission on Human and Peoples' Rights' (2019) 19 *African Human Rights Law Journal 43-61.*

101. African Commission on Human and People's Rights, Principles and Guidelines on the Right to a Fair Trial and Legal Assistance in Africa (2003) (African Principles).

102. In this regard the African Principles above n 101 recommends:

> '(a) The independence of judicial bodies and judicial officers must be guaranteed in a country's constitution and laws.
>
> (b) A military tribunal that does not use the duly established procedure of the legal process may not displace the jurisdiction of ordinary judicial bodies.
>
> (c) Decisions by judicial bodies should not be subject to revision except through judicial review.
>
> (d) All judicial bodies shall be independent from the Executive branch and any method of judicial selection shall safeguard the independence and impartiality of the Judiciary. The establishment of an independent body for the process of judicial appointments is encouraged.

(98.) Principle 5 addresses the concept of an impartial tribunal and emphasises that judicial officers 'shall decide matters before them without any restrictions, improper influence, inducements, pressure, threats or interference, direct or indirect, from any quarter or for any reason'.

The United Nations' Basic Principles on the Independence of the Judiciary

(99.) The UN Basic Principles, which were endorsed by consensus by the UN General Assembly, reiterate the established guarantees of judicial independence, including security of tenure; appropriate safeguards for the appointment and removal of judicial officers; dismissal only on just cause; the finality of judicial decisions (save for further judicial review); and the ability of judicial officers to make decisions without improper influence from any quarter.[103]

> (e) Judicial independence includes security of tenure for Judges or members of judicial bodies and Judges should not be appointed under fixed-term contracts.
>
> (f) The removal or suspension of Judges should only be on account of gross misconduct incompatible with judicial office, or for mental incapacity.
>
> (g) Judicial officers facing disciplinary, suspension or removal proceedings shall be entitled to guarantees of a fair hearing, including legal representation, and to an independent review of decisions of disciplinary, suspension or removal hearings. The procedures for the discipline of judicial officers shall be prescribed by law.'

103. Of relevance for present purposes are these principles from the UN Basic Principles above n 84:

> '(a) Judicial independence shall be guaranteed by the state and enshrined in the country's Constitution or laws.
>
> (b) All governmental and other institutions have the obligation to respect the independence of the Judiciary.
>
> (c) Judicial decisions should be made without improper influences, pressures, threats or interference and they shall not be subject to revision, save through judicial review.
>
> (d) Everyone has the right to be tried by Courts or tribunals using established procedures.
>
> (e) Ordinary Courts or judicial tribunals shall therefore not be displaced by bodies which do not use duly established legal procedures.

Bangalore Principles of Judicial Conduct

(100.) The Bangalore Principles were adopted at the Round Table Meeting of Chief Justices held in The Hague on 25 and 26 November 2002.[104] Our courts have cited these Principles and they are seen as a benchmark for judicial independence in our law.[105] The Bangalore Principles lay particular emphasis on judicial independence and require that the exercise of the judicial function is free of any extraneous influences, inducements, pressures, threats or interference, direct or indirect, from any quarter or for any reason. It also requires that judges are free from influence by the Executive and Legislative branches of government and 'must also appear to a reasonable observer to be free therefrom.'[106]

(101.) The Commentary on the Bangalore Principles notes the following in respect of judicial independence. Judicial independence refers to both the individual and the institutional independence required for decision-making. To establish whether the Judiciary can be considered independent of the other branches of government, regard is usually had to, among others: the manner of appointment of members, their term of office, their conditions

---

> (f) Any method of judicial selection shall safeguard against judicial appointments for improper motives.
>
> (g) The term of Judges, their independence, security and conditions of service shall be adequately secured by law.
>
> (h) Judges shall have guaranteed tenure and they shall be subject to suspension or removal only for reasons of incapacity or behaviour that renders them unfit to discharge their duties.
>
> (i) A charge or complaint made against a Judge in their judicial and professional capacity shall be processed expeditiously and fairly under an appropriate procedure.
>
> (j) The Judge shall have the right to a fair hearing.
>
> (k) All disciplinary, suspension or removal proceedings shall be determined in accordance with established standards of judicial conduct.'

104. Section 1.1 of Bangalore Principles above n 85.

105. See, among others, *Hlophe vs Judicial Service Commission [2022] ZAGPJHC 276; [2022] 3 All SA 87 (GJ) at paras 125-6.*

106. Bangalore Principles above n 85 at Value 1 para 1.3.

of service, the existence of guarantees against outside pressures, and the question whether the court presents an appearance of independence. Judges must not be perceived to be subject to improper external influence. Lastly, judges should be answerable for their decisions regarding the merits of a case solely by way of judicial review or appeal.[107]

(102.) For present purposes, the second important principle under the Bangalore Principles is that of impartiality. Judges must perform their judicial duties without favour, bias or prejudice. A judge who is not independent (on an institutional basis) cannot be impartial, and impartiality must exist both in fact and perception. The latter is measured by the standard of a reasonable observer.

Summary and Conclusions on International Obligations

(103.) To sum up:

(a.) South Africa has binding international obligations to ensure that legal proceedings are conducted before a competent, independent and impartial judicial body, and—

(i.) where such body is a military Court, the same principles of competence, independence, and impartiality ought to apply; and

(ii.) independent and impartial tribunals require, among others:

(aa.) security of tenure for judicial officers;

(ab.) procedures for the appointment and removal of Judges that safeguard independence;

(ac.) removal of Judges only on just cause;

107. Commentary on the Bangalore Principles of Judicial Conduct (Bangalore Commentary) (2007).

(ad.) fair trial rights afforded to Judges being disciplined or removed;

(ae.) actual independence from the Executive;

(af.) the ability of the judicial officer to make decisions without improper influence, inducements, pressure, threats or interference; and

(ag.) objective impartiality.

(b.) South Africa has further committed to the principle of judicial independence by agreeing to adhere to principles set out by international bodies. These include the principles set out by the Africa Commission in the African Principles and by the Human Rights Committee in General Comment No.32, set out earlier.

(104.) The inescapable conclusions to be drawn from international law and jurisprudence are these: the guarantee of judicial independence ought also to be afforded to military courts. This is particularly so where the military courts have jurisdiction over criminal cases, including cases such as rape and sexual assault. These courts must be given the same independence guarantees as ordinary courts determining such matters.[108] The internationally accepted standard of independence that must be afforded to these courts requires independence in relation to the Executive,[109] and in relation to the military hierarchy.[110] There must be safeguards against actual and perceived

108. Article 7(d) read with Article 26 of the African Charter above n 83.

109. Article 7(d) of the African Charter above n 83, as interpreted by Principle 4(g) of the African Principles above n 101.

110. Principle 13 of the Decaux Principles above n 81 and Bangalore Commentary above n 107 at para 38.

partiality,[111] and in the appointment of military judges.[112] Security of tenure is key, and this excludes fixed-term contracts.[113]

(105.) There must be clear protection against external pressures and an ability to decide matters without any restrictions, improper influence, inducements, pressure, threats or interference, direct or indirect, from any quarter or for any reason.[114] A further key requirement is actual and perceived independence.[115] Judicial decisions must not be subject to revision other than by a superior court.[116] Removal or suspension of judges may only be on account of gross misconduct incompatible with judicial office, or for mental incapacity.[117] Lastly, there must be appropriate suspension and disciplinary procedures for judges, prescribed by law, which includes judicial officers being entitled to guarantees of a fair hearing and provisions for an independent review of decisions of disciplinary or removal hearings.

(106.) Against the backdrop then of our jurisprudence and the requirement imposed on our country to take steps to secure the independence of the

---

111. Article 7(d) of the African Charter above n 83, as applied in *Lekwot above n 98 and Koso above n 96; Article 14 of the ICCPR above n 82, as interpreted in General Comment No.32 above n 86 at para 21; Bangalore Principles above n 85 Value 1 at para 1.3; Bangalore Principles above n 85 Value 2 at para 2.1; and Bangalore Commentary above n 107 at paras 51-2.*

112. Article 7(d) of the African Charter above n 83, as interpreted by Principle 4(h) of the African Principles above n 101; Article 10 of the UN Basic Principles above n 84; and Bangalore Commentary above n 107 at para 26.

113. Article 7(d) of the African Charter above n 83; Article 14 of the ICCPR above n 82, as interpreted in General Comment No.32 above n 86 at para 19; Article 11 and 12 of the UN Basic Principles above n 84; and Bangalore Commentary above n 107 at para 26(a).

114. Article 7(d) of the African Charter above n 83, as interpreted by Principle 5 of the African Principles above n 101; *Koso above n 96; Article 2 of the UN Basic Principles above n 84; and Bangalore Principles above n 85 Value 1 at para 1.1.*

115. Bangalore Commentary above n 107 at 42 paras 37-8.

116. Article 7(d) of the African Charter above n 83, as interpreted by Principle 4(f) of the African Principles above n 101; and Article 4 of the UN Basic Principles above n 84.

117. Article 7(d) of the African Charter above n 83, as interpreted by Principle 4(p) of the African Principles above n 101; Article 14 of ICCPR above n 82, as interpreted in General Comment No.32 above n 86 at para 20; and Article 17 of the UN Basic Principles above n 84.

Judiciary in its constitution or laws, in fulfilment of its international legal obligations, the question is whether the relevant provisions of the MDSMA and Defence Act have succeeded in doing so.

First Challenge: Sections 101 and 102 of the Defence Act

(107.) This challenge relates to Executive-initiated and Executive-driven boards of inquiry. These Sections, as formulated, are not specifically targeted at military courts and military judges, but their wide language on its face could be applied to them. To that extent, the challenge must be upheld. It is not permissible under our Constitution for the Executive to have the power to initiate and control boards of inquiry to investigate judicial officers' fitness and the conduct of their cases, as occurred in this case. The involvement of officials of the SANDF in making decisions relating to boards of inquiry, insofar as they pertain to military courts and military judges, plainly offends the principle of separation of powers and subverts the independence of military courts. Boards of inquiry are unquestionably Executive-initiated right from the outset and they are Executive-driven. The boards are convened by the Minister or the Secretary of Defence or the Chief of the Defence Force under Section 101 of the Defence Act. Section 101(2) affords the same power to the Chief of a Service or Division. The Executive has wide-ranging powers in convening a board of inquiry under a convening order which will designate the board's members and their orders.[118]

(108.) This Executive control over the convening and conduct of military courts is constitutionally offensive:

(a.) It is contrary to the central plank of judicial independence, that no external influence to sway a military judge to decide a case fairly, impartially and without fear or favour is permitted.

---

118. Section 101(4) of the Defence Act provides:

> 'A board of inquiry must be convened by means of a written Convening Order and must consist of so many persons who are in the employ of the Department of Defence as the person convening the Board may determine, but where a Board is convened by a military officer it must consist of at least one officer and as many warrant officers, non-commissioned officers or civilians who are in the employ of the Department of Defence as the officer convening the Board may determine.'

(b.) Exclusive Executive control over the investigating of judicial officers is inherently unconstitutional. The position here is similar to that of Magistrates, in regard to which this Court in *Van Rooyen* ruled that the initiation of an investigation into their conduct should be held under the auspices of an independent body, not the Executive.[119]

(c.) There is clear potential for abuse where, as here, officials who fall under the Executive have full control over the composition of a board of inquiry, its terms of reference and the manner in which it conducts its business.

(d.) Sections 101 and 102 enable boards of inquiry to be composed in their entirety of members who are not judicial officers – *Van Rooyen* held that this is inconsistent with judicial independence.[120]

(109.) To cure this constitutional defect, reading down is preferable. This can be done by, as the Applicant suggests, reading the phrases 'any matter', 'any member or employee' and the 'affairs of any institution' as excluding military judges, and the same should be done in respect of Section 137 of the Code,[121] read with Rule 79 of the MDSMA Rules.[122]

---

119. *Van Rooyen above n 14 at para 206.*

120. Id at para 195.

121. Section 137 of the Code, being First Schedule to the Defence Act 44 of 1957, headed 'Attendance of witnesses at and composition of boards of inquiry', reads:

> '(1) The president of any board of inquiry convened under Section 134 or 135 may, in the prescribed manner, subpoena any person in Namibia, whether or not otherwise subject to this Code, to attend such board of inquiry and, subject to subsection (2), to give evidence or to produce any document or thing in such person's possession or under such person's control.
>
> (2) No witness is required to answer any question or to produce any document or thing at any board of inquiry which such witness could not be compelled to answer or produce in proceedings before a civil Court.
>
> (3) The composition of boards of inquiry, the method of convening such Boards and the procedure to be followed by such Boards are as prescribed.'

122. Rule 79 of the MDSMA Rules, headed 'Collation of evidence during pre-trial

Second Challenge: Section 15 of the MDSMA

(110.) This challenge concerns the brief, renewable terms of military judges. On their own version, the Respondents have acknowledged that military judges are appointed, at the Minister's prerogative, for brief, renewable terms. This is a complete answer to the High Court's and Supreme Court of appeal's quibbling about whether the 'reassignment' of military judges in fact amounts to renewable terms – the SANDF

---

investigation phase', reads:

> '(1) The prosecution counsel, disciplinary adjutant or military police investigating official must obtain any required statement or evidence, including visiting any person for such purpose, from any person whether subject to this Act or not.
>
> (2) A disciplinary adjutant or prosecution counsel conducting a pre-trial investigation may—
>
> (a) procure the attendance of witnesses;
>
> (b) have witnesses summoned to give evidence or to produce a document or item thereat;
>
> (c) administer oaths or affirmations;
>
> (d) admit sworn and unsworn statements into evidence; and
>
> (e) collate evidence into the pre-trial investigation in accordance with subsection (3).
>
> (3) A pre-trial investigation must comprise of, if applicable—
>
> (a) a cover sheet reflecting the reference of the pre-trial investigation;
>
> (b) an index with page numbering;
>
> (c) a certified copy of the account of warning or account of arrest;
>
> (d) a certified copy of the certificate of surrender or arrest, in the prescribed form, if applicable;
>
> (e) original statements or certified copies of original statements; and
>
> (f) documentary evidence.
>
> (4) Where an incident leads to a report of misconduct and an account of warning or account of arrest, such incident must be investigated under this Part.'

itself calls it renewable terms and, on the objective facts, that is exactly what it is.

(111.) In *Justice Alliance*, this Court emphasised that non-renewable terms for judges is an essential prerequisite of structural independence.123 Absent non-renewability, there is the risk that public confidence in military judges is undermined. The Court observed:

> '[N]on-renewability is the bedrock of security of tenure and a dyke against judicial favour in passing judgment. Section 176(1) gives strong warrant to this principle in providing that a Constitutional Court judge holds office for a non-renewable term. Non-renewability fosters public confidence in the institution of the judiciary as a whole, since its members function with neither threat that their terms will not be renewed nor any inducement to seek to secure renewal.'[124]

(112.) The assignment of renewable terms is furthermore opaque, without clearly cognisable objective criteria; instead it is premised on the unconstrained discretion and carte blanche of the Minister and Adjutant General, glibly referred to by the Respondents as their 'prerogative'. This unconstrained discretion, coupled with opaque requirements, has been held by this Court to be inconsistent with the central guarantee of independence.[125]

(113.) The Supreme Court of Appeal erred in requiring evidence substantiating the averment by the Applicant that 'military judges may be inclined to temper their reviews or adjust their judgments to secure further assignments'.[126] The

---

123. *Justice Alliance above n 17 at para 73 and fn 72, citing the Canadian case of Leblanc above n 57 at paras 38-9, 43-4 and 59.*

124. Id.

125. *AmaBhungane Centre for Investigative Journalism NPC vs Minister of Justice and Correctional Services [2021] ZACC 3; 2021 (3) SA 246 (CC); 2021 (4) BCLR 349 (CC) at para 92 citing Justice Alliance above n 17 at para 65 where this Court stated: 'The designation by a member of the Executive in ill-defined circumstances or circumstances that completely lack description does not conduce to a reasonable perception of independence'.*

126. Supreme Court of Appeal judgment above n 6 at para 57. In this passage the judgment uses the word 'reviews' (as I have quoted it), though perhaps it is a typographical error and 'views' was intended.

Applicant merely had to show that a reasonable, well-informed person would not have confidence that military judges are protected from these threats due to their short, renewable assignments.[127] Here, the undisputed (or, at best for the SANDF, the indisputable) facts demonstrate that the Applicant was in fact subjected to a variety of threats and pressure. He was the only military judge not to be reassigned in 2017, implementing the threats to do so that started in 2014.

(114.) Military judges are the only full-time judicial officers who are appointed for short, renewable terms, notwithstanding their significant geographical and penal jurisdiction. This is constitutionally unpalatable. Lastly, renewable terms for military judges are out of step with recent developments in comparable constitutional democracies, including Canada, New Zealand and the United Kingdom.

(115.) In this instance, reading down Section 15 by precluding renewable judicial terms is not a satisfactory solution to this constitutionally impermissible arrangement. This is because the difficulty may be that reading down will only preclude 'renewable' terms and not 'short' terms as well. Conceivably, with a reading-down, a military judge could, for example, be appointed for a non-renewable one-year period. It might be said that, as long as the period is not renewable, it does not matter how short it is, since the prospect of renewal is removed as a perverse incentive. The question is what exactly the term 'non-renewable' means. Conceivably, an officer may be appointed as a military judge for a one-year term in year one, and then again reappointed in year three after a lapse of one year from the expiry of their first term. Conversely, 'non-renewable' could mean that the officer can never be reappointed as a military judge.

(116.) A further question is whether adequate security of tenure might not also be achieved by relatively long terms, like renewable five-, eight-, or ten-year terms. A reading-down is not permanent, in the sense that Parliament can enact a different regime as long as it is consistent with this judgment, but the problem relates to appointments made during the period of the reading-down.

---

127. *Sonke above n 35 at paras 78-80.*

The SANDF might be unwilling to appoint military judges until a specified retirement age, but likewise might be unwilling to have short-term appointees removed permanently from the pool of future appointments, possibly depending on how big the pool is. An interim, temporary solution might be longer renewable appointments; or the right to reappoint after a lapse of a certain period. Those possible solutions cannot be achieved by a reading-down.

(117.) Another issue is that in terms of Section 15 an assignment is for a fixed period 'or coupled to a specific deployment, operation or exercise'. If, for example, SANDF members are deployed in a peace-keeping operation in Angola, can the authorities appoint a military judge to preside over a military court in Angola, during the period of that operation, whose assignment as a military judge will terminate when that operation ends? If a military judge is so appointed, may they then not be reappointed when that operation terminates, even if it terminates after only six months? It is conceivable that potential candidates for military judgeships may be reluctant to accept deployment in those circumstances.

(118.) A further potential difficulty with a reading-down is that Section 15 does not apply only to military judges: it applies also to directors and prosecution, defence and review counsel. Short renewable terms may be acceptable in respect of them and there has been no argument to the contrary at the hearing in this Court. In light of all these difficulties, the only viable solution is a reading-in, not a reading-down. It is not enough, as would be the case with Sections 101 and 102 of the Defence Act, to say that the assignments contemplated in Section 15 do not include assignments of military judges. Plainly there is a need for a statutory provision that provides for the term of appointment of military judges, and Section 15 is that provision. It is not objectionable that military judges are appointed 'for a fixed term' – the problem is renewability. It is consequently necessary to declare Section 15 constitutionally invalid to the extent that it does not provide adequate security of tenure for military judges, to suspend the declaration for two years, and to have a temporary reading-in.

(119.) The most appropriate way of addressing all these concerns is to allow for a person to be assigned as a military judge for a period not exceeding one year on a non-renewable basis. Further assignment of that person as a military judge may occur only after the lapse of a period of not less than two years since their last assignment. The rationale behind these time-related provisions is to avoid short, renewable terms of appointment. The objection to those type of appointments bears repetition – first, it undermines public confidence inasmuch as non-renewability is an essential component of structural independence; and second, absent cognisable objective criteria it affords the Executive (the Minister and the Adjutant-General) unconstrained discretion in assigning military judges.

Third Challenge: Section 17 of the MDSMA

(120.) The Applicant challenges the power of the Executive to remove military judges. As stated, the Minister may remove a military judge for cause on the recommendation of the Adjutant General. The latter is, like the Minister, a member of the Executive. It is unconstitutional for the Executive to have the power to remove military judges without independent oversight or control. Our courts have repeatedly set their face against removal for cause where such cause is not subject to 'independent review and determination by a process at which the judge affected is afforded a full opportunity to be heard.'[128]

(121.) At present, military judges are the only judicial officers that may be removed in this fashion. This is in stark contrast to the procedure for the removal of judges of the superior courts and Magistrates. The position here also stands in contrast to that in the United Kingdom, New Zealand, and Canada. It is no answer to say, as the High Court did, that boards of inquiry provide the required independent oversight mechanism in cases of removal. For the reasons enunciated, boards of inquiry lack independence.

(122.) It is not possible to cure the constitutional invalidity through a reading down of the provision. The Section must therefore be declared unconstitutional and the declaration ought to be suspended for 24 months for Parliament to attend to the constitutional deficiency. In the interim, there

---

128. See generally, among others, *De Lange above n 31 and Van Rooyen above n 14 which both cite Valente above n 38 at 698.*

must be a reading down of the Section until Parliament cures the invalidity through remedial legislation.

(123.) It is in my view unobjectionable, as an interim arrangement during the period of suspension, to have the Minister devise their own processes for an inquiry into the fitness of a military judge, on the condition that it is an independent inquiry. There is no harm in leaving the composition of the inquiry body to the Minister, but its independence is crucial. A further important caveat is that a military judge may not be removed except on the recommendation of the independent inquiry.

Conclusion and Costs

(124.) Leave to appeal must be granted and the appeal against the order of the Supreme Court of Appeal must be upheld. An important consideration regarding costs is that the Applicant has only attained partial success. The Applicant was unsuccessful in his opposition to the state parties' review application, and he does not appeal that order in this Court. In respect of his counter-application, the Applicant has not persisted with some of the relief which was dismissed in the courts below. Those are his prayers declaring that the Board of Enquiry established in respect of him is unlawful, and declaring the proceedings instituted by the state parties in the High Court to be unlawful and unconstitutional. In the premises, a 50/50 allocation is a fair allocation of costs in respect of the matters where the Applicant had won and lost respectively. Thus, the Applicant should be awarded 50% of his costs in the High Court and the Supreme Court of Appeal. Based on the trite Biowatch[129] principle, in respect of the other 50% of the costs he should bear no liability. The Applicant is entitled to all his costs in this Court.

Order

(125.) I make the following order:

---

129. *Biowatch Trust vs Registrar Genetic Resources [2009] ZACC 14; 2009 (6) SA 232 (CC); 2009 (10) BCLR 1014 (CC) at para 21.*

1. Leave to appeal is granted.

2. The appeal is upheld.

3. The order of the Supreme Court of Appeal is set aside to the extent that the Court dismissed the Applicant's appeal against the High Court's refusal to grant the declarations of statutory invalidity sought by the Applicant in his counter-application in the High Court.

4. The costs orders made in the Supreme Court of Appeal in relation to costs in that Court and in the High Court are set aside.

5. It is declared that:

(a.) Sections 101 and 102 of the Defence Act 42 of 2002 are unconstitutional and invalid to the extent that they permit members of the Executive to convene boards of inquiry to investigate military judges and the content and merits of their judgments and rulings. Pending the coming into operation of remedial legislation, the phrases 'any matter', 'any member or employee' and the 'affairs of any institution' in Section 101 and 102 of the Defence Act and Section 136 of the Military Disciplinary Code, read with Rule 79 of the Military Discipline Supplementary Measures Act's Rules, must be read as excluding military Judges.

(b.) Section 15 of the Military Discipline Supplementary Measures Act 16 of 1999 is unconstitutional and invalid to the extent that it empowers the Minister of Defence and Military Veterans (Minister), acting on the recommendation of the Adjutant General, to assign judges for renewable periods.

(c.) The existing practice of assigning judges for renewable periods of one to two years is unconstitutional and unlawful. Pending the coming into operation of remedial legislation, the assignment of a military judge may not be renewed until the lapse of at least two years since that person's last assignment.

(d.) Section 17 of the Military Discipline Supplementary Measures Act 16 of 1999 is unconstitutional and invalid to the extent that it empowers the Minister, acting on the recommendation of the Adjutant General, to remove a military judge and that the Minister may do so without any independent inquiry into the fitness of the military judge to hold office.

(e.) Pending the coming into operation of remedial legislation, the Minister may devise processes for an inquiry into the fitness of a military judge and the composition of the inquiry body, provided that:

i. it is an independent inquiry; and

ii. a military judge may not be removed except on the recommendation of the independent inquiry.

(f.) The declarations of constitutional invalidity above are suspended for a period of 24 months to allow remedial legislation to be enacted and brought into operation.

6. The first Respondent is ordered to pay half of the costs of the Applicant in the Supreme Court of Appeal and the High Court, including the costs of two counsel where so employed.

7. The first Respondent is ordered to pay the costs of the Applicant in this Court, including the costs of two counsel where so employed.

For the Applicant: G. Marcus SC, C. McConnachie, M. Marongo and M. Kritzinger instructed by Griesel Vanzanten Attorneys

For Respondents: E. Tsatsi SC and C. Kwinda instructed by State Attorney

For the Amicus Curiae: E. Webber and E. Van Heerden instructed by Legal Resources Centre

(2025) I FLR 136 (India)

Supreme Court of India

Criminal Appeals 5267 and 5268 of 2024

Om Prakash Yadav vs Niranjan Kumar Upadhyay & Others

Composition of Court: Justice J.B. Pardiwala and Justice Manoj Misra

Date of Decision: 13 December, 2024

Counsel for the Applicant: Mr. Ravindra Singh
Counsel for the Respondent: No.1: Mr. R. Basant
Counsel for the Respondent No.3,4,5: Ms. Nanita Sharma

Summary

The judgment addressed the applicability of Section 197 of CrPC, which requires prior sanction to prosecute public servants for acts performed in the discharge of their official duties. The case stemmed from the alleged murder of Om Prakash Yadav's brother in 2007, where certain police officers, including Niranjan Kumar Upadhyay, were accused of fabricating evidence and registering a false case to shield the main accused. The Allahabad High Court had quashed the proceedings against the officers, citing the absence of prior sanction under Section 197. However, the Supreme Court ruled that actions such as fabricating evidence and lodging false cases were manifestly illegal and beyond the scope of official duties, thereby not warranting protection under Section 197. The Court emphasized that legal protections for public servants do not extend to unlawful acts performed under the guise of authority. Overturning the High Court's decision, the Supreme Court allowed the criminal proceedings against the officers to continue, underscoring the principle that public officials must remain accountable for actions outside the lawful scope of their duties. This judgment reinforces the boundaries of legal immunity for public servants and upholds accountability for misuse of power.

Headnotes

Facts: On 12 October 2007, Om Prakash Yadav lodged a First Information Report (FIR) with the Dakshin Police Station in Firozabad, Uttar Pradesh, alleging that his brother, Suman Prakash Yadav, was murdered at around 8:30 a.m. near Suhagnagar Crossing. During the incident, Suman's young son, Harsh, was grievously injured. The FIR named several accused, including Ashok Dixit, and charged them under various sections of the Indian Penal Code (IPC), namely murder (Section 302) and conspiracy (Section 120-B). On the same day, at approximately 9:30 a.m., the police in Gwalior, Madhya Pradesh, registered another FIR under the Madhya Pradesh Excise Act, alleging that Ashok Dixit was arrested for possession of illegal liquor. This FIR was allegedly fabricated by police officers, including Niranjan Kumar Upadhyay, to provide Dixit with an alibi for the murder. The fabricated FIR claimed that Dixit was arrested at Thatipur Crossing in Gwalior, approximately 160 km away from Firozabad, at a time that made it impossible for him to commit the murder. Subsequent investigations revealed discrepancies in the Gwalior FIR, leading to allegations that the officers involved conspired with Dixit to obstruct justice. These events culminated in criminal proceedings against the officers, which the Allahabad High Court later quashed on the grounds of lack of prior sanction under Section 197 Code of Criminal Procedure (CrPC) which provides for seeking sanction of the government for prosecuting government servants for offences committed while acting in official capacity in discharge of duties, prompting Om Prakash Yadav to appeal to the Supreme Court.

Issue(s): Whether the offence or the act alleged to have been committed by the respondent nos. 1, 3, 4 and 5 respectively could be said to have been done "while acting or purporting to act in the discharge of official duty"?

Contentions of the parties: The appellant contended that the police officers, including Niranjan Kumar Upadhyay, had conspired to fabricate evidence and create a false alibi for the main accused, Ashok Dixit, by registering a bogus FIR under the Madhya Pradesh Excise Act. He argued that these acts were not performed in the discharge of official duties, as no public servant's duty includes committing unlawful acts like fabricating evidence or obstructing justice. He emphasized that such manifestly illegal acts fall outside the protective scope of Section 197, which shields public servants from prosecution without prior sanction only for bona fide actions linked to their official roles. It was further highlighted that the fabricated FIR undermined the murder investigation in Firozabad and sought to obstruct justice for the heinous crime committed against his brother. Conversely, the respondents argued that their actions were connected to their official roles and thus required prior sanction under Section 197 CrPC for prosecution. They claimed no direct involvement in registering the false FIR and maintained that their actions, if any, were carried out in their official capacity. They also pointed out procedural deficiencies, including delayed statements of witnesses and insufficient evidence linking them to the alleged conspiracy. The respondents asserted that prosecuting them without prior sanction would be improper, particularly given their retirement and the elapsed time since the incident. They further argued that the High Court was correct in quashing the criminal proceedings due to the absence of required sanction.

Held: The Supreme Court extensively analysed whether the actions of the respondents, alleged to have fabricated evidence and created a false alibi to shield an accused in a murder case, could be considered acts performed in the discharge of their official duties under Section 197. The Court emphasized that Section 197 provides protection to public servants from prosecution for actions reasonably connected with their official duties, ensuring they can act fearlessly without apprehension of false or vexatious litigation. However, it clarified that this protection does not extend to acts that are purely private, malicious, or outside the scope of official functions. The Court assessed the nature and intent of the respondents' actions, highlighting that creating a false alibi and obstructing justice could not be construed as acts done in the legitimate discharge of public duties. While the High Court had quashed the proceedings against the respondents citing the absence of sanction under Section 197, the Supreme Court scrutinized whether the alleged actions were intrinsic to their official roles or were personal acts of misconduct. The judgment reaffirmed that the applicability of Section 197 depends on whether there exists a reasonable connection between the alleged act and the discharge of official duties. Acts aimed at shielding an accused in a criminal case, done under the pretence of official capacity but with ulterior motives, do not attract the protection of this section. The Court's decision delineates the boundaries of legal immunity for public servants, ensuring accountability while preserving their ability to perform genuine official functions. The Court further elaborated on the broader principles of Section 197, cautioning against its misuse as a shield for wrongful acts under the guise of public office and reiterated the importance of balancing the need to protect public servants from frivolous litigation with the imperative to hold them accountable for acts done outside their official capacities. It underscored that immunity under Section 197 is not absolute and should not be construed to include every act committed by a public servant while holding office, especially where the act is wholly unconnected to the legitimate discharge of their duties. The reasoning reinforces the principle of accountability within public service, ensuring that legal immunity is not misappropriated to obstruct justice. Hence, the court allowed the present appeal and set aside the order of the High Court.

Case Laws Cited

Dr. Hori Ram Singh vs The Crown [AIR 1939 FC 43]; Gill and Another vs The King [AIR 1948 PC 128]; Albert West Meads vs The King [AIR 1948 PC 156]; Shreekantiah Ramayya Munipalli vs State of Bombay [(1954) 2 SCC 992]; Amrik Singh vs State of Pepsu [AIR 1955 SC 309]; Matajog Dobey vs H.C. Bhari [AIR 1956 SC 44]; Dhannjay Ram Sharma vs M.S. Uppadaya and Others [AIR 1960 SC 745]; P. Arulswami vs State [(1967) 1 SCR 201], Harihar Prasad vs State of Bihar [(1972) 3 SCC 89]; B. Saha and Others vs M.S. Kochar [(1979) 4 SCC 177]; State of Maharashtra vs Dr. Budhikota Subbarao [(1993) 3 SCC 339]; R. Balakrishna Pillai vs State of Kerala and Another [(1996) 1 SCC 478]; Shambhoo Nath Misra vs State of U.P. and Others [(1997) 5 SCC 326]; State of Orissa through Kumar

Raghvendra Singh and Others vs Ganesh Chandra Jew [(2004) 8 SCC 40]; Devinder Singh and Others vs State of Punjab through CBI [(2016) 12 SCC 87]; Parvat Singh and Others vs State of Madhya Pradesh [(2020) 4 SCC 33]; S.K. Zutshi and Another vs Bimal Debnath and Another [(2004) 8 SCC 31]; K. Kalimuthu vs State [(2005) 4 SCC 512]; Sankaran Moitra vs Sadhna Das and Another [(2006) 4 SCC 584]; Choudhury Parveen Sultana vs State of West Bengal and Another [(2009) 3 SCC 398]; Urmila Devi vs Yudhvir Singh [(2013) 15 SCC 624]; Rajib Ranjan vs R. Vijaykumar [(2015) 1 SCC 513]; Inspector of Police and Another vs Battenapatla Venkata Ratnam and Another [(2015) 13 SCC 87]; Surinderjit Singh Mand and Another vs State of Punjab and Another [(2016) 8 SCC 722]; Pukhraj vs State of Rajasthan and Another [(1973) 2 SCC 701]; State of Bihar vs Kamla Prasad Singh and Others [(1998) 5 SCC 690]; Bakhshish Singh Brar vs Gurmej Kaur and Another [(1987) 4 SCC 663]; P.K. Pradhan vs State of Sikkim [(2001) 6 SCC 704]; Birbal Nath vs State of Rajasthan [2023 SCC OnLine SC 1396]

JUDGMENT

Jb Pardiwala, J

(1.) Leave granted.

(2.) These appeals arise out of the common judgment and order passed by a learned Single Judge of the High Court of Judicature at Allahabad dated 19 April 2018 in Criminal Misc. Writ Application Nos. 4080 of 2009 and 32494 of 2009 respectively filed by the Respondent Nos. 1, 3, 4 and 5 respectively under Section 482 of the Code of Criminal Procedure, 1973 (for short, the CrPC) whereby the High Court allowed the applications and quashed the proceedings of Case No. 67 of 2008 *(State vs Niranjan Kumar Upadhyay) as* well as Case No. 67-A of 2009 *(State vs Ram Prakash Gunkar and Ors.)* pending before the CJM, Firozabad, both arising out of Case Crime No. 617 of 2007 registered for the offence punishable under Sections 147, 148, 149, 307, 302, 201 and 120-B respectively of the Indian Penal Code, 1860 (for short, the IPC) with the Dakshin Police Station, District Firozabad, Uttar Pradesh.

Factual Matrix

(3.) On 12 October 2007, at 09:15 a.m., Om Prakash Yadav (hereinafter, the Appellant) lodged a First Information Report (hereinafter, 'FIR') as Case Crime No. 617 of 2007 for the offence punishable under Sections 147, 148, 149, 302 and 307 of IPC respectively with the Dakshin Police Station, Firozabad, Uttar Pradesh, against Surender Singh Gurjar, Veerbhan Gurjar, Ashok Dixit, Pappu Dixit, Sanjay Dixit and three others. The FIR alleged that the Appellant's brother, Suman Prakash Yadav who was a teacher at the Tilak Inter College, Firozabad, was killed and his brother's son Harsh aged about 4 ½ years was grievously injured by the aforesaid accused persons by indiscriminately firing with their handguns near the Suhagnagar Crossing, at 08:30 a.m., on 12 October 2007. The Appellant claimed that the incident was witnessed by him and several others.

(4.) On the same day, another FIR was registered as Case Crime No. 967 of 2007 at the Murar Police Station, Gwalior, Madhya Pradesh, for the offence punishable under Section 34 of the Madhya Pradesh Excise Act, 1915 (hereinafter, the Excise Act) against Ashok Dixit who is the main accused of Case Crime No. 617 of 2007. The FIR which was lodged by Head Constable Ram Baran Singh Yadav (hereinafter, Respondent No.5) stated that based on the information received from an informant while patrolling the area, the accused Ashok Dixit was arrested for carrying 12 bottles of illegal foreign liquor near the Thatipur Crossing. It was stated therein that the Respondent No. 5 along with ASI Ram Prakash Gunkar (hereinafter, Respondent No. 4) and Head Constable Vijay Bahadur Singh (hereinafter, Respondent No. 3) of the Thatipur Chauki, Murar Police Station, had seized the illegal liquor and arrested the accused at around 09.30 hrs on 12 October 2007. It was further added that the accused, Ashok Dixit, was later released on bail by the Station House Officer (hereinafter, SHO), DS Khushawa of the Murar Police Station, on the same day, upon furnishing the necessary surety since the offence under Section 34 of the Excise Act was a bailable one. On 26 October 2007, the concerned IO is said to have submitted a charge sheet in connection with Case Crime No. 967 of 2007 against Ashok Dixit before the Chief Judicial Magistrate (hereinafter, CJM), Gwalior.

(5.) The investigating officer (hereinafter, IO) at Dakshin, Firozabad undertook further investigation and recorded the statements of several witnesses under Section 161 CrPC in connection with Case Crime No. 617 of 2007. On 5 January 2008, the Charge Sheet No. 3 of 2008 was submitted before the CJM, Firozabad, against 12 persons namely Ashok Dixit, Pappu Dixit, Sanjay Dixit, Surender Singh Gurjar, Veerbhan Gurjar, Sandeep, Swadesh Bhardwaj, Ashu, Suresh, Pancham, Rajesh and Devender. However, the charge sheet stated that the investigation against Niranjan Kumar Upadhyay (hereinafter, Respondent No. 1), Respondent No.3, Respondent No. 4, Respondent No. 5 and two other individuals in regard to the FIR registered for the offence under Section 34 of the Excise Act in Murar, Gwalior allegedly for the purpose of shielding the accused, Ashok Dixit, was still pending.

(6.) Subsequently, on 23 January 2008, the IO at Dakshin, Firozabad recorded the statements of SHO DS Khushawa, Respondent No. 3, Respondent No. 4, and Respondent No. 5 respectively of the Murar Police Station, Gwalior under Section 161 of CrPC.

(7.) Soon thereafter, on 30 January 2008, the IO at Dakshin, Firozabad moved an application before the CJM, Gwalior, Madhya Pradesh, requesting that the proceedings in Case No. 15003 of 2007 relating to the Case Crime No. 967 of 2007 under Section 34 of the Excise Act filed against the accused Ashok Dixit, pending before him, be stayed. The application alleged that the Respondent No. 1 who was posted in Gwalior as town inspector (for short, TI) was a relative of the accused Ashok Dixit. It was further alleged that the Respondent Nos. 1, 3, 4 and 5 respectively had conspired to shield the accused from the offence of murder by creating a bogus case under Section 34 of the Excise Act with the sole object of providing the accused with an alibi for the crime alleged to have been committed in Firozabad. The incident in Firozabad occurred at 08:30 a.m. while the incident in Gwalior occurred at 09:30 a.m. on the same day. The distance between Gwalior and Firozabad being 160 kilometers, the same could not have been covered in a duration of one hour by road. The application stated that, since the accused, Ashok Dixit, might confess his guilt in connection with the offence under Section 34 of the Excise Act with a view to save himself from the offence of murder, the proceedings in Case Crime No. 617 of 2007 pending before the CJM,

Firozabad might get adversely affected if the proceedings in Case No. 15003 of 2007 were allowed to be continued.

(8.) Upon due consideration of the aforesaid application, the CJM, Gwalior vide its order dated 5 February 2008, directed the SHO of the Murar Police Station, Gwalior, to furnish a report before the Court. On 12 February 2008, the statements of Respondent Nos. 3, 4 and 5 respectively, were recorded by the SHO of the Murar Police Station, Gwalior and an enquiry report was furnished on 17 February 2008 before the CJM, Gwalior. Upon perusal of the enquiry report, the CJM, Gwalior vide its order dated 23 February 2008 rejected the application dated 20 January 2008 filed by the IO at Dakshin, Firozabad, as being baseless.

(9.) On 14 April 2008, the IO at Dakshin, Firozabad filed an application before the CJM, Firozabad for the issuance of non-bailable warrant against the Respondent Nos. 1, 3, 4 and 5 respectively along with two other persons. In pursuance of the said application, on 21 April 2008, the CJM, Firozabad issued a non-bailable warrant against the aforesaid six accused which included the Respondent Nos. 1, 3, 4 and 5 respectively, herein. However, it is the case of the IO at Firozabad that the Respondent Nos. 1, 3, 4 and 5 were absconding and therefore, proceedings under Sections 82 and 83 CrPC respectively were also initiated and completed against them.

(10.) On 2 May 2008, the IO at Dakshin, Firozabad filed an application before the DIG, Gwalior, Madhya Pradesh through the DIG, Agra, Uttar Pradesh, requesting sanction for prosecution of the Respondent Nos. 1, 3, 4 and 5 respectively. Further, on 7 May 2008, the superintendent of police, Firozabad, also sent a letter to the DIG, Gwalior, requesting for the sanction for prosecution under Section 197 CrPC so that the Respondents could be charge-sheeted.

(11.) In the meantime, the Respondent No.1 preferred Criminal Misc. Writ Petition No. 10181 of 2008 before the High Court of Allahabad and vide order dated 23 July 2008, the arrest of Respondent No. 1 was stayed.

(12.) On 30 July 2008, the superintendent of police, Firozabad, addressed one another letter to the DIG, Gwalior in the form of a reminder to accord sanction under Section 197 CrPC for prosecuting the Respondents herein. However, on 2 August 2008, the DIG, Gwalior replied to the superintendent of police, Firozabad, informing him that sanction for prosecution cannot be granted till the disposal of the trial in connection with Case Crime No. 967 of 2007 registered at the Murar Police Station, Gwalior for the offence under Section 34 of the Excise Act.

(13.) On 28.08.2008, the Appellant filed a Misc. Criminal Case. No. 5971 of 2008 under Section 482 CrPC before the High Court of Madhya Pradesh at Gwalior for quashing the criminal proceedings concerning Case No. 15003 of 2007 arising out of Case Crime No. 967 of 2007 registered for the offence under Section 34 of the Excise Act pending before the Court of CJM, Gwalior. In the alternative, it was prayed that the proceeding be stayed till a decision is arrived at in the case pending against Ashok Dixit before the CJM, Firozabad, concerning Case Crime No. 617 of 2007. The High Court vide its order dated 25 August 2009 stayed the proceedings in Case No. 15003 of 2007 by observing as follows:

> '12. In the light of the above legal position, the Appellant who is a complainant in the criminal case in connection with Crime No. 617 of 2007 registered against Respondent No.2 at Firozabad has locus standi to file this petition under Section 482 of Cr.P.C. Now legal aspect and circumstances of the case is to be considered. Suppose for the sake of argument, if Respondent No. 2 admits his guilt in the case of Excise Act pending in the Court of CJM Gwalior what will be its effect? He will have a good ground of alibi that at the time of alleged murder of Appellant's brother he was not present at Firozabad but was present at Gwalior which is 160 km away from Firozabad. So it will cause a great prejudice in that case and on the other hand, in the interest of justice, if proceedings pending in the Court of CJM Gwalior are stayed, it will not cause any prejudice to Respondent No. 2. Moreover, it will avoid conflicting judgments of two courts. Therefore, it is good case for invoking inherent powers of the court.
>
> 13. Considering the facts and circumstances of the case, petition is allowed and further proceedings pending in the Court of CJM Gwalior in connection with Excise Act pending in the CJM Gwalior concerning Case

No. 15003 of 2007 are hereby stayed till disposal of the Criminal Case pending at Firozabad concerning Crime No.617 of 2007.'

(Emphasis supplied)

(14.) After a period of almost one year, on 25 October 2008, the IO at Dakshin, Firozabad recorded the statements of two persons i.e., Ramesh Yadav and Barelal under Section 161 CrPC. Both stated that they had witnessed the Respondent No. 1 being directly involved in the creation of a false case under Section 34 of the Excise Act in order to provide the accused Ashok Dixit the benefit of an alibi. Soon thereafter, on 3 November 2008, a supplementary Charge Sheet No. 3A of 2008 in case Crime No. 617 of 2007 was filed against the Respondent no. 1 for the offence punishable under Sections 147, 148, 149, 307, 302, 201 and 120-B IPC respectively for being involved in hatching a conspiracy of murder that occurred in Firozabad. It was the case of the IO at Firozabad that the charge sheet was filed since he had found out that the Respondent No. 1 was not posted at the Murar Police Station, Gwalior at the time of the arrest of Ashok Dixit for the offence under Section 34 of the Excise Act and therefore, the provision of sanction under Section 197 CrPC would not be attracted against the Respondent No. 1. It is pertinent to observe here that it is the case of the Respondent No. 1 herein that the Charge Sheet No. 3A of 2008 was backdated to 3 November 2008 when in fact it was actually filed on 24 November 2008 before the Magistrate.

(15.) The mother of Respondent No.1, while alleging that the Appellant was trying to falsely implicate the Respondent No. 1 in the case of murder, moved an application before the DIG, Firozabad, requesting that the investigation be transferred from the Dakshin Police Station to some other police station. The DIG, Firozabad vide order dated 11 November 2008 directed the Senior Superintendent of Police, Firozabad (for short, SSP) to look into the matter. Thereafter, the SSP called for a status report on the case from the circle officer vide letter dated 14 November 2008. The status report submitted by the circle officer revealed that while the Respondent No. 1 had obtained a stay on his arrest from the High Court, the arrest of the other accused remained pending and the investigation was still going on. Upon consideration of the same, the SSP, Firozabad, vide order dated 20 November 2008 transferred the investigation from the Dakshin Police Station to the Uttar Police Station at Firozabad, with immediate effect.

(16.) The CJM, Firozabad took cognisance of the Charge Sheet No. 3A of 2008 vide order dated 24 November 2008. Immediately, on 28 January 2009, the Respondent No. 1 preferred Criminal Misc. Application No. 4080 of 2009 under Section 482 CrPC before the High Court of Allahabad seeking to quash the proceedings in Case No. 67 of 2008 (State vs Niranjan Kumar Upadhyay) arising out of the above charge sheet in Case Crime No. 617 of 2007, pending before the CJM, Firozabad.

(17.) Later, on 25 February 2009, the charge sheet bearing No. 30 of 2009 was filed in the case of the Respondent Nos. 3, 4 and 5 respectively for the offence under Sections 147, 148, 149, 307, 302, 201 and 120-B IPC respectively for being involved in the conspiracy to commit murder of the Appellant's brother at Firozabad. The CJM, Firozabad took cognisance of the same vide order dated 10 August 2009. On 29 November 2009, the Respondent Nos. 3, 4 and 5 respectively also preferred an application being the Criminal Misc. Application No. 32494 of 2009 under Section 482 CrPC before the High Court of Allahabad seeking to quash the proceedings of Case No. 67A of 2009 (State vs Ram Prakash Gunkar and Ors.) arising out of the said charge sheet in Case Crime No. 617 of 2007 pending before the CJM, Firozabad.

(18.) During the pendency of the aforesaid two applications filed under Section 482 CrPC before the High Court, the Court of Additional District and Sessions Judge, Firozabad, completed the Sessions Trial No. 753 and 753A of 2008 respectively and vide the judgment & order dated 10 July 2015, held all the 12 accused, including Ashok Dixit, guilty of the offences under Sections 147, 148, 149, 307, 302 and 120-B IPC with which they were charged. The relevant observations made by the trial Court are reproduced hereinbelow:

> '...The "plea of alibi" taken by accused Ashok Dixit that on the day of incident he was lodged in jail u/s 34, Excise Act at PS Murar, district Gwalior was with the inconsistent report of the Murar police officials and after investigation IO has submitted its report to SSP, Gwalior and JM, Gwalior and stated that the case was false. The above mentioned police

officials have been suspended after conducting a departmental investigation also they have been named for conspiring the death along with accused Ashok Dixit in the charge sheet that has been presented before CJM, Firozabad in which they have been charged u/s 302, 120B I.P.C...

It is correct that the distance of 160 kilometres cannot be covered in one hour and if accused Ashok Dixit was at Murar, Gwalior at 9.30 a.m., then he cannot be involved in the commission of incident at Firozabad at 8.30 a.m. It was contended in this regard on behalf of the prosecution that accused Ashok Dixit is a cunning criminal. He showed his presence there colluding with Murar Police Station, Gwalior in order to escape himself from the offence of murder. The investigator SHO Shri Baldhari Singh made enquiries after going there, then the whole matter was found forged and the investigator gave an application to SSP Gwalior in this regard and also submitted an application before JM Gwalior Madhya Pradesh and keeping the investigation in progress, it was found that in order to save accused Ashok Dixit from the heinous crime like murder, the forged arrest and his release on bail has been shown by the police of Murar police station. SSP Gwalior, on investigation, finding the whole case forged, has suspended all the officials involved in the said matter and initiated departmental inquiry against them and after collecting the evidence in the said case, a charge sheet has been filed in the Court of CJM Firozabad against the said police officials Niranjan Upadhyay, TI Police Station Murar, Gwalior and Shailendra Singh and Triloki Gaur and ASI PP Gunkar, Head Constable Vijay Bahadur and Head Constable Rambaran Yadav under Section 147, 148, 149, 307, 302, 201, 120B IPC with regard to give cooperation in the conspiracy of murder under Section 120B IPC. A case No. 67 A/2008 *State vs Niranjan and Ors.* is pending in that regard in the Court of CJM Firozabad and the warrant of the arrest of the accused persons have been issued. The said file pending in the Court of CJM was summoned on behalf of the prosecution in this regard, which is available on the file of the instant session trial which makes it clear that accused Ashok Dixit has shown his presence at 9.30 a.m. on the day of incident showing his arrest under Section 34 of Excise Act in order to escape from the case of murder of Suman Prakash colluding with the police officials of Police Station Murar, District

Gwalior, Madhya Pradesh which was found forged in the investigation and charge sheet has been filed against the said police officials involving them in the conspiracy of murder and in order to save accused Ashok Dixit from punishment, the case of the same is pending in the Court of CJM, Firozabad and warrant of arrest against all the police officials have been issued and SSP Gwalior has suspended them and departmental inquiry has been initiated against them. All these police officials are absconding. Arrest warrants have been issued against them by CJM Court, Firozabad. The copy of charge sheet of Case No. 67 A/2008 *State vs Niranjan and Ors.* pending in the Court of CJM has also been filed on record behalf of the prosecution. The proceedings of case No. 15003/2007 *State vs Ashok Dixit* under Section 34 of Excise Act, Police Station Murar pending before the CJM Court has been stayed by order dated 25 August 2009 by the Hon'ble High Court, bench at Gwalior passed in Misc. Case No. 5971. The copy of the order passed by the Hon'ble High Court bench at Gwalior is filed on record from 613B/25 to 613B/30. SLP has been filed against the said order before the Hon'ble Supreme Court which was not admitted for hearing, the copy of the same is filed on record at 613B/31, Therefore, no profit of case under Section 34 of Excise Act cannot be given to accused Ashok Dixit and his presence at Murar, District Gwalior at the time of incident under the case of 34 Excise Act has been found forged and the accused has made a forged plea of alibi colluding with the police officials.'

(Emphasis supplied)

(19.) The High Court at Allahabad heard the Criminal Misc. Writ Application Nos. 4080 of 2009 and 32494 of 2009 analogously and disposed them vide the common judgment and order dated 19 April 2018. The High Court quashed the proceedings in Case Nos. 67 of 2008 and 67A of 2009 respectively essentially on the ground that sanction to prosecute the Respondent Nos. 1, 3, 4, and 5 respectively under Section 197 CrPC was necessary & since it had not been obtained, the trial cannot proceed. The relevant observations are reproduced hereinbelow:

'<u>Admittedly, the Applicants are public servant and case was registered under Section 34 Excise Act against main accused of the murder in the</u>

> discharge of public duty but the sanction to prosecute for the offence committed at Firozabad was not granted by the State of MP to prosecute the Applicants for the offence committed within the jurisdiction of the Police Station, Dakhin at Firozabad (UP) as is evident from the Annexure SA-I and SA-II to the supplementary affidavit. In the above circumstances, it ought not to be proper to allow the proceedings to be continued against the Applicants and in case, the proceeding is allowed to continue against the Applicants, it would be nothing but misuse of process of law.

In view of what has been submitted and discussed above, the applications have substance and are liable to be allowed.

> Accordingly, the applications are allowed and the proceedings pending before CJM, Firozabad as Case No. 67 of 2008 (*State vs Niranjan Kumar Upadhyay*) as well as Case No. 67A of 2009 (*State vs Ram Prakash Gunkar and Ors.*) in connected application arising out of Case Crime No. 617 of 2007 under Sections 147, 148, 149, 307, 302, 201, 120B IPC, PS Dakshin, District Firozabad are hereby quashed.'
>
> (Emphasis supplied)

(20.) In such circumstances referred to above, the Appellant (complainant) is here before this Court with the present appeal.

Submission on Behalf of the Appellant

(21.) Mr Ravindra Singh, the learned senior counsel appearing for the Appellant submitted that the plea of alibi which was taken by the accused Ashok Dixit on the ground that his arrest in connection with the offence under Section 34 of the Excise Act was effected on 12 October 2007, at 9.30 a.m., by the officials of the Murar Police Station, Gwalior, Madhya Pradesh, has been appropriately considered by the Trial Court at Firozabad in Sessions Trial No. 753 and 753A of 2008. However, the said plea of alibi was outrightly rejected by the Trial Court by way of its well-reasoned judgment. The Trial Court categorically observed that the accused Ashok Dixit in connivance with the police officials of the Murar Police Station, Gwalior had managed to get a false case registered under Case Crime No. 967 of 2007 related to Section

34 of the Excise Act. The Trial Court had further observed that during the investigation, the presence and arrest of Ashok Dixit in Murar, Gwalior was found to be false & bogus and therefore, charge sheet came to be filed against those police officials for acting in collusion with Ashok Dixit. Furthermore, those police officials have also been suspended and a departmental enquiry has been initiated against them. Therefore, it was submitted that the Respondent No. 1 cannot assert that he has been erroneously implicated in Case Crime No. 617 of 2007 registered for the offence under Sections 147, 148, 149, 307, 302, 201 & 120-B of IPC with the Dakshin Police Station, Firozabad, Uttar Pradesh.

(22.) The counsel submitted that the High Court fell in serious error while passing the impugned order. The High Court could be said to have travelled beyond its jurisdiction by quashing the criminal proceedings against the Respondents on the ground that the Trial Court has already decided the case against Ashok Dixit and the other accused. The Trial Court in Sessions Trial Nos. 753 and 753A of 2008 respectively arising out of Case Crime No. 617of 2007 held Ashok Dixit guilty of the offence of murder of the Appellant's brother.

(23.) The counsel submitted that the High Court erroneously quashed the criminal proceedings against the Respondents saying that the accused Respondents being public servants, the sanction to prosecute for the alleged offence is a must. It was submitted that the act of hatching a conspiracy to commit murder and creating a plea of alibi by instituting a false case, cannot be said to be done in the exercise of discharge of official duty. It was further submitted that no sanction is required under Section 197 CrPC to prosecute an erring Government official/Respondent No. 1 herein for the reason that the Respondent No. 1 was not posted at the Murar Police Station, Gwalior where the Case Crime No. 967 of 2007 was registered.

(24.) It was also submitted that the Respondent No. 1 had managed with the police officials of the Murar Police Station, Gwalior, to get a false FIR being Case Crime No. 967 of 2007 registered under Section 34 of the Excise Act and thereby falsely showed the presence of Ashok Dixit at Murar, Gwalior on 12 October 2007 at 9.30 a.m. i.e., on the same day on which the Case Crime No. 617 of 2007 was registered at the Dakshin Police Station,

Firozabad in respect of the murder of the Appellant's brother. Furthermore, the Respondent No. 1 had also influenced the other Respondents to release a person under the Excise Act from the Thatipur Chowki of the Murar Police Station without producing the said person before the concerned court, in order to save Ashok Dixit.

(25.) The learned counsel relied upon the police statements of Ramesh Yadav and Barelal dated 25 October 2008. They as independent witnesses have categorically stated that while they were at Thatipur, Gwalior, 'Niranjan Upadhyay came out from car along with other person and said that Ashok Dixit you do not worry, I will protect you from murder case but you follow me and starts roaming in Thatipur, Gwalior along with 10–12 cartons of whisky.....' The same makes it clear that the Respondent No. 1 was also actively involved in the lodging of a false FIR.

(26.) In such circumstances referred to above, the learned counsel submitted that there being merit in his appeal, the same may be allowed and the impugned order passed by the High Court be set aside.

Submissions on Behalf of the Respondent No. 1

(27.) Mr R Basant, the learned senior counsel appearing for the Respondent No. 1 submitted that there is nothing to indicate that the Respondent No. 1 was directly or indirectly responsible for the registration of Case Crime No. 967 of 2007 in any manner, since he was neither posted at the Murar Police Station nor he had instructed any of the concerned officials to register such an FIR. In fact, the Respondent No. 1 was posted at District Shivpuri which is 120 km away from Gwalior at the time of filing the Case Crime No. 967 of 2007 on 12 October 2007.

(28.) The counsel submitted that the Respondent No. 1 had neither filed the FIR in Case Crime No. 967 of 2007 at the Murar Police Station, Gwalior nor was he associated with the said police station in any manner. However, assuming without conceding that the said FIR was registered at the behest of Respondent No. 1, sanction for prosecution with respect to Case Crime No. 617 of 2007 is required. It is an admitted fact that sanction was refused by the DIG, Gwalior vide its letter dated 2 August 2008.

(29.) The counsel further submitted that there are bleak chances of conviction of the Respondent No. 1 for the following reasons: (a) the Respondent No. 1 was not posted at the Murar Police Station, Gwalior where the Case Crime No. 967 of 2007 was registered, (b) the Respondent No. 1 is 72 years old and no purpose would be served if the Respondent No. 1 was made to face trial at this stage when the Case Crime No. 617 of 2007 was admittedly filed in the 2007, (c) the Trial Court has already convicted all the accused including Ashok Dixit by way of its judgment in 10 July 2015, (d) Respondent No. 1 has retired from police service in 2015 and 9 years have passed since then, (e) No departmental inquiry was initiated against Respondent No. 1 for the alleged act of registration of Case Crime No. 967 of 2007 at the Murar Police Station, Gwalior, and (f) there is nothing to indicate that the Respondent No. 1 is related to the accused Ashok Dixit.

(30.) The counsel submitted that the charge sheet should be read as a whole and there exists no circumstance or evidence to warrant any assumption of involvement of Respondent No. 1 in connection with Case Crime No. 617 of 2007 for the alleged offence of conspiracy to commit murder. This is so because there are only two statements of witnesses recorded under Section 161 CrPC and such statements were recorded after a period of one year i.e., on 25 October 2008 from the date of registration of Case Crime No. 617 of 2007 i.e., on 12 October 2007. These two statements are the sole basis for instituting a prosecution against the Respondent No. 1. Furthermore, the said witnesses were not examined in the trial whereby the 12 accused including Ashok Dixit stood convicted vide order dated 10 July 2015.

(31.)It was also submitted that there is a material contradiction in the case of the prosecution. The statements of the two witnesses i.e., Ramesh and Barelal suggest that the Respondent No. 1 was seen with Ashok Dixit in Gwalior since they had verbatim deposed that they had heard Respondent No. 1 telling Ashok Dixit that they would create a false plea of alibi. However, the eyewitnesses have all deposed that Ashok Dixit was present at the place of the incident in Firozabad where the firing had occurred. These two contradictory statements confirm the presence of Ashok Dixit in Firozabad and also in Gwalior and are therefore, *ex-facie* derogatory to each other.

(32.) The counsel submitted that Section 201 CrPC would not apply to the instant facts and circumstances. There is no allegation that the Respondent No. 1 had conspired with the other co-accused persons for the offence of murder and the only allegation that surfaces from the charge sheet is that a false alibi was provided in order to shield Ashok Dixit by registering an FIR under the Excise Act in Gwalior. The said alleged Act was made after the commission of the offence of murder and there is nothing on record to even remotely suggest that the Respondent No. 1 had knowledge about the incident of murder.

(33.) In light of the above, the counsel submitted that the impugned Judgment and Order of the High Court quashing the criminal proceedings against the Respondent No. 1 may not be interfered with.

Submissions on Behalf of the Respondent Nos. 3, 4 and 5

(34.) Ms Nanita Sharma, the learned counsel appearing for the Respondent Nos. 3, 4, and 5 respectively submitted that the Uttar Pradesh Police was bent upon falsely implicating her clients for the offence under Sections 302 and 120-B IPC. This is evident from the following: (a) the statements of Ramesh Yadav and Barelal were recorded under Section 161 CrPC after a gap of one year from the date of the offence committed at Firozabad i.e., 12 October 2007, (b) the address of Barelal as recorded by the IO while recording his statement under Section 161 CrPC was found to be incorrect and as per the information of the Sarpanch, no person with the name of Barelal had ever lived at the said address. The permanent address of the witness Barelal was not in existence even as per the certificate given by the parshad of the area on 28 December 2008, (c) Ramesh Yadav had also never lived at the address which was given by him to the IO during his statement recorded under Section 161 CrPC and the same was clear from the certificate issued by the Sarpanch of Bada Gaon, Murar Police Station, Gwalior.

(35.) The counsel also submitted that the Respondent Nos. 3, 4 and 5 respectively had never been named in the FIR registered in Case Crime No. 617 of 2007 nor their names were ever disclosed by any of the witnesses whose statements had been recorded by the IO under Section 161 CrPC after the commission of the offence at Firozabad. It was never pointed out that there was any conspiracy between the Respondents and the main accused, Ashok Dixit. It was submitted that the Respondent nos. 3, 4 and 5 respectively or their family members are neither relatives nor known to the accused, Ashok Dixit, in any manner.

(36.) The counsel submitted that the IO at Firozabad has falsely implicated the Respondent Nos. 3, 4 and 5 respectively in the murder case which occurred at Firozabad even though they had no role to play in the case. They have been implicated only because of the rivalry between the two police establishments and the refusal of the DIG, Gwalior to grant sanction to prosecute them. It was submitted that the Respondents had only performed their duty without suspecting any kind of manipulation in both the arrest and release of Ashok Dixit because they were merely following the instructions of their superior officer i.e., the TI (SHO), DS Khushawa of the Murar Police Station.

(37.) The counsel in the last submitted that the High Court was justified in quashing the criminal proceedings against the Respondent Nos. 3, 4 and 5 for want of sanction.

Issues(s) for Determination

(38.) Having heard the learned counsel appearing for the parties and having gone through the materials on record, the only issue that falls for our consideration is:

a. Whether the CJM, Firozabad could have taken cognisance of the Charge Sheet No. 3A of 2008 and Charge Sheet No. 30 of 2009 respectively against the Respondent Nos. 1, 3, 4 and 5 respectively, in the absence of the grant of sanction for prosecution under Section 197 CrPC. In other words, whether the offence or the act alleged to have been committed by the Respondent Nos. 1, 3, 4 and 5 respectively could be said to have been done 'while acting or purporting to act in the discharge of official duty'.

Analysis

(39.) Section 197 CrPC reads as under:

> '**197. Prosecution of Judges and public servants. —**
>
> (1) When any person who is or was a Judge or Magistrate or a public servant not removable from his office save by or with the sanction of the Government is accused of any offence alleged to have been committed by him while acting or purporting to act in the discharge of his official duty, no Court shall take cognisance of such offence except with the previous sanction save as otherwise provided in the Lokpal and Lokayuktas Act, 2013 (1 of 2014)—
>
> (a.) in the case of a person who is employed or, as the case may be, was at the time of commission of the alleged offence employed, in connection with the affairs of the Union, of the Central Government;
>
> (b.) in the case of a person who is employed or, as the case may be, was at the time of commission of the alleged offence employed, in connection with the affairs of a state, of the State Government:
>
> Provided that where the alleged offence was committed by a person referred to in clause (b) during the period while a Proclamation issued under clause (1) of Article 356 of the Constitution was in force in a state, clause (b) will apply as if for the expression "State Government" occurring therein, the expression "Central Government" were substituted.
>
> Explanation. — For the removal of doubts it is hereby declared that no sanction shall be required in case of a public servant accused of any offence alleged to have been committed under Section 166A, Section 166B, Section 354, Section 354A, Section 354B, Section 354C, Section 354D, Section 370, Section 375, 3 [Section 376A, Section 376AB, Section 376C, Section 376D, Section 376DA, Section 376DB] or Section 509 of the Indian Penal Code (45 of 1860).
>
> (2) No court shall take cognisance of any offence alleged to have been committed by any member of the Armed Forces of the Union while acting

or purporting to act in the discharge of his official duty, except with the previous sanction of the Central Government.

(3) The State Government may, by notification, direct that the provisions of subsection (2) shall apply to such class or category of the members of the forces charged with the maintenance of public order as may be specified therein, wherever they may be serving, and thereupon the provisions of that subsection will apply as if for the expression "Central Government" occurring therein, the expression "State Government" were substituted.

(3A) Notwithstanding anything contained in subsection (3), no court shall take cognisance of any offence, alleged to have been committed by any member of the Forces charged with the maintenance of public order in a state while acting or purporting to act in the discharge of his official duty during the period while a Proclamation issued under clause (1) of Article 356 of the Constitution was in force therein, except with the previous sanction of the Central Government.

(3B) Notwithstanding anything to the contrary contained in this Code or any other law, it is hereby declared that any sanction accorded by the State Government or any cognisance taken by a court upon such sanction, during the period commencing on the 20th day of August, 1991 and ending with the date immediately preceding the date on which the Code of Criminal Procedure (Amendment) Act, 1991 (43 of 1991), receives the assent of the President, with respect to an offence alleged to have been committed during the period while a Proclamation issued under clause (1) of Article 356 of the Constitution was in force in the State, shall be invalid and it shall be competent for the Central Government in such matter to accord sanction and for the Court to take cognisance thereon.

(4) The Central Government or the State Government, as the case may be, may determine the person by whom, the manner in which, and the offence or offences for which, the prosecution of such Judge, Magistrate or public servant is to be conducted, and may specify the Court before which the trial is to be held.'

(40.) The 41st Report of the Law Commission of India contextualises the object behind the enactment of Section 197 CrPC by pointing out that it enables the more important categories of public servants, performing onerous and responsible functions, to act fearlessly by protecting them from false, vexatious or *mala fide prosecutions*. Under the erstwhile Code of Criminal Procedure, 1898, the ambit of the Section was considered a bit too wide since it read – 'is accused as such Judge or public servant of any offence'. However, to offer more precision, the Amending Act of 1923 inserted the phrase – 'is accused of any offence alleged to have been committed by him while acting or purporting to act in the discharge of his official duty'. The same has been retained in the statute books till today despite the provision undergoing several amendments over the period of time.

(41.) As rightly acknowledged by the Law Commission, the meaning of the word'acting or purporting to act' in Section 197 CrPC has been well settled by a legion of decisions of the Federal Court, the Privy Council and the Supreme Court and any difficulty that may be felt lies only in the actual application of the principles laid down in these decisions to the facts and circumstances of a particular case. In other words, the question whether a particular act is done by a public servant in the discharge of his official duty is substantially one of fact, which is to be determined in the unique circumstances of each case.

(42.)The applicability of Section 197 CrPC has been the subject of judicial interpretation in several cases. One of the first and foremost case laws which examined the pith of the expression 'any act done or purporting to be done' was the Federal Court decision in *Dr Hori Ram Singh vs The Crown* reported in AIR 1939 FC 43. Their Lordships were called upon to consider the applicability of Section 270 of the Government of India Act, 1935 which albeit not identical, but was similar to Section 197 CrPC. The Court held that while the offence under Section 409 IPC as regards the criminal breach of trust by a public servant would not require consent from the Governor for it cannot be done or purported to be done in the execution of his duty, yet the offence under Section 477A IPC as regards the falsification of accounts would require the Governor's consent. The words 'purported to be done' was interpreted as follows:

'**Extent of the Protection.** Obviously, the section does not mean that the very act which is the gravamen of the charge and constitutes the offence should be the official duty of the servant of the Crown. Such an interpretation would involve a contradiction in terms, because an offence can never be an official duty. The words as used in the section are not "in respect of any official duty" but "in respect of any act done or purporting to be done in the execution of his duty." The two expressions are obviously not identical. The offence should have been committed when an act is done in the execution of duty or when an act purports to be done in the execution of the duty. The reference as obviously to an offence committed in the course of an action, which is taken or purports to be taken in compliance with an official duty, and is in fact connected with it. The test appears to be not that the offence is capable of being committed only by a public servant and not by anyone else, but that it is committed by a public servant in an act done or purporting to be done in the execution of his duty. The section cannot be confined to only such acts as are done by a public servant directly in pursuance of his public office, though in excess of the duty or under a mistaken belief as to the existence of such duty. Nor is it necessary to go to the length of saying that the act constituting the offence should be so inseparably connected with the official duty as to form part and parcel of the same transaction. If the act complained of is an offence, it must necessarily be not an execution of duty, but a dereliction of it. What is necessary is that the offence must be in respect of an act done or purported to be done in execution of duty, that is in the discharge of an official duty. It must purport to be done in the official capacity with which he pretends to be clothed at the time, that is to say under the cloak of an ostensibly official act, though, of course, the offence would really amount to a breach of duty. An act cannot purport to be done in execution of duty unless the offender professes to be acting in pursuance of his official duty and means to convey to the mind of another the impression that he is so acting.

The section is not intended to apply to acts done purely in a private capacity by a public servant. It must have been ostensibly done by him in his official capacity in execution of his duty, which would not necessarily be the case merely because it was done at a time when he held such office, nor even necessarily because he was engaged in his official business at the time. For instance, if a public servant accepts as a reward a bribe in his office while actually engaged in some official work, he is not accepting it even in his official capacity, much less in the execution of any official duty, although it is quite certain that he could never have been able to take the bribe unless he were the official in charge of some official work. He does not even pretend to the person who offers the bribe that he is acting in the discharge of his official duty, but merely uses his official position to obtain the illegal gratification.'

(Emphasis supplied)

(43.) His Lordship, Sulaiman, J, clarified that it is not imperative for the very act which is at the center of the charge to be the official duty of the public servant. This would lead to the inference that an offence can never be part of one's official duty and defeat the very intent behind the enactment of the provision. Instead, the essence of the provision was that the offence must be in respect of an act done or purported to be done in the execution of duty i.e., in the discharge of an official duty. Although the offence would really amount to a breach of duty, it must purport to be done in the official capacity with which the official pretended to be clothed at the time. However, it was made clear that the provision must not be applied to acts done purely in a private capacity by a public servant but only to those acts ostensibly done by him in his official capacity and in execution of his duty. Therefore, merely because the act was committed at a time when he held such office or when he was engaged in his official business would not make the Section automatically applicable.

(44.) His Lordship, Varadachariar, J, in his concurring opinion, expressed that the question of whether or not the act complained of is one 'purporting to be done in execution of his duty' as a public servant is substantially one of fact which is to be determined with reference to the act complained of along with the attendant circumstances. It would not be wise nor desirable to lay down any hard and fast tests in this regard.

(45.) The Judicial Committee of the *Privy Council in Gill and Another vs The King reported* in AIR 1948 PC 128 was faced with deciding whether sanction was required under Section 197 CrPC for the prosecution of a public servant charged with the offence of bribery and/or conspiracy to take bribes. The Court was of the opinion that it was impossible to distinguish or differentiate between Section 270 of the Government of India Act, 1935 and Section 197 CrPC, at least in relation to offences of this character. Therefore, the decision in *Dr Hori Ram Singh* (supra) would be of great assistance in cases pertaining to Section 197 as well. It was observed that a public servant can only be said to act or purport to act in the discharge of his official duty, if his act is as such as to lie within the scope of his official duty. Therefore, the test may well be whether the public servant, if challenged, can reasonably claim that, what he does, he does in virtue of his office. The relevant observations are reproduced hereinbelow:

> ' "A public servant can only be said to act or to purport to act in the discharge of his official duty, if his act is such as to lie within the scope of his official duty. Thus, a judge neither acts nor purports to act as a judge in receiving a bribe, though the judgment which he delivers may be such an act: nor does a Government medical officer act or purport to act as a public servant in picking the pocket of a patient whom he is examining, though the examination itself may be such an act. The test may well be whether the public servant, if challenged, can reasonably claim that, what he does, he does in virtue of his office" Applying such a test to the present case, it seems clear that Gill could not justify the acts in respect of which he was charged as acts done by him by virtue of the office that he held. Without further examination of the authorities their Lordships, finding themselves in general agreement with the opinion of the Federal Court in the case cited, think it sufficient to say that in their opinion no sanction under Section 197 of the Code of Criminal Procedure was needed.'
>
> (Emphasis supplied)

(46.) In *Albert West Meads vs The King* reported in AIR 1948 PC 156, the Privy Council echoed the view taken in Gill (supra) and held that the appellant in that case could not justify that the act of fraudulently misapplying money entrusted to his care as a public servant was an act done by him by virtue of his office.

(47.) In *Shreekantiah Ramayya Munipalli vs State of Bombay* reported in (1954) 2 SCC 992, this Court stressed that each case must be decided in its own facts. Herein, the Bench opined that Section 197 CrPC can never be applied if it is construed too narrowly since it is no part of an official's duty to commit an offence and the language of the provision must be given its true meaning. However, it is not the duty but the act which has to be examined because an official act can be performed in the discharge of official duty as well as in the dereliction of it. The relevant observations are as follows:

> '14. Now it is obvious that if Section 197 of the Criminal Procedure Code is construed too narrowly it can never be applied, for of course it is no part of an official's duty to commit an offence and never can be. But it is not the duty we have to examine so much as the act, because an official act can be performed in the discharge of official duty as well as in dereliction of it. The Section has content and its language must be given meaning. ...'
>
> (Emphasis supplied)

(48.) In *Amrik Singh vs State of Pepsu* reported in AIR 1955 SC 309, the appellant was charged under Section 465 IPC for forging the thumb-impression of an individual and under Section 409 IPC for the criminal misappropriation of a certain sum. The Court opined that if the act complained of is directly concerned with the official duty of the public servant so that, if questioned, it could be claimed to have been done by virtue of the office, then sanction would be necessary. This would be irrespective of whether it was, in fact, a proper discharge of his duties because that would really be a matter of defence on the merits which would have to be investigated at trial and not be examined at the stage of granting sanction for prosecution. Therefore, the test as to whether sanction is necessary to prosecute a public servant will depend on whether the acts complained of are so integrally connected with his duties as a public servant. If they do, then sanction is a requisite and there cannot be any uniform rule that an offence of criminal misappropriation or criminal breach of trust would always be outside the scope of Section 197 CrPC. The relevant observations are reproduced hereinbelow:

> '7. The result of the authorities may thus be summed up : It is not every offence committed by a public servant that requires sanction for prosecution under Section 197(1) of the Code of Criminal Procedure; nor even every act done by him while he is actually engaged in the performance of his

> official duties; but if the act complained of is directly concerned with his official duties so that, if questioned, it could be claimed to have been done by virtue of the office, then sanction would be necessary; and that would be so, irrespective of whether it was, in fact, a proper discharge of his duties, because that would really be a matter of defence on the merits, which would have to be investigated at the trial, and could not arise at the stage of the grant of sanction, which must precede the institution of the prosecution.
>
> 8. ...In our judgment, even when the charge is one of misappropriation by a public servant, whether sanction is required under Section 197(1) will depend upon the facts of each case. If the acts complained of are so integrally connected with the duties attaching to the office as to be inseparable from them, then sanction under Section 197(1) would be necessary; but if there was no necessary connection between them and the performance of those duties, the official status furnishing only the occasion or opportunity for the acts, then no sanction would be required.
>
> xxx xxx xxx
>
> 11. ...The result then is that whether sanction is necessary to prosecute a public servant on a charge of criminal misappropriation, will depend on whether the acts complained of hinge on his duties as a public servant. If they do, then sanction is requisite. But if they are unconnected with such duties, then no sanction is necessary.
>
> (Emphasis supplied)

(49.) A five-Judge Bench of this Court in *Matajog Dobey vs H.C. Bhari* reported in AIR 1956 SC 44 acknowledged that slightly differing tests had been laid down under Section 197 CrPC but the difference in those tests were only in language and not in substance. The Court laid down a more refined test that there must be a reasonable connection between the act done and the discharge of the official duty and the act must bear such relation to the duty that the accused could lay a reasonable, but not a pretended or fanciful claim, that he did it in the course of the performance of his duty. Therefore, what one must ascertain is whether the act and the official duty are so interrelated such that it can be reasonably postulated that it was done in the performance of the official duty, though possibly in excess of the needs and requirements of the situation. The relevant observations are as follows:

> '17. Slightly differing tests have been laid down in the decided cases to ascertain the scope and the meaning of the relevant words occurring in Section 197 of the Code; "any offence alleged to have been committed by him while acting or purporting to act in the discharge of his official duty". But the difference is only in language and not in substance. <u>The offence alleged to have been committed must have something to do, or must be related in some manner with the discharge of official duty. No question of sanction can arise under Section 197, unless the act complained of is an offence; the only point to determine is whether it was committed in the discharge of official duty. There must be a reasonable connection between the act and the official duty. It does not matter even if the act exceeds what is strictly necessary for the discharge of the duty, as this question will arise only at a later stage when the trial proceeds on the merits. What we must find out is whether the act and the official duty are so inter-related that one can postulate reasonably that it was done by the accused in the performance of the official duty, though possibly in excess of the needs and requirements of the situation. ...</u>
>
> xxx xxx xxx
>
> 19. The result of the foregoing discussion is this: <u>There must be a reasonable connection between the act and the discharge of official duty; the act must bear such relation to the duty that the accused could lay a reasonable, but not a pretended or fanciful claim, that he did it in the course of the performance of his duty.'</u>
>
> (Emphasis supplied)

(50.) Furthermore, in *Dhannjay Ram Sharma vs M.S. Uppadaya and Ors.* reported in AIR 1960 SC 745, it was clarified that the mere fact that an opportunity to commit an offence is furnished by the official duty is not such a connection of the offence with the performance of such duty, so as to justify even remotely the view that the acts complained of are within the scope of the application of Section 197 CrPC.

(51.) This Court in *P. Arulswami vs State* reported in (1967) 1 SCR 201 was also concerned with an offence under Section 409 IPC and it was opined that the act must be directly concerned and connected with the official duties of the public servant such that it could be claimed to have been done by virtue of his office. Furthermore, it is the 'quality' of the act that must be emphasised on. The act must not be totally unconnected with the official duty. Only if it falls either within the scope and range of the official duties, or is in excess of it, then Section 197 CrPC would stand attracted. The Court had stated as thus:

> '...It is not therefore every offence committed by a public servant that requires sanction for prosecution under Section 197(1) of the Criminal Procedure Code; nor even every act done by him while he is actually engaged in the performance of his official duties; but if the act complained of is directly concerned with his official duties so that, if questioned, it could be claimed to have been done by virtue of the office, then sanction would be necessary. It is the quality of the act that is important and if it falls within the scope and range of his official duties the protection contemplated by Section 197 of the Criminal Procedure Code will be attracted. An offence may be entirely unconnected with the official duty as such or it may be committed within the scope of official duty. Where it is unconnected with the official duty there can be no protection. It is only when it is either within the scope of the official duty or in excess of it that the protection is claimable...'
>
> (Emphasis supplied)

(52.) In *Harihar Prasad Etc. vs State of Bihar* reported in (1972) 3 SCC 89 the appellants were alleged to have entered into a criminal conspiracy for committing the offences of criminal breach of trust and cheating in respect of a large amount of government money earmarked for a development project. The Court opined that sanction under Section 197 CrPC would not be necessary since it is no part of the duty of a public servant while discharging his official duties, to enter into a criminal conspiracy or to indulge in criminal misconduct and observed as thus:

> '66. The next point was with regard to consent or sanction. There is no doubt that in respect of BP Sinha consent was properly given by the Deputy

Commissioner. So consent was also given in respect of N.K. Banerjee and Harihar Prasad by the Chief Secretary. This is not a case of sanction or consent under Section 196-A of the Code of Criminal Procedure. On the question of the applicability of Section 197 of the Code of Criminal Procedure, the principle laid down in two cases, namely, *Shreekantiah Ramayya Munipalli vs State of Bombay* [AIR 1955 SC 287] and *Amrik Singh vs State of Pepsu* [AIR 1955 SC 309] was as follows:

> "It is not every offence committed by a public servant that requires sanction for prosecution under Section 197(1) of the Criminal Procedure Code; nor even every act done by him while he is actually engaged in the performance of his official duties; but if the act complained of is directly concerned with his official duties so that, if questioned, it could be claimed to have been done by virtue of the office, then sanction would be necessary."

The real question therefore is whether the acts complained of in the present case were directly concerned with the official duties of the three public servants. As far as the offence of criminal conspiracy punishable under Section 120-B, read with Section 409 of the Penal Code, 1860 is concerned and also Section 5(2) of the Prevention of Corruption Act, are concerned they cannot be said to be of the nature mentioned in Section 197 of the Code of Criminal Procedure. To put it shortly, it is no part of the duty of a public servant, while discharging his official duties, to enter into a criminal conspiracy or to indulge in criminal misconduct. Want of sanction under Section 197 of the Code of Criminal Procedure is, therefore, no bar.'

(Emphasis supplied)

(53.) In *B. Saha and Ors. vs M.S. Kochar* reported in (1979) 4 SCC 177, the Appellants were charged for the offences under Sections 409 and 120-B IPC. The Court opined that while it is not an invariable proposition of law that the act of criminal misappropriation or conversion cannot be inseparably intertwined with the performance of the official duty, yet in the facts of the present case, the alleged act of criminal misappropriation could not reasonably be said to be imbued with the colour of office or having a direct connection with the duties of the Appellants as public servants. Therefore, sanction was not considered necessary. While observing so, the Court stated that the expression 'any offence alleged to have been committed by him while acting or purporting to act in the discharge of his official duty' must neither be construed narrowly nor widely and the right approach would be to arrive at a balance between the two extremes. Therefore, the sine qua non for the applicability of this Section is that the offence charged, be it one of commission or omission, must be committed by the public servant either in his official capacity or under the colour of the office held by him such that there is a direct or reasonable connection between the act and the official duty. The relevant observations are as thus:

> '17. The words "any offence alleged to have been committed by him while acting or purporting to act in the discharge of his official duty" employed in Section 197(1) of the Code, are capable of a narrow as well as a wide interpretation. If these words are construed too narrowly, the Section will be rendered altogether sterile, for, "it is no part of an official duty to commit an offence, and never can be". In the wider sense, these words will take under their umbrella every act constituting an offence, committed in the course of the same transaction in which the official duty is performed or purports to be performed. The right approach to the import of these words lies between these two extremes. While on the one hand, it is not every offence committed by a public servant while engaged in the performance of his official duty, which is entitled to the protection of Section 197(1), an act constituting an offence, directly and reasonably connected with his official duty will require sanction for prosecution under the said provision. As pointed out by Ramaswami, J, in *Baijnath vs State of MP* [AIR 1966 SC 220, 227 : (1966) 1 SCR 210 : 1966 Cri LJ 179] , "it is the quality of the act that is important, and if it falls within the scope and range of his official duties, the protection contemplated by Section 197 of the Criminal Procedure Code will be attracted."
>
> 18. In sum, the sine qua non for the applicability of this Section is that the offence charged, be it one of commission or omission, must be one which has been committed by the public servant either in his official capacity or under colour of the office held by him.'

(Emphasis supplied)

(54.) This Court in *State of Maharashtra vs Dr Budhikota Subbarao* reported in (1993) 3 SCC 339 elaborated on how the balance between a narrow and wide construction of Section 197 CrPC can be maintained. The Court opined that the Section must be construed strictly while determining its applicability to any act or omission in the course of service and its operation has to be limited only to those acts which are discharged in the 'course of duty'. However, once any act or omission has been found to have been committed by a public servant in the discharge of his duty then a liberal and wide construction can be given to the particular act, so far as its official nature is concerned. For instance, a public servant is not entitled to indulge in criminal activities in the discharge of his duty and to that extent, the Section must be construed narrowly and in a restricted manner. However, once it is established that the act or omission was done by the public servant while discharging his duty, then the scope of it being 'official' should be interpreted such that the objective of the Section is advanced in favour of the public servant.

(55.) In *R. Balakrishna Pillai vs State of Kerala and Another* reported in (1996) 1 SCC 478, the appellant who was the then Minister for Electricity for the State of Kerala was alleged to have entered into a criminal conspiracy to sell electricity to an industry in the State of Karnataka without the consent of the Government of Kerala. The Court stressed that the quality of the act must be looked into and there can be no general proposition that whenever there is a charge of criminal conspiracy levelled against a public servant, the protection under Section 197 CrPC would have no application. The question of whether the act complained of had a direct nexus with the discharge of official duties would depend on the facts of each case and it was stated as thus:

> '6. ...The question whether the acts complained of had a direct nexus or relation with the discharge of official duties by the public servant concerned would depend on the facts of each case. There can be no general proposition that whenever there is a charge of criminal conspiracy levelled against a public servant in or out of office the bar of Section 197(1) of the Code would have no application. Such a view would render Section 197(1) of the Code specious. Therefore, the question would have to be examined in the facts of each case. ..."
>
> (Emphasis supplied)

(56.) In *Shambhoo Nath Misra vs State of UP and Ors.* reported in (1997) 5 SCC 326, allegations of fabrication of record and misappropriation of public funds were made against the accused public servant. The Court while holding that sanction was not necessary in the facts of the case re-affirmed that the public servant's act must be in furtherance of the performance of his official duties and only if the act or omission is integral to the performance of the public duty, he would be entitled to protection under Section 197 CrPC. While stating so, the Court elaborated on the objective behind the enactment of the provision and clarified that the protection of sanction is an assurance to an honest and sincere officer so that he can perform his public duty honestly and to the best of his ability. The threat of prosecution would demoralise them and therefore, the requirement of sanction by the competent authority or the appropriate Government can serve as a shield only for such honest officers who carry out their duty with an aim to further public interest. The Court also rightly cautioned that, however, such an immunity cannot be utilised by public servants to camouflage the commission of a crime under the supposed colour of public office.

(57.) This Court's reasoning in *State of Orissa and Ors. vs Ganesh Chandra* Jew reported in (2004) 8 SCC 40 was further adopted in a few other landmark decisions including *SK Zutshi and Another vs Bimal Debnath and Another* reported in (2004) 8 SCC 31 and *K. Kalimuthu vs State* reported in (2005) 4 SCC 512. The Court in *Ganesh Chandra Jew* (supra) considered the scope of the expression 'official duty' and stated that the protective cover of the Section must not be extended to every act or omission done by a public servant in service but be restricted to only those acts or omissions which are done by a public servant in the discharge of his 'official' duty. The scope can be widened further by also extending protection to those acts or omissions which are done in the 'purported' exercise of 'official' duty i.e., under the colour of office, but not more.

(58.) Dr Arijit Pasayat, J, went on to state that the protection given under Section 197 CrPC must not be viewed as limitless. This protection has certain limits and is available only when the alleged act done is reasonably connected with the discharge of his official duty and not merely a cloak for doing the objectionable act. However, if the public servant acted in excess of his official duty but there exists a reasonable connection between the act and the performance of his official duty, the excess cannot be a sufficient ground to deprive him of the protection under Section 197 CrPC. Therefore, it was re-iterated that it is the 'quality' of the act which is important and such an act must fall within the scope and range of the public servant's official duty. While there cannot be any universal rule to determine whether there exists a reasonable connection between the act done and the official duty, one 'safe and sure test' in this regard would be to consider if the omission or neglect on part of the public servant to commit the act complained of could have made him answerable for a charge of dereliction of his official duty. If the answer to this question is in the affirmative, the protection under Section 197 CrPC can be granted since there was every connection with the act complained of and the official duty of the public servant. The relevant observations are as follows:

> '7. This protection has certain limits and is available only when the alleged act done by the public servant is reasonably connected with the discharge of his official duty and is not merely a cloak for doing the objectionable act. If in doing his official duty, he acted in excess of his duty, but there is a reasonable connection between the act and the performance of the official duty, the excess will not be a sufficient ground to deprive the public servant of the protection. The question is not as to the nature of the offence such as whether the alleged offence contained an element necessarily dependent upon the offender being a public servant, but whether it was committed by a public servant acting or purporting to act as such in the discharge of his official capacity. Before Section 197 can be invoked, it must be shown that the official concerned was accused of an offence alleged to have been committed by him while acting or purporting to act in the discharge of his official duties. It is not the duty which requires examination so much as the act, because the official act can be performed both in the discharge of the official duty as well as in dereliction of it. The act must fall within the scope and range of the official duties of the public servant concerned. It is the quality of the act which is important and the protection of this Section is available if the act falls within the scope and range of his official duty. There cannot be any universal rule to determine whether there is a reasonable connection between the act done and the official duty, nor is

> it possible to lay down any such rule. One safe and sure test in this regard would be to consider if the omission or neglect on the part of the public servant to commit the act complained of could have made him answerable for a charge of dereliction of his official duty. If the answer to this question is in the affirmative, it may be said that such act was committed by the public servant while acting in the discharge of his official duty and there was every connection with the act complained of and the official duty of the public servant...'
>
> (Emphasis supplied)

(59.) In *Sankaran Moitra vs Sadhna Das and Another* reported in (2006) 4 SCC 584, the appellant police officer was accused of killing the complainant's husband while carrying out a lathi-charge near the polling-booth on an election day. While the Bench in its majority opinion had held that the appellant was acting in the discharge of his official duty, C.K. Thakker, J, in his minority opinion had stated that the act complained of had no nexus, reasonable connection or relevance to the official act or duty of such public servant and was otherwise, illegal, unlawful and high-handed. He went on to state that it is not only the 'power' but the 'duty' of the court to apply its mind to the factual situation before it. The Courts must ensure that on the one hand, the public servant is protected if the case is covered by Section 197 CrPC and on the other hand, that appropriate action would be allowed to be taken if the provision is not attracted and the accused is trying to take undue advantage of the Section under the guise of his position as a public servant. The relevant observations are as thus:

> '67. From the aforesaid decisions, in my opinion, the law appears to be well settled. The primary object of the legislature behind Section 197 of the Code is to protect public officers who have acted in discharge of their duties or purported to act in discharge of such duties. But, it is equally well settled that the act said to have been committed by a public officer must have reasonable connection with the duty sought to be discharged by such public officer. If the act complained of has no nexus, reasonable connection or relevance to the official act or duty of such public servant and is otherwise illegal, unlawful or in the nature of an offence, he cannot get

shelter under Section 197 of the Code. In other words, protection afforded by the said Section is qualified and conditional.

68. Mr Tulsi, no doubt, submitted that the Appellant was a police officer. He was on duty. He had received a message about rioting and law and order situation at Beliaghata. He, therefore, had gone to the spot pursuant to the said message, in police uniform, in police jeep to deal with the situation. All the ingredients of Section 197 of the Code were thus satisfied and the High Court was wrong in not applying the said provision.

69. I am unable to agree with Mr Tulsi. In my judgment, it is precisely in such cases that the Court is called upon to consider whether the public servant was acting or purporting to act in discharge of his duty or it was merely a cloak for doing illegal act under the excuse of his status as a public servant and by taking undue advantage of his position, he was committing an offence or an unlawful act. In such situations, when the question comes up for consideration before a Court of law as to the applicability or otherwise of Section 197 of the Code, it is not only the power but the duty of the Court to apply its mind to the fact situation before it. It should ensure that on the one hand, the public servant is protected if the case is covered by Section 197 of the Code and on the other hand, appropriate action would be allowed to be taken if the provision is not attracted and under the guise of his position as public servant, he is trying to take undue advantage.'

(Emphasis supplied)

(60.) In *Choudhury Parveen Sultana vs State of West Bengal and Another* reported in (2009) 3 SCC 398 the appellant's husband had suffered grievous injury in a shoot-out for which a case was registered and police investigation was undertaken. The appellant had filed a complaint before the Magistrate that the respondent no. 2 (Investigating Officer) and the co-accused visited her house under the pretext of conducting an investigation, threatened her and her husband to make a tutored statement and had also tried to obtain the husband's signature on a blank paper under threatening circumstances. While the Magistrate had taken cognisance, the High Court had quashed the proceedings for want of sanction. In such circumstances, the following observations were made:

> '18. The direction which had been given by this Court, as far back as in 1971 in Bhagwan Prasad Srivastava case [(1970) 2 SCC 56 : 1970 SCC (Cri) 292 : (1971) 1 SCR 317] holds good even today. <u>All acts done by a public servant in the purported discharge of his official duties cannot as a matter of course be brought under the protective umbrella of Section 197 CrPC. On the other hand, there can be cases of misuse and/or abuse of powers vested in a public servant which can never be said to be a part of the official duties required to be performed by him.</u> As mentioned in Bhagwan Prasad Srivastava case [(1970) 2 SCC 56 : 1970 SCC (Cri) 292 : (1971) 1 SCR 317] the underlying object of Section 197 CrPC is to enable the authorities to scrutinise the allegations made against a public servant to shield him/her against frivolous, vexatious or false prosecution initiated with the main object of causing embarrassment and harassment to the said official. <u>However, as indicated hereinabove, if the authority vested in a public servant is misused for doing things which are not otherwise permitted under the law, such acts cannot claim the protection of Section 197 CrPC and have to be considered dehors the duties which a public servant is required to discharge or perform. Hence, in respect of prosecution for such excesses or misuse of authority, no protection can be demanded by the public servant concerned.</u>
>
> 19. In the instant case, certain deeds and acts have been attributed to Respondent 2 and another accused, which cannot be said to have been part of the official duties to be performed by Respondent 2. Hence, in our view, Respondent 2 was not entitled to the protection of Section 197 CrPC in respect of such acts.'
>
> (Emphasis supplied)

The Court, while stating that the respondent no. 2 was not entitled to the protection under Section 197 CrPC, was of the view that if the authority which has been vested in a public servant is misused or abused for committing acts which are not otherwise permitted under the law, one cannot claim recourse under Section 197 CrPC. In such circumstances, the acts committed must be considered dehors the duties which a public servant is required to discharge or perform.

(61.) In *Urmila Devi vs Yudhvir Singh* reported in (2013) 15 SCC 624, a complaint was filed by M alleging that the appellant and R were living in an illicit relationship. Therefore, the respondent Sub-Divisional Magistrate directed the Tehsildar to enquire into the matter and also directed the DSP concerned to conduct a special investigation. It was alleged that the respondent had forcibly entered the house of the appellant at 10.00 p.m. with his investigation team, equipped with video cameras, to carry out a search of the appellant's house. It was further alleged that R was forced to remove his clothes in front of the other officials and that both the appellant and R were taken to a Civil Hospital where they were forced to undergo a medical examination against their will. The medical examination of the appellant was also alleged to have been conducted by a male doctor. Furthermore, it was alleged that when the appellant and R filed a complaint against M, the respondent threatened them to withdraw the same. The Court stated that none of the acts alleged against the respondent, can by any stretch of imagination, be held to have been carried out in his capacity as an Executive Magistrate. Hence, the invocation of Section 197 CrPC was wholly uncalled for. While emphasising that the test of direct and reasonable connection between the official duty of the accused and the acts allegedly committed by him is the true test, the Court stressed that public functionaries cannot, under the cloak of the purported discharge of official duties, resort to the harassment and humiliation of the citizens on the pretext of a complaint having been received by them. The relevant observations are reproduced hereinbelow:

> '63. The test of direct and reasonable connection between the official duty of the accused and the acts allegedly committed by them is, therefore, the true test to be applied while deciding whether the protection of Section 197 CrPC is available to a public servant accused of the commission of an offence. The High Court has not adverted to this test nor has it held that there existed a direct and reasonable connection between the official duty being discharged by the accused public servant and the acts committed by him. The High Court has on the contrary misdirected itself when it said that the accused had only committed an act of omission towards his official duties which entitled him to the protection of Section 197 of the Code.

65. It is difficult to appreciate what the High Court meant by saying that the acts of the accused were "at best acts of omission towards official duty". It was not the case of the respondent before the High Court nor is it his case before us that the complaint filed by Maya Devi disclosed any offence which could be taken cognisance of by him as an Executive Magistrate or investigated by the police. Assuming that the complainant and RC Chopra were living together even when they were not married to each other, the complaint regarding any such relationship could be filed only by the wife of RC Chopra, or the husband of the complainant Urmila Devi. The complaint filed by Maya Devi could not provide a valid basis for the SDM, the Tehsildar or the Deputy Superintendent of Police concerned to barge into the house of the complainant, humiliate or harass her or drag her to the police station without the registration of any case or subject her to an uncalled for medical examination. The test of direct and reasonable connection between the official duty of the respondent Sub-Divisional Magistrate and the police officers concerned and the acts complained of thus fails in the present case especially because there is not even a semblance of a lawful justification forthcoming from the respondent for what he did. Entering the house of a woman, after sunset with a posse of police force, carrying video cameras conducting an unwarranted search of the house, humiliating and invading the privacy of the complainant, insulting and humiliating RC Chopra by asking him to undress and dragging both of them to the police station for medical examination against their wishes, especially when male doctors were asked to examine the complainant which added insult to injury, all remain unsupported by any lawful justification and have no connection with the duties that were cast upon the respondent as a public servant, even if a complaint alleging an adulterous relationship between the appellant and RC Chopra had been received by the SDM. The alleged acts of the respondent cannot, therefore, be said to be in discharge of his official duties or in the purported discharge of such duties.

66. Public functionaries cannot under the cloak of purported discharge of official duties resort to harassment and humiliation of the citizens on the pretext of a complaint having been received by them, especially when the same does not disclose the commission of any offence triable by the

Executive Magistrate or cognisable by the police; nor was there any other proceeding in connection with which such conduct could be justified in law. The plea of the respondent that the prosecution was barred under Section 197 CrPC has, therefore, to be rejected.'

(Emphasis supplied)

(62.) In *Rajib Ranjan vs R. Vijaykumar* reported in (2015) 1 SCC 513, a complaint was filed against the appellant public officials for conspiracy to create false documents. This Court had held that even while discharging official duties, if a public servant enters into a criminal conspiracy or indulges in criminal misconduct, such a misdemeanor must not be treated as an act in the discharge of his official duties in order to grant protection under Section 197 CrPC and elaborated as follows:

'15. The sanction, however, is necessary if the offence alleged against the public servant is committed by him "while acting or purporting to act in the discharge of his official duties". In order to find out as to whether the alleged offence is committed while acting or purporting to act in the discharge of his official duty, the following yardstick is provided by this Court in Budhikota Subbarao [*State of Maharashtra vs Budhikota Subbarao*, (1993) 3 SCC 339 : 1993 SCC (Cri) 901 : (1993) 2 SCR 311] in the following words : (SCC p. 347, para 6)

"6. ... If on facts, therefore, it is prima facie found that the act or omission for which the accused was charged had reasonable connection with discharge of his duty then it must be held to be official to which applicability of Section 197 of the Code cannot be disputed."

16. This principle was explained in some more detail in *Raghunath Anant Govilkar vs State of Maharashtra* [(2008) 11 SCC 289 : (2009) 1 SCC (Cri) 130] , which was decided by this Court on 8 February 2008 in SLP (Crl.) No. 5453 of 2007, in the following manner: (SCC pp. 298- 99, para 11)

"11. '7. ... "66. ... On the question of the applicability of Section 197 of the Code of Criminal Procedure, the principle laid down in two cases, namely, *Shreekantiah Ramayya Munipalli vs State of Bombay* [AIR 1955 SC 287 :

1955 Cri LJ 857] and *Amrik Singh vs State of Pepsu* [AIR 1955 SC 309 : 1955 Cri LJ 865] was as follows : (Amrik Singh case [AIR 1955 SC 309 : 1955 Cri LJ 865] , AIR p. 312, para 8)

'8. ... It is not every offence committed by a public servant that requires sanction for prosecution under Section 197(1) of the Criminal Procedure Code; nor even every act done by him while he is actually engaged in the performance of his official duties; but if the act complained of is directly concerned with his official duties so that, if questioned, it could be claimed to have been done by virtue of the office, then sanction would be necessary....'

The real question therefore, is whether the acts complained of in the present case were directly concerned with the official duties of the three public servants. As far as the offence of criminal conspiracy punishable under Section 120-B read with Section 409 of the Penal Code is concerned and also Section 5(2) of the Prevention of Corruption Act, are concerned they cannot be said to be of the nature mentioned in Section 197 of the Code of Criminal Procedure. To put it shortly, it is no part of the duty of a public servant, while discharging his official duties, to enter into a criminal conspiracy or to indulge in criminal misconduct. Want of sanction under Section 197 of the Code of Criminal Procedure is, therefore, no bar." [Ed. : As observed in *Harihar Prasad vs State of Bihar*, (1972) 3 SCC 89, 115, para 66 : 1972 SCC (Cri) 409.]' [Ed. : Quoted from *State of Kerala vs V. Padmanabhan Nair*, (1999) 5 SCC 690, 692, para 7 : 1999 SCC (Cri) 1031.]"

17. Likewise, in *Shambhoo Nath Misra vs State of UP* [(1997) 5 SCC 326 : 1997 SCC (Cri) 676 : AIR 1997 SC 2102] , the Court dealt with the subject in the following manner : (SCC p. 328, para 5)

"5. The question is when the public servant is alleged to have committed the offence of fabrication of record or misappropriation of public fund, etc. can he be said to have acted in discharge of his official duties? It is not the official duty of the public servant to fabricate the false record and misappropriate the public funds, etc. in furtherance of or in the discharge of his official duties. The official capacity only enables him to fabricate the record or misappropriate the public fund, etc. It does not mean that it is integrally connected or inseparably interlinked with the crime committed in the course of same transaction, as was believed by the learned Judge. Under these circumstances, we are of the opinion that the view expressed by the High Court as well as by the trial Court on the question of sanction is clearly illegal and cannot be sustained."

18. The ratio of the aforesaid cases, which is clearly discernible, is that even while discharging his official duties, if a public servant enters into a criminal conspiracy or indulges in criminal misconduct, such misdemeanour on his part is not to be treated as an act in discharge of his official duties and, therefore, provisions of Section 197 of the Code will not be attracted. In fact, the High Court has dismissed the petitions filed by the appellant precisely with these observations, namely, the allegations pertain to fabricating the false records which cannot be treated as part of the appellants' normal official duties. The High Court has, thus, correctly spelt out the proposition of law. The only question is as to whether on the facts of the present case, the same has been correctly applied.'

(Emphasis supplied)

(63.) The purpose behind the enactment of Section 197 CrPC must not be to shield corrupt officials and this was the position taken in *Inspector of Police and Another vs Battenapatla Venkata Ratnam* and Another reported in (2015) 13 SCC 87. Here, the Respondents while working as Sub-Registrars in various offices of the State of Andhra Pradesh had conspired with stamp vendors, document writers and other staff to manipulate the registers and had gotten the documents registered with the old value of the respective properties, resulting in wrongful gain to themselves and loss to the Government. Such acts were held to not be in the discharge of their official duty. The observations made are reproduced hereinbelow:

'11. The alleged indulgence of the officers in cheating, fabrication of records or misappropriation cannot be said to be in discharge of their official duty. Their official duty is not to fabricate records or permit evasion of payment of duty and cause loss to the revenue. Unfortunately, the High Court missed these crucial aspects. The learned Magistrate has correctly taken the view that if at all the said view of sanction is to be considered, it could be done at the stage of trial only.'

(Emphasis supplied)

(64.) This Court in *Surinderjit Singh Mand and Another vs State of Punjab and Another* reported in (2016) 8 SCC 722 was faced with a factual scenario wherein an accused was allegedly arrested in a theft case by the Appellant police officers on 24 June 1999 but was formally and officially shown to have been arrested only on 28 June 1999. Prosecution was initiated against the Appellant officers on the basis of an FIR registered at the instance of the mother of the accused in relation to the alleged illegal detention of the accused for the period from 24 June 1999 to 28 June 1999. While holding that no sanction to prosecute was required in the circumstances of an illegal detention, this Court observed as thus:

> '23. Having given our thoughtful consideration to the contention advanced at the hands of the learned counsel for the Respondents, we are of the view that the decision rendered by this Court in *PP Unnikrishnan* case *[PP Unnikrishnan vs Puttiyottil Alikutty*, (2000) 8 SCC 131 : 2000 SCC (Cri) 1460] is clear and emphatic. The same does not leave any room for making any choice. It is apparent that the official arrest of Neeraj Kumar in terms of the provisions of the Code, referred to hereinabove, would extend during the period from 28 June 1999 to 30 June 1999. The above period of apprehension can legitimately be considered as having been made "while acting or purporting to act in the discharge of their official duties". The factual position expressed by the Appellants is that Neeraj Kumar was not detained for the period from 24 June 1999 to 28 June 1999. His detention during the above period, if true, in our considered view, would certainly not emerge from the action of the accused while acting or purporting to act in the discharge of their official duties. If it emerges from the evidence adduced before the trial Court that Neeraj Kumar was actually detained during the period from 24 June 1999 to 28 June 1999, the said detention cannot be taken to have been made by the accused while acting or purporting to act in the discharge of their official duties. More so, because it is not the case of the Appellants that they

had kept Neeraj Kumar in jail during the period from 24 June 1999 to 28 June 1999. If they had not detained him during the above period, it is not open to anyone to assume the position that the detention of Neeraj Kumar, during the above period, was while acting or purporting to act in the discharge of their official duties. Therefore, in the peculiar facts and circumstances of this case, based on the legal position declared by this Court in PP Unnikrishnan case [PP Unnikrishnan vs Puttiyottil Alikutty, (2000) 8 SCC 131 : 2000 SCC (Cri) 1460], we are of the considered view that sanction for prosecution of the accused in relation to the detention of Neeraj Kumar for the period from 24 June 1999 to 28 June 1999 would not be required before a Court of competent jurisdiction takes cognisance with reference to the alleged arrest of Neeraj Kumar. We therefore hereby, endorse the conclusions drawn by the High Court to the above effect.'

(Emphasis supplied)

(65.) Thus, the legal position that emerges from a conspectus of all the decisions referred to above is that it is not possible to carve out one universal rule that can be uniformly applied to the multivarious facts and circumstances in the context of which the protection under Section 197 CrPC is sought for. Any attempt to lay down such a homogenous standard would create unnecessary rigidity as regards the scope of application of this provision. In this context, the position of law may be summarized as under:

(i.) The object behind the enactment of Section 197 CrPC is to protect responsible public servants against institution of possibly false or vexatious criminal proceedings for offences alleged to have been committed by them while they are acting or purporting to act in their official capacity. It is to ensure that the public servants are not prosecuted for anything which is done by them in the discharge of their official duties, without any reasonable cause. The provision is in the form of an assurance to the honest and sincere officers so that they can perform their public duties honestly, to the best of their ability and in furtherance of public interest, without being demoralised.

(ii.) The expression 'any offence alleged to have been committed by him while acting or purporting to act in the discharge of his official duty' in Section 197 CrPC must neither be construed narrowly nor widely and the correct approach would be to strike a balance between the two extremes. The Section should be construed strictly to the extent that its operation is limited only to those acts which are discharged in the 'course of duty'. However, once it has been ascertained that the act or omission has indeed been committed by the public servant in the discharge of his duty, then a liberal and wide construction must be given to a particular act or omission so far as its 'official' nature is concerned.

(iii.) It is essential that the Court while considering the question of applicability of Section 197 CrPC truly applies its mind to the factual situation before it. This must be done in such a manner that both the aspects are taken care of viz., on one hand, the public servant is protected under Section 197 CrPC if the act complained of falls within his official duty and on the other, appropriate action be allowed to be taken if the act complained of is not done or purported to be done by the public servant in the discharge of his official duty.

(iv.) A public servant can only be said to act or purport to act in the discharge of his official duty, if his act is such that it lies within the scope and range of his official duties. The act complained of must be integrally connected or directly linked to his duties as a public servant for the purpose of affording protection under Section 197 CrPC. Hence, it is not the duty which requires an examination so much as the 'act' itself.

(v.) One of the foremost tests which was laid down in this regard was – whether the public servant, if challenged, can reasonably claim that, what he does, he does in virtue of his office.

(vi.) Later, the test came to be re-modulated. It was laid down that there must be a reasonable connection between the act done and the discharge of the official duty and the act must bear such relation to the duty such that the accused could lay a reasonable, but not a pretended or fanciful claim, that his actions were in the course of performance of his duty. Therefore, the sine qua non for the applicability of this Section is that the offence charged, be it one of commission or omission, must be committed by the public servant either in his official capacity or under the colour of the office held by him such that there is a direct or reasonable connection between the act and the official duty.

(vii.) If in performing his official duty, the public servant acts in excess of his duty, the excess by itself will not be a sufficient ground to deprive the public servant from protection under Section 197 CrPC if it is found that there existed a reasonable connection between the act done and the performance of his official duty.

(viii.) It is the 'quality' of the act that must be examined and the mere fact that an opportunity to commit an offence is furnished by the official position would not be enough to attract Section 197 CrPC.

(ix.) The legislature has thought fit to use two distinct expressions 'acting' or 'purporting to act'. The latter expression means that even if the alleged act was done under the colour of office, the protection under Section 197 CrPC can be given. However, this protection must not be excessively stretched and construed as being limitless. It must be made available only when the alleged act is reasonably connected with the discharge of his official duty and not merely a cloak for doing the objectionable act.

(x.) There cannot be any universal rule to determine whether there is a reasonable connection between the act done and the official duty, nor is it possible to lay down such a rule. However, a 'safe and sure test' would be to consider if the omission or neglect on the part of the public servant to commit the act complained of would have made him answerable for a charge of dereliction of his official duty. If the answer to this question is in the affirmative, the protection under Section 197 CrPC can be granted since there was every connection with the act complained of and the official duty of the public servant.

(xi.) The provision must not be abused by public servants to camouflage the commission of a crime under the supposed colour of public office. The benefit of the provision must not be extended to public officials who try to take undue advantage of their position and misuse the authority vested in them for committing acts which are otherwise not permitted in law. In such circumstances, the acts committed must be considered dehors the duties which a public servant is required to discharge or perform.

(xii.) On an application of the tests as aforesaid, if on facts, it is prima facie found that the act or omission for which the accused has been charged has a reasonable connection with the discharge of his official duty, the applicability of Section 197 CrPC cannot be denied.

(66.) At the cost of repetition, we say that the position of law on the application of Section 197 CrPC is clear – that it must be decided based on the peculiar facts and circumstances of each case. This Court has held in a legion of decisions that any misuse or abuse of powers by a public servant to do something that is impermissible in law like threatening to provide a tutored statement or trying to obtain signatures on a blank sheet of paper; causing the illegal detention of an accused; engaging in a criminal conspiracy to create false or fabricated documents; conducting a search with the sole object of harassing and threatening individuals, amongst others, cannot fall under the protective umbrella of Section 197 CrPC.

(67.) In light of the same, it follows that when a police official is said to have lodged a false case, he cannot claim that sanction for prosecution under Section 197 CrPC was required since it can be no part of the official duty of a public official to lodge a bogus case and fabricate evidence or documents in connection with the same. On examining the quality of the act, it is evident that there exists no reasonable or rational nexus between such an act and the duties assigned to the public servant for the claim that it was done or purported to be done in the discharge of his official duty. The mere fact that an opportunity to register a false case was furnished by the official duty would certainly not be sufficient to apply Section 197 CrPC. Allowing so, would enable the accused to use their status as public servants as a facade for doing an objectionable, illegal and unlawful act and take undue advantage of their position. If the Case Crime No. 967 of 2007 registered at the Murar Police Station, Gwalior, by Respondent Nos. 3, 4 and 5 respectively, was a false case, then there is no doubt that the refusal to grant sanction would not operate as a bar for their prosecution. Moreover, as far as the case of Respondent No. 1 is concerned, it is an undisputed fact that he was not even posted as the SHO or TI at the Murar Police Station when the said false case was registered. The same is evident from the affidavit submitted by the IO at Firozabad before the High Court. Additionally, the Respondent No. 1 has himself admitted in his submissions before us that he was in fact posted at District Shivpuri which is 120 km away from Gwalior during the relevant time. Therefore, any act or offence committed by the Respondent No. 1 in the present case can safely be said to have been outside the scope of his official duty which obviates the question of sanction for his prosecution.

(68.) Having said the above, the question whether sanction is required or not is a question that may arise at any stage of the proceeding. There might arise situations where the complaint or the police report may not disclose that the act constituting the offence was done or purported to be done in the discharge of official duty. However, the facts subsequently coming to light may establish the necessity for sanction. That the necessity of sanction may also reveal itself in the course of the progress of the case as was laid out in Matajog (supra) as follows:

> '20. Is the need for sanction to be considered as soon as the complaint is lodged and on the allegations therein contained? At first sight, it seems as though there is some support for this view in *Hori Ram* case [(1939) FCR 159, 178] and also in *Sarjoo Prasad vs King-Emperor* [(1945) FCR 227]. Sulaiman, J says that as the prohibition is against the institution itself, its applicability must be judged in the first instance at the earliest stage of institution. Varadachariar, J also states that the question must be determined with reference to the nature of the allegations made against the public servant in the criminal proceeding. But a careful perusal of the later parts of their judgments shows that they did not intend to lay down any such proposition. Sulaiman, J refers (at P-179) to the prosecution case as disclosed by the complaint or the police report and he winds up the

> discussion in these words: "Of course, if the case as put forward fails or the defence establishes that the act purported to be done is in execution of duty, the proceedings will have to be dropped and the complaint dismissed on that ground". The other learned Judge also states at p. 185, "At this stage we have only to see whether the case alleged against the Appellant or sought to be proved against him relates to acts done or purporting to be done by him in the execution of his duty". It must be so. The question may arise at any stage of the proceedings. The complaint may not disclose that the act constituting the offence was done or purported to be done in the discharge of official duty; but facts subsequently coming to light on a police or judicial inquiry or even in the course of the prosecution evidence at the trial, may establish the necessity for sanction. Whether sanction is necessary or not may have to be determined from stage to stage. The necessity may reveal itself in the course of the progress of the case.'
>
> (Emphasis supplied)

(69.) In *Pukhraj vs State of Rajasthan and Another* reported in (1973) 2 SCC 701, the 2nd Respondent was alleged to have abused and kicked his clerk who was his subordinate and was charged under Sections 323 and 504 IPC. The Court opined that such an act cannot be said to be in the purported exercise of his duty and held that sanction under Section 197 CrPC was not necessary. However, it was also observed that the necessity of sanction may reveal itself in the course of progress of the case and that it would be open to the accused to place materials on record during the trial for showing what his duty was and also that the acts complained of were so interrelated to his duty that protection under Section 197 CrPC must be granted to him. It was observed as follows:

> '3. We must also make it clear that this is not the end of the matter. As was pointed out in *Sarjoo Prasad vs King-Emperor* [AIR 1946 FC 25 : 1954 FCR 227 : 47 Cri LJ 838] referring to the observations of Sulaiman, J in Hori Ram Singh case the mere fact that the accused proposes to raise a defence of the act having purported to be done in execution of duty would not in itself be sufficient to justify the case being thrown out for want of sanction. At this stage we have only to see whether the acts alleged against

the 2nd respondent can be said to be in purported execution of his duty. But facts subsequently coming to light during the course of the judicial inquiry or during the course of prosecution evidence at the trial may establish the necessity for sanction. Whether sanction is necessary or not may have to depend from stage to stage. The necessity may reveal itself in the course of the progress of the case [see observations in *Matajog Dobey vs H.C. Bhari*]. In *Bhagwan Prasad Srivastava vs N.P. Misra* also it was pointed out that it would be open to the Appellant (the 2nd Respondent in this case) to place the material on record during the course of the trial for showing what his duty was and also that the acts complained of were so inter-related with his official duty so as to attract the protection afforded by Section 197 CrPC.'

(Emphasis supplied)

(70.) In *B. Saha (supra)*, the Court went on to observe that they have no quarrel with the proposition that the question of sanction under Section 197 CrPC can be raised and considered at any stage of the proceedings. Moreover, it was also stated that in considering the question whether or not sanction for prosecution was required, it is not necessary for the Court to confine itself to the allegations in the complaint, and it can take into account all the material on record at the time when the question is raised and falls for consideration. Similar to the rationale adopted in *B. Saha (supra), this Court in State of Bihar vs Kamla Prasad Singh and Ors.* reported in (1998) 5 SCC 690 also re-affirmed that while determining whether the public servant was 'acting in the discharge of his official duty', the Court must consider not only the allegations made in the complaint but also other materials available on record.

(71.) In *Bakhshish Singh Brar vs Gurmej Kaur and Another* reported in (1987) 4 SCC 663, the petitioner police officer along with 14 other persons was charged under Sections 148, 149, 302, 323 and 325 IPC for allegedly causing hurt to the complainant and also causing the death of her son. This Court had emphasised that a balance has to be struck between protecting public servants from being harassed in criminal prosecutions and protecting the rights of the citizens against unlawful acts of public servants. This must be done by examining as to what extent and how far is a public servant working in the discharge or purported discharge of his duties and whether the public servant had exceeded his limit. Having said so, it was observed that criminal trials must also not be stayed in all cases at the preliminary stage because that will cause great damage to the evidence. The relevant observations are reproduced hereinbelow:

> '6. In the instant case, it is alleged that grievous injuries were inflicted upon the complainant and as a result of injuries one of the alleged accused had died. The question is while investigating and performing his duties as a police officer was it necessary for the petitioner to conduct himself in such a manner which would result in such consequences. It is necessary to protect the public servants in the discharge of their duties. They must be made immune from being harassed in criminal proceedings and prosecution, that is the rationale behind Section 196 and Section 197 of the CrPC. But it is equally important to emphasise that rights of the citizens should be protected and no excesses should be permitted. "Encounter death" has become too common. In the facts and circumstance of each case protection of public officers and public servants functioning in discharge of official duties and protection of private citizens have to be balanced by finding out as to what extent and how far is a public servant working in discharge of his duties or purported discharge of his duties, and whether the public servant has exceeded his limit. It is true that Section 196 states that no cognisance can be taken and even after cognisance having been taken if facts come to light that the acts complained of were done in the discharge of the official duties then the trial may have to be stayed unless sanction is obtained. But at the same time it has to be emphasised that criminal trials should not be stayed in all cases at the preliminary stage because that will cause great damage to the evidence.'

(Emphasis supplied)

(72.) This Court in *P.K. Pradhan vs State of Sikkim* reported in (2001) 6 SCC 704 re-emphasised that for invoking protection under Section 197 CrPC, the acts of the accused must be such that it cannot be separated from the discharge of the official duty. However, if there was no reasonable connection between the act and the performance of those duties, and the official status only furnishes the occasion or opportunity for the illegal act, then no sanction would be required. The Court acknowledged that the question of sanction can be raised at any time after cognisance i.e., maybe immediately after cognisance or framing of charge or even at the time of conclusion of trial and after conviction as well. However, there may be certain cases where it may not be possible to decide the question of sanction effectively without giving opportunity to the defence to establish that what he did, he did in the discharge of official duty. In such cases, the question of sanction must be left open to be decided in the main judgment which may be delivered upon conclusion of the trial. The relevant observations are as follows:

> '15....It is well settled that question of sanction under Section 197 of the Code can be raised any time after the cognisance; maybe immediately after cognisance or framing of charge or even at the time of conclusion of trial and after conviction as well. But there may be certain cases where it may not be possible to decide the question effectively without giving opportunity to the defence to establish that what he did was in discharge of official duty. In order to come to the conclusion whether claim of the accused that the act that he did was in course of the performance of his duty was a reasonable one and neither pretended nor fanciful, can be examined during the course of trial by giving opportunity to the defence to establish it. In such an eventuality, the question of sanction should be left open to be decided in the main judgment which may be delivered upon conclusion of the trial.
>
> 16. In the present case, the accused is claiming that in awarding contract in his capacity as Secretary, Department of Rural Development, Government of Sikkim, he did not abuse his position as a public servant and works were awarded in favour of the contractor at a rate permissible under law and not low rates. These facts are required to be established which can be done at the trial. Therefore, it is not possible to grant any relief to the appellant at this stage. However, we may observe that during the course of trial, the court below shall examine this question afresh and deal with the same in the main judgment in the light of the law laid down in this case without being prejudiced by any observation in the impugned orders.'
>
> (Emphasis supplied)

(73.) This Court in *Devinder Singh vs State of Punjab* reported in (2016) 12 SCC 87 had observed that sometimes certain questions about the requirement of sanction cannot be decided without evidence and questions like the good faith or bad faith of the public servant can be decided on the conclusion of trial. The relevant observations made are reproduced hereinbelow:

> '39.8. Question of sanction may arise at any stage of proceedings. On a police or judicial inquiry or in course of evidence during trial. Whether sanction is necessary or not may have to be determined from stage to stage and material brought on record depending upon facts of each case. Question of sanction can be considered at any stage of the proceedings. Necessity for sanction may reveal itself in the course of the progress of the case and it would be open to the accused to place material during the course of trial for showing what his duty was. The accused has the right to lead evidence in support of his case on merits.
>
> 39.9. In some cases, it may not be possible to decide the question effectively and finally without giving opportunity to the defence to adduce evidence. Question of good faith or bad faith may be decided on conclusion of trial.
>
> 40. In the instant cases, the allegation as per the prosecution case is that it was a case of fake encounter or death caused by torture whereas the defence of the accused person is that it was a case in discharge of official duty and as the deceased was involved in the terrorist activities and while maintaining law and order the incident has taken place. The incident was in the course of discharge of official duty. Considering the aforesaid principles in case the version of the prosecution is found to be correct, there is no requirement of any sanction. However, it would be open to the accused persons to adduce the evidence in defence and to submit such other materials on record indicating that the incident has taken place in discharge of their official duties and the orders passed earlier would not come in the way of the trial Court to decide the question afresh in the light of the aforesaid principles from stage to stage or even at the time of conclusion of the trial at the time of judgment. As at this stage it cannot be said which version is correct. The trial court has prima facie to proceed on the basis of the prosecution version and can re-decide the question afresh in case from the evidence adduced by the prosecution or by the accused or in any other manner it comes to the notice of the court that there was a reasonable nexus of the incident with discharge of official duty, the court shall re-examine the question of

sanction and take decision in accordance with law. The trial to proceed on the aforesaid basis.'

(Emphasis supplied)

(74.) The legal position that emerges from the discussion of the aforesaid case laws is that:

(i.) There might arise situations where the complaint or the police report may not disclose that the act constituting the offence was done or purported to be done in the discharge of official duty. However, the facts subsequently coming to light may establish the necessity for sanction. Therefore, the question whether sanction is required or not is one that may arise at any stage of the proceeding and it may reveal itself in the course of the progress of the case.

(ii.) There may also be certain cases where it may not be possible to effectively decide the question of sanction without giving an opportunity to the defence to establish that what the public servant did, he did in the discharge of official duty. Therefore, it would be open to the accused to place the necessary materials on record during the trial to indicate the nature of his duty and to show that the acts complained of were so interrelated to his duty in order to obtain protection under Section 197 CrPC.

(iii.) While deciding the issue of sanction, it is not necessary for the Court to confine itself to the allegations made in the complaint. It can take into account all the material on record available at the time when such a question is raised and falls for the consideration of the Court.

(iv.) Courts must avoid the premature staying or quashing of criminal trials at the preliminary stage since such a measure may cause great damage to the evidence that may have to be adduced before the appropriate trial court.

(75.) In the present case, we are concerned with the allegation of registering an FIR i.e., Case Crime No. 967 of 2007 for the offence under Section 34 of the Excise Act at the Murar Police Station, Gwalior, Madhya Pradesh at the instance of the accused Respondents so as to facilitate one Ashok Dixit in raising the plea of alibi in Case Crime No. 617 of 2007 filed at the Dakshin Police Station, Firozabad, Uttar Pradesh for the murder of the Appellant's brother. The Appellant's brother was shot dead at 8.30 a.m. on 12 October 2007 in Firozabad, Uttar Pradesh and the arrest of the accused Ashok Dixit for the offence under the Excise Act is said to have been made at 9.30 a.m. on the very same day in Gwalior, Madhya Pradesh. Evidently the accused in both the cases i.e., Ashok Dixit could not have been simultaneously present at both the places on the same day, especially when the distance between the two locations is 160 km and such a distance cannot be covered by road in one hour. This is precisely the reason why the Appellant asserts that the case registered at Gwalior is false or in other words concocted.

(76.) It is relevant to note that the Trial Court vide its order dated 10 July 2015 held the accused, Ashok Dixit along with 11 others guilty of murder of the Appellant's brother. In doing so, the Trial Court had made some pertinent observations regarding the registration of the case under the Excise Act by the accused Respondents. The Trial Court had arrived at a categorical finding that the second FIR was registered as a result of collusion by the present accused Respondents with Ashok Dixit. It has been observed that the IO at Dakshin, Firozabad after thorough investigation had found out that the entire case was concocted and hence, the charge sheets giving rise to Case Nos. 67 of 2008 and 67A of 2009 had been filed against the accused Respondents for being involved in the conspiracy of murder. The Trial Court also observed that the accused Respondents had been suspended by the SSP, Gwalior and a departmental inquiry had been initiated against them. Adding to the above, the High Court of Madhya Pradesh vide order dated 25 August 2009 had also stayed the proceedings in Case No. 15003 of 2007 (*State vs Ashok Dixit*) under Section 34 of the Excise Act which is pending before the CJM, Gwalior for the reason that a decision in that case might cause severe prejudice to the case of murder of the Appellant's brother.

(77.) The statements of the Respondent Nos. 3, 4 and 5 respectively recorded earlier by the IO at Dakshin, Firozabad during the course of his investigation on 23 January 2008 and later by the SHO of the Murar Police Station, D.S.

Khushawa on 12 February 2008, under Section 161 CrPC, are the only pieces of evidence that have been adduced before us for our consideration. Those statements reveal that – (a) amongst the two panchas of arrest and seizure namely, Shailendra Singh and Triloki Gaur in the alleged false second case i.e., Case Crime No. 967 of 2007, Triloki Gaur was the former driver of the Respondent No. 1, (b) the Respondent No. 1 had arrived at the Murar Police Station shortly after the alleged arrest of Ashok Dixit and had conversed with the SHO of the Murar Police Station, D.S. Khushawa, (c) the Respondent No. 1 also had a conversation with the person arrested by the accused Respondents, and (d) the Respondent No. 1 had asked the SHO of the Murar Police Station, D.S. Khushawa, to release the arrested person on bail stating that he was his relative. However, it is settled law that a statement recorded under Section 161 CrPC does not constitute substantive evidence and can only be utilised for the limited purpose of proving contradictions and/or omissions as envisaged under Section 145 of the Evidence Act, 1872. This has been laid down in a catena of decisions including in *Parvat Singh and Ors. vs State of Madhya Pradesh* reported in (2020) 4 SCC 33 which observed as follows:

> '13.1...However, as per the settled proposition of law a statement recorded under Section 161 CrPC is inadmissible in evidence and cannot be relied upon or used to convict the accused. As per the settled proposition of law, the statement recorded under Section 161 CrPC can be used only to prove the contradictions and/or omissions. Therefore, as such, the High Court has erred in relying upon the statement of PW 8 recorded under Section 161 CrPC while observing that the Appellants were having the lathis.'
>
> (Emphasis supplied)

(78.) The aforesaid position of law was reiterated in *Birbal Nath vs State of Rajasthan* reported in 2023 SCC OnLine SC 1396 which observed as thus:

> '19. Statement given to police during investigation under Section 161 cannot be read as an "evidence". It has a limited applicability in a Court of Law as prescribed under Section 162 of the Code of Criminal Procedure (CrPC).

> 20. No doubt statement given before police during investigation under Section 161 are "previous statements" under Section 145 of the Evidence Act and therefore can be used to cross examine a witness. But this is only for a limited purpose, to "contradict" such a witness. Even if the defence is successful in contradicting a witness, it would not always mean that the contradiction in her two statements would result in totally discrediting this witness. It is here that we feel that the learned Judges of the High Court have gone wrong.'
>
> (Emphasis supplied)

(79.) Moreover, the statements of the two independent witness i.e., Ramesh Yadav and Barelal recorded on 25 October 2008 by the IO at Dakshin, Firozabad, implicating the Respondent No. 1, cannot be taken as a gospel truth either, especially when they were not examined in the Session Trial Nos. 753 and 753A of 2008 respectively which resulted in the conviction of the accused Ashok Dixit. Therefore, we are a bit hesitant to rely on the version of events as stated under these statements recorded under Section 161 CrPC at this stage. It would be best left for the trial Court to decide the truthfulness and veracity of these statements which allegedly prove the case of the prosecution.

(80.) Furthermore, the Respondent No. 1 has contended that no departmental inquiry was ever initiated against him in relation to the registration of Case Crime No. 967 of 2007. However, the Trial Court in its order dated 10 July 2015 has made an observation that the Respondent Nos. 1, 3, 4 and 5 respectively were suspended and also subjected to an inquiry. Whether the departmental inquiry was initiated against all the accused Respondents or just some of them and the exact findings of the inquiry is also an aspect where there exists some ambiguity.

(81.) Having said so, on the other hand, the Respondent Nos. 3, 4 and 5 respectively have also not adduced any credible evidence before us to prima facie establish that it was Ashok Dixit who was arrested at 9.30 a.m. at Murar, Gwalior; that the illegal liquor carried by him was seized, and that he was later released from the Murar Police Station on the directions of SHO, D.S. Khushawa upon furnishing a surety. It is true that the offence contemplated under Section 34 of the Excise Act is bailable and that any accused under the said offence would be entitled to be released on bail from the police station. However, bearing in mind that there exist serious suspicion as to whether an arrest was ever made to begin with and if made, whether it was Ashok Dixit who was indeed arrested, we find ourselves unable to arrive at an appropriate decision at this stage due to lack of reliable and credible evidence to verify the same. The Respondent Nos. 3, 4 and 5 respectively have stated that the accused had identified himself to be Ashok Dixit upon arrest and it is unclear whether the identity of the said accused was further duly verified while the case was registered under the Excise Act. Despite the Appellant's allegation that the release of the said accused on bail from the police station was done hurriedly, almost immediately after arrest, in order to conceal the identity of the person who was released and that an unconnected stranger might have been released from the police station, no other material which substantiates the bona fides of Respondent Nos. 3, 4 and 5 have been made available before us at the present moment.

(82.) It is the case of the IO at Dakshin, Firozabad that sanction for prosecution of the accused Respondents was not granted by the DIG, Gwalior citing the pendency of Case No. 15003 of 2007 in Case Crime No. 967 of 2007 registered for the offence under the Excise Act before the CJM, Gwalior. However, those proceedings have been stayed by the High Court of Madya Pradesh vide order dated 25 August 2009 and therefore, the question of sanction can be re-visited, if found necessary.

(83.) As far as Respondent No. 1 is concerned, it is made clear that there would be no requirement for sanction since he was not acting in the discharge of his official duty by virtue of not being posted at Murar Police Station, Gwalior at the relevant time when the alleged false case was registered. As a consequence, the extent of the involvement of Respondent No. 1 in the alleged conspiracy to murder can be determined by the Trial Court upon a further examination of the evidence adduced before itself. However, so far as the Respondent Nos. 3, 4 and 5 respectively are concerned, if the case of the prosecution that they had also played a dubious role in registering a false case is correct then the requirement of sanction would not be a sin qua non for proceeding further with the criminal proceedings. However, the defence must be given an opportunity to rebut the same by leading appropriate evidence.

(84.) At this juncture on a prima facie examination of the materials adduced before us, we are of the opinion that the criminal proceedings pending before the CJM, Firozabad as Case Nos. 67 of 2008 and 67A of 2009 should not have been quashed at such a preliminary stage. In cases where there is a legitimate doubt as regards whether sanction for prosecution under Section 197 CrPC is required or not, the progress of the trial must not be hampered or unnecessarily delayed. Therefore, the CJM, Firozabad had rightly taken cognisance of the two charge sheets vide its orders dated 24 November 2008 and 10 August 2009 respectively. The High Court committed an error in failing to consider this aspect while quashing the proceedings in Case No. 67 of 2008 and 67A of 2009 respectively vide its impugned order.

(85.) In view of the aforesaid discussion, the trial Court is directed to proceed with the trial and at any stage of the trial if the evidence suggests that the acts complained of were indeed done or purported to be done in the discharge of official duty by Respondent Nos. 3, 4 and 5 respectively or that the FIR registered by them was not bogus, the trial may be stayed for want of sanction. Therefore, the question of sanction only qua Respondent Nos. 3, 4 and 5 respectively is left open to be appropriately decided by the Trial Court at a suitable stage, in accordance with the law, without being prejudiced by any of the observations made in this order as well as in the order passed by the High Court. As these proceedings arise from a case registered more than 16 years ago, the Trial Court is directed to proceed with the trial and conclude it expeditiously preferably within one year from today.

Conclusion

(86.) In light of the aforesaid, the appeals filed by the Appellant are allowed and the impugned order passed by the High Court is set aside.

(87.) We dispose of the present appeals in light of the aforesaid directions.

(88.) Pending application(s), if any, shall stand disposed of.

J.B. Pardiwala, J
Manoj Misra, J

New Delhi
13 December 2024

(2025) I FLR 195 (India)

The Supreme Court of India

Civil Appeal 1943 of 2022

Lt Col Suprita Chandel vs Union of India and Others

Composition of Court: Justice B.R. Gavai and Justice K.V. Viswanathan

Date of Decision: 9 December 2024

Counsel for the Appellant: Mrs. Vibha Dutta Makhija, Senior Advocate with Mr Rakesh Kumar, Advocate on Record

Counsel for the Respondents: Mr. K.M. Nataraj, Additional Solicitor General of India, with Mr. R. Bala, Senior Advocate, Mr. Mukesh Kumar Maroria, Advocate on Record, Mr. Vatsal Joshi, Advocate, Mr. Sanjay Kumar Tyagi, Advocate, Mr. S.S. Rebello, Advocate, Mr. Anuj Srinivas Udupa, Advocate, Mr. Akshay Amritanshu, Advocate and Mr. Siddhant Kohli, Advocate

Summary

This case involved Appellant's application for a permanent commission in the Army Dental Corps. An amendment to the regulations made her ineligible. A group of similarly situated candidates in the Army Dental Corps filed a petitio challenging their ineligibility under the new regulations because they qualified under the previous regulation at the time it was effective. The Armed Forces Tribunal (AFT) granted them relief and ruled the old regulation should apply to them. However, the AFT denied Appellant's application because she did not join the original applicants though her situation was substantially similar. The Supreme Court of India ruled that the decision of the AFT in the earlier case should also apply to the Appellant and once a point of law is decided, others who are similarly placed must not be asked to litigate separately on the same issue.

Headnotes

<u>Facts:</u> Appellant received a short service commission in the Army Dental Corps on 10 August 2008. She qualified to sit for exams for a permanent commission. However, before she could do so, the respondents amended the regulations making her ineligible. Prior to the amendment, the regulation provided that anyone less that 28 years of age could sit for the exam for a permanent commission, but that age limit would be extended to 30 years of age if the candidate had prior commission service and held the requisite qualifications recognized by the Dental Council of India. The amended regulation raised the age extension to 35 years of age but replaced the qualifications. Instead, candidates under the new regulation must have a Masters in Dental Surgery for the extension to be granted. A group of similarly situated applicants filed a petition in the AFT because they qualified under the previous regulation. The AFT granted them relief and allowed them to qualify under the previous regulation. The applicant in this case did not join in that petition because she was on maternity leave at the time. However, when she separately filed a case in the AFT, the same was dismissed by the tribunal.

<u>Issue:</u> Whether a previous order of the AFT should apply to those similarly situated without one having to initiate separate petitions?

<u>Contention of the Parties:</u> Appellant argued that the AFT's order should be quashed, and she should be allowed to qualify for a permanent commission under the previous order of the AFT because she did, in fact, qualify for a permanent commission under the previous regulations. Moreover, her situation was substantially similar to that of the other petitioners in whose favour the AFT had decided.

Respondents argued that the AFT's order dismissing the petition filed by the Appellant should be upheld because she did not join the original petition, and she delayed filing her application.

Held: Applicant was wrongly excluded from the relief the AFT had granted to the original applicants because she was in a substantially similar situation and those who are similarly situated should be given the same benefit as others. The Court held that the Appellant should be considered for a permanent commission with all benefits dated from the grant of the original applicants' commission dated 22 January 2014. The Supreme Court also specifically observed that "it is a well settled principle of law that where a citizen aggrieved by an action of the government department has approached the court and obtained a declaration of law in his/her favour, others similarly situated ought to be extended the benefit without the need for them to go to court."

Cases Cited

Amrit Lal Berry vs. Collector of Central Excise, New Delhi and Ors., (1995) 4 SCC 714.
K.I. Shepherd & Ors. vs. Union of India & Ors. (1987) 4 SCC 431.
State of Maharashtra and Another vs. Chandrakant Anant Kulkarni & Ors. (1981) 4 SCC 130.

JUDGMENT

K.V. Viswanathan, J

(1.) This appeal challenges the order of the Armed Forces Tribunal (AFT) Regional Bench, Lucknow dated 5 January 2022 in Original Application No. 241 of 2021. By the said order, the AFT dismissed the application of the Appellant and declined her prayer for reliefs similar to the ones granted by the judgment dated 22 January 2014 of the AFT Principal Bench in O.A. No. 111 of 2013 and batch, to the Applicants therein. The Appellant claims that those Applicants were identically situated with her.

(2.) The Appellant on 10 March 2008 was commissioned as a Short Service Commissioned Officer in the Army Dental Corps (AD Corps). She was at that time 27 years 11 months and 28 days of age. The regulation, as it then stood, entitled her to three chances for taking up the departmental examination for permanent commission. It also provided extension of age limit. The relevant clauses, namely, Para 12 of Army Instruction 15 of 79 and Para 4(a) and 4(b) of AI 37 of 78 read as under:

> '...Officers granted Short Service Commission will be given three chances for taking up the departmental examination for permanent commission. Two chances will be given after completion of 2 years of service and before completion of 4 years of service and third chance in extended tenure after completion of 5 years of service and before completion of 8 years of service provided they fulfil the conditions of eligibility as laid down in AI 37/78, as amended.'

Paras 4(a) and 4(b) of Annexure 'A' to the AI 37/78

> '(a.) Candidates must not have attained 28 years of age on 31 December of the year of receipt of application from them. This age limit may be extended upto 30 years by the Government of India on the recommendation of the AD Corps Selection Board in the case of candidates with additional Post-Graduate qualifications.
>
> (b.) A candidate with previous commissioned service in the Army Dental Corps will be entitled to extension of the above age limits as given below:-
>
> Full period of previous reckonable service if such service was rendered while in possession of dental qualification recognized by the Dental Council of India (vide para 3 above).'

(Emphasis supplied)

(3.) It is undisputed that the Appellant could not qualify in the first two chances on completion of two years of service and four years of service respectively. On 15 November 2012, her services were extended for another five years. By 9 March 2013 the Appellant had completed five years of service and was eligible to avail of her third chance, subject to age relaxation up to the full period of reckonable service.

(4.) However, on 20 March 2013, amendments were carried out to clause 4(a) and 4(b) of AI 37 of 78 as amended in AI 15 of 79, inasmuch as, while Para 4(a) was amended, Para 4(b) came to be deleted. The amended Para 4(a) of AI 37 of 78 introduced on 20 March 2013, reads as under:

> '(a) Para 4(a) of Annexure 'A' to AI 37/78
>
> Candidates must not have attained 30 years of age on 31 December of the year of receipt of application form from them for Departmental Permanent Commission. The age limit may be extended up to 35 years in respect of those candidates who are in receipt of PG qualification of Masters in Dental Surgery duly recognised by Dental Council of India, at the time of initial commission to Army Dental Corps.'

(5.) The net result was the Appellant was deprived of her third chance since the extension was capped at 35 years and was confined to those who were in receipt of PG qualification of Masters in Dental Surgery on and from 20 March 2013.

(6.) According to the Appellant, officers similarly situated with the Appellant who were also not given an opportunity to appear for the clinical test and interview, in view of the amendment, quickly moved applications before the AFT, Principal Bench in O.A. No. 111 of 2013 and batch of matters raising various contentions and contended that they have been wrongly deprived of availing the third chance for no fault of theirs. Though the amendments to the policy were upheld, the Principal Bench of the AFT granted relief in the following terms in the said batch of matters.

> '35. The other contention of the learned counsel for the Petitioners is that the Government can grant age relaxation in the given facts and circumstances of the case. It is trite that the Government has the power to relax the upper age limit if it is found that operation of the Rule or policy has hardship on the persons working in the Corps. Nothing has been shown that the Government has no power to relax the upper age limit. Now coming to the

question as to whether the operation of the policy has hardship, it would be seen that an exception was provided for SSC Officers for giving the benefit by extending the upper age limit. It is also admitted by the Respondents in Para-41 of their counter that one-time age relaxation in the upper age limit has been granted in the case of an AMC officer who had joined as SSC Officer prior to the issuance of the impugned amendment. By deletion of Para-4(b) some of the SSC Officers became ineligible for permanent absorption. The Petitioners, who were working in the Corps continuously, expected to be given three chances to seek their permanent absorption. However, due to impugned amendment, they have been denied these chances. Therefore, as one-time exception, the Government can relax the upper age limit in respect of those Petitioners who have become ineligible on account of the impugned amendment.

36. In view of the above discussions, all the four petitions stand partly allowed with following directions:-

(1.) The impugned policy of 2013 is held to be intra *vires*.

(2.) A direction is issued to the Respondents to consider the case of the Petitioners, who were eligible in the year 2012 but became ineligible in the year 2013 for grant of permanent absorption on account of amendment of policy after clubbing the selection of 2012 with 2013. Their case shall be considered in terms of the previous policy.

(3.) A further direction is issued to the Respondents to grant one-time age relaxation in favour of the Petitioners for seeking permanent absorption as has been done in the case of AMC officers who had joined as SSC Officer prior to the issuance of the impugned amendment. The entire exercise for consideration of the Petitioners for grant of permanent commission shall be completed within a period of two months from the date of receipt of a copy of this order. The Petitioners' case thereafter shall be considered by the ensuing Board for their permanent absorption in the Corps.'

(7.) According to the Appellant, she could not join the Applicants therein in the litigation as she was in her advance stage of pregnancy and while posted at Bareilly, she proceeded on maternity leave on 16 May 2013. The Appellant delivered a child on 1 July 2013.

(8.) Consequent to the order of the Principal Bench, permanent commissions were granted to officers who were eligible prior to the amendment to avail a third chance but could not avail in view of the amendment of 20 March 2013. The Appellant was not considered because she was not part of the Original Application.

(9.) A representation submitted by the Appellant on 6 September 2014 did not yield any favourable result and was rejected with the following endorsement on 15 September 2014:

> '(1.) Ref advance copy of your application No DS- 12301/05/2004 dated 6 September 2014.
>
> (2.) As per directions of MoD communicated vide DGAFMS letter No12252/CC/AKJ/DGAFMS/LC dated 12 August 2014, hon'ble Armed Forces Tribunal (Principal Bench). New Delhi has granted "one-time" age relaxation in the eligibility criteria "only to the Petitioners". Hon'ble AFT has further clarified that this order will not form a precedence.
>
> (3.) For your info please.'

(Emphasis Supplied)

(10.) At the outset itself, we may say that the phrase 'only to the Petitioners' in the order rejecting the representation is patently erroneous. While the AFT Principal Bench granted relief to the Petitioners, it did not prohibit the department from considering similarly situated persons. Another representation was disposed of on 9 November 2017, inter alia, on the primary ground that she did not meet the criterion. In the meantime, the Appellant's services were further extended for a period of four years on 31 October 2017.

(11.) The Appellant thereafter filed Original Application No. 241 of 2021 before the AFT, Regional Bench, Lucknow seeking relief similar to the ones granted to the batch of Petitioners in O.A. 111 of 2013 by AFT, Principal Bench, New

Delhi which attained finality. For the sake of completion of record, it should be mentioned that the Appellant had in 2014 itself moved to the Armed Forces Tribunal by filing an application in Diary No. 1761 of 2014. However, the said application was withdrawn with liberty to move afresh. Thereafter, again she filed O.A. 70 of 2017 before the Principal Bench which was again withdrawn with liberty to move the appropriate Tribunal. It was thereafter that after making the representation on 4 October 2017 which was rejected on 9 November 2017 and after returning from the Arunachal Pradesh posting and further after the Covid-19 ordeal had reasonably subsided in January 2021, she moved the AFT, Regional Bench, Lucknow by filing O.A. No. 241 of 2021, which has been dismissed by the impugned order.

(12.) The only reasoning given in the impugned order is in the following terms.

> '(d) The Applicant was not a Petitioner in those petitions filed before AFT (PB), New Delhi, therefore, Applicant cannot be granted any relief with regard to relaxation of age limit which is clarified by AFT (PB) in its judgment dated 22 January 2014 that "an officer is not entitled to be absorbed permanent, if he/she has crossed the upper age limits". The benefit of age relaxation was granted to the Petitioners of Original Applications who were eligible in the year 2012 but became ineligible in the year 2013 for grant of permanent absorption on account of amendment of policy after clubbing the selection of 2012 with 2013 considering the terms of the previous policy and were granted one time age relaxation.'

(13.) We have heard Ms Vibha Datta Makhija, learned senior counsel for the Appellant and Mr R Balasubramanian, learned senior counsel for the Respondents. Having considered the submissions of the learned counsels and perused the records, we are of the opinion that the Appellant is entitled to parity with those Applicants who succeeded before the AFT, Principal Bench in O.A. No. 111 of 2013. We say so for the following reasons.

(14.) It is a well settled principle of law that where a citizen aggrieved by an action of the government department has approached the court and obtained a declaration of law in his/her favour, others similarly situated ought to be extended the benefit without the need for them to go to court. [See *Amrit Lal Berry vs Collector of Central Excise, New Delhi and Others* (1975) 4 SCC 714]

(15.) In *K.I. Shephard and Ors. vs Union of India and Others* (1987) 4 SCC 431, this Court while reinforcing the above principle held as under:

> '19. The writ petitions and the appeals must succeed. We set aside the impugned judgments of the Single Judge and Division Bench of the Kerala High Court and direct that each of the three transferee banks should take over the excluded employees on the same terms and conditions of employment under the respective banking companies prior to amalgamation. The employees would be entitled to the benefit of continuity of service for all purposes including salary and perks throughout the period. We leave it open to the transferee banks to take such action as they consider proper against these employees in accordance with law. Some of the excluded employees have not come to Court. There is no justification to penalise them for not having litigated. They too shall be entitled to the same benefits as the Petitioners. ....'
>
> (Emphasis Supplied)

(16.) No doubt, in exceptional cases where the Court has expressly prohibited the extension of the benefit to those who have not approached the Court till then or in cases where a grievance in personam is redressed, the matter may acquire a different dimension, and the department may be justified in denying the relief to an individual who claims the extension of the benefit of the said judgment.

(17.) That is not the situation here. In the submissions too, the Respondents have not been able to point out any valid justification as to how the Applicants who obtained the benefit from the AFT, Principal Bench in O.A. No. 111 of 2013 and batch are not identically situated with the Appellant. Like the Applicants who succeeded, the Appellant was also ripe for the third chance before the amended para-4(a) of AI No. 37 of 1978 was introduced on 20 March 2013. The Principal Bench of the AFT in O.A. No. 111 of 2013 after clearly holding that the Applicants therein were denied the third chance directed consideration of their cases for permanent absorption by granting one-time age relaxation by considering them under the unamended policy.

(18.) The Respondent authorities on their own should have extended the benefit of the judgment of AFT, Principal Bench in O.A. No. 111 of 2013 and batch to the Appellant. To illustrate, take the case of the valiant Indian soldiers bravely guarding the frontiers at Siachen or in other difficult terrain. Thoughts on conditions of service and job perquisites will be last in their mind. Will it be fair to tell them that they will not be given relief even if they are similarly situated, since the judgment they seek to rely on, was passed in the case of certain Applicants alone who moved the Court? We think that would be a very unfair scenario. Accepting the stand of the Respondents in this case would result in this Court putting its imprimatur on an unreasonable stand adopted by the authorities.

(19.) The stand of the Department relying on the judgment of this Court in *State of Maharashtra and Another vs Chandrakant Anant Kulkarni and Others*, (1981) 4 SCC 130 to contend that mere reduction in chance of consideration did not result in deprivation of any right does not appeal to us. The Appellant's case is founded on the principle of discrimination. What is sauce for the goose ought to be sauce for the gander. If the Applicants in O.A. No. 111 of 2013 whom we find are identically situated to the Appellant were found to be eligible to be given a third chance for promotion, because they acquired eligibility before the amendment to AI No. 37 of 1978 on 20 March 2013, we find no reason why the Appellant should not be treated alike.

(20.) The order dated 13 March 2014 in the application for clarification of the AFT, Principal Bench, order of 22 January 2014 and the order dated 19 May 2014 in the review relied upon in the counter affidavit do not in any manner dilute the case of the Appellant herein. In fact, the order dated 13 March 2014 fully supports the Appellant since it extended the benefit to those persons who acquired the eligibility in 2013. As far as the order in review dated 19 May 2014 directing that there would be no dilution in the laid down criterion and the further direction that the order in review shall not form a precedent does not imply that the main order of 22 January 2014 of the Principal Bench, AFT, should not be extended to similarly situated individuals like the Appellant, who has been knocking the doors for relief since September 2014.

(21.) We see no delay in the Appellant approaching the tribunal. The Appellant has been seeking justice from 2014 and the only delay between 2017 to 2021 after the withdrawal of the earlier applications with liberty, was due to the fact that between August 2017 and 2019 she was posted in Arunachal Pradesh and it was during this time that the Appellant made a second representation. Thereafter, the period between March 2020 and January 2021 was on account of Covid-19 pandemic. In any event, since a clear case of discrimination has been made out, we do not want to non-suit the Appellant on the ground of delay. We say so on the special facts of this case.

(22.) We also find that the Appellant—a woman officer—has continuously worked since 2007 and even as late as on 31 October 2017, she was granted extension of another four years of service, and she continues to be in service thereafter also on account of the status quo granted by this Court on 8 March 2022. Not only this, the Appellant was awarded Commendation Card by the Chief of Army Staff on 14 January 2019. It is also undisputed that the Appellant has had a distinguished service and is now posted as Lieutenant Colonel in the Army Dental Corps at Agra.

(23.) We hold that the Appellant was wrongly excluded from consideration when other similarly situated officers were considered and granted permanent commission. Today, eleven years have elapsed. It will not be fair to subject her to the rigours of the 2013 parameters as she is now nearly 45 years of age. There has been no fault on the part of the Appellant.

(24.)On the peculiar facts of this case and since nothing adverse has been placed on record with regard to performance of the Appellant, in exercise of powers under Article 142 of the Constitution, we direct that the Appellant ought to be given Permanent Commission. We direct that the Appellant's case be taken up for grant of Permanent Commission and she be extended the benefit of Permanent Commission with effect from the same date the similarly situated persons who obtained benefits pursuant to the judgment dated 22 January 2014 in O.A. No. 111 of 2013 of the Principal Bench of the AFT. All consequential benefits like seniority, promotion and monetary benefits, including arrears shall be extended to the Appellant. The above directions shall be implemented within a period of four weeks from today.

(25.) The appeal is allowed and the order of the AFT, Regional Bench, Lucknow, dated 5 January 2022 in O.A. No. 241 of 2021 is quashed and set aside. No costs.

B.R. Gavai, J
K.V. Viswanathan, J

New Delhi
9 December 2024

(2025) I FLR 207 (India)

Supreme Court of India

Civil Appeal No. 13730 of 2024

Union of India & Ors. vs Saroj Devi

Composition of the Court: Justice Abhay S. Oka and Justice Augustine George Masih

Date of Decision: 3 December 2024

Counsel for the Appellant: Mr. Vikramjeet Banerjee, A.S.G., Mr. Mukesh Kumar Maroria, Advocate on Record, Ms. Arunima Dwivedi, Advocate, Mr. Shetty Uday Kumar Sagar, Advocate, Ms. Vishakha, Advocate, Mr. Bhuvan Mishra, Advocate

Counsel for the Respondents: Mr. K Parameswar, Senior Advocate, Mr. A K Trivedi, Advocate, Mr. Vaibhav Trivedi, Advocate, Ms. Kanti, Advocate, Ms. Raji Gururaj, Advocate, Mr. Shreenivas Patil, Advocate, Ms. Chitransha, Advocate, Mr. G Anandan, Advocate, Mr. B Sasikumar, Advocate, Mrs. Harini Ramsankar, Advocate, M/S Ram Sankar & Co, Advocate on Record

Summary

Naik Inderjeet Singh, an Indian Army soldier, tragically died on 23 January 2013, while on duty in the Line of Control for Area Domination Patrol. He experienced cardiopulmonary arrest due to breathing difficulties in extreme climate conditions. He was declared dead upon reaching Chowkibal's Medical Inspection (MI) room. Although his death was initially classified as a "battle casualty," it was later reclassified as a "physical casualty attributable to military service." His widow received terminal benefits and a Special Family Pension but was denied Liberalised Family Pension (LFP) which is granted to deaths in operational areas. Consequently, she filed an application before the Armed Forces Tribunal to challenge the denial of LFP. The Tribunal ruled in her favour, granting her LFP and ex-gratia payment. The Union of India challenged the decision of the AFT stating that LFP can only be granted in deaths in actual operations as held by the Supreme Court in another decision. The Supreme Court of India ruled in favor of the widow and dismissed the appeal filed by the Union of India with costs, holding her entitled to benefits and also observing that in the earlier decision cited by the Union of India, the death of the service-member had occurred due to a heart attack in a room.

Headnotes

<u>Facts:</u>-The respondent was the widow of Naik Inderjeet Singh, who was employed by the Indian Army from 1996 until his death on 23 January 2013. On the morning of his death, the deceased was on duty near the Line of Control along the Anti Infiltration Obstacle System. The deceased began to complain of breathlessness while on duty and was found to be in critical condition by the regimental medical officer. As a result of the climatic conditions, he could not be air evacuated as needed and had to be evacuated on foot. Upon reaching Chowkibal's MI room, he was declared dead because of cardiopulmonary arrest. The deceased's death was classified as a "battle casualty," then later classified as a "physical casualty" attributable to military service. The respondent was granted terminal benefits and a Special Family Pension. However, she was denied a Liberalised Family Pension (LFP). The respondent filed an original application with the Armed Forces Tribunal (AFT), seeking to quash the order denying the LFP and praying for the same to be granted with interest. The Tribunal ruled in favor of the respondent, granting the LFP. The Union of India appealed. The appeal was dismissed with a judgment in favor of the respondent, granting her Rs.50,000.

<u>Issue(s):</u> Should the deceased's death be classified as a "battle casualty" thereby entitling her to LFP? The question was answered in the affirmative by the Supreme Court of India

Reasoning: The appellants/Union of India argued that LFP should be granted when a soldier dies in the circumstances mentioned in categories D and E of paragraph 4.1 of the Government letter dated 31 January 2001 which required the soldier to have died in actual operations to be entitled to LFP. However, this court held that the deceased's death should be classified as a "battle casualty" as it fell within the said definition as per "Army Order 1 of 2003", clause (g) of Appendix A which defines a "battle casualties" to include those occurring on the Line of Control, even if the death is ultimately caused by extreme climate conditions. The Court observed that because the deceased soldier died while on duty near the Line of Control in extreme climate conditions, the death should have been classified as a "battle casualty" thereby entitling the widow to LFP. The judgments cited by the Union of India to contest the claim were distinguished by Court. It was held that in the case Kanchan Dua Vs Union of India, the soldier had died in his room and in Radhika Devi Vs Union of India the solider had not died due to extreme climatic conditions. The court also strongly observed that "the respondent ought not to have been dragged to this court" and granted Rs.50,000 in costs to the respondent-widow.

Held: The Civil Appeal filed by the Union of India dismissed. Compensation granted to respondent.

JUDGMENT

Abhay S. Oka, J

(1.) Leave granted.

Factual Aspect

(2.) The Respondent is the widow of late Nk Inderjeet Singh (for short, 'the deceased'). The deceased was employed in the Indian Army on 27 February 1996. He was part of an Area Domination Patrol. The Area Domination Patrol was launched from Manjit Main to Rangwar Post for domination of the Rangwar Gap in the proximity of the Line of Control (for short, 'LC') along the Anti Infiltration Obstacle System (for short,'AIOS'). A fence built by the Indian Army to prevent cross-border infiltration is known as AIOS. He complained of breathlessness during duty in extreme climatic conditions from 1.00 a.m. to 3.30 a.m. on 23 January 2013. He was taken to the nearby Rangwar Post. The regimental medical officer found the condition of the deceased very critical. He could not be air-evacuated due to bad weather. Therefore, he was evacuated on foot. When he was taken to Chowkibal's MI room, he was declared dead. The cause of death was cardiopulmonary arrest. His death was initially classified as a 'battle casualty' but was later classified as a 'physical casualty' attributable to military service. The Respondent was granted all terminal benefits, including a Special Family Pension. As she was denied a Liberalised Family Pension (LFP), she filed an Original Application before the Armed Forces Tribunal (for short, the Tribunal). The Respondent sought quashing of the order dated 10 February 2016, by which the benefit of LFP was denied to her. She prayed for a direction to grant her LFP with interest. The Appellants opposed the Original Application. Ultimately, by the impugned judgment dated 23 August 2019, the Tribunal allowed the application and directed that the Respondent be granted LFP and ex-gratia lumpsum amount payable in case of battle casualties dying in harness. The present appeal takes exception to the said judgment and order.

Submissions

(3.) Shri Vikramjeet Banerjee, learned Additional Solicitor General, pointed out that LFP is governed by the order dated 31 January 2001 issued by the Director (Pensions) of the Ministry of Defence, Government of India. He submitted that LFP is granted in case of death of an Armed Forces personnel under the circumstances mentioned in categories D and E of paragraph 4.1 of the order dated 31 January 2001. He submitted that, admittedly, category D does not apply to the deceased. He submitted that the case of the deceased is not covered by any of the clauses in category E. He submitted that as the deceased died due to cardiopulmonary arrest, his case was classified as a 'physical casualty' attributable to military service, and, therefore, the Respondent was paid a Special Family Pension. He relied on this Court's decisions in the case of *Kanchan Dua vs Union of India and Anr.*[1], *and Radhika Devi vs Union of India and Ors.*[2] He submitted that the present case is covered by both decisions. He submitted that the view taken by the tribunal is entirely erroneous.

(4.) Shri K. Parameshwar, learned senior counsel appearing for the Respondent, supported the impugned judgment by relying upon documents annexed to the counter affidavit.

Consideration of Submissions

(5.) We must deal with the factual aspects. In paragraph 4.3 of the Original Application filed by the Respondent, the following are the averments made:

> '4.3 That while the husband of the Applicant was posted in J&K and was part of Area Domination Patrol which was launched from Manjit Main to Rangwar Post for domination of Rangwar Gap in the proximity of LC and along the AIOS in extreme climatic condition on 23 January 2013 from 01.00 hrs to 03.30 hrs. The husband of the Applicant complained of breathlessness and was taken to Rangwar Post where he was given First Aid. The condition of the husband of the Applicant deteriorated and was required for immediate evacuation, but due to the inclement weather, air evacuation could not be done and husband of the Applicant was taken on foot to Chowkibal where he was declared dead. The Commanding Officer of the Unit has issued a Battle Casualty Certificate on 23 January 2013 whereby the death of the husband of the Applicant has been treated as Battle Casualty.'

In the reply filed to the Original Application, the Appellants did not dispute the correctness of the averments made in paragraph 4.3. The Appellants could not have disputed the said facts as they were also mentioned in the certificate issued by the Commanding Officer.

(6.) There is no dispute that the grant of LFP is governed by the order dated 31 January 2001 issued by the Director (Pensions). The said order applies to those who were in service as of 1 January 1996 or joined service thereafter.

---

1. (2020) 18 SCC 709

2. (2020) 18 SCC 715

Clause 6.1 of the order dated 31 January 2001 reads thus:

> **'6. Liberalised Family Pension (LFP)**
>
> 6.1 In case of death of an Armed Forces Personnel under the circumstances mentioned in categories "D" & "E" of para 4.1 above, the eligible member of the family shall be entitled to Liberalised Family Pension equal to reckonable emoluments last drawn as defined in para 3.1 above, both for officers and PBOR. Liberalised Family Pension at this rate shall be admissible to the widow in the case of officers and to the nominated heir in the case of PBOR until death or disqualification.
>
> ....'

(7.) In the present case, the Respondent has not contended that the case of the deceased falls in category D. The tribunal accepted that the case falls in category E, which reads thus:

> **'Category E**
>
> **Death or disability arising as a result of:-**
>
> (a.) Enemy action in international war.
>
> (b.) Action during deployment with a peacekeeping mission abroad.
>
> (c.) Border skirmishes.
>
> (d.) During laying or clearance of mines including enemy mines as also minesweeping operation.
>
> (e.) On account of accidental explosions of mines while laying operationally oriented mine-field or lifting or negotiating minefield laid by enemy or own forces in operational areas near international borders or the line of control.
>
> (f.) **War-like situations, including cases which are attributable to/aggravated by:-**
>
> (i.) Extremist acts, exploding mines etc. while on way to an operational area.

(ii.) Battle inoculation training exercises or demonstration with live ammunition.

(iii.) Kidnapping by extremists while on operational duty.

(g.) An act of violence/attack by extremists, anti-social elements, etc.

(h.) Action against extremists, antisocial elements, etc. Death/ disability while employed in the aid of civil power in quelling agitation, riots or revolt by demonstrators will be covered under this category.

(i.) Operations specially notified by the Government from time to time.'

(Emphasis added)

A perusal of the reply filed to the Original Application shows that the stand of the Appellants is that clause (f) of category E is not applicable as the death of the deceased was attributable to military service and was classified as a 'physical casualty'. It was contended that the death was not treated as a 'battle casualty'. The stand taken is that the case of the deceased was not covered by clause (f) of category E as it was not a case of 'battle casualty' as the deceased died due to cardiopulmonary arrest. Therefore, the only question to be decided is whether the case will be covered by the category of 'battle casualty'.

(8.) It is brought on record that initially, the Commanding Officer had categorised the death as a 'Battle Casualty', and later on, it was changed to a 'physical casualty'. To the counter filed by the Respondent, a copy of Army Order 1 of 2003 has been annexed as Annexure R-6. The circumstances for the classification of physical/battle casualties have been incorporated in Appendix 'A'. In Appendix 'A', category 1 is of battle casualties. Clause (g) thereto reads thus:

> '(g) Casualties occurring while operating on the International Border or Line of Control due to natural calamities and illness caused by climatic conditions.'

(9.) Coming to the facts of the case, it is not disputed that on the date of the death, the deceased was posted with his battalion in Jammu and Kashmir as part of Operation Rakshak. He was part of an Area Domination Patrol for domination of the Rangwar Gap in the proximity of LC. He was doing duty from 1.00 a.m. to 3.30 a.m. The certificate issued by the Commanding Officer records the following facts:

(a.) The deceased was working in extreme climatic conditions on the date of his death;

(b.) He was part of Operation Rakshak, and he was also part of the routine Area Domination Patrol close to LC. There were extreme climatic conditions at that place; and

(c.) When the deceased became breathless, his condition was such that he needed immediate evacuation. However, immediate evacuation by air could not be done due to bad weather conditions. Ultimately, he was taken on foot, and when the team carried him to Chowkibal's MI room, he was declared dead.

(10.) Thus, the death can be attributed to illness caused by extreme climatic conditions. Hence, as per clause 1 (g) of Appendix 'A' of the Army Order 1 of 2003, the case will fall in 'Battle Casualties'. The reason is that the deceased was operating near LC in extreme climatic conditions. He was part of Operation Rakshak and was on duty near LC. The casualty caused by illness due to climatic conditions is covered by clause 1 (g). In this case, the Respondent's husband was a victim of illness caused by extreme climatic conditions. Therefore, the case of the deceased will fall in the category of 'Battle Casualties'.

(11.) Clause (f) of category E is attracted when death arises as a result of war-like situations. The definition of death as a result of war-like situations is an inclusive definition, and the case cannot remain confined to sub-clauses (i) to (iii) of category E (f). In this case, the death has occurred as a result of a war-like situation prevailing near LC. Therefore, we concur with the view taken by the Tribunal that clause (f) of category E was applicable.

(12.) The decisions in the cases of *Kanchan Dua vs Union of India and Anr.*[3] and *Radhika Devi vs Union of India and Ors.*[4] have been decided on the basis of the peculiar facts of the cases. The same can have no application to the facts of this case. In the first case, the deceased was found dead in his room. In the second case, the death was not caused by extreme climatic conditions.

(13.) In our view, in a case like this, the Respondent ought not to have been dragged to this Court, and the decision-making authority of the Appellants ought to have been sympathetic to the widow of a deceased soldier who died in harness. Therefore, we propose to impose costs quantified as Rs. 50,000/-, which will be payable to the Respondent.

(14.) Accordingly, the appeal is dismissed. The directions contained in paragraph 13 of the impugned judgment shall be implemented within a maximum period of three months from today. We direct the Appellants to pay the costs quantified as Rs. 50,000/- to the Respondent within a period of two months from today.

Abhay S. Oka, J
Augustine George Masih, J

New Delhi
3 December 2024

---

3. (2020) 18 SCC 709

4. (2020) 18 SCC 715

(2025) I FLR 216 (India)

Punjab and Haryana High Court

Civil Writ Petition 3676 of 2023

Omvati Devi vs Union of India and Others

Composition of Court: Justice Sureshwar Thakur and Justice Sudeepti Sharma

Date of decision: 29 November 2024

Counsel for the Petitioner: Mr. Navdeep Singh with Ms. Roopan Atwal and Ms. Srishti Sharma, Advocates
Counsel for the Respondent: Ms. Anita Balyan, Advocate for Union of India

Summary

Petitioner prayed before the High Court for the grant of Special Family Pension which was denied by the military and then by the Armed Forces Tribunal (AFT). The husband of Petitioner, Hav Ramvir, was enrolled in the Army on 16 August1983. He was allegedly murdered by Signalman P.K. Dey of the same unit on 02 January 2003. The Petitioner was granted Ordinary Family Pension and not Special Family Pension which is granted in cases of deaths in service which are treated "attributable to or aggravated by service" although the death was declared as "attributable" by the military authroities. She moved an application for grant of Special Family Pension, which was rejected by the accounts branch on the pretext that the husband of the Petitioner was allegedly murdered when he was attempting unnatural sex on the accused and hence, was neither attributable to nor became aggravated by military service. She challenged the denial before the AFT, however, the Tribunal vide order dated 08 March 2021 dismissed the said petition, while concluding that the death of the late husband of the applicant has no causal connection with the military service, so she is not entitled to any Special Family Pension. She then challenged the order of the AFT before the High Court.

Headnotes

Facts: The husband of the present petitioner while being stationed on duty with the Armored Brigade Signal Company, Ratnu Chak, was murdered by a co-soldier namely Sigmn Parshant Kumar Dey. Though the death was declared "attributable to service", Special Family Pension was denied to her on the pretext that her late husband was allegedly attempting unnatural sex on the accused.

Issue: Was the death of the husband of the Petitioner the result of military service?

Held: Uncontrovertedly, the deceased soldier was murdered by co-soldier Parshant Kumar Dey, while his performing duties with the Armored Brigade Signal Company, Ratnu Chak. Therefore, his demise is to be declared to be holding a causal connection with military service. It was also noted that the theory of unnatural sex was also not found correct by the criminal court and the accused was acquitted. The impugned order as passed by the Tribunal concerned, was quashed and set aside with a direction to grant Special Family Pension to the petitioner along with interest @ 7% per annum.

It was further held that the family members of the deceased soldier, who faces a fatal assault from a co-soldier, and that too while his performing duties would be entitled to Special Family Pension by treating the death as "attributable to service" and if they are denied the same, it would result in unjust snatchings of the rights ensuing to the surviving members of the deceased soldiers. Moreover, the denial founded on the above conjectural reasons is required to be discountenanced.

JUDGMENT

Sureshwar Thakur, J

(1.) Through the instant writ petition, the Petitioner herein prays for the setting aside of the order dated 8 March 2021 (Annexure P-1), as passed by the learned Armed Forces Tribunal concerned, wherebys, the prayer made by the Petitioner for the grant of Special Family Pension to her was denied.

Factual Background

(2.) The husband of the Petitioner namely, Hav. Ramvir, was enrolled in the army (Corps of Signals) on 16 August 1983. He was allegedly murdered by Signalman P.K. Dey of the same unit on 2 January 2003 to prevent unnatural sex, as became attempted upon him, by the deceased husband of the Petitioner. The Petitioner was granted ordinary Family Pension. She moved an application for grant of Special Family Pension, which was rejected by the PCDA (Pensions) Allahabad, thus, on the ground that the death of her late husband was owing to the wound/injury, which was neither attributable to nor became aggravated by military service. She submitted an appeal against the order of the PCDA (Pensions) Allahabad, which was vide order dated 6 July 2011 also rejected by the 1st Appellate Authority, on the ground that the death of her husband was not in any way related to military duties, and, therefore is not attributable to military service.

(3.) Feeling aggrieved, the Petitioner filed O.A., before the tribunal concerned for the grant of Special Family Pension. However, the learned tribunal vide order dated 8 March 2021 dismissed the said O.A., while concluding that the death of the late husband of the Applicant has no causal connection with the military service, so she is not entitled to any Special Family Pension.

(4.) Feeling dissatisfied from the afore dis-affirmative order, the Petitioner has filed thereagainst the instant writ petition.

Inferences of this Court

(5.) Admittedly, the husband of the present Petitioner while being stationed on duty with the Armoured Brigade Signal Company, Ratnu Chak, was murdered by a co-soldier namely Sigmn Parshant Kumar Dey. The trial in respect of the offences (supra) became conducted by the Court of 1st Additional Sessions Judge, Jammu. On conclusion of the said trial, a verdict of acquittal became recorded.

(6.) Though, it is contended by the present Respondent that the accused soldier though propagated that in his committing the offence of murder, he became instigated by an ill act of the deceased soldier, comprised in his attempting to make him succumb to his desire of his indulging in un-natural sex with him. However, a reading of the verdict passed by the learned 1st Additional Sessions Judge, Jammu, which becomes appended with the instant writ petition, rather does disclose, that the said defence was neither propagated nor the said defence became accepted. In consequence, the said plea is deemed to be holding no credit worthiness.

(7.) Be that as it may, since un-controvertedly, the deceased soldier was murdered by co-soldier Parshant Kumar Dey, while his performing duties with the Armored Brigade Signal Company, Ratnu Chak. Therefore, his demise is to be declared to be holding a causal connection with his rendering military service. The said conclusion, is but, invincible and was required to be so drawn even by the learned Tribunal in the O.A. (supra). However, the Tribunal concerned without bearing in mind the above factum, thus on mere surmises concluded, that there was no causal connection inter-se the performance of duties by the deceased soldier, thus with his being murdered by a co-soldier, despite reiteratedly when the said commission of murder occurred during the performance of duties by the deceased solider with the Armored Brigade Signal Company, Ratnu Chak. Resultantly therebys there was but the apposite inter-se causal connection besides the lethal assault thus was attributable to rendition of military service.

(8.) If the above inference is not recorded, thereupon, the family members of the deceased soldier, who faces a fatal assault from a co-soldier, and that to while his performing duties, but would be deprived qua the benefits of Special Family Pension. Since the said benefits are to be endowed to the surviving family members of the deceased soldier, who suffers fatal injuries, while his evidently performing duties. However, if they are yet denied the same, it would result in unjust snatchings of the rights ensuing to the surviving members of the deceased soldiers. Moreover, even the denial on supra premise rather is not so explicitly stated in the relevant regulations, which become extracted hereinafter. Therefore, the denial founded on the above conjectural reasons is required to be discountenanced.

> **'Special Family Pension**
>
> **213. A special family pension may be granted to the family of an individual if his death was due to or hastened by**
>
> **(a) a wound, injury or disease which was attributable to military service,**
>
> **OR**
>
> **(b) the aggravation by military service of a wound, injury or disease, which existed before or arose during military service.'**

Final Order of this Court

(9.) In aftermath, this Court finding merit in the writ petition is constrained to allow the same.

(10.) The impugned order as passed by the Tribunal concerned, is quashed and set aside but with a direction to the Respondents to grant Special Family Pension to the Petitioner from the date, the said benefit accrued to her alongwith interest @ 7% per annum.

(11.) Since the main case itself has been decided, thus, all the pending application(s), if any, also stand(s) disposed of.

Sureshwar Thakur, J
Sudeepti Sharma, J

29 November 2024

(2025) I FLR 221 (India)

Punjab and Haryana High Court

Criminal Writ Petition 275/2024

Colonel Jagpreet Singh Bakshi and Another vs Union of India and Others

Composition of the Court: Justice Sureshwar Thakur and Justice Sudeepti Sharma

Date of Decision: 12 November 2024

Counsel for the Petitioners: Mr. Rajesh Sehgal, Mr. Arun Singla and Mr. Navdeep Singh
Counsel for the Respondents: Mr. Rohit Verma, Senior Panel Counsel, Union of India

Summary

The petitioners who were serving Army officers, were alleged to have committed procedural and financial irregularities in 2018. A series of Courts of Inquiry (CsOI) were convened, culminating in disciplinary proceedings and a General Court Martial (GCM) convened in January 2023. The petitioners challenged the GCM's legality, particularly on limitation grounds, before the Armed Forces Tribunal (AFT). The AFT dismissed their petition, declaring it non-maintainable but also deciding the case on merits. The AFT erred by deciding the case on merits after deeming it non-maintainable. This prejudiced their rights to contest the findings before the competent authority, creating a *fait accompli.* The High Court held that the Petition was maintainable and also set aside the AFT's order and remanded the matter for a fresh decision. The AFT was directed to reconsider the case on merits, ensuring procedural propriety and avoiding prejudice to the petitioners' rights. This judgment underscores the expansive jurisdiction of the AFT and reiterates that tribunals must ensure procedural fairness and avoid prejudicial findings when declaring petitions non-maintainable.

Headnotes

Facts: The petitioners, two serving Army officers, were accused of procedural lapses and financial irregularities in a tendering process in August 2018. A Court of Inquiry was convened to investigate the allegations. The first Court of Inquiry could not assemble and was replaced by another inquiry on 19 July 2019. Findings of the new inquiry (dated 25 September 2019) held the petitioners blameworthy. The General Officer Commanding 11 Corps directed disciplinary proceedings on 24 February 2020. The findings of the 2019 inquiry were set aside by the Armed Forces Tribunal (AFT) in 2020. Fresh inquiries were convened in 2021 after the second inquiry was cancelled. A charge sheet was issued on 03 January 2023 under Section 52(f) of the Army Act, 1950. A General Court Martial was convened on 06 January 2023 and assembled on 14 January 2023. The petitioners raised a plea of limitation, which was rejected by the Court Martial on 13 May 2023. The petitioners filed OA No. 862 of 2023 challenging the rejection order by the Court Martial on limitation. The AFT dismissed the OA on both maintainability and merits on 13 December 2023. The AFT held that under Section 15 of the AFT Act it did not have the jurisdiction to hear an appeal against an order passed by a Court Martial unless it is the final order that has been confirmed. Hence, the petitioners sought to challenge the AFT's decision in the High Court.

Issue(s): Whether the AFT possessed the jurisdiction to adjudicate an appeal filed against an order of the Court Martial which was not a final finding or sentence that had been conformed and whether the AFT had also erred in deciding the Original Application (O.A.) on merits after declaring it non-maintainable?

Reasoning: The AFT acted improperly by ruling on merits after declaring the petition non-maintainable. This was a material irregularity and a breach of procedural propriety. The decision on merits effectively prejudiced the petitioners' ability to contest the inquiry findings before the competent authority. The AFT is vested with plenary jurisdiction under Section 15 of the Armed Forces Tribunal Act, 2007, to entertain appeals against any order, decision, finding, or sentence passed by a court-martial or related matters. The AFT's interpretation that it lacked jurisdiction due to the absence of a confirmation order under Section 153 of the Army Act, 1950, was incorrect. The expressions in Section 15(1) and (2) are broad, allowing the AFT to entertain disputes even before a confirmation order is passed. No statutory provision curtails this jurisdiction.

Held: The writ petition was allowed. The impugned order passed by the AFT quashed and set aside by the High Court and the matter remanded back for a fresh decision. The AFT was directed to reconsider the case on merits, ensuring procedural propriety and avoiding prejudice to the petitioners' rights.

JUDGMENT

Sureshwar Thakur, J

(1.) Through the instant writ petition, the Petitioners herein pray for setting aside of the order dated 13 December 2023 (Annexure P-6) as passed by the learned Armed Forces Tribunal concerned (hereinafter for short called as the AFT), whereby, the O.A. filed by the Petitioners has been dismissed on the grounds of maintainability as well as on merits.

Factual Background

(2.) The Petitioners both serving as Army Officers were alleged to have committed certain irregularities in the tendering process in August 2018, which resulted in the convening of Court of Inquiry. Owing to certain administrative reasons, the said Court of Inquiry could not assemble and thus vide order dated 19 July 2019, a fresh Court of Inquiry was ordered. The said Court of Inquiry gave its findings on 25 September 2019, whereby the Applicants were held blameworthy for certain procedural lapses and financial irregularities. The said Court of Inquiry was submitted on 28 September 2019 to the HQ 11 Corps. The general commanding 11 Corps, perused the same and issued directions dated 24 February 2020 for initiation of disciplinary proceedings against the Applicants. Further, the said Court of Inquiry was challenged before the Principal Bench vide O.A. No. 1175 of 2020 and vide order dated 28 November 2020 passed by the AFT concerned, the said Court of Inquiry was set aside. Thereafter, another Court of Inquiry was ordered on 1 January 2021. The said Court of Inquiry was cancelled owing to administrative reasons.

(3.) Thereafter, vide order dated 6 January 2021 another Court of Inquiry was convened. On completion of the said Court of Inquiry, the findings as became recorded thereins were submitted before the competent authority. On the basis of the said Court of Inquiry, directions dated 16 September 2021 were issued by the competent authority viz. General Officer Commanding 11 Corps, that disciplinary action be initiated against the Applicants. Accordingly, Summary of Evidence was recorded and charge sheet dated 3 January 2023 was issued under Section 52 (f) of the Army Act, 1950. Vide order dated 6 January 2023, a General Court-Martial was convened and assembled on 14 January 2023 for trial of the Applicants.

(4.) On behalf of the Applicants, a plea that the bar of limitation is attracted though became raised. However, the same was rejected vide order dated 13 May 2023.

(5.) Feeling aggrieved, the Petitioners filed O.A. No. 862 of 2023 under Sections 14 and 15 of the Armed Forces Tribunal Act, 2007 (hereinafter for short called as the Act), challenging the afore rejection order. The said O.A. became dismissed vide order dated 13 December 2023, on the ground qua the same being non-maintainable. Further, the AFT concerned dismissed the same on merits also.

Submissions of the Learned Counsel for the Petitioners

(6.) The learned counsel for the Petitioners submit that the learned AFT after reaching a conclusion on the O.A. (supra) as became laid before it, qua the same being not maintainable, yet has untenably proceeded to pronounce an order on merits. Therefore, it is contended that the making of a decision on the merits of the *lis*, rather was required to be done by the competent authority, than by the learned AFT concerned. As such, it is contended that the entering into the merits of the lis and also the makings of a decision thereons, has also resulted in a grave prejudice becoming visited upon the present Petitioners, to the extent that therebys the present Petitioners would be estopped to, before the Competent Authority, thus contest the lis on merits.

Inferences of this Court

(7.) The sum and substance of the said submission, is that, the learned AFT after declaring the petition to be premature and thus concomitantly declaring it to be also not maintainable, has yet proceeded to decide the O.A., on merits, wherebys, the apposite findings recorded by the Court of Inquiry, thus become upheld. Resultantly therebys the present Petitioners, in case they assumingly convince the Court of Inquiry, about the validity of their espousal, whereupon, the Court of Inquiry may proceed to not confirm the preliminary Inquiry Report. However, through the making of a decision on the merits of the *lis*, evidently the Petitioners become barred to effectively contest the *lis* on merits before the Court of Inquiry, therebys, the Petitioners naturally became condemned unheard and/or therebys the confirming authority rather would become presented with a *fiat accompli*. The said was required to be obviated by the learned AFT concerned. Consequently, the makings of a decision on the merits of the *lis*, naturally is a sequel of gross non-application of mind besides becomes ridden with a gross material impropriety. Moreover, the vice of illegality also becomes ingrained in the decision on merits, as became recorded on the lis (supra).

(8.) **For the reasons to be assigned hereinafter, the decision recorded on the Original Application, thus by the learned AFT, after an interpretation being made of the provisions carried in Section 15 of the Act, is quashed and set aside and the lis is remanded to the learned AFT for a fresh decision on merits.**

(9.) Since this Court declares the O.A., to be maintainable, therebys the consequent effect thereof, is that, the decision on merits of *lis*, is also required to be re-made by the learned AFT concerned. The reason for concluding so, but irrespective of what has been stated (supra), is that, once jurisdictional competence vested in the learned AFT, to within the ambit of subsection (1) of Section 15 of the Act, thus make a decision qua validity of the preliminary findings, as become recorded by the Court of Inquiry. Therefore, for the able exercisings of the said vested statutory jurisdictional competence in the learned AFT concerned, thus the latter is required to be re-visiting even the merits of the lis. Furthermore, therebys there would be no supra inter-se conflict inter-se the inference, that once the O.A., has been declared to be not maintainable; therebys, there was no requirement for the learned AFT concerned, thus to either enter into the merits of the *lis* or to make a decision thereons.

(10.) For fully understanding the controversy at hand, it is necessary to extract the provisions embodied in Section 15 of the Act, provisions whereof are extracted hereinafter.

> '**15. Jurisdiction, powers and authority in matters of appeal against court-martial.**
>
> (1) Save as otherwise expressly provided in this Act, the Tribunal shall exercise, on and from the appointed day, all the jurisdiction, powers and authority exercisable under this Act in relation to appeal against **any order, decision, finding or sentence passed by a court-martial or any matter connected therewith or incidental thereto.**
>
> (2) Any person aggrieved by an order, decision, finding or sentence passed by a court-martial may prefer an appeal in such form, manner and within such time as may be prescribed.
>
> (3) The Tribunal shall have power to grant bail to any person accused of an offence and in military custody, with or without any conditions which it considers necessary:

Provided that no accused person shall be so released if there appears reasonable ground for believing that he has been guilty of an offence punishable with death or imprisonment for life.

(4.) The Tribunal shall allow an appeal against conviction by a court-martial where—

(a) the finding of the court-martial is legally not sustainable due to any reason whatsoever; or

(b) the finding involves wrong decision on a question of law; or

(c) there was a material irregularity in the course of the trial resulting in miscarriage of justice,

but, in any other case, may dismiss the appeal where the tribunal considers that no miscarriage of justice is likely to be caused or has actually resulted to the Appellant:

Provided that no order dismissing the appeal by the tribunal shall be passed unless such order is made after recording reasons therefore in writing.

(1) The Tribunal may allow an appeal against conviction, and pass appropriate order thereon.

(2) Notwithstanding anything contained in the foregoing provisions of this Section, the Tribunal shall have the power to—

(a) substitute for the findings of the court-martial, a finding of guilty for any other offence for which the offender could have been lawfully found guilty by the court-martial and pass a sentence afresh for the offence specified or involved in such findings under the provisions of the Army Act, 1950 (46 of 1950) or the Navy Act, 1957 (62 of 1957) or the Air Force Act, 1950 (45 of 1950), as the case may be; or

(b) if sentence is found to be excessive, illegal or unjust, the Tribunal may—

(i.) remit the whole or any part of the sentence, with or without conditions;

(ii.) mitigate the punishment awarded;

(iii.) commute such punishment to any lesser punishment or punishments mentioned in the Army Act, 1950 (46 of 1950), the Navy Act, 1957 (62 of 1957) and the Air Force Act, 1950 (45 of 1950), as the case may be;

(c) enhance the sentence awarded by a court-martial:

Provided that no such sentence shall be enhanced unless the Appellant has been given an opportunity of being heard;

(d) release the Appellant, if sentenced to imprisonment, on parole with or without conditions;

(e) suspend a sentence of imprisonment;

(f) pass any other order as it may think appropriate.

Notwithstanding any other provisions in this Act, for the purposes of this Section, the Tribunal shall be deemed to be a criminal court for the purposes of Sections 175, 178, 179, 180, 193, 195, 196 or 228 of the Indian Penal Code (45 of 1860) and Chapter XXVI of the Code of Criminal Procedure, 1973 (2 of 1974)'

(11.) The provisions embodied in subsection (1) of Section 15 of the Act are relevant for deciding the instant controversy. Importantly, an interpretation is required to be imparted to the statutory expressions '**any order, decision, finding or sentence passed by a court-martial or any matter connected therewith or incidental thereto**', as become carried thereins. The learned AFT concerned after making an interpretation of the above statutory expressions, as exist in the provisions (supra), ultimately concluded, but after alluding to the provisions embodied in Section 153 of the Army Act, provisions whereof also become extracted hereinafter, that since the provisions embodied in Section 153 (supra) echo, that unless a confirmation order is made in respect of any finding or in respect of awarding any sentence by the general, district or summary general, court-martial, thereupon, the appositely rendered incriminatory finding or the sentence awarded rather shall be invalid, qua therebys the O.A., being not maintainable rather for wants of makings of an apposite confirmation order.

> **'153. Finding and sentence not valid, unless confirmed – No finding or sentence of a general, district or summary general, court-martial shall be valid except so far as it may be confirmed as provided by this Act.'**

(12.) Resultantly it was concluded that uptos, the makings of an order of confirmation by the competent authority in respect of the sentence awarded or finding recorded, thus the aggrieved becomes barred to access the AFT concerned.

(13.) The interpretation (supra) made by the AFT concerned, on a combined and conjunct reading being made to the expression (supra) as occur in the subsection (1) of Section 15 of the Act, with the provisions engrafted in Section 153 of the Army Act, but arises from a lack of a complete incisive and in-depth understanding of the provisions (supra).

(14.) The reason for this Court contrarily assigning to the expressions **'any order, decision, finding or sentence passed by a court-martial or any matter connected therewith or incidental thereto'** as exist in the provisions (supra), that therebys there is conferment of jurisdiction in the AFT, to entertain a petition against any order decision, finding or sentence passed by a court-martial or any matter connected therewith or incidental thereto, thus inter alia ensues on the following grounds.

a.) The jurisdiction conferred thereunders vis-à-vis the AFT concerned, especially when the AFT is a specially created judicial body, thus is for determining the disputes relating to the personnel, who serve respectively in the Army, Navy or Air Force. Therefore, therebys rather a plenitude of competent jurisdiction becomes ably conferred vis- à-vis the AFT concerned. The expanse of the jurisdiction conferred vis-à-vis the Armed Forces Tribunals concerned, when becomes so amply endowed, through the swathe of the expression **'any order, decision, finding or sentence passed by a court-martial or any matter connected therewith or incidental thereto'**, which plain speakingly is but of a plenitude genre. Necessarily, therebys the said expressions invest an able jurisdiction in the AFT, to entertain, thus any motion laid in the prescribed form, which becomes directed against any order, decision finding or sentence passed by a court-martial or any matter connected therewith or incidental thereto.

b.) Moreover, the said provisions are also required to be read in conjunction with subsection (2) of Section 15, whereins, it becomes explicitly expressed that, an aggrieved from an order, decision, finding or sentence passed by a court-martial, becomes endowed the privilege to prefer an appeal in the form of an O.A., becoming constituted before the AFT concerned. Obviously even the supra provision became ably recoursed by the present Petitioner, as the O.A., was constituted in a proper prescribed form.

c.) Now in case the legislature intended to curb the plenitude or the swathe of the able jurisdiction conferred upon the AFT, through the expressions (supra), as exist respectively in subsection (1) and in subsection (2) of Section 15 of the Act, therebys a specific statutory provision was also required to be also incorporated in the apposite special statute. However, since no special statutory provision exists in the special statute (supra) wherebys becomes restricted, rather the plenitude or the swathe of the jurisdiction conferred upon the AFT concerned, as imminently emerges, from the width of the expression(s) (supra), which but covers also any order, decision, finding or sentence passed by a court-martial or any matter connected therewith or incidental thereto. Therefore, it is to be concluded that the provisions incorporated in Section 153 of the Army Act, which state that unless confirmation order is made in respect of an awarding of any sentence by the general, district or summary general, court-martial thereupon, the incriminatory finding or the sentence awarded shall be invalid, are to be construed to be neither restricting nor curtailing the jurisdiction (supra) conferred in the AFT concerned. Contrarily, the (supra) provisions existing in the Army Act are to succumb and/or to become construed to become bridled by the swathe of the jurisdiction conferred upon the AFT concerned.

(15.) However, yet when this Court for reasons (supra) has stated that the said decision on merits, was to be made only after the petition becoming declared to be maintainable. Contrarily, when even after the petition becoming declared as non-maintainable, thus the learned Tribunal yet has proceeded to make a decision on the merits of the *lis*, which is but adversarial to the present Petitioners. However, when this Court has declared the O.A., to be maintainable, therebys a fresh decision on the merits of the *lis*, is required to be made upon the O.A.

Final Order of this Court

(16.) In aftermath, the writ petition is allowed. The impugned order dated 13 December 2023 (Annexure P-6) is quashed and set aside. The *lis* is remanded to the AFT concerned for the making of a fresh decision thereons, even on merits. The said re-decision on merits shall be made by the Bench of the AFT concerned, without it becoming influenced by the earlier made decision on the merits of the *lis*.

(17.) Since the main case itself has been decided, thus, all the pending application(s), if any, also stand(s) disposed of.

Sureshwar Thakur, J
Sudeepti Sharma, J

12 November 2024

(2025) I FLR 232 (India)

Supreme Court of India

Civil Appeal No. 6186 of 2018

S. P. Pandey vs Union of India & Ors.

Composition of Court: Justice Pamidighantam Sri Narasimha and Justice Sandeep Mehta

Date of Decision: 21 October 2024

Counsel for the Appellant: Ms. Vanshaja Shukla, Advocate, Mr. Ansh Narayan Tripathi, Advocate, Mr. Nitin Bhardwaj, Advocate on Record
Counsel for the Respondents: Mr. R Bala, Senior Advocate, Mr. Mukesh Kumar Maroria, Advocate on Record, Mr. Rohit Pandey, Advocate, Mr. Ishaan Sharma, Advocate, Mr. Prahlad Singh, Advocate, Mr. Annirudh Sharma, Ii, Advocate, Mr. Mrigank Pathak, Advocate

Summary

The appellant, a radar fitter in the Indian Air Force, was punished with an Admonition for overtaking vehicles at a railway crossing and using insubordinate language to a superior officer. The appellant filed a statutory complaint, which led to an investigation that concluded that the allegations were false. The Tribunal set aside the punishment, finding that the officer's actions were disproportionate and vindictive. The Supreme Court agreed with the Tribunal's findings and awarded the appellant Rs. 1 lakh in compensation for the unnecessary litigation and distress caused. The Court noted that "the balance and proportion that needs to be maintained between such an infraction and its punishment will always be at the core of good governance."

Headnotes

Facts: The appellant, Pandey, was an Airman in the Indian Air Force as a Radar Fitter. On or around 17 May 10, Pandey overtook several vehicles with his motorcycle while waiting at a closed crossing. A Squadron Leader confronted Pandey for overtaking the vehicles, confiscated his keys, and ordered him to report to the Guard Room for violating good order and Air Force discipline. The Squadron Leader contended that an argument ensued, which is when Pandey used insubordinate language. As a result, Pandey was given an order of Admonition. The initial Admonition was canceled and expunged. However, a new trial ordered the same charges and resulted in another order of Admonition. Pandey's appeals through the Air Force were rejected, so he appealed to the Armed Forces Tribunal. The Tribunal set aside the Admonition, finding the punishment to be disproportionate to the offence. However, the Tribunal did not compensate Pandey for his distress throughout the unnecessary litigation. Pandey appealed to the Supreme Court who agreed with the Tribunal and also granted Rs. 1 lakh in compensation for the unnecessary litigation.

Issue(s): When there is clear and convincing evidence of unnecessary litigation and distress, can an appellant recover monetary compensation? The answer is yes. Will an order of Admonition be set aside where there is evidence of vindictiveness in a charge? The answer is yes.

Reasoning by the Armed Forces Tribunal: While the Armed Forces Tribunal did not order for compensation, they did find that the Admonition should be set aside. It is important to note their reasoning, as the Supreme Court upholds their conclusion. The Tribunal explains that there is no doubt that every Airman is expected to uphold the highest degree of discipline inside and outside of his service place. However, many other motorists had overtaken a long queue of cars to position themselves closer to an area. It appeared that the Squadron Leader took too strict of an action in a public place over a trivial issue. Even if Pandey would have committed a wrong in a public place, the context required the Squadron Leader to handle the situation more appropriately and proportionately. It is also relevant that Pandey was guaranteed twice that the Admonition would be expunged. Despite that, the respondent continued by charging Pandey again. This gave an indication of vindictiveness that could have been instigated by the officer. Therefore, the punishment of admonition was set aside. However, the Tribunal held that Pandey was unable to make a case for compensation. Therefore, compensation was not granted by the Tribunal.

Held: The Civil Appeal is allowed. Compensation for a wrongful order was granted, and the order to set aside admonition was upheld.

ORDER

Pamidighantam Sri Narasimha, J

(1.) The Appellant is not satisfied that the Armed Forces Tribunal, Jaipur has allowed his O.A. and quashed the order of Admonition passed against him on 18 January 2011. He demands compensation for the wrongful order by filing the present appeal. We agreed with him and for reasons to follow, allowed the appeal and granted compensation.

(2.) Facts of the case are that the Appellant was enrolled in the Indian Air Force in 1997 as Airman in the trade of Radar Fitter. At the relevant time, he was posted on the strength of 333 TRU C/o 5 FBSU, Air Force where he commenced work from 16 November 2009.

> 2.1 The incident in question occurred on 17 May 2010, at about 14.20 hrs when he was returning home from duty. On his way back, he had to stop at a railway crossing in a civil area which was closed. The gate was closed due to transit of a train. The allegation against the Appellant is that, instead of waiting behind the vehicles already in line at the railway crossing, he overtook all the vehicles, went straight ahead and parked his motorcycle in front of the railway gate.
>
> 2.2 Respondent No. 7 a Sqn Ldr (Squadron Leader) who was also waiting for the railway barrier to open, approached the Appellant and in 'exercise of the responsibility' conferred on officers of the air forces under para 565 of

the Regulations questioned the Appellant for overtaking all vehicles, pulled out the motorcycle keys and directed the him to park his motorcycle in Guard Room. The Respondent No. 7 handed over the keys to Duty NCO and informed the Appellant that his motorcycle is being confiscated for not following Good Order and Air Force discipline. This led to an argument between the Appellant and Respondent No. 7 wherein the Appellant allegedly used insubordinate language (*yah kaya gundagardi hai*) contrary to Air Force discipline. Respondent No. 7 ordered closed arrest of the Appellant and informed the Commanding Officer and the Adjutant of the Unit. Charge sheet for two offences, i.e. 'Violation of Good Order and Air Force Discipline" and 'Use of insubordinate language to a superior officer' was drawn against the Appellant.

2.3 The charge was tried by Officiating Commanding Officer on 18 May 2010 and an order of Admonition was passed on the same day. However, Respondent No. 4 the Station Commander 5 FBSU sought sanction for expunction of punishment entry from the documents of the Appellant and to proceed with de novo trial of the Appellant for the above alleged misconduct on the technical ground that sanction under Section 83 of the Air Force Act, 1950 was not obtained.

2.4 The Appellant preferred a statutory complaint dated 24 May 2010. This led to a formal investigation as ordered by Respondent No. 4 to bring out the fact of allegation made by the Appellant against Respondent No. 7 and it was reported that the allegations made by the Appellant were false. However, by letter dated 23 June 2010 the Appellant was assured that punishment dated 18 May 2010 would be cancelled and the Admonition entry will be expunged from the record. Relevant portion of letter of Squadron Leader Fit Cdr HRM Ft dated 23 June 2010 is as under:-

'REPLY TO ROG APPLICATION

1. Reference is made to your application dated 24 May 2010.

2. You, are interviewed by the Station Commander in two sessions on 18 and 21 June 2010 and all the issues brought out by you were addressed. Formal investigation was ordered to bring out the fact of

the allegations made by you against Sqn Ldr H.V. Pandey (27441) F (P). From the FI, it is clear that allegation made against Sqn officer were false. You were told by the Stn Cdr that punishment given to you dated 18 May 2010 by CO 333 TRU will be cancelled and entry will be expunged from the documents.

3. Application being devoid of merit, is disposed, herewith.

4. You are requested to give written acknowledgement regarding receipt of disposal of your application.'

(Emphasis supplied)

(3.) Consequently, by order dated 24 June 2010 the Appellant was intimated that charges raised against him have been expunged under 33(1) of the Regulation and punishment entry has been deleted from his service documents. The order reads as follows:

'Tel: AFNET/7742 333TRU, AF
C/0 56 APO PIN-937333
333 TRU/C 951/2/P1 24 June 2010
742490-K Cpl S.P. Pandey Rad Fit

EXPUNGEMENT OF PUNISHMENT

1. Reference is made to 5 FBSU, AF letter No 5FBSU/C 102/1/P1 dated 23 Jun 10.

2. It is intimated that the punishment awarded to you by the undersigned on 18 May 10 in connection with the charge sheet raised by Sqn Ldr HV Pandey ((27441) F (P) of 4 Sqn has been expunged under Rule 33 (1) of the Regulation of the Air Force. The punishment entry has been deleted from the conduct sheet of your service documents.

3. This is for your information.

Sd/- zz
R. Putatunda)
Fit Lt CO'

(4.) This litigation would not have survived if the above referred letter had been given effect to. That didn't happen. Wing Commander V.K. Mohan proceeded de novo against the same charge and ordered for recording of Summary of Evidence on 30 June 2010. The Appellant preferred a representation to the Air Officer Commanding-in-Chief with the prayer to stay operation of order dated 30 June 2010 for recording of Summary of Evidence and prohibit the Commanding Officer to conduct the second trial for the same charges. The representation preferred by the Appellant was rejected by Chief of Air Staff vide order dated 6 January 2011.

(5.) In the circumstances, a second Admonition Order was passed against the Appellant dated 18 January 2011. He appealed to Respondent No. 2 and even this was rejected on 28 April 2011. The representation to the Chief of Air Staff for reconsideration of order dated 6 January 2011 which was also rejected on the ground of it being repetitive in nature.

(6.) Being aggrieved, the Appellant approached the Armed Forces Tribunal by filing an Original Application. After hearing the Appellant and the Respondents and having gone through the materials and records before it, the Tribunal set aside the punishment of 'Admonition' passed against the Appellant vide order dated 18 January 2011. It is important to extract the conclusion of the Tribunal, the relevant part of the order is extracted as follows:

> '11. Before proceeding further we may recall that the punishment awarded to the Petitioner is of 'Admonition'. Learned counsel for the Respondents submitted that on date, the Petitioner has retired from service and any further indulgence would gain no fruitful result even if the punishment of 'Admonition' is set aside and now the issue involved remains only of academic interest.
>
> 12. Be that as it may, we feel it worth mentioning that from the sequence of events on record, it is evident that the entire episode got triggered by the fact that in a civil area, i.e. at a railway crossing, the Petitioner, like many other service/civil motor cyclists had overtaken the long queue of cars to position themselves in front row, close to the railway crossing barrier. No

doubt, it is expected of every Air Warrior/Airman to uphold highest degree of discipline inside and outside his service place. But at the same time, from the events noticed hereinbefore, it is borne out that the Petitioner had overtaken the parked four wheelers and motorcycles on a public road near the railway crossing barrier and had parked his motorcycle in the front row, may be to avoid rush of traffic when the barrier opened. It appears that this gesture of the Petitioner was taken as an affront by the Sqn Ldr HV Pandey and he approached the Petitioner from the rear and forcefully took away the keys of the motorcycle; confiscated the motorcycle on the ground that the Petitioner violated traffic rules and general road discipline, ordered the Petitioner to report to the Guard Room and took the Applicant in custody. It was on his orders the Petitioner was locked in a cell. The strict action taken by Sqn Ldr HV Pandey in a public place over a trivial issue cannot at the same time be appreciated. Even if in the opinion of Sqn Ldr HV Pandey the Petitioner had committed some wrong in public place, the circumstances of the case required him to have advised the Petitioner to mend his ways in future keeping in view the high discipline and dignity of the Air Force. But the manner in which the whole incident was highlighted in full public gaze, and consequent action taken by him, permitting a trivial happening to escalate out of proportion, cannot be appreciated. An offence is an officer and his behaviour should also be officer-like. His behaviour has to set up an example. The incident could have been handled by the officer more appropriately.

13. From the record, it is revealed that the Petitioner was assured in writing on two occasions that the punishment entry will be expunged. Despite that, the Respondent chose to proceed afresh. It gives an indication of vindictiveness and perhaps it was instigated by the officer.

14. For reasons mentioned hereinabove, we are of the considered view that the Summary of Evidence and punishment of 'Admonition' awarded to the Applicant deserve to be set aside.

15. Accordingly, punishment of 'Admonition' dated 18 January 2011 awarded to the Petitioner is set aside. Impugned order dated 28 April 2011 (Annexure-27 to the petition), and order dated 6 January 2010

(Annexure-25 to the petition) are also set side. Consequences to follow. So far as prayer of the Petitioner for directing Sqn Ldr H.V. Pandey, Respondent No. 7 to pay compensation to the Petitioner is concerned, we find that the Petitioner has not been able to make out a case, hence rejected.

16. TA is disposed of accordingly.'

6.1 It is apparent from the findings of the Tribunal that the Respondent No. 7, took the incident personally and forcefully confiscated the keys of the motorcycle and ordered the Appellant to report to the Guard Room. The Tribunal also notices that he was taken into custody. The Tribunal also recorded that at the instance of Respondent No. 7 the Appellant was locked in the cell. While deprecating the conduct of Respondent No. 7 for adopting such a severe action over a trivial issue, the Tribunal opined that the officer of a rank of Squadron Leader could have given a proper advice to the Appellant, to rectify his actions, keeping in view the high discipline and dignity of Air Force. However, the manner in which Respondent No. 7 conducted himself was not appreciated. While deprecating the conduct of Respondent No. 7 the Tribunal also came to the conclusion that the Appellant was subjected to harassment and humiliation giving an impression of vindictiveness at the instance of the concerned officers. It is for this reason the tribunal had no hesitation in setting aside the punishment. The tribunal set aside the order of Admonition dated 18 January 2011. It also set aside the order dated 28 April 2011, whereby the Appellant's statutory appeal had been dismissed. Lastly, the Tribunal also set aside the order dated 6 January 2010, wherein the Air Force Commander had rejected the Appellant's representation. Thus, the decision and the findings of the Tribunal have attained finality.

6.2 However, for reason that the Tribunal rejected the prayer for compensation, the present appeal filed by the Appellant. We have gone through the material on record, findings of the Tribunal and noted the submissions of Ms Vanshaja Shukla, counsel for the Appellant and by Mr R. Bala, senior counsel for the Respondents.

(7.) The initial service of the Appellant for 14 long years, from its commencement in 1997 to 2011 was unblemished. This is an admitted fact. From the unfortunate incident on 17 May 2010, the Appellant's life was embroiled in defending in the disciplinary proceedings and contesting the case before the Tribunal. The disproportionate measure adopted by the Respondents, the assurance of expunging the Admonition, withdrawal of the same and then the retrial, leading to imposition of the punishment caused great amount of distress.

(8.) The findings of the Tribunal are categorical. It found that the matter was escalated beyond proportion and there is also an element of vindictiveness in the action taken against the Appellant. More than anything, the lone battle of the Appellant against the unfair and arbitrary treatment meted out to him, we think is the cause and reason for the indignation. The institution did not protect him, instead it put its full force behind Respondent No. 7. Fortunately, the Tribunal set the record straight.

(9.) Ms Vanshaja Shukla, counsel appearing on behalf of the Appellant has submitted the financial loss that has occurred to the Appellant and prayed for appropriate compensation.

(10.) Small excesses like overtaking the vehicle of one's senior at a railway crossing may be an incident of indiscipline in defence services, but the balance and proportion that needs to be maintained between such an infraction and its punishment will always be at the core of good governance. If the balance is not maintained, the distinction between bad governance, impropriety, unfairness and inhuman treatment is not much. The tribunal is right in holding that a small incident has unnecessarily grown beyond proportion.

(11.) When the institutions that we build grow beyond proportion, officers act mechanically and many a times helplessly, ignore the simple and readily available remedies that are available in our normal lives. We would have thought that an incident like this would have ended if a senior officer had at the right time intervened and resolved the issue by taking into account the emotional aspect of the dispute. Perhaps a simple apology by Respondent No. 7 would have gone a long way, but that did not happen, and we are now called upon to assess the economic value of the indignity and proceed to grant monetary compensation to him. We are aware of how insignificant the monetary value of loss of dignity could be, but legal remedies that they are, enable us to settle it only as a measure, a token of our concern and in recognition of a citizen's identity and dignity.

(12.) Having considered the facts and circumstances of the case and having noted the specific and clear findings of the Tribunal, we direct the Respondents to pay an amount of Rs. 1 lakh to the Appellant towards compensation for having suffered an unnecessary and a long-drawn litigation that was foisted on him. The amount may be paid within a period of 30 days from the date of this order.

(13.) The Civil Appeal is disposed of in the above-mentioned terms.

Pamidighantam Sri Narasimha, J
Sandeep Mehta, J

New Delhi
21 October 2024

(2025) I FLR 242 (United States of America)

The U.S. Court of Appeals for the Armed Forces

Crim. App. No. 20210647

Isac D. Mendoza, Staff Sergeant vs United States

Composition of Court: C.J. Ohlson, J. Hardy, J. Johnson, J. Sparks and J. Maggs (Five Judge Bench)

Date of Decision: 7 October 2024

Counsel for the Appellant: Captain Matthew S. Fields, Colonel Philip M. Staten, Major Bryan A. Osterhage, and Jonathan F. Potter, Esq., Captain Carol K. Rim.
Counsel for the Respondent (Appellee): Captain Anthony J. Scarpati, Colonel Christopher B. Burgess, Lieutenant Colonel Jacqueline J. DeGaine, and Major Chase C. Cleveland.

Summary

The Appellant (a member of the army) was charged with performing non-consensual sexual assault on JW, a fellow member of the army, when she was extremely intoxicated. The Government brought a charge under Article 120(b)(2)(A) of the Uniform Code of Military Justice (UCMJ) which penalizes engaging in a sexual act with a person capable of consenting, but did not consent to the act. The Appellant was convicted by the military judge, which was upheld in appeal by the Army Court of Criminal Appeals (ACCA). The

Appellant thereby preferred another appeal before the Court of Appeal for the Armed Forces challenging his conviction. The main grounds of his challenge were that the Government charged him under Article 120(b)(2)(A), UCMJ but presented evidence to prove JW's incapacity to consent on the ground of her extreme intoxication, which is provided under another provision, viz., Article 120(b)(3)(A), UCMJ, thereby conflating two separate theories of criminal liability. This deprived him of the constitutional right to know which offence and which criminal liability he needs to prepare his defense for. The court accepted the Appellant's argument regarding the violation of due process and held that the aforesaid Articles of the UCMJ create separate theories of criminal liability, which cannot be conflated. However, it refrained from ruling upon the legal sufficiency of the Appellant's conviction and remanded the matter to the ACCA for a fresh appraisal.

Headnotes

Facts: The Appellant (accused) and JW (victim) were members of the army who were stationed at Kenya. The alleged incident of sexual assault without the consent of the victim took place on 11 July 2020. On this day, when JW went off-post, she allegedly consumed a considerable amount of alcohol with her fellow soldiers. It was stated that when she returned to the barracks, where the Appellant was also present, she continued to drink heavily to the point that she eventually blacked out. She came to her senses the next morning when the Appellant, whom she did not recognize, knocked on her barracks room door to return her shoes. Soon, she realized that her underwear was changed and her tampon was pushed all the way inside. This alarmed her and she suspected that a non-consensual sexual act had been committed on her person. She reported the incident to the concerned officer and was later subjected to a sexual assault forensic examination which confirmed the presence of semen matching the Appellant's DNA profile. Meanwhile, the Appellant initially denied engaging in any sexual activity with JW and claimed that she had merely passed out on his bed and later took a shower in his room. However, he subsequently confessed to the US Army Criminal Investigation Division (CID) agent that he had sexual intercourse with JW and that she was extremely intoxicated, though he did not state that she withheld consent. The investigation unearthed CCTV footage which showed JW, heavily under the influence of alcohol, being supported by the Appellant to his room. Witnesses' testimony also corroborated JW's intoxicated state.

Issues: (1) Whether the Appellant's conviction under Article 120(b)(2)(A), UCMJ which criminalizes engaging in a sexual act with a person capable of consenting, who did not consent to the act, is legally sufficient?

(2.) Whether the Appellant being charged under Article 120(b)(2)(A) instead of under Article 120(b)(3)(A) of the UCMJ, which criminalizes engaging in a sexual act who is incapable of consenting due to impairment by any drug, intoxicant or other similar substance and that condition is known or reasonably should be known by the person, amounts to a due process violation?

Contentions of Parties: The Appellant's contentions rest upon two broad heads: firstly, that the evidence presented by the prosecution is legally insufficient to sustain a conviction for the charge of sexual assault without consent. This is because JW's lack of consent was proved by circumstantial evidence, without presenting any affirmative evidence on the point. Secondly, that the government has conflated two different and inconsistent criminal theories by charging the Appellant under Article 120(b)(2)(A) instead of under Article 120(b)(3)(A) of the UCMJ; which raises significant due process concerns. It was contended that he was deprived of the right to fair notice as to the nature of allegation against which he was required to defend himself. In other words, the Government charged him for one offence but presented evidence for another offence.

The Government pleaded that there is sufficient evidence to prove that the impugned sexual act was non-consensual. JW's high level of intoxication, coupled with other evidence (CCTV footage, Appellant's confession and witnesses' testimony) is legally sufficient to prove the Appellant's guilt beyond reasonable doubt. With respect to the Appellant's second contention, the Government rebuts the due process concerns raised by the Appellant by arguing that a charge under Article 120(b)(2)(A) of the UCMJ can be proved by showing a "lack of consent" of JW due to extreme intoxication. There are provisions which may provide for overlapping, and sometimes multiple theories of criminal liability. The Appellant was prosecuted and tried for the offence which he had committed and there has been no violation of due process.

Held: (1) Majority opinion (J. Hardy, joined by Chief Judge Ohlson and Judge Johnson)

A. Burden of proof – Whether can be discharged by circumstantial evidence – Circumstantial evidence in sexual assault cases

Prosecution can meet its burden of proving the guilt of an accused by circumstantial evidence. Direct evidence not imperative. The Appellant's argument that a conviction in sexual assault cases cannot be solely based upon circumstantial evidence, and at least some affirmative evidence to prove the absence of consent must be presented, cannot be accepted. The rule that a conviction can be based upon circumstantial evidence is not qualified by any conditions and does not entertain any exceptions for an offence/class of offences.

B. Interpretation of Article 120(b)(2)(A) and Article 120(b)(3)(A), UCMJ – Theories of criminal liability – *Mens rea* as an essential ingredient

Article 120(b)(2)(A) and Article 120(b)(3)(A) of the UCMJ establish separate theories of criminal liability. The former criminalizes sexual assault without consent of a person who is capable of consenting while the latter criminalizes sexual assault on a person who is incapable of consenting due to being intoxicated, in addition to the requirement of proving mens rea on part of the accused that he had knowledge about such condition of the victim. The Government's contention that it can prove a lack of consent under Article 120(b)(2)(A) by proving that the victim was intoxicated is legally untenable as such a wide interpretation of this provision would render Article 120(b)(3)(A) superfluous and of no effect. The Government's act of bringing the charge under Article 120(b)(2)(A) also bypasses the requirement of proving *mens rea* under Article 120(b)(3)(A) on part of the Appellant. Hence, there has been a violation of the constitutional right of the Appellant to know what offense and what legal theory he will be tried and convicted for.

C. Legal sufficiency – Rule thereof – Misapplication by ACCA

A presumption is made in favor of the prosecution with respect to the evidence presented in legal sufficiency cases. The evidence must be examined as per a "reasonable trier of fact." As a rule, the appellate court does not decide whether the conviction of the accused was legally sufficient, but merely decides whether the lower courts' verdicts display a correct application of legal principles. In the present case, it is unclear how the ACCA took into consideration the evidence regarding intoxication of the accused. The Government did not establish that the accused knew that JW was incapable of consenting and it tried to prove his guilt based on the incorrect understanding that if her extreme intoxication is proved, her lack of consent and the requisite *mens rea* on the part of the accused is also proved. The reason for this lack of clarity is that the ACCA did not have the benefit of this decision which has declared, as a rule of law, that the aforesaid two Articles of the UCMJ create separate theories of criminal liability. ACCA's judgement was therefore, set aside and the matter remanded back for fresh consideration of the legal and factual sufficiency of conviction of the accused in light of the now settled proposition of law.

D. Interpretation of statutes – Principles to be applied – Canon of surplusage

While interpreting the provisions of a statute, the court must first examine whether the language of the statute is plain and unambiguous. If it is so, the provision must be given effect to as it is. However, if the language is ambiguous, the court must assess the context in which the language has been used as well as the broader context of the statute as a whole. An attempt must be made to harmonize the provisions. The canon of surplusage must be applied, which states that courts should give effect to every word in a provision, and should not adopt an interpretation which renders another provision of no-effect.

2) Part-dissent (J. Sparks)

J. Sparks agrees with the majority over the finding that Article 120(b)(2)(A) and Article 120(b)(3)(A) of the UCMJ establish different theories of criminal liability. However, he disagrees with the decision of remanding the matter back to the ACCA. In his opinion, even if the legal sufficiency test is applied, which entails viewing the evidence in the light most favorable to the prosecution, the Government has been unable to prove the lack of consent of JW in indulging in the sexual act. Moreover, the violation of due process (by the Government charging the Appellant for the wrong offence and presenting evidence for a different offence in trial) cannot be cured by remanding the matter. Therefore, he favors a dismissal of the Appellant's conviction with prejudice instead of the majority's decision to remand the matter to the ACCA.

3) Part-dissent (J. Maggs)

J. Maggs concurs with the majority over the interpretation of the two Articles but dissents on the ground that the matter should be remanded to the ACCA solely to determine the factual sufficiency of the charge. The legal sufficiency of a lack of consent is adequately proved through the evidence on record.

Case laws cited

1) By J. Hardy

United States vs Smith, 83 M.J. 350, 359 (C.A.A.F. 2023); *United States vs King*, 78 M.J. 218, 221 (C.A.A.F. 2019); *Jackson vs Virginia*, 443 U.S. 307, 319 *(1979)*; *United States vs Long*, 81 M.J. 362, 368 (C.A.A.F. 2021); *United States vs Kearns*, 73 M.J. 177, 182 (C.A.A.F. 2014); *United States vs Young, 64 M.J.* 404, 407 (C.A.A.F. 2007); *Holland vs United States*, 348 U.S. 121, 140 (1954); *Desert Palace, Inc. vs Costa, 539 U.S. 90, 100* (2003); *United States vs Lopez de Victoria*, 66 M.J. 67, 73 (C.A.A.F. 2008); *United States vs McPherson*, 73 M.J. 393, 395 (C.A.A.F. 2014); *Robinson vs Shell Oil Co.*, 519 U.S. 337, 341 (1997); *United States vs Kelly*, 77 M.J. 404, 407 (C.A.A.F. 2018); *United States vs Christian*, 63 M.J. 205, 208 (C.A.A.F. 2006); *United States vs Sager*, 76 M.J. 158, 161 (C.A.A.F. 2017); *Yates vs United States*, 574 U.S. 528, 543 (2015); *Roberts vs Sea-Land Services, Inc.*, 566 U.S. 93, 111; *Duncan vs*

Walker, 533 U.S. 167, 174 (2001); *Leocal vs Ashcroft*, 543 U.S. 1, 12 (2004); *United Staes vs Elespuru*, 73 M.J. 326, 330 (C.A.A.F. 2014); *United States vs Riggins*, 75 M.J. 78, 83 (C.A.A.F. 2016); *United States vs Clark*, 75 M.J. 298, 300 (C.A.A.F. 2016); *United States vs Leak*, 61 M.J. 234, 241 (C.A.A.F. 2005); *United States vs Thompson*, 83 M.J. 1, 5 (C.A.A.F. 2022); *United States vs Nerad*, 69 M.J. 138, 147 (C.A.A.F. 2010).

2) By J. Sparks

United States vs King, 78 M.J. 218, 221 (C.A.A.F. 2019); *United States vs Gutierrez*, 73 M.J. 172, 175 (C.A.A.F. 2014); *United States vs Bennitt*, 72 M.J. 266, 268 (C.A.A.F. 2013); *United States vs Robinson*, 77 M.J. 294, 298 (C.A.A.F. 2018); *United States vs Navrestad*, 66 M.J. 262, 269 (C.A.A.F. 2008); *Jackson vs Virginia*, 443 U.S. 307, 319 (1979); *United States vs Elespuru*, 73 M.J. 326, 330 (C.A.A.F. 2014); *United States vs Motsenbocker*, No. 201600285, 2017 CCA LEXIS 539, *17 (N-M. Ct. Crim. App. Aug 10, 2017); *United States vs Morton*, 69 M.J. 12, 16 (C.A.A.F. 2010).

3) By J. Maggs

United States vs Brown, 84 M.J. 124, 127 (C.A.A.F. 2024); *United States vs Wilson*, 76 M.J. 4, 6 (C.A.A.F. 2017); *United States vs Smith*, 83 M.J. 350, 359 (C.A.A.F. 2023); *United States vs Long*, 81 M.J. 362, 364 (C.A.A.F. 2021).

Judge Hardy delivered the opinion of the Court, in which Chief Judge Ohlson and Judge Johnson joined. Judge Sparks filed a separate opinion, concurring in part and dissenting in part and in the judgment. Judge Maggs filed a separate opinion, concurring in part and dissenting in part.

Judge Hardy delivered the opinion of the Court.

After a night of socialising and heavy drinking with other soldiers, JW blacked out, leaving her with no further memories until the following morning. An investigation by the United States Army Criminal Investigation Division (CID) established that later that night, JW and Appellant went to Appellant's barracks room where Appellant performed a sexual act upon JW. Under the theory that JW did not consent to the act, the Government charged Appellant with sexual assault in violation of Article 120(b)(2)(A), Uniform Code of

Military Justice (UCMJ), 10 U.S.C. § 920(b)(2)(A) (2018).[1] Notably, the Government did not charge Appellant with a sexual assault under Article 120(b)(3)(A), UCMJ, which would have required the Government to prove both that Appellant committed a sexual act on JW when JW was incapable of consenting to the sexual act due to impairment by any drug, intoxicant, or other similar substance and that Appellant knew or should have known that JW was incapable of consenting.

At trial, the Government presented evidence of JW's extreme intoxication and argued to the military judge sitting alone both that JW would not have consented to sexual intercourse with Appellant and that she was incapable of consenting to sexual intercourse due to her high level of intoxication. The military judge found Appellant guilty, contrary to his plea, of one specification of sexual assault in violation of Article 120, UCMJ, and the United States Army Court of Criminal Appeals (ACCA) affirmed. *United States vs Mendoza,* No. ARMY 20210647, 2023 CCA LEXIS 198, at *10, 2023 WL 3540415, at *4 (A. Ct. Crim. App. May 8, 2023) (unpublished).

Before this Court, Appellant challenges the legal sufficiency of his conviction on the grounds that the Government failed to introduce affirmative evidence of the lack of consent beyond a reasonable doubt. We disagree with Appellant that direct evidence of JW's lack of consent was necessary for his conviction to be legally sufficient, but we do agree with his secondary argument that Article 120(b)(2)(A), UCMJ, and Article 120(b)(3)(A), UCMJ, create separate theories of criminal liability. Article 120(b)(2)(A), UCMJ, criminalises engaging in a sexual act with a person capable of consenting who did not consent, and Article 120(b)(3)(A), UCMJ, criminalises engaging in a sexual act with a person who is incapable of consenting due to impairment by any drug, intoxicant, or other similar substance when the accused knows or should have known that the person was incapable of consenting.

In this case, the Government elected not to charge Appellant with sexual assault under Article 120(b)(3)(A), UCMJ (a sexual act upon a person incapable of consenting), and instead charged Appellant with sexual assault under Article 120(b)(2)(A), UCMJ (a sexual act upon a person capable of

1. Appellant was also charged with and acquitted of a second specification of abusive sexual contact in violation of Article 120, UCMJ.

consenting who did not consent). Nevertheless, at trial the Government presented significant evidence of JW's extreme intoxication and argued that JW's inability to consent established the absence of consent. The Government's approach—which conflated two different and inconsistent theories of criminal liability—raises significant due process concerns. Because the ACCA's decision upholding Appellant's conviction does not explain how or why the evidence of JW's intoxication factored into its analysis, we reverse the decision of the ACCA and remand the case for the court to reconsider its legal and factual sufficiency analysis in light of this opinion.

Background

In July 2020, Appellant and JW were both stationed at Camp Casey, Korea. On 11 July 2020, JW went off-post to eat and drink with fellow soldiers. When the group returned to the barracks, they joined other soldiers, including Appellant, who were socialising outside. JW testified that she recalled coming back to the barracks, seeing the other soldiers outside, and continuing to drink with them before she eventually blacked out.

JW's next memory was waking up the following morning to Appellant knocking on her barracks room door to return her shoes. JW did not recognise Appellant and did not know why he was at her door. JW went back to sleep and woke up to Appellant again knocking at her door to ask if she was okay.

Afterwards, JW went to the bathroom and 'realised something was wrong'. JW noticed that she was not wearing the underwear she had been wearing the night before and that her tampon was pushed all the way inside her to the extent that she could not reach the string. JW testified that she had never inserted a tampon so far, and that she would never have sex with her tampon in or when she was on her period. Realising that something was wrong and starting to panic, JW went to the barracks Charge of Quarters (CQ) desk to try to identify Appellant and learn what happened the night before.

The CQ noncommissioned officer (NCO) testified that JW was crying and was very upset when she came to the CQ desk. The CQ NCO contacted a Sexual Harassment/Assault Response and Prevention (SHARP) program representative, who later met with JW and arranged for her to file a report and to receive a sexual assault forensic examination (SAFE) at the troop medical clinic.

While she was waiting to be taken to the medical clinic, JW went to her friend, Specialist (SPC) RL, to ask what had happened the night before. SPC RL testified that JW was upset, crying, and confused when they spoke. After JW left for the clinic, SPC RL and his NCO spoke to Appellant after hearing reports of his interactions with JW the previous night. Appellant told SPC RL and his NCO that JW had fallen asleep in his bed. During their conversation, JW called SPC RL, who handed the phone to Appellant. JW asked Appellant what happened, and he replied that nothing happened, and that she had locked herself in his bathroom. Appellant then requested to accompany SPC RL and his NCO to the clinic to see JW. On the way, Appellant told SPC RL that JW had taken a shower in his room and then put her shirt on backwards. At the parking lot of the clinic, Appellant told a CID agent who was conducting canvassing interviews that JW had been in his room the night before.

During a later interview with the CID agent, Appellant admitted to having sexual intercourse with JW in his bedroom. He acknowledged that JW was extremely intoxicated at the time and that she was incapable of consenting because of her intoxication. Appellant also admitted that he 'was in control the whole time' during intercourse; however, he never admitted that JW verbally or physically withheld consent. US Army Criminal Investigation Laboratory testing of cervical swabs taken from JW during her SAFE exam confirmed the presence of semen matching Appellant's DNA profile.

Evidence collected by CID during its investigation, including CCTV footage from the barracks, helped reconstruct the events at the barracks during the period when JW blacked out. Witnesses testified that they saw JW drink and socialise with other soldiers, including Appellant, while displaying symptoms of intoxication, including slurred speech and unsteady movements. Some soldiers also noted JW's flirtatious behavior with Appellant and others. The CCTV footage from the barracks showed that JW walked unsteadily with Appellant to his room while Appellant grabbed her crotch. Later, the footage captured JW and Appellant exiting his room with JW's arms seemingly draped over Appellant's shoulders for support. JW testified that she remembered nothing of her encounter with Appellant.

A military judge sitting as a general court-martial convicted Appellant of one specification of sexual assault in violation of Article 120(b)(2)(A), UCMJ, and sentenced him to a dishonorable discharge, thirty months of confinement, and reduction to the grade of E-1. The convening authority approved the sentence and waived automatic forfeitures of all pay and allowances for six months for the benefit of Appellant's wife.

On appeal before the ACCA, Appellant argued that the evidence was factually insufficient because the Government 'produced no evidence that the victim did not consent to sexual intercourse'. Mendoza, 2023 CCA LEXIS 198, at *8, 2023 WL 3540415, at *3. The ACCA rejected this argument, explaining that several factors led it to find Appellant's conviction factually sufficient, 'including but not limited to: the victim's high level of intoxication, [A]ppellant's statement to CID, eyewitness testimony, and the CCTV footage'. Id., 2023 WL 3540415, at *3. Because the ACCA was 'convinced of [A]ppellant's guilt beyond a reasonable doubt', it affirmed his conviction. Id. at *10, 2023 WL 3540415, at *3-4 (citation omitted) (internal quotation marks omitted).

We granted review to determine whether Appellant's conviction for sexual assault without consent was legally sufficient. United States vs Mendoza, 84 M.J. 105 (CAAF 2023) (order granting review).

Discussion

In most legal sufficiency cases, which we review *de novo*, the Court asks 'whether, after viewing the evidence in the light most favourable to the prosecution, any rational trier of fact could have found the essential elements of the crime beyond a reasonable doubt'. United States vs Smith, 83 M.J. 350, 359 (CAAF 2023) (citations omitted) (internal quotation marks omitted). Because the Court draws every reasonable inference from the evidence in favor of the prosecution, '[t]he standard for legal sufficiency involves a very low threshold to sustain a conviction'. *United States vs King,* 78 M.J. 218, 221 (CAAF 2019) (alteration in original) (citations omitted) (internal quotation marks omitted). This deferential standard impinges upon the factfinder's discretion '"only to the extent necessary to guarantee the fundamental protection of due process of law"'. Id. (quoting Jackson vs Virginia, 443 US 307, 319 (1979)).

This case, however, departs from the usual 'reasonable trier of fact' analysis because Appellant challenges the legal sufficiency of his sexual assault conviction on two unusual grounds. First, Appellant argues that the evidence was legally insufficient because the Government relied solely on circumstantial evidence to prove that JW did not consent to the sexual activity. In Appellant's view, the Government's failure to present any 'affirmative' evidence of JW's lack of consent means that no rational factfinder could legally find him guilty under Article 120(b)(2)(A), UMCJ.

In the alternative, Appellant argues that his conviction was legally insufficient because the Government violated his due process rights by conflating two different theories of criminal liability under Article 120, UCMJ, during his court-martial. Appellant asserts that Article 120(b)(2)(A), UCMJ, and Article 120(b)(3)(A), UCMJ, establish separate theories of liability, and that the Government robbed him of his due process right to fair notice by arguing that JW was incapable of consenting due to alcohol intoxication without charging Appellant with sexual assault under Article 120(b)(3)(A), UCMJ. In Appellant's view, because the Government charged him under Article 120(b)(2)(A), UCMJ, (sexual assault without consent), he had no notice that he needed to defend himself from the Government's allegation that JW was incapable of consenting. We consider each of Appellant's arguments in turn.

A. Article 120(b)(2)(A) does not require 'affirmative' evidence

This Court has repeatedly held that the Government may meet its burden of proving an accused's guilt beyond a reasonable doubt with circumstantial evidence. *United States vs Long,* 81 M.J. 362, 368 (CAAF 2021); see also King, 78 M.J. at 221 (first citing *United States vs Kearns,* 73 M.J. 177, 182 (CAAF 2014); then citing *United States vs Young,* 64 M.J. 404, 407 (CAAF 2007)). Nevertheless, Appellant argues that this principle works differently in sexual assault cases, which—in Appellant's view—require 'at least a single fact related to affirmative non-consent in order to deem a conviction for sexual assault without consent legally sufficient'. Reply Brief of Appellant at 13, *United States vs Mendoza,* No. 23-0210 (CAAF Jan. 12, 2024) (emphasis in original).

We disagree. The President has instructed that findings of guilt 'may be based on direct or circumstantial evidence', without mention of any exception for certain offences. Rule for Court-Martial (RCM) 918(c). And in *Long*—a case involving rape and other sex offenses—we recognised that 'the Government is free to meet its burden of proof with circumstantial evidence'. 81 M.J. at 368 (alteration in original removed) (internal quotation marks omitted) (quoting *King*, 78 M.J. at 221). The President's instructions and our case law are consistent with the Supreme Court's guidance that circumstantial evidence 'is intrinsically no different from testimonial evidence'. *Holland vs United States*, 348 US 121, 140 (1954); see also *Desert Palace, Inc. vs Costa*, 539 US 90, 100 (2003) ('we have never questioned the sufficiency of circumstantial evidence in support of a criminal conviction, even though proof beyond a reasonable doubt is required'). Accordingly, we reiterate once again that the absence of direct evidence of an element of an offence does not prevent a finding of guilty for that offense from being legally sufficient.

B. Article 120(b)(2)(A) and Article 120(b)(3)(A) establish separate theories of liability[2]

Appellant's alternative argument requires us to examine Article 120(b)(2)(A), UCMJ, to determine whether the Government can prove sexual assault 'without the consent' of the victim by establishing that the victim was incapable of consenting. This Court reviews questions of statutory interpretation *de novo*. *United States vs Lopez de Victoria, 66 M.J. 67, 73 (CAAF 2008)*. The first step in statutory interpretation cases 'is to determine whether the language at issue has a plain and unambiguous meaning with regard to the particular dispute in the case'. *United States vs McPherson, 73 M.J. 393, 395 (CAAF 2014)* (citation omitted) (internal quotation marks omitted). '[I]f the statutory language is unambiguous and the statutory scheme is coherent and consistent', the inquiry is done. Id. 'Whether the statutory language is ambiguous is determined "by reference to the language itself, the specific context in which that language is used, and the broader context of the statute as a whole".' *Id. (quoting Robinson vs Shell Oil Co.*, 519 US 337, 341 (1997)).

---

2. All statutory references in this part of the opinion are to Article 120, UCMJ, 10 U.S.C. § 920 (2018), unless otherwise indicated. For readability purposes, we refer to 'subsection (b)(2)(A)' and 'subsection (b)(3)(A)' for Article 120(b)(2)(A), UCMJ, and Article 120(b)(3)(A), UCMJ, respectively.

When we engage in this analysis, the Court '"typically seeks to harmonise independent provisions of a statute"'. *United States vs Kelly*, 77 M.J. 404, 407 (CAAF 2018) (quoting *United States vs Christian*, 63 M.J. 205, 208 (CAAF 2006)). To this end, this Court employs the surplusage canon, which requires 'that, if possible, every word and every provision is to be given effect and that no word should be ignored or needlessly be given an interpretation that causes it to duplicate another provision or to have no consequences'. *United States vs Sager*, 76 M.J. 158, 161 (CAAF 2017).

1. Text of Article 120(b), UCMJ

Article 120(b), UCMJ, criminalises sexual assault in the military and defines multiple ways in which the Government may prove the offence. Article 120(b), UCMJ, provides in relevant part:

> '(b.) SEXUAL ASSAULT.—Any person subject to this chapter who—
>
> (1.) commits a sexual act upon another person by—
>
> (A.) threatening or placing that other person in fear;
>
> (B.) making a fraudulent representation that the sexual act serves a professional purpose; or
>
> (C.) inducing a belief by any artifice, pretense, or concealment that the person is another person;
>
> (2.) commits a sexual act upon another person—
>
> (A.) (without the consent of the other person; or
>
> (B.) when the person knows or reasonably should know that the other person is asleep, unconscious, or otherwise unaware that the sexual act is occurring; or
>
> (3.) commits a sexual act upon another person when the other person is incapable of consenting to the sexual act due to—
>
> (A.) impairment by any drug, intoxicant, or other similar

substance, and that condition is known or reasonably should be known by the person; or

(B.) a mental disease or defect, or physical disability, and that condition is known or reasonably should be known by the person;

is guilty of sexual assault and shall be punished as a court-martial may direct.'

The Article defines 'consent' as 'a freely given agreement to the conduct at issue by a competent person' and explicitly states that '[a]ll the surrounding circumstances are to be considered in determining whether a person gave consent'. Article 120(g)(7)(A), (C), UCMJ. The Article separately defines 'incapable of consenting' as meaning that a person is 'incapable of appraising the nature of the conduct at issue' or 'physically incapable of declining participation in, or communicating unwillingness to engage in, the sexual act at issue'. Article 120(g)(8), UCMJ.

In this case, the Government charged Appellant under Article 120(b)(2)(A), UCMJ, which criminalises sexual assault 'without the consent' of a victim. The Government defends its choice by arguing that the plain language of subsection (b)(2)(A) permits it to meet its burden of proof with evidence of JW's lack of capacity to consent due to her level of intoxication. The Government dismisses Appellant's due process concerns, arguing that he was convicted of precisely the crime with which he was charged—sexual assault without consent—and that nothing prevents Congress from enacting overlapping criminal statutes that provide the Government with multiple theories of liability.

Our analysis begins, as it must, with the text of the statute. It is true, as the Government argues, that the language of subsection (b)(2)(A) does not expressly foreclose the Government from proving that JW did not consent by presenting evidence that she was incapable of consenting. But it is also true, as Appellant argues, that nothing in the language of subsection (b)(2)(A)—or in any other part of the Article—forecloses Appellant's interpretation that subsection (b)(2)(A) presumes that the victim was capable of consenting. However, when we look beyond the specific language of subsection (b)(2)(A) and examine the 'the specific context in which that language is used, and the broader context of the statute as a whole', we do not believe that subsection (b)(2)(A) can be read as broadly as the Government suggests. *McPherson,* 73 M.J. at 395 (internal quotation marks omitted) (quoting *Robinson,* 519 US at 341).

Our analysis is guided by this Court's decision in *Sager,* 76 M.J. 158. There, the Court examined the language of Article 120(b)(2)(B), UCMJ, which criminalised a sexual act upon another person 'when the person knows or reasonably should know that the other person is asleep, unconscious, or otherwise unaware that the sexual act is occurring'. *Id.* at 161. The Court rejected the Government's argument that the phrase 'asleep, unconscious, or otherwise unaware' created a single theory of criminal liability. Id. at 161–62. Noting Congress's use of the disjunctive 'or' and applying the 'ordinary meaning' canon of statutory construction, the Court held that 'asleep', 'unconscious', and 'otherwise aware' reflected separate theories of liability. Id. ('In ordinary use the word "or". . . . marks an alternative which generally corresponds to the word "either". ' (alteration in original) (internal quotation marks omitted) (quoting Earl T. Crawford, *The Construction of Statutes* § 188 (1940))). The Court further noted that the Government's theory would violate the canon against surplusage, by stripping the words 'asleep', 'unconscious', and 'or' of any meaning. Id. at 162 ('[T]he canon against surplusage is strongest when an interpretation would render superfluous another part of the same statutory scheme.' (quoting *Yates vs United States,* 574 US 528, 543 (2015))).

The same logic applies to the Government's argument in this case. Under the Government's theory, every sexual act committed upon a victim who is incapable of consenting under subsection (b)(3)(A) would also qualify as a sexual assault under subsection (b)(2)(A) because the victim did not consent. The Supreme Court, however, has repeatedly instructed that Courts must 'give effect, if possible, to every word of a statute'. See, e.g., *Roberts vs Sea-Land Services,* Inc., 566 US 93, 111 (internal quotation marks omitted) (quoting *Duncan vs Walker,* 533 US 167, 174 (2001)). The Government's preferred approach would defy this guidance by rendering subsection (b)(2)(A) 'practically devoid of significance', Leocal vs Ashcroft, 543 US 1, 12 (2004), and relegating subsection (b)(3)(A) to mere surplusage without any purpose or effect.

Rendering subsection (b)(3)(A) as surplusage would be especially problematic because it would allow the Government to circumvent the mens rea requirement that Congress specifically added to the offense of sexual assault of a victim who is incapable of consenting. To achieve a conviction under subsection (b)(3)(A), the Government must prove not only that the victim was incapable of consenting but also that the victim's condition was known or reasonably should have been known by the accused. However, because subsection (b)(2)(A) only requires that the sexual act be performed 'without the consent' of the victim (regardless whether the accused knew or should have known of that condition), if the Government can establish the absence of consent by proving that the victim was incapable of consenting, then the Government can obtain an incapable-of-consent conviction under subsection (b)(2)(A) without proving the accused's mens rea beyond a reasonable doubt. Indeed, this is exactly what may have happened in Appellant's case. The military Judge may have convicted Appellant of sexual assault on the theory that JW was incapable of consenting without the Government proving that Appellant knew or should have known that she was incapable. We agree with Appellant that this possibility raises serious due process concerns.

To avoid these concerns, and consistent with the language and structure of Article 120, UCMJ, we hold that subsection (b)(2)(A) and subsection (b)(3)(A) establish separate theories of liability. Subsection (b)(2)(A) criminalises the performance of a sexual act upon a victim who is capable of consenting but does not consent. Subsection (b)(3)(A) criminalises the performance of a sexual act upon a victim who is incapable of consenting to the sexual act due to impairment by any drug, intoxicant, or other similar substance when the victim's condition is known or reasonably should be known by the accused. Of course, nothing prevents the Government from charging a defendant with both offenses under inconsistent factual theories and allowing the trier of fact to determine whether the victim was capable or incapable of consenting. See *United Staes vs Elespuru*, 73 M.J. 326, 330 (CAAF 2014) (recognising that the "complexity of Article 120, UCMJ, . . . make[s] charging in the alternative an unexceptional and often prudent decision"). But what the Government cannot do is Charge One offense under one factual theory and then argue a different offense and a different factual theory at trial. Doing so robs the defendant of his constitutional "right to know what offense and under what legal theory he will be tried and convicted." United States vs Riggins, 75 M.J. 78, 83 (CAAF 2016) (citation omitted) (internal quotation marks omitted).

2. Legal Sufficiency of Appellant's Conviction

To convict Appellant of sexual assault in violation of Article 120(b)(2)(A), UCMJ, the Government was required to prove beyond a reasonable doubt that Appellant: (1) committed a sexual act upon JW, and (2) that Appellant did so 'without the consent' of JW. Here, it is undisputed that Appellant committed a sexual act upon JW. And even though there is no direct evidence that Appellant engaged in sexual intercourse 'without the consent' of JW, the Government presented significant circumstantial evidence on the point.3 Nevertheless, we agree with Appellant that some of the Government's arguments at trial raise significant due process concerns about his conviction.[4]

To prove the absence of consent, trial counsel:

- Argued not only that JW would not have consented but also that JW was incapable of consenting due to alcohol intoxication.
- Presented the testimony of an expert witness who estimated that JW's blood alcohol level was between 0.175 and 0.19 at the time of the sexual act and opined that JW would have had diminished mental capacity.
- Pointed to the testimony of multiple witnesses, saying '[e]veryone who had any interaction with [JW] knew she was too intoxicated to function that night', and that their testimony confirmed that JW 'met the definition of an incompetent person before the accused took her to his room'.

---

3. This evidence includes: (1) testimony that JW had no prior relationship with Appellant; (2) testimony that JW would never have sex while on her period; (3) testimony that JW would not have pushed a tampon so far inside of herself; (4) testimony that JW made a morning-after report to the CQ desk after she realised something was wrong; (5) testimony that JW was upset; (6) testimony that Appellant initially denied that he had engaged in any sexual acts with JW; and (7) testimony that JW locked herself in Appellant's bathroom.

4. In his supplement to his petition for review, Appellant asked this Court to decide whether his 'conviction for sexual assault without consent should be reversed'? Appellant argued both that his conviction was legally insufficient and that there had been a constructive amendment to the charged offence. This Court granted review only of the legal sufficiency issue. *Mendoza, 84 M.J. at 105 (order granting review). Accordingly, we consider any due process concerns only through the narrow lens of legal sufficiency.*

- Argued that the barracks CCTV footage showed that when JW went to Appellant's room, she 'was completely out of it. She's stumbling. She's walking into the walls, bumping into objects, and she has no idea what's going on here'.
- Pointed to Appellant's own statements in which Appellant admitted that JW was 'really drunk' and that 'she wasn't able to give consent'.

The Government's arguments before this Court also make clear that the Government presented this evidence at trial to establish that JW was incapable of consenting and therefore there was an absence of consent.[5] But as we explained above, that is a different theory of criminal liability and a different offence than the one the Government charged.

Under the actual charged offense, Article 120(b)(2)(A), UCMJ, it is not clear how the evidence of JW's intoxication factored into either the decision of the military Judge or the opinion of the ACCA. With respect to the military Judge, the Government states: 'Whether Ms JW was completely incapacitated by alcohol or whether she was merely intoxicated to a point that her resistance was significantly reduced was a question of fact properly before the military Judge for consideration.' But nothing in the record indicates whether the military Judge found that JW was capable of consenting but did not, or that JW was incapable of consenting and thus could not. Similarly, in upholding the factual sufficiency of Appellant's conviction, the ACCA relied on several factors, including 'the victim's high level of intoxication'. *Mendoza*, 2023 CCA LEXIS 198, at *8, 2023 WL 3540415, at *3. The ACCA's express reliance on the evidence of JW's intoxication—without any explanation of how or why that evidence factored into its analysis—raises serious questions about the legal and factual sufficiency of Appellant's conviction.

5. See Brief of Appellee at 8, *United States vs Mendoza*, No. 23-0210 (CAAF Dec. 26, 2023) ('evidence that a victim could not consent, is also evidence that they did not consent'); id. at 12 ('The service Courts of criminal appeals (CCAA) [sic] agree that the Government may meet its burden of proving "without consent" by relying mainly on evidence of extreme intoxication' (footnote omitted)); id. at 20 ('the direct evidence of incapacitation through intoxication, on its own, is overwhelming evidence that Ms JW did not consent'); id. at 21 ('If someone is incapable of giving consent, clearly this is a factor in determining whether there was consent.').

Of course, we are mindful that the ACCA did not have the benefit of our decision holding that Article 120(b)(2)(A), UCMJ, and Article 120(b)(3)(A), UMCJ, establish separate theories of liability. This likely explains the lack of clarity in the ACCA's decision with respect to how it viewed and used the evidence of JW's intoxication. And although this Court does not review the factual sufficiency of convictions when we review cases under Article 67, UCMJ, 10 U.S.C. § 867 (2018), we 'retain the authority to review factual sufficiency determinations of the CCAs for the application of "correct legal principles", but only as to matters of law'.[6] *United States vs Clark*, 75 M.J. 298, 300 (CAAF 2016) (quoting United States vs Leak, 61 M.J. 234, 241 (CAAF 2005)). Indeed, in the past we have remanded cases when there is an 'open question' whether the CCA's factual sufficiency analysis applied correct legal principles. *United States vs Thompson*, 83 M.J. 1, 5 (CAAF 2022) (quoting *United States vs Nerad*, 69 M.J. 138, 147 (CAAF 2010)).

In our view, the ACCA's opinion presents an open question whether it improperly considered the evidence of JW's intoxication as proof of JW's inability to consent and therefore proof of the absence of consent. To be clear, our holding—that subsection (b)(2)(A) and subsection (b)(3)(A) create separate theories of liability—does not bar the trier of fact from considering evidence of the victim's intoxication when determining whether the victim consented. See Article 120(g)(7)(C), UCMJ ('All the surrounding circumstances are to be considered in determining whether a person gave consent.'). Nothing in the Article bars the Government from offering evidence of an alleged victim's intoxication to prove the absence of consent.[7] Conversely, nothing bars the defense from offering the same evidence to sow reasonable doubt.8 But what

---

6. Congress amended Article 67(c), UCMJ, in 2021, but that amendment only applies to offences that occurred on or after 1 January 2021. William M (Mac) Thornberry National Defense Authorization Act for Fiscal Year 2021, Pub. L. No. 116-283, § 542(e)(2), 134 Stat. 3388, 3612-13. Because the alleged offence in this case occurred in July 2020, the amended Article does not apply to this case. This opinion makes no comment on what changes, if any, that amendment had on this Court's authority to review the factual sufficiency of offences committed after 1 January 2021.

7. In this case, the Government argues that evidence of a victim's intoxication may be used to show that alcohol was used 'to reduce a victim's resistance'. Brief of Appellee at 17 n.12, *United States vs Mendoza, No. 23-0210 (CAAF 26 December 2023) (citation omitted) (internal quotation marks omitted).*

the Government can- not do is prove the absence of consent under Arti- cle 120(b)(2)(A), UCMJ, by merely establishing that the victim was too intoxicated to consent.

In this case, the Government argued that the evidence established both that JW would not have consented to the sexual act and that she was incapable of consenting to the sexual act. The ACCA's opinion affirming Appellant's conviction did not specify whether the ACCA found that JW was capable of consenting, stating only that the evidence established that Appellant engaged in sexual intercourse with a victim whom he knew to be 'highly intoxicated'. *Mendoza*, 2023 CCA LEXIS 198, at *10, 2023 WL 3540415, at *3. Recognising the significance of our holding with respect to Article 120(b)(2)(A), UCMJ, and the prominent role intoxication evidence played in Appellant's trial, we believe that the ACCA should reconsider the factual and legal sufficiency of Appellant's conviction in light of this opinion. Remanding to the ACCA will also give the parties a full and fair opportunity to be heard on the legal and factual sufficiency of Appellant's conviction under Article 120(b)(2)(A), UCMJ.

We therefore set aside the ACCA's decision and remand the case for a new review under Article 66, UCMJ, 10 U.S.C. § 866 (2018). We express no view on whether the evidence is factually or legally sufficient to support Appellant's conviction for a violation of Article 120(b)(2)(A), UCMJ, and instead leave that question for the ACCA to decide.

Conclusion

The decision of the United States Army Court of Criminal Appeals is set aside. The record of trial is returned to the Judge Advocate General of the Army for remand to the United States Army Court of Criminal Appeals for a new factual and legal sufficiency review under Article 66, UCMJ, 10 U.S.C. § 866 (2018).

Judge SPARKS, concurring in part and dissenting in part and in the judgment.

I join part II(B)(1) of the majority opinion because I agree with the majority that Article 120(b)(2)(A), UCMJ, and Article 120(b)(3)(A),

UCMJ, create separate theories of criminal liability. 10 U.S.C. § 920 (2018). The majority acknowledges, correctly in my opinion, that '[t]he Government's approach—which conflated two different and inconsistent theories of criminal liability—raises significant due process concerns'. *United States vs Mendoza,*__M.J.__,__(3) (CAAF 2024). And I am in complete agreement with the majority that:

> 'what the Government cannot do is charge one offence under one factual theory and then argue a different offence and a different factual theory at trial. Doing so robs the defendant of his constitutional "right to know what offence and under what legal theory he will be tried and convicted." '

Id. at__(13) (quoting *United States vs Riggins,* 75 M.J. 78, 83 (CAAF 2016)). The majority even goes so far as to explain that in this case '[t]he military judge may have convicted Appellant of sexual assault on the theory that JW was incapable of consenting without the Government proving that Appellant knew or should have known that she was incapable'. Id. at__(12–13). Again, I agree.

It is in deciding where we go from this point that the majority and I disagree. Instead of finding that the evidence is legally insufficient or that Government violated Appellant's due process right to fair notice by arguing an uncharged factual and legal theory of liability at trial and testing the error for prejudice, the majority instead concludes that the appropriate remedy in this case is to remand the case to the United States Army Court of Criminal Appeals (ACCA) for a new legal and factual sufficiency review in which the ACCA can explain 'how or why the evidence of JW's intoxication factored into its analysis'. *Id.* at__(3). With this I cannot agree.

First, I believe that the majority misconstrues Appellant's argument when it claims that he 'argues that the evidence was legally insufficient because the Government relied solely on circumstantial evidence'. *Id.* at__(6–7). Appellant does not argue that the Government can never prove lack of consent by circumstantial evidence. Rather, he argues that when the Government charges 'without consent' the burden of proof rests upon the Government to present legally sufficient evidence that affirmatively points to a lack of consent vice evidence that points to a lack of capacity to consent—a separate factual and legal theory. Brief of Appellant at 19–20, *United States vs Mendoza*, No. 23–0210 (CAAF 27 November 2023).[8] In short, Appellant argues that the Government failed to present legally sufficient evidence that the victim did not consent, despite the evidence presented that she may have been incapable of consent. He further argues that to affirm his conviction using evidence of an uncharged factual and legal theory would violate his due process right to fair notice. I agree—and I believe the majority does as well.

Nevertheless, the majority concludes that the correct result here is to remand this case to the ACCA for a new legal and factual sufficiency review in light of this opinion. Just how the ACCA's review must change is not entirely clear. On the one hand, the majority states, '[u]nder the actual charged offence, Article 120(b)(2)(A), UCMJ, it is not clear how the evidence of JW's intoxication factored into either the decision of the military judge or the opinion of the ACCA'. *Mendoza*,__M.J. at__(15). However, the majority later explains that its holding 'does not bar the trier of fact from considering evidence of the victim's intoxication when determining whether the victim consented'. Id. at__(16–17) ("All the surrounding circum- stances are to be considered in determining whether a person gave consent.' (internal quotation marks omitted) (quoting Article 120(g)(7)(C))). To that end, the majority does not appear concerned that the ACCA considered evidence of JW's intoxication, but only 'whether it improperly considered the evidence of JW's intoxication as proof of JW's inability to consent and therefore proof of the absence of consent'. *Id*. at (16) (emphasis added).

The majority's focus on whether the ACCA properly considered evidence of JW's intoxication in determining whether the Government presented sufficient evidence to convict Appellant of the charged crime ignores the real issue in this case—the Government's violation of Appellant's due process

8. Similarly, in dissenting from the ACCA opinion in this case, Senior Judge Walker explained, '[t]he charged offence requires the Government to affirmatively prove the victim did not consent and the Government failed to satisfy its burden on this essential element.' *United States vs Mendoza*, No. ARMY 20210647, 2023 CCA LEXIS 198, at *14, 2023 WL 3540415, at *5 (A. Ct. Criminal Appeal 8 May 2023) (unpublished) (Walker, SJ, dissenting). Senior Judge Walker further explained, '[t]he Government cannot rely exclusively on the victim's lack of memory due to intoxication as a proxy for satisfying its burden to prove a lack of consent, which is what occurred in this case.' Id. at *15, 2023 WL 3540415, at *6.

right to fair notice by charging Appellant with sexual assault without consent, but arguing at trial that he was guilty because JW was incapable of consent. This does not merely raise serious due process concerns. This is a violation of Appellant's due process right to fair notice. No explanation from the ACCA about how it considered the evidence of JW's intoxication will change the fact that Appellant's due process rights were violated at trial, long before this case reached the ACCA.

For the reasons explained below, I believe that the only options in this case are for this Court to find the evidence legally insufficient or, if the evidence is legally sufficient, to find that the Government violated Appellant's due process right to fair notice. Both routes require reversal. Neither leads to a second legal and factual sufficiency review by the ACCA. After reviewing the record in this case, I find the evidence is legally insufficient to affirm Appellant's conviction and would dismiss this case with prejudice. I therefore respectfully dissent.

Background

Given the nature of legal sufficiency review and the low bar to uphold a conviction, I believe it is necessary to explain the facts in detail. I apologise for restating facts already addressed by the majority, but I believe it is necessary to paint the complete picture of this case before reviewing the legal question at issue.

Appellant and JW were both stationed at Camp Casey, in South Korea. On the evening of 11 July 2020, JW went out to dinner with friends. She testified about what she remembers from that night after getting back from dinner as follows: 'I remember getting back to the barracks, there's a whole bunch of people out front drinking and whatnot, and I remember seeing Sergeant [B] from S2, and he had a bottle of vodka. I remember drinking that and that's the last thing I remember from that night.'

She testified that her final memories from that evening were around 11:00 p.m. The next thing she remembered was waking up to a knock on her barrack's room door the following morning.

It is undisputed that JW was intoxicated that evening. It is also undisputed that JW has no memory of having sex with Appellant and could not testify whether she consented to having sex with Appellant. Instead, her testimony consisted of claims that she would not have consented to sex with Appellant under the circumstances, including her lack of a social relationship with Appellant and the fact that she was menstruating at the time.

Video evidence presented at trial clearly shows Appellant and JW entering Appellant's room at approximately 2:08 a.m. on 12 July 2020. Before entering the room, JW appeared to be intoxicated, but seemed aware of what was happening and was able to walk on her own. As they approached Appellant's room, Appellant touched JW's crotch. This touching constituted the basis for the abusive sexual contact specification of which Appellant was found not guilty.

Appellant and JW remained in the room for slightly more than one hour, leaving the room at 3:11 a.m. At that point, JW was leaning on Appellant as they walked back to her room. While JW was not walking on her own, she was walking with Appellant's assistance and not simply being carried by Appellant, who is smaller in stature than JW.

JW awoke the following morning to a knock on her door. She answered the door and was greeted by Appellant, who returned her shoes to her. According to JW, she did not recognise Appellant and had no prior social interaction with him. She went back to sleep but awoke again to Appellant knocking. This time he asked if she was sure she was okay. It was at this point that JW realised she was no longer wearing her underwear from the previous night, despite still wearing her pants from the previous night.[9] She went to the bathroom and discovered that her tampon had been pushed all the way inside her body. JW began to panic and eventually went to the hospital and underwent a sexual assault forensic examination, which included obtaining DNA swabs from her vagina. According to her testimony at trial, JW 'filed a report just to figure out what had happened'. The DNA test confirmed that she and Appellant engaged in sexual intercourse.

---

9. JW admitted at trial that the sports bra and underwear she had been wearing the previous night were located on the floor of her room. JW's testimony also suggests that she had been wearing a pad rather than a tampon on the night of the assault, because she describes the photo showing her underwear as 'that is a photo of the underwear I was wearing with the pad I had been wearing'. JW also admitted that she could not recall when she put her tampon in, claiming 'it would have been the day prior', which suggests it happened during the period of time for which she has no memory.

A. Appellant's Confession

Appellant was interviewed by Army Criminal Investigation Division Special Agent (SA) Dereck Williams. SA Williams first spoke to Appellant when he was canvassing the barracks. During this informal interview in the parking lot, Appellant told SA Williams that JW had been in his room the prior night. After later identifying Appellant as a suspect, SA Williams formally interrogated Appellant in a recorded interview.

During the interview Appellant admitted that JW was extremely intoxicated, but he initially denied having sexual relations with her. After being confronted with the CCTV footage of them entering his room, Appellant admitted that they had sex, but claimed it was consensual. He then admitted that he knew she was too intoxicated to consent and made a written confession. In his written confession, Appellant explained that he and JW began to flirt while they were drinking in the day room:

> 'She leaned in and was whispering in my ear and kissing my neck and I pulled away initially however, became overwhelmed with emotion to give in and ignore all the signs and my own words [warning SGT RC that she was intoxicated]. I invited her down to my room and she followed in the process [I] groped her groin and thigh in the hallway. When we came into the room she initially sat on the bed and I the couch after a bit of conversation I got up to get a beer and we kissed, while kissing I asked her "is this okay?" she replied "show me what you got." We both began to remove clothing individually and I proceeded to lie down on the bed, she proceeded to give me oral sex and then I asked her to lie on her back. I then asked her to get on top [sic] of me, then I asked her to once again lie on her back. . . .She then went into the bathroom and closed the door and turned the shower on while she went to throw up. She did not throw up and [I] knocked on the door asking if she was ok twice both time [sic] she said she was ok. She opened the door the second time and fell back onto the toilet and I had to help her up, she then fell back again and I then helped her up out of the bathroom and onto my sink.'

In response to specific questions from SA Williams, Appellant admitted that JW was '[o]verly intoxicated', that she was not capable of giving consent when they had sex, and that he knew 'it was wrong to conduct sex acts on SPC [JW] when she was incapable of giving consent'.

B. The Charge

The Government charged Appellant with committing a sexual act upon JW, by penetrating her vulva with his penis, without her consent, in violation of Article 120(b)(2)(A), UCMJ. Appellant was not charged with sexual assault while the victim was incapable of consenting due to impairment by an intoxicant, in violation of Article 120(b)(3)(A), UCMJ.[10]

C. Trial

At trial, the Government argued that the evidence would show that Appellant committed the charged sexual acts without JW's consent. JW testified that she did not remember having sex with Appellant, but that she would never have had sex while on her period, nor would she have had sex with her tampon in.

The Government presented expert testimony from Dr RW, an expert in forensic biology with an emphasis on the effects of alcohol on behaviour. Dr RW testified that a 'blackout' from drinking can involve either partial or total memory loss for a portion of the drinking episode. He explained that blackouts typically occur at a blood alcohol content (BAC) of .14 or higher, with total memory loss typically occurring at .2 or higher. Dr RW estimated the victim's BAC on the night in question was between .175 and .19.

Additionally, Dr RW testified that individuals in a state of blackout can still engage in voluntary behaviour. Dr RW explained that after a blackout individuals attempt to piece together what happened during that period of time:

> 'And oftentimes they're doing that based on their own personal values. So oftentimes it's, you know, I typically do this, but, you know, so that must be what happened kind of situation. So that's how a person often tries to put together the pieces of the memory. And then oftentimes they may

10. The Government also charged Appellant with one specification of abusive sexual contact without consent, in violation of Article 120(d), UCMJ, for touching JW's groin without her consent. Appellant was found not guilty of that specification.

> find out from another person, when finding out what exactly happened during that memory, that it might not be what they expected because of alcohol.'

Dr RW also explained that 'as the blood alcohol level increases, a person may become more reckless, acts in sexually provocative ways or aggressive, and it also impairs a person's reaction time, comprehension, and motor movements'.

Dr RW viewed the CCTV footage in this case and commented upon JW's demeanour before and after she entered Appellant's room:

> 'So in reviewing the CCTV footage, I noticed there's a significant difference when [JW] left her room, I guess it was at about 1:47 and started to walk with—to [Appellant's] actual room. She was much more—she didn't appear to have a solid gait. So she had an uneven gait. She seemed a little bit staggery, but she was in stark contrast to what you saw once she left [Appellant's room], where she appeared to be much more sedated, where she was hanging on him and kind of being dragged along a little bit more. So that was just a stark difference between the two. And with that, it just made me think, you know, it's very much like the biphasic effects of alcohol . . . we call it the biphasic effects because you actually see a rise in the BAC, and during that rise, that's usually called the ascending limb, that's more stimulating. That's the more outgoing, the more talkative. And each person's slope can be different depending on what they're drinking or their weight. A lot of different factors.
>
> And then once a person stops drinking, there's about 30 to 45 minutes where the alcohol is being absorbed just to a person to reach their peak. That's their peak BAC And then at that point, the body starts to, you know—really the liver, starts to process and get rid of all that alcohol in the system. And that's when you start to see some of those withdrawal. Essentially, your body's going into alcohol withdrawal, the sedating effects. So you see a lot more of the person nodding off. A person really, really just looking sedated compared to what they were like when they were actually consuming alcohol.'

Finally, Dr RW testified that JW had Benadryl in her system, which could explain her steep decline from the point of entering Appellant's room to the time she left, if she took it during the time she was in her own room around 1:45 a.m.

D. Government's Closing Argument

During closing argument trial counsel argued, '[w]ith regard to consent, as you heard, [the victim] would not consent. *She could not*. She did not consent'. (Emphasis added.) Trial counsel also argued, the victim 'testified that she would not consent under those circumstances'. As trial counsel continued, he seemed to conflate blacking out with an inability to consent, claiming, JW 'could not consent under the circumstances. As she testified, she blacked out before 1:45 a.m., while she was still outside, before Specialist [L] went to retrieve her.'

When he discussed the legal definition of consent, trial counsel focused on the definition of 'competent person' and all the evidence the military judge should consider to conclude that JW was not competent to consent to the sexual acts in question. 'In other words,' he concluded, 'every eyewitness confirmed that Specialist [JW] was [sic] clearly— met the definition of an incompetent person before the accused took her to his room. And most importantly is that the accused knew it too.'

For all intents and purposes, the Government's argument at trial was that JW did not consent to the charged sexual acts because she was not competent to consent given her state of intoxication. The Government never argued, nor did JW testify, that JW ever gave any indication to Appellant that her participation in the sexual acts was not voluntary. Rather, the Government's sole theory of the case was that JW 'could not consent under the circumstances'.

Discussion

A. Standard of Review

This Court reviews questions of legal sufficiency *de novo*. *United States vs King*, 78 M.J. 218, 221 (CAAF 2019). ' "The test for legal sufficiency is whether, after viewing the evidence in the light most favourable to the prosecution, any rational trier of fact could have found the essential elements of the crime beyond a reasonable doubt." '[11] *United States vs Gutierrez,* 73 M.J. 172, 175 (CAAF 2014) (quoting United States vs Bennitt, 72 M.J. 266, 268 (CAAF 2013)). 'This legal sufficiency assessment draw[s] every reasonable inference from the evidence of record in favor of the prosecution.' King, 78 M.J. at 221 (alteration in original) (internal quotation marks omitted) (quoting *United States vs Robinson,* 77 M.J. 294, 298 (CAAF 2018)). As such, '[t]he standard for legal sufficiency involves a very low threshold to sustain a conviction.' Id. (quoting United States vs Navrestad, 66 M.J. 262, 269 (CAAF 2008) (Effron, CJ, joined by Stucky, J, dissenting)). 'The criterion thus impinges upon "jury" discretion only to the extent necessary to guarantee the fundamental protection of due process of law.' *Jackson vs Virginia,* 443 US 307, 319 (1979).

In order to meet its low burden of establishing legal sufficiency in this case, the Government relies on evidence that JW was incapable of consenting to prove that she did not consent. As the majority opinion acknowledges, 'there is no direct evidence that Appellant engaged in sexual intercourse "without the consent" of JW.' *Mendoza,* M.J. at __ (13–14). Nonetheless, the Government interprets the theories of sexual assault without consent and sexual assault while the victim is incapable of consent under Article 120 as overlapping. Like the majority, I reject this interpretation for a number of reasons.

First, the Government's argument that proof of incapacity necessarily means proof of a lack of consent violates the statutory interpretation canon against surplusage by rendering all theories of sexual assault other

11. The majority claims that this case 'departs from the usual "reasonable trier of fact" analysis because Appellant challenges the legal sufficiency of his sexual assault conviction on two unusual grounds'. *Mendoza,* __ M.J. at __ (6). However, the majority fails to explain what different standard we must now use. I disagree on this point and note that Appellant's arguments are not so unusual. Appellant simply argues that the evidence used by the Government in this case is not legally relevant because it supports an uncharged theory of liability and is therefore insufficient to support a finding of guilty. The fact that we must determine whether Appellant is correct that the Government cannot use evidence of an uncharged legal theory to prove a charged legal theory does not change the ultimate question of whether the Government did, in fact, present legally sufficient evidence for a rational trier of fact to find every element of the charge beyond a reasonable doubt.

than without consent superfluous. Second, contrary to the Government's argument, the legal theories of lack of consent and incapacity are legally contradictory rather than overlapping. And third, the Government violates a defendant's due process right to fair notice when it convicts him using a legal theory that was not charged.

B. The Government Argued at Trial That the Victim Was Incapable of Consenting

In this case, Appellant argues that there is no evidence in the record that JW did not consent to the sexual activity. On the other hand, the Government argues that 'there was ample direct evidence that [JW] was incapable of consent and strong circumstantial evidence that [JW] did not consent'. Brief of Appellee at 11, *United States vs Mendoza,* No. 23-0210 (CAAF Dec. 26, 2023). However, as explained above, the Government's argument to this Court that there is strong circumstantial evidence that JW did not consent was never made at trial. Rather, the Government's entire argument at trial was that JW was incompetent and therefore could not consent to sex.

The Government now argues to this Court that 'evidence that a victim could not consent, is also evidence that [she] did not consent'. *Id.* at 8. Therefore, we must determine whether evidence of a victim's incompetence necessarily proves a lack of consent in the context of Article 120(b)(2)(A) before we can determine whether the Government presented enough evidence to reach the low threshold of legal sufficiency for a charge of sexual assault without consent. For the reasons explained below, I believe that evidence of a victim's incompetence is not evidence of a lack of consent.

C. Canon Against Surplusage

I agree with the majority that the Government's interpretation of Article 120, UCMJ, violates the canon against surplusage. While I wish to avoid repeating the majority opinion's analysis, I still find it necessary to examine the statutory scheme of Article 120, UCMJ, before moving on to the next portion of my opinion in order to be clear about what relevance, if any, evidence of JW's intoxication has to proving a charge of without consent.

Congress has articulated multiple legal theories of sexual assault. These can be broken down into three basic categories: (1) sexual assault when a victim is physically capable of consent but not legally capable of consent due to circumstances created by the accused;[12] (2) sexual assault when the victim is capable of consenting and does not consent;[13] and (3) sexual assault when the victim is physically incapable of consent and that condition is known or reasonably should be known by the accused.[14]

According to the Government's interpretation of Article 120, all theories of sexual assault committed when the victim is legally or physically incapable of consent could be charged under the single theory that the victim did not consent. If, as the Government argues, evidence of an inability to consent is evidence of a lack of consent, the Government could prove a lack of consent by proving that the victim was legally or physically incapable of consenting to the alleged conduct. Were this the case, there would be no need for the Government to ever charge sexual assault when a victim is incapable of consent because it could simply prove a charge of sexual assault without consent using evidence of legal or physical incapacity.

Because the Government's interpretation would make every part of the statute articulating a theory of criminality except 'without consent' unnecessary, the majority correctly rejects this interpretation.

---

12. Article 120(b)(1)(A), UCMJ—'threatening or placing that other person in fear'; Article 120(b)(1)(B), UCMJ—'making a false representation that the sexual act serves a professional purpose'; or Article 120(b)(1)(C), UCMJ—'inducing a belief by any artifice, pretense, or concealment that the person is another person'.

13. Article 120(b)(2)(A), UCMJ—'without . . . consent'.

14. Article 120(b)(2)(B), UCMJ—'when the person knows or reasonably should know that the other person is asleep, unconscious, or otherwise unaware'; Article 120(b)(3)—

> commits a sexual act upon another person when the other person is incapable of consenting to the sexual act due to—
>
> > (A) impairment by any drug, intoxicant, or other similar substance, and that condition is known or reasonably should be known by the person; or
> >
> > (B) a mental disease or defect, or physical disability, and that condition is known or reasonably should be known by the person.

Furthermore, as the majority opinion points out, allowing the Government to charge sexual assault without consent and to argue an incapacity theory would allow the Government to avoid the obligation of proving beyond a reasonable doubt that the victim was actually incapable of consenting, and that the accused knew or reasonably should have known of the victim's incapacity, which I will address in the next section.

D. Lack of Consent and Incapacity Are Contradictory Theories of Criminality

The majority and I agree that Articles 120(b)(2)(A) and 120(b)(3)(A) present distinct factual and legal theories of sexual assault. However, as the majority points out, 'nothing prevents the Government from charging a defendant with both offences under inconsistent factual theories and allowing the trier-of-fact to determine whether the victim was capable or incapable of consenting'. *Mendoza*, __ M.J. at __ (13) (citing *United States vs Elespuru*, 73 M.J. 326, 330 (CAAF 2014)). Therefore, I find it necessary to examine the distinctions between these separate factual and legal theories of liability to determine the legal and logical relevance of the evidence presented in this case. As the majority points out, the majority's holding 'does not bar the trier-of-fact from considering evidence of the victim's intoxication when determining whether the victim consented'. *Id.* at __ (16–17) (citing Article 120(g)(7)(C), UCMJ). Given this permissible use of circumstantial evidence, we must examine whether direct evidence of JW's intoxication constitutes logically and legally relevant circumstantial evidence that JW did not, in fact, consent to the sexual activity in this case.

To prove a charge of sexual assault without consent the Government is required to prove that (1) the accused committed a sexual act upon the victim; and (2) the victim did not consent to the sexual act. Manual for *Courts-Martial, United States* pt. IV, para 60.b.(2)(d) (2019 ed.) (*MCM*). In order to prove a charge of sexual assault while the victim is incapable of consent the Government must prove that (1) the accused committed a sexual act upon the victim; (2) while the victim is incapable of consenting; and (3) the accused knew or reasonably should have known the victim was incapable of consenting. *MCM* pt. IV, para. 60.b.(2)(e).

According to Article 120(g)(7), UCMJ:

'(A) The term "consent" means a freely given agreement to the conduct at issue by a competent person. An expression of lack of consent through words or conduct means there is no consent. Lack of verbal or physical resistance does not constitute consent. Submission resulting from the use of force, threat of force, or placing another person in fear also does not constitute consent. A current or previous dating or social or sexual relationship by itself or the manner of dress of the person involved with the accused in the conduct at issue does not constitute consent.

(B) A sleeping, unconscious, or incompetent person cannot consent. A person cannot consent to force causing or likely to cause death or grievous bodily harm or to being rendered unconscious. A person cannot consent while under threat or in fear or under the circumstances described in sub-paragraph (B) or (C) or subsection (b)(1).

(C) All the surrounding circumstances are to be considered in determining whether a person gave consent.'

Furthermore, the term 'incapable of consenting' means the person is:

'(A) incapable of appraising the nature of the conduct at issue; or

(B) physically incapable of declining participation in, or communicating unwillingness to engage in, the sexual act at issue.'

Article 120(g)(8), UCMJ.

In his articulation of the elements of these offences, the President has explained that legal incapacity offences require proof of the specific circumstances (e.g., placing the victim in fear) that result in the legal incapacity to consent. MCM pt. IV, para. 60.b.(2)(a)–(c). He has also explained that physical incapacity offences require specific proof that the victim was incapable of consent. *MCM* pt. IV, para. 60.b.(2)(e)–(f). In contrast, a charge of sexual assault without consent does not require the Government to prove that the victim was capable of consenting. *MCM* pt. IV, para. 60.b.(2)(d). The Government acknowledges this in its brief when it admits 'the Government had no requirement to prove that the victim was competent; only that she did not, in fact, consent'. Brief of Appellee at 28, *United States vs Mendoza,* No. 23-0210 (CAAF 26 December 26, 2023) (alterations in original removed) (internal quotation marks omitted) (quoting *United States vs Motsenbocker*, No. 201600285, 2017 CCA LEXIS 539, *17 (N-M. Ct. Crim. App. 10 August 2017) (unpublished)).

While it may at first blush appear logical to argue that proving the victim was incapable of consenting necessarily proves that the victim did not consent—or that evidence of JW's intoxication constitutes circumstantial evidence that she did not consent—we need look no further than the majority's explanation of the two offences to reject this argument. 'Article 120(b)(2)(A), UCMJ, criminalises engaging in a sexual act with a person capable of consenting who did not consent, and Article 120(b)(3)(A), UCMJ, criminalises engaging in a sexual act with a person who is incapable of consenting . . . .' *Mendoza*, __ M.J. at (3). If this is so, and I believe it is, then evidence establishing the victim's incapacity necessarily disproves an allegation of sexual assault without consent. Thus, a closer look reveals that these two theories of criminality are legally contradictory rather than overlapping. Indeed, if Articles 120(b)(2)(A) and 120(b)(3)(A) constitute different and inconsistent theories of liability, as the majority claims, they must be different in the proof required and not in name only if the canon against surplusage is to mean anything.

Any incapacity theory of sexual assault requires the Government to prove beyond a reasonable doubt the victim's legal or physical incapacity. When charged under an incapacity theory the accused could offer proof of the victim's competence as a defence. For example, in Riggins, the Appellant was able to disprove what the Government charged in the original sexual assault specifications 'by demonstrating that, at the time of the sexual activity, [the victim] was not in fear'. 75 M.J. at 82. On appeal, this Court explained that incapacity and lack of consent are different legal theories of liability because 'the fact that the Government was required to prove a set of facts that resulted in [the victim]'s *legal inability* to consent was not the equivalent of the Government bearing the affirmative responsibility to prove that [the victim] *did not, in fact, consent*'. *Id*. at 84.

In contrast, as the Government acknowledges, when it charges sexual assault without consent it has no obligation to prove that the victim was competent. Unlike an incapacity theory of criminality, evidence of the victim's competency would offer no defence under a without consent theory. In other words, a charge of sexual assault without consent is equivalent to the

Government stipulating that the victim was competent to consent under the circumstances alleged. This is the root of the due process problem in this case. The Government charged the only theory of sexual assault for which proof of the victim's competency to consent is not a defence, then argued at trial that the victim was incapable of consenting.

Consistent with the Government's acknowledgment that a charge of sexual assault without consent does not require the Government to prove the victim's competency, it seems apparent to me that the Government would be unable to charge both theories of sexual assault—without consent and incapacity—in the alternative without necessarily disproving one charge at trial in order to prove the other. This is precisely what Appellant is getting at when he argues that the Government is required to present direct evidence of a lack of consent in order to prove sexual assault under Article 120(b)(2)(A). If the Government seeks to meet its burden using circumstantial evidence, it is the Government's burden to demonstrate the logical relevance of such evidence to prove an element of the charge—e.g., that evidence of intoxication makes it less likely that the victim would consent.

The majority alludes to the long-standing practice of allowing the Government to plead in the alternative to accommodate any contingencies of proof. *Mendoza*, __ M.J. at __ (13) (citing *Elespuru*, 73 M.J. at 330).[15] On this point, I would simply provide a cautionary note to military Judges. Should they encounter such pleadings, at the close of the evidence they should make a careful determination as to which offence is supported by the evidence and which one may not be supported. Then only one of these contingent offences should be sent to the trier-of-fact. After all, '[i]t is the Government's responsibility to determine what offence to bring against an accused. Aware of the evidence in its possession, the Government is presumably cognisant of which offences are supported by the evidence and which are not'. *United States vs Morton*, 69 M.J. 12, 16 (CAAF 2010).

Having explained the distinct and inconsistent nature of without consent and incapacity theories of liability, I now turn to the evidence in this case

---

15. In *Elespuru, this Court evaluated the Appellant's argument that his convictions for abusive sexual contact and wrongful sexual contact were multiplicious, not whether conflicting theories of liability violate the due process right to fair notice. 73 M.J. at 327.*

and examine whether the Government presented legally sufficient evidence of JW's lack of consent.

E. The Government Failed to Prove Sexual Assault Without Consent

First, it has been well established that the Government argued at trial and on appeal that JW was legally incapable of consent on the night in question. If that is the case, the Government is legally incapable of proving Appellant's guilt under Article 120(b)(2)(A), UCMJ. However, despite the Government's argument on this point, no court has found as a matter of law that JW was incapable of consent. Therefore, we must now examine whether the evidence presented at trial is sufficient to prove that JW did not, in fact, consent.

It bears restating that there is no direct evidence that JW did not consent to the sexual activity that took place. The Government argues, however, that there is 'strong circumstantial evidence that [JW] did not consent'. Brief of Appellee at 11, *United States vs Mendoza*, No. 23-0210 (CAAF 26 December 2023). Similarly, the majority, despite not reaching the question of legal sufficiency, claims that there is 'significant circumstantial evidence on this point'. *Mendoza*, __ M.J. at __ (13–14). According to the majority:

> 'This evidence includes: (1) testimony that JW had no prior relationship with Appellant; (2) testimony that JW would never have sex while on her period; (3) testimony that JW would not have pushed a tampon so far inside of herself; (4) testimony that JW made a morning-after report to the CQ desk after she realised something was wrong; (5) testimony that JW was upset; (6) testimony that Appellant initially denied that he had engaged in any sexual acts with JW; and (7) testimony that JW locked herself in Appellant's bathroom.'

Id. at __ (14 n.3).

In making this assertion, the majority neglects important facts and makes much of evidence that is subject to multiple explanations. For example, Appellant's initial denial of engaging in sexual acts with JW could be interpreted as evidence of consciousness of guilt for engaging in sex with someone he believed was not capable of consenting—as he explained in his confession and the Government argued at trial—or it could be interpreted as evidence that he did not want to confess to extramarital sexual conduct. But it is not enough for the Government to prove that Appellant had a guilty conscience, it must prove the specific elements of the crime for which Appellant feels guilty.

Appellant did admit that he knew JW was incapable of consenting. But at no point during the interview was Appellant provided with a legal definition of incapacity. While Appellant's confession provides strong evidence that JW may have been too intoxicated to consent, it does not establish that she did not consent. Indeed, his confession describes JW as actively engaging in the sexual acts, rather than being unable to appreciate the nature of the conduct or unable to decline participation therein. See Article 120(g)(7) ('"incapable of consenting" means the person is (A) incapable of appraising the nature of the conduct at issue; or (B) physically incapable of declining participation in, or communicating unwillingness to engage in, the sexual act at issue').

Similarly, evidence that JW and Appellant lacked a prior relationship, testimony from JW that she would never have sex on her period and would never push a tampon so far inside herself, and evidence that JW seemed upset all ignore the overwhelming evidence that JW was intoxicated on the night in question and acting in ways uncharacteristic of her normal behaviour.

Nor does JW's immediate report provide any evidence that JW did not consent to the sexual acts in question. Rather than reporting a sexual assault, JW testified at trial that she 'filed a report just to figure out what had happened'. It is precisely because of JW's inability to testify that she was sexually assaulted that the Government must prove its case by circumstantial evidence.

The Government argues that the JW's intoxication is simply part of 'all [the] surrounding circumstances [that] are to be considered in determining whether a person gave consent'. Brief of Appellee at 17, No. 23-0210 (CAAF 26 December 2023) (internal quotation marks omitted) (quoting Article 120(g)(8)). To that end, the ACCA pointed to 'the victim's high level of intoxication' as evidence supporting a finding of guilty. *Mendoza,* 2023 CCA LEXIS 198, at *8, 2023 WL 3540415, at *3. However, this conclusion is at best questionable and at worst contradicted by the expert testimony presented in this case. Specifically, the Government's expert witness Dr RW testified that 'as the blood alcohol level increases, a person may become more reckless, acts in sexually provocative ways or aggressive, and it also impairs a person's reaction time, comprehension, and motor movements'. Dr RW did not testify that an increased BAC makes a person less likely to consent to sexual activity.

Dr RW also estimated that JW's B.A.C. was between .175 to .19, which would result in her not acting like her 'usual self'. Indeed, Sergeant RC testified that on the night in question JW 'wasn't acting like herself. Most of the encounters I've had with her she's more of just kind of an introverted, more to herself type person. This time she was more outgoing [and] started becoming flirtatious in a way'. Given the expert and lay testimony presented at trial, evidence of JW's intoxication provides more basis for reasonable doubt than it does circumstantial evidence that she did not consent.

While the Government points to testimony from JW that she would not have consented under these circumstances, the video evidence in this case shows she and Appellant entered his room together while they appear to be flirting, both intoxicated. In fact, the military Judge—the sole fact-finder in this case—found Appellant not guilty of the charge of abusive sexual contact alleged to have occurred just before they entered Appellant's barracks room. The CCTV footage and Appellant's admissions leave no doubt that the touching took place, so we are left to conclude that the military Judge did not believe JW did not consent to the touching in the hallway, nor that she was incapable of consenting as she entered Appellant's room (as the Government argued at trial).

Despite this finding by the military Judge that necessarily finds that JW consented to sexual contact moments before entering Appellant's room, the Government would have us conclude that the evidence is sufficient for a rational trier-of-fact to conclude beyond a reasonable doubt that she did not consent to sexual acts that took place at some point after entering the room. Given JW's lack of memory regarding whether or not she consented, the expert testimony from Dr RW regarding the effects of alcohol and JW's level of intoxication, and the substance of Appellant's confession, I cannot conclude that the evidence supports a finding that JW did not consent.

In sum, after viewing the evidence in the light most favourable to the prosecution, I cannot conclude that any rational trier-of-fact could have found the essential elements of the crime beyond a reasonable doubt.

Conclusion

Without consent and incapacity to consent are two separate theories of criminal liability. The Government made the decision to charge Appellant with sexual assault without consent and therefore could not prove Appellant's guilt by proving that JW was incapable of consent. The fact of the matter is the Government charged Appellant with the wrong offence and proceeded to trial with evidence that supported a different uncharged offence. A due process violation occurred at trial that a remand to the lower Court simply cannot cure. Further, having reviewed the record in this case, I cannot conclude that a rationale trier-of-fact could be satisfied beyond a reasonable doubt that JW did not consent to the sexual acts that took place after she entered Appellant's room.

For these reasons, I respectfully dissent from the decision to remand and would dismiss Appellant's conviction with prejudice.

Judge MAGGS, concurring in part and dissenting in part.

I concur with the Court's interpretation of Article 120(b)(2)(A), Uniform Code of Military Justice (UCMJ), 10 U.S.C. § 920(b)(2)(A) (2018). I disagree, however, with one aspect of the Court's disposition of this appeal. Specifically, while the Court remands the case for both a new legal and factual sufficiency review, I would hold that the evidence is legally sufficient and remand solely for a new factual sufficiency review. I therefore respectfully concur in part and dissent in part.

Background

In the supplement to his petition for review, Appellant asked this Court to decide '[w]hether [his] conviction for sexual assault without consent should be reversed?' He asserted that this Court should set aside the decision of the United States Army Court of Criminal Appeals (ACCA) because the evidence was legally insufficient. In the alternative, Appellant contended that allowing his conviction to stand based on the evidence admitted at trial would amount to a constructive amendment of the charged offence.

This Court granted review of a modified version of the question that Appellant presented in his supplement, namely, '[w]hether Appellant's conviction for sexual assault without consent was legally sufficient'. *United*

States vs Mendoza, 84 M.J. 105 (CAAF 2023) (order granting review). The parties' briefs, accordingly, focus on the legal sufficiency of the evidence of lack of consent under Article 120(b)(2)(A), UCMJ. The Court, however, does not answer the granted question but instead remands the case so that the ACCA may perform both a new legal sufficiency review and a new factual sufficiency review.

Legal Sufficiency

Questions of legal sufficiency are reviewed de novo. United States vs Brown, 84 M.J. 124, 127 (CAAF 2024) (citing *United States vs Wilson,* 76 M.J. 4, 6 (CAAF 2017)). Accordingly, this Court has the ability and authority to decide whether the evidence is legally sufficient without any further review by the ACCA. I see no prudential reason not to do so in this case given that we specified the issue of legal sufficiency and that the parties thoroughly briefed this issue.

As the Court correctly explains, the bar for finding the evidence to be legally sufficient is 'very low'. *United States vs King,* 78 M.J. 218, 221 (CAAF 2019) (internal quotation marks omitted) (citation omitted). We must consider 'whether, after viewing the evidence in the light most favourable to the prosecution, any rational trier-of-fact could have found the essential elements of the crime beyond a reasonable doubt'. *United States vs Smith,* 83 M.J. 350, 359 (CAAF 2023) (internal quotation marks omitted) (quoting *United States vs Robinson,* 77 M.J. 294, 297–98 (CAAF 2018)).

The Court properly holds in this case that evidence that the victim was incapable of consenting because of intoxication generally cannot prove lack of consent in a case charged under Article 120(b)(2)(A), UCMJ. This holding implicates the legal sufficiency of the evidence for finding Appellant guilty because, as one of the ACCA judges observed, the 'Government's primary evidence of lack of consent in this case was the victim's lack of memory due to intoxication and outward manifestation of intoxication'. *United States vs Mendoza,* No. ARMY 20210647, 2023 CCA LEXIS 198, at *12, 2023 WL 3540415, at *4 (A. Ct. Criminal Appeal 8 May 2023) (Walker, SJ, dissenting) (unpublished). But even if all of the intoxication evidence must be put aside, the record in this case still contains other evidence potentially relevant to the issue of consent. This Court may determine whether this other evidence is legally sufficient to sustain the finding that Appellant is guilty. *United States vs Long*, 81 M.J. 362, 364 (CAAF 2021) (assessing legal sufficiency in this manner).

The other evidence in this case includes: (1) testimony that JW (the alleged victim) had no prior relationship with Appellant; (2) testimony that JW would never have sex while on her period; (3) testimony that JW would not have pushed a tampon so far inside of herself; (4) testimony that JW made a morning-after report to the Charge of Quarters (CQ) desk after she realised something was wrong; (5) testimony that JW was upset; (6) testimony that Appellant initially denied that he had engaged in any sexual acts with JW; and (7) testimony that JW locked herself in Appellant's bathroom. Based on this other evidence, I would hold that a rational trier-of-fact could have found that the element of lack of consent under Article 120(b)(2)(A), UCMJ, was proven beyond a reasonable doubt. Accordingly, I would answer the granted question in the affirmative, and I would not remand the case to the ACCA for further review of the legal sufficiency of the evidence.

Factual Sufficiency

While I would decide that the evidence was legally sufficient, I concur with the Court's decision to remand the case for a new factual sufficiency review. Although the granted question and the briefs in this appeal do not address factual sufficiency, our new clarification of the relationship between Article 120(b)(2)(A), UCMJ, and Article 120(b)(3)(A), UCMJ, raises the question of whether the ACCA may have erred in its factual sufficiency analysis. Because this Court cannot review questions of factual sufficiency *de novo*, Appellant is entitled to have the ACCA perform a proper factual sufficiency review in the first instance.

(2025) I FLR 284 (India)

Supreme Court of India

Union of India & Others vs Lt Col Rahul Arora

Composition of Court: Prashant Kumar Mishra and Prasanna Bhalachandra Varale, JJ

Date of Decision: 9 September 2024

Counsel for the Appellant: Mr. R. Bala
Counsel for the Respondent: Mr. G.S. Ghuman

Summary

Respondent was an officer of the Army Medical Corps of the Indian Army. He was dismissed from service following the accusation of a solider that he changed the soldier's status from "unfit" to "fit" following the soldier's payment of money to him. Respondent was charged with violating the law on three charges involving intent to defraud and altering a document, absenting himself without leave and for conduct unbecoming of an officer and the character expected of his position.

Respondent was found guilty on two of the three charges by the General Court Martial (GCM) and this decision was upheld by the Armed Forces Tribunal (AFT). Respondent challenged the order of the AFT before the High Court of Punjab & Haryana. The High Court allowed the writ petition of the Respondent on the ground that an officer junior to the Respondent was placed as a Judge Advocate in the trial, which was in violation of law laid down by the Supreme Court. The dismissal of the Respondent and the order of the AFT was set-aside by the High Court.

Headnotes

Facts: Besides the legal issue of the appointment of an officer as the Judge Advocate who was junior than the accused, it was also noted by the Supreme Court that it had been observed by the High Court that the Appellant and Respondent had submitted two different convening orders. The Appellant's order contained reasons for appointing a junior officer as Judge Advocate, but the document produced by the Respondent did not. It was further observed that the one produced by the Appellant had been altered after despatch.

Issue: Can a Judge Advocate, who is inferior in rank, legally offer advice to the Court Martial against a superior officer in a GCM? Were the prerequisites of bringing a junior officer as a Judge Advocate met?

Contentions of the Parties: The Appellant submitted that there is no blanket prohibition on appointing an officer of lower rank than the charged officer to serve as Judge Advocate in a Court Martial. Appellant further contended that the judgment of the Supreme Court of India in Charanjit Singh Gill carved out an exception that when a superior officer is not available, a junior officer can serve as Judge Advocate. Appellant then cited S.P.S. Rajkumar for the proposition that a Court Martial is not invalidated by the appointment of a Judge Advocate. The Respondent contented that the prerequisites of bringing a junior officer as a Judge Advocate were not met and the judgment of the High Court was in line with what had been held by the Supreme Court of India in Charanjit Singh Gill.

Held: It was held by the Supreme Court that the legal position is well settled that non-recording of reasons of appointment of an officer junior in rank as a Judge Advocate in the convening order invalidates the Court Martial proceedings and that the High Court had not committed any error of law in holding so. Civil Appeal filed by the Union of India dismissed.

Case Law Cited

Union of India vs Charanjit Singh Gill, 2000 (5) SCC 742

Union of India vs S.P.S Rajkumar, 2007 (6) SCC 407

JUDGMENT

Prashant Kumar Mishra, J

This appeal is directed against the order dated 21 May 2014 passed by the High Court of Punjab & Haryana in CWP No. 20380 of 2012. Under the said order, the High Court has set aside the order passed by the Armed Forces Tribunal, Chandigarh[1], which has dismissed the appeal of the Respondent and upheld the findings and sentence awarded by the General Court-Martial[2].

(2.) The Respondent was first commissioned in the Army Medical Corps[3] as medical officer from 29 May 1978 to 31 July 1983. He was again commissioned as regular officer in AMC on 25 February 1987. In 1996, he was designated as Graded ENT Specialist and was then upgraded as classified Specialist ENT in the year 2001. In the month of February 2002, the Respondent was posted with Military Hospital, Secunderabad wherein he was required to examine new recruits being forwarded by various training centres.

(3.) In September, 2002 one Recruit/Soldier/GD K. Siddaiah alleged that the Respondent paid money for reviewing its remarks 'unfit' to 'review after 15 days'. The statement of the recruit was recorded by one Maj. Mrs RMB Mythilly who initiated AFMSF-7. The Respondent was charge-sheeted, and three charges were framed against him, namely:

> '(i) The Respondent, an ENT Specialist at a Military Hospital, had, for extraneous consideration declared an army recruit, K. Siddaiah, as 'fit' after previously declaring him 'unfit'. Consequently, the first charge against him was under Section 57(c) of the Army Act for knowingly and with intent to defraud altering a document/remarks in the AFMSF-7.
>
> (ii) The second charge was under Section 39(a) of the Army Act for absenting himself without leave from 11 April 2004 to 19 April 2004.

1.'AFT'.

2.'GCM'.

3.'AMC'.

(iii) The third charge was under Section 45 of the Army Act for conduct unbecoming of an officer and the character expected of his position.'

(4.) Upon conclusion of trial by GCM and upon finding two out of three charges proven, the Respondent was dismissed from service against which he preferred proceedings before AFT, which upheld the findings of guilt and the sentence of dismissal from service as awarded by the GCM. It is this order of the AFT which was assailed by the Respondent before the High Court. The High Court allowed the writ petition preferred by the Respondent solely on the ground that an officer junior to the Respondent has acted as Judge Advocate in the GCM contrary to the law laid down by this Court in *Union of India & Anr. vs Charanjit Singh Gill*[4].

(5.) Assailing the impugned order of the High Court, Shri R. Bala, learned Senior Advocate for the Appellant/Union of India has argued that there is no blanket prohibition on appointing an officer of lower rank than the charged officer to serve as Judge Advocate in a court-martial. He would strenuously urge that in *Charanjit Singh Gill* (supra), this Court has carved out an exception to the effect that 'a Judge Advocate appointed with the court-martial should not be an officer of a rank lower than that of the officer facing the trial unless the officer of such rank is not (having due regard to the exigencies of public service) available and the opinion regarding non-availability is specifically recorded in the convening order'. According to learned senior counsel, the present case falls within the above exception inasmuch as non-availability of an officer of equivalent or higher rank was specifically recorded in the convening order. It is also argued, referring to Army Rule 103 that a court-martial shall not be invalid merely by reason of any invalidity in the appointment of the Judge Advocate officiating thereat. Reference is made to *Union of India vs S.P.S. Rajkumar and Ors.*[5]

(6.) Per contra, Shri G.S. Ghuman, learned counsel appearing for the Respondent would submit that one Major Rajiv Dutta was appointed as a Judge Advocate in the court-martial, who was junior in rank to the Respondent. This

4. 2000 (5) SCC 742.

5. 2007 (6) SCC 407.

was informed to the Respondent by forwarding certified copy of the convening order under the Army Rules 33 (7) and 34 and the same was also received by the Respondent on 7 October 2014. Both the copies were filed with the written statement. In these orders, the prerequisites of bringing the appointment of an officer equivalent or junior to the rank of the Respondent was not mentioned, therefore, the High Court has taken the correct view in the matter by referring to *Charanjit Singh Gill* (supra).

(7.) In the present appeal, we are only concerned with the legality of the appointment of Judge Advocate who was admittedly junior to the Respondent, therefore, we are not dwelling on the facts of the case or merits of the charges.

(8.) Before the High Court, two different convening orders were produced. One by the Appellant and the other one by the Respondent. While the documents submitted by the Appellant contained the reasons for appointing a junior as the Judge Advocate whereas in the convening order submitted by the Respondent no such reason was mentioned. After comparing the documents, the High Court has recorded a finding that the convening order Annexure R-I (produced by the Appellant before the High Court) has been altered after the same was dispatched and received by the Headquarters Artillery Centre, Hyderabad. The High Court noted that Annexure P-I is identically worded, but in the second page, the words 'in my opinion having due regard to the exigencies of public service an officer of equal or superior rank to the accused is not available to act as Judge Advocate' are additional. The High Court specifically observed that once a document has been put in the course of transmission by the General Officer Commanding, Andhra Pradesh, Tamil Nadu, Karnataka and Kerala Area, the same could not be changed/altered or modified except after recording that there was a mistake, which needs correction. Once dispatched by the officer signing the same, the communication of the document is complete and any alteration in the document is unauthorised.

(9.) In the above circumstances, it is quite apparent that the reason for culling out exception as held permissible by this Court in *Charanjit Singh Gill* (supra), was not mentioned in the document while the same was dispatched by the issuing authority and supplied to the Respondent. Subsequent mentioning of the reason in the other document, after putting signatures by the issuing authority, was unauthorised and impermissible, the High Court has correctly held that the convening order suffers from incurable defect as held by this Court in *Charanjit Singh Gill* (supra) in the following words:

> '16. It is true that a Judge Advocate theoretically performs no function as a Judge but it is equally true that he is an effective officer of the Court conducting the case against the accused under the Act. It is his duty to inform the Court of any defect or irregularity in the charge and in the constitution of the Court or in the proceedings. The quality of the advice tendered by the Judge Advocate is very crucial in a trial conducted under the Act. With the role assigned to him a Judge Advocate is in a position to sway the minds of the members of the court-martial as his advice or verdict cannot be taken lightly by the persons composing the Court who are admittedly not law-knowing persons. It is to be remembered that the courts-martial are not part of the judicial system in the country and are not permanent courts.
>
> 18. In view of what has been noticed hereinabove, it is apparent that if a "fit person" is not appointed as a Judge Advocate, the proceedings of the court-martial cannot be held to be valid and its finding legally arrived at. Such an invalidity in appointing an 'unfit' person as a Judge Advocate is not curable under Rule 103 of the Rules. If a fit person possessing requisite qualifications and otherwise eligible to form part of the General Court-Martial is appointed as a Judge Advocate and ultimately some invalidity is found in his appointment, the proceedings of the court-martial cannot be declared invalid. A "fit person" mentioned in Rule 103 is referable to Rules 39 and 40. It is contended by Shri Raval, learned Additional Solicitor General that a person fit to be appointed as Judge Advocate is such officer who does not suffer from any ineligibility or disqualification in terms of Rule 39 alone. It is further contended that Rule 40 does not refer to disqualifications. We cannot agree with this general proposition made on behalf of the Appellant inasmuch as sub-rule (2) of Rule 40 specifically provides that members of a court-martial for trial of an officer should be of a rank not lower than that of the officer facing the trial unless such officer is not available regarding which specific opinion is required to be recorded in the convening order. Rule 102 unambiguously provides that "an officer

> who is disqualified for sitting on a court-martial, shall be disqualified for acting as a Judge Advocate at that court-martial". A combined reading of Rules 39, 40 and 102 suggests that an officer, who is disqualified to be a part of a court-martial, is also disqualified from acting and sitting as a Judge Advocate at the court-martial. It follows, therefore, that if an officer lower in rank than the officer facing the trial cannot become a part of the court-martial, the officer of such rank would be disqualified for acting as a Judge Advocate at the trial before a GCM. Accepting a plea to the contrary would be invalidating the legal bar imposed upon the composition of the Court in sub-rule (2) of Rule 40.
>
> 20. The purpose and object of prescribing the conditions of eligibility and qualification along with desirability of having members of the court-martial of the rank not lower than the officer facing the trial is obvious. The law-makers and the rule-framers appear to have in mind the respect and dignity of the officer facing the trial till guilt is proved against him by not exposing him to the humiliation of being subjected to trial by officers of lower rank. The importance of the Judge Advocate as noticed earlier being of a paramount nature requires that he should be such person who inspires confidence and does not subject the officer facing the trial to humiliation because the accused is also entitled to the opinion and services of the Judge Advocate. Availing of the services or seeking advice from a person junior in rank may apparently be not possible ultimately resulting in failure of justice.'

(10.) The legal position is thus well settled in *Charanjit Singh Gill* (supra) that non-recording of reasons of appointment of an officer junior in rank as a Judge Advocate in the convening order invalidates the court-martial proceedings. The High Court has not committed any error of law in holding so in the facts and circumstances of the case.

(11.) The next argument raised by the Appellant taking shelter of Army Rule 103 is referred only to be rejected for the reason that the protection under this rule is available only where a fit person has been appointed as a Judge Advocate. If the person so appointed is not fit to act and perform the duties of the Judge Advocate as held in *Charanjit Singh Gill* (supra), Rule 103 would not come to the rescue of the Appellant. Moreover, such argument has already been rejected by this Court in paragraph 18 of the report in *Charanjit Singh Gill* (supra).

(12.) In view of the forgoing discussion, we find no substance in this civil appeal which deserves to be and is hereby dismissed.

Prashant Kumar Mishra, J
Prasanna Bhalachandra Vale,J

New Delhi
9 September 2024

(2025) I FLR 292 (India)

The High Court of Delhi

Writ Petition (Civil) 3294/2023

Rajneesh vs Union of India

Composition of Court: Justice Rekha Palli and Justice Shailinder Kaur

Date of Decision: 28 August 2024

Counsel for the Petitioner: Mr. Vinod Dahiya, Mr. Saaransh Sharma and Mr. Vandana Dahiya, Advocates
Counsel for Union of India: Mr. Rishabh Sahu, Senior Panel Counsel with Mr. Sameer Sharma, Adv.

Summary

Following the petitioner's dismissal from service in the Border Security Force (BSF), he filed a petition under Article 226 of the Constitution of India. His petition emanated from the Summary Security Force Court (SSFC) proceedings, which convicted him on the basis of his purported "plea of guilty" for his alleged role in smuggling of "phensedyl" from Bangladesh to India. Following his dismissal, the petitioner first filed a statutory petition before the Inspector General, BSF. Following the dismissal of the statutory petition, the petitioner sought quashing of the impugned orders and prayed for reinstatement in service with all due benefits accruing to him. The merits of the case notwithstanding, the petitioner's counsel argued the findings of the SSFC should be set-aside due to procedural defects. As for the SSFC proceedings, the petitioner contended they were conducted without complying with the BSF Act and Rules. The respondents contended that there were no procedural defects and all proceedings were conducted in strict compliance with the BSF Act and Rules, and that the petitioner was provided ample opportunity to defend himself. The court noted the powers vested in the High Courts under Article 226 of the Constitution of India are limited. However, the exercise of these powers is certainly warranted in cases where there is an error of jurisdiction, or violation of principles of natural justice, or if any manifest error of law is apparent on the face of record. It is also warranted in cases where the order impugned has been passed in a malafide manner or with bias. The court held that Rule 63 of the BSF Rules was violated, which prevented the petitioner from having enough time to prepare his defence and that the proceedings were rushed to the point of becoming a mere formality and mechanical. The court further held that in light of the facts and circumstances of the case, dismissal from service awarded to the petitioner was vitiated. The court reasoned that because the proceedings were conducted in blatant violation of Rule 63(6) and Rule 142(2) of BSF Rules, the impugned orders were liable to be set aside. The court directed the respondent to reinstate the petitioner into service with all consequential benefits while retaining the right of the respondent to conduct a *de novo* trial within 3 months. The court then underscored the prevalence of a lackadaisical attitude while conducting SSFC proceedings. It emphasized the importance of strict adherence to the procedures due to the serious impact the charges have, on not only the personnel, but their families as well.

Headnotes

Facts: This case follows the petitioner's plea of guilty for his alleged role in the smuggling of "phensedyl" from Bangladesh to India and, consequently, his dismissal from service vide the impugned order dated 19.01.2022. The petitioner thereafter filed a statutory petition before the Inspector General, Border Security Force (BSF), which was dismissed vide the other impugned order dated 05.04.2022. Before the smuggling incident, the petitioner had received 12 "Good" decoration rewards with no adverse remarks in his service of 9 years 8 months, and 5 days. This case largely hinges on the propriety of the Record of Evidence (ROE) and Charge-Sheet presented to the petitioner. The ROE was completed after an inordinate delay. The ROE was to be completed on 05.12.2021 but was completed only on 24.12.2021. Further, the Charge-Sheet was not presented to the petitioner 24 hours before the commencement of the trial by the SSFC. Ultimately, the SSFC completed the petitioner's trial in barely 50 minutes on 19.01.2022

Issue: Whether the petitioner has been fairly tried by the SSFC with due compliance of BSF Act and Rules particularly, when the petitioner disputes having pleaded guilty?

Reasoning: First, the court reasoned that the exercise of the powers under Article 226 of the Constitution of India was certainly warranted in cases where there is an error of jurisdiction, or violation of principles of natural justice, or if any manifest error of law apparent on the face of record. The court further reasoned that Article 226 was not in conflict with military codes that governed the action against the petitioner.

Next, the court found that failure to provide the petitioner with ROE and Charge-Sheet 24 hours before the commencement of SSFC violated Rule 63 and reduced the petitioner's trial to an empty formality. The court noted that these trials must be held in accordance with the principles of natural justice and the laid down procedure, so as to enable the disciplinary authority to take an informed decision.

The court next addressed the petitioner's plea of guilty. The court pointed to the original records of the SSFC which indicated the trial was conducted in a slipshod manner with the Commandant, who was the Presiding Officer, having prepared the record of the SSFC proceedings in advance in violation of Rule 142(2). The court held that in light of the facts, it was constrained to hold that either the petitioner never pleaded guilty to the Charge or his plea of guilty as recorded by the Court was not voluntary. As such, the right of the petitioner to have a fair trial before the SSFC was violated, and he was condemned unheard without following the principles of natural justice.

Held: The SSFC proceedings, including the award of sentence of dismissal from service awarded to the petitioner, were vitiated. The court held the proceedings were conducted in blatant violation of Rule 63(6) and Rule 142(2) of BSF Rules and the ruling should be set aside. The court further emphasized that these proceedings must be given due regard to the rules and procedures outlined in the BSF Act and Rules. The court charged Presiding Officers with the duty to understand that these trials are not just mere formalities but are a fundamental aspect of ensuring justice and maintaining discipline in the Force by following the prescribed procedure. This duty is of utmost importance in order to safeguard the rights of the accused as well as the commitment of the Force in upholding the rule of law and maintaining the highest standards of discipline within its ranks. Failure thereof will only result in a miscarriage of justice, for both the individuals as well as the Force.

JUDGMENT

Shalinder Kaur, J

(1.) The present petition under Article 226 of the Constitution of India emanates from the Summary Security Force Court (SSFC) proceedings which convicted the Petitioner on the basis of his purported 'plea of guilty' for his alleged role in smuggling of 'phenesdyl' from Bangladesh to India and consequently, awarded him dismissal from service vide the impugned order dated 19 January 2022, against which a statutory petition filed by him before the Inspector General, Border Security Force (BSF) came to be dismissed vide the other impugned order dated 5 April 2022. Thus, the Petitioner has sought quashing of the impugned orders besides praying for reinstatement in service with all due benefits accruing to him.

(2.) Brief facts are such, the Petitioner joined the BSF as a Constable (General Duty) on 15 May 2012. While being posted to perform his duties at 158th Battalion, BSF at Border Out Post (BOP) in Khararmath, he was, on the night of 2/3 October 2021, detailed for 'Ambush Cum Patrolling' (ACP) between 00.01 to 06.00 hours at duty point 36A at BOP, Khararmath. During the said period, an incident of smuggling took place, wherein the Petitioner has been alleged to have facilitated in the act of smuggling of phenesdyl syrup from Bangladesh to India.

(3.) Based on this incident, a Record of Evidence (ROE) was held, upon consideration whereof, the Commandant notified the Petitioner on 17 January 2022 that he would be tried by the SSFC under Sections 70 and 74 of the BSF Act, 1968 on a charge under Section 40 of the BSF Act for acts 'prejudicial to the good order and discipline of the Force'. A copy of the charge sheet was served on the Petitioner on 18 January 2022 and the SSFC proceedings were thereafter held on 19 January 2022. Upon conclusion of trial, the Petitioner was held guilty of the charge on the basis of a 'plea of guilty' and was consequently dismissed from service without pensionary benefits.

(4.) It is the case of the Petitioner that on 20 January 2022, when he was instructed to put his signatures on certain documents before receiving the copy of the SSFC's order, it was the first time that he came to know that he had been held guilty under Section 40 of the BSF Act and had been dismissed from the service. The Petitioner upon learning about his dismissal, filed a statutory petition against the said order of dismissal on 4 February 2022 under Rule 28A of the BSF Rules before the inspector general (IG), Frontier Headquarter, BSF, South Bengal. However, the IG, BSF dismissed his petition vide order dated 5 April 2022, in the meanwhile Deputy Inspector General (DIG) SHQ, Kolkata, BSF, had confirmed the sentence during the pendency of the first appeal before the IG.

(5.) Dissatisfied with the aforesaid order, the Petitioner on 9 May 2022 submitted an application/request letter for a personal hearing to the Director General (DG), BSF, Delhi, seeking a fresh fair trial and his reinstatement in service. However, this application/request letter came to be dismissed on 14 June 2022, leading to the filing of the present petition.

Submissions of the Parties

(6.) Mr Vinod Dahiya, learned counsel for the Petitioner contended that even though the findings of the SSFC have also been assailed on merits, the same are liable to be set aside on the sole ground of procedural defects itself. The

SSFC proceedings, he contended have been conducted without complying with the BSF Act and Rules. In fact, even the ROE proceedings of the SSFC were also vitiated, having been completed after an inordinate delay. The ROE, he submitted, was to be completed on 5 December 2021 but was completed only on 24 December 2021.

(7.) To point out the defects further, the learned counsel submitted that there was a blatant violation of Rule 63(6) of the BSF Rules, a copy of the charge sheet was not supplied to the Petitioner 24 hours before the commencement of the trial by the SSFC as contemplated under the said Rule. Therefore, non-compliance with Rule 63(6), he contended, had led to gross injustice, thereby impairing the right of the Petitioner to have sufficient time to prepare his defence.

(8.) He submitted that the Petitioner was not given any opportunity to prove his defence, instead the Commandant coerced him to plead 'guilty'. Even though, the signatures of the Petitioner were obtained on the said plea of 'guilty', he was not made aware of its contents and therefore, the SSFC proceedings ran contrary to Rule 142(1) and (2) rendering the said plea of 'guilty' invalid. Moreso, the SSFC completed the trial in barely 50 minutes on 19 January 2022, which in itself is sufficient to establish that the trial was conducted hastily and in a mechanical manner thereby giving a complete go-bye even to the rules of natural justice, leading to miscarriage of justice. Additionally, the Petitioner was denied an opportunity to appoint 'friend of the accused' during the SSFC trial, as required by the BSF Rules and was instead forced into accepting Inspector Ram Khilari Yadav as the 'friend of the accused'.

(9.) The learned counsel asserted that even Rule 134 of BSF Rules was violated as evidence was not recorded or explained in a language that the Petitioner understood, whereas it was incumbent upon the commandant to enquire from the Petitioner about the language he was conversant with so as to enable him to understand the evidence on record. He contended that the findings of SSFC were based on no substanital evidence and there is no material on record to sustain or corroborate the charge leveled against the Petitioner. He, therefore, urged that the punishment awarded to him by the

SSFC, which was conducted not only in blatant violation of the mandatory statutory provisions but also without giving the Petitioner an opportunity to prove his defence, be set aside.

(10.) Mr Dahiya further submitted that to assail the findings of the SSFC, the Petitioner filed a statutory appeal to IG, which was also decided in a casual manner by simply relying on the order of the SSFC without appreciating the facts of the case, the material on record and the testimony of the witnesses, which would have shown that the Petitioner had been erroneously charged and held guilty. Further, the DIG, SHQ, BSF, Kolkata, he contended, had confirmed the sentence without even considering the fact that the Petitioner's appeal before the IG was pending. Moreso, his request letter to the DG was also rejected in a mechanical manner without going through the facts and circumstances of the case.

(11.) Learned counsel finally submitted that the Respondent miserably failed to acknowledge that the Petitioner had received 12 'Good' decoration rewards with no adverse remarks in his service of 9 years 8 months and 5 days. Based on his outstanding service record, the punishment of dismissal imposed on him was even otherwise disproportionate.

(12.) Learned counsel by citing the following decisions, contended that in these facts and circumstances, the Petitioner's 'dismissal' was unjust and warrants quashing by this Court:

(i.) *Constable Uma Shankaran vs Union of India and Ors.*: 2019 SCC OnLine Del 7739.

(ii.) *Ex. Head Constable Moti Singh vs Union of India and Ors.*: 2017 SCC OnLine Del 7523.

(13.) On the other hand, while refuting the pleas of the Petitioner, Mr Rishabh Sahu, learned counsel for the Respondent contended that there was overwhelming evidence on record to prove the involvement of the Petitioner in cross border smuggling of 'phensedyl'. Moreover, during the ROE which was conducted with utmost due diligence, the Petitioner was afforded an opportunity to make a statement in his defence to which he declined. Thus, after examining the ROE, the Commandant decided to hold the SSFC. The entire disciplinary process was conducted by scrupulously following the provisions of BSF Act and Rules and there were no procedural deficiencies, whatsoever.

(14.) Learned counsel further submitted that the Petitioner had received the copy of the charge sheet and the ROE well before 24 hours from commencement of the trial as required by Rule 63(6) of BSF Rules. The Petitioner was given ample opportunities to defend himself at every stage and the Court of Inquiry had also been conducted fairly wherein the Petitioner was found blameworthy for being involved in smuggling having connived with a civilian.

(15.) Learned counsel submitted that the SSFC proceedings were initiated on 19 January 2022 and during the trial, the charge sheet was read over to the Petitioner in the language, he understood. Thereupon, the Court explained to the Petitioner, the meaning of the charge and ensured that he understood the nature of charge to which he voluntarily pleaded guilty. He was also briefed about the difference in procedure, if he did not plead guilty. Moreso, his signatures and that of his friend were taken in compliance of provision of Rule 142(2) of BSF Rules. Accordingly, the SSFC trial was based on the Petitioner's voluntary plea of'guilty', which was concluded in a short time, only on account of him having pleaded guilty.

(16.) In addition to the above, the learned counsel contended that the Petitioner had failed to point out any irregularity in the procedure that was followed by the ROE and the SSFC or how the sentence awarded to him did not commensurate with the gravity of the offence he was charged with, to which he pleaded guilty. He submitted that merely having a clean record could not ameliorate the severity of the offence and does not absolve the Petitioner of the serious charge proved against him. The Petitioner, as a member of the Armed Forces deployed to combat trans-border crimes including smuggling, failed in his duties by colluding with the smugglers and also attempted to involve fellow personnel in these illegal activities. This conduct violated the highest standards of discipline and morality expected from a BSF personnel. He, therefore, prayed that the present petition be dismissed, being devoid of merits.

Analysis and Conclusion

(17.) We have carefully considered the submissions addressed on behalf of the parties and perused the record submitted before us.

(18.) At the outset, we may deal with the contention of learned counsel for the Respondent that under Article 226 of the Constitution of India, the High Court does not function as an Appellate Court to re-evaluate the evidence and may only review the decision-making process to determine if any infirmity existed that would invalidate the decision of SSFC. It is the Respondent's plea that as no such infirmity exists in the present case, there was no occasion to exercise the extraordinary jurisdiction under Article 226 of the Constitution of India.

(19.) In order to appreciate the plea of the Respondent, it would be apposite to note that though the scope of interference in exercise of extraordinary powers vested in the High Courts under Article 226 of the Constitution of India is limited, the exercise of these powers is certainly warranted in cases where there is an error of jurisdiction or violation of principles of natural justice or if any manifest error of law apparent on the face of record as also in a case where the order impugned has been passed malafidely or with a bias. This Court is conscious of the fact that military and paramilitary personnel are governed by Special Statutes, which are complete Codes in themselves and the procedure prescribed therein is to be followed in cases governed by these statutes. The same, in our considered opinion, does not place an embargo on this Court to exercise its powers under Article 226 where a case is found to be squarely covered by the aforesaid parameters, as held in a catena of decisions of the Hon'ble Supreme Court as well as Co-ordinate Benches of this Court.

(20.) In this background, the issue that we are required to adjudicate is whether the Petitioner has been fairly tried by the SSFC with due compliance of BSF Act and Rules particularly, when the Petitioner disputes to have pleaded 'guilty'.

(21.) Before us, the learned counsel for the Petitioner strenuously urged that the Petitioner was placed under open arrest on 18 January 2022 and was in the evening provided with incomplete copies of the ROE and charge sheet and that the SSFC commenced its proceedings at 12.00 hrs on the very next day i.e. on 19 January 2022, within less than 24 hours of him being provided with the copies of the aforesaid. Thus, making it extremely difficult for the Petitioner to understand the nuances of the charge as also the procedure and to appear before SSFC to adequately defend himself in this limited period of time, the learned counsel emphasised that the SSFC proceedings be set aside on this ground alone.

(22.) It is not in dispute that on 29 November 2021, the Commandant ordered for preparing the ROE, which was forwarded to him on 25 December 2021, the said record is running into 29 pages with 9 witnesses having been examined on behalf of the Respondent. On 17 January 2022, the Petitioner was conveyed vide a written communication that he would be tried by SSFC on 19 January 2022 at 10.30 hours on the charge leveled against him under Section 40 of the BSF Act. The said communication, apart from intimating the Petitioner to furnish the name of the person to be appointed as his 'friend of accused' and granting him a liberty to engage a legal practitioner to assist him for his defence, also records that a copy of the charge sheet as also the ROE were enclosed therewith. However, according to the Petitioner, not only incomplete copies of the ROE and charge sheet were provided to him but he was also not given full 24 hours' time for examining the said documents leading to clear infraction of Rule 63(6).

(23.) In this regard, we may notice that the provision regarding the preparation of defence by the accused person is prescribed under Rule 63 of BSF Rules which, inter-alia, includes the procedure to be followed by SSFC while holding the trial. Rule 63 (1) reads as under:

> '(1) An accused, who has been remanded for trial, shall be afforded proper opportunity for preparing his defence and shall be allowed proper communication with his defending officer or counsel and with his witnesses.'

(24.) Rule 63(4) further reads:

> '(4) as soon as practicable after a decision has been taken to place the accused on trial and in any case not less than four days before his trial he shall be given:

(a.) copy of the charge sheet;

(b.) an unexpurgated copy of the record or abstract of evidence showing the passages (if any), which have been expurgated in the copy sent to the senior member;

(c.) notice of any additional evidence which the prosecution intends to adduce; and

(d.) if the accused so requires, a list of the ranks names and units of the members who are to form the Court and of any waiting members.'

(25.) Rule 63(6), in particular, lays down:-

> '(6) the provisions of sub-rules (2) and (3) shall not apply in relation to a trial before a Summary Security Force Court and in relation to such a trial the period of four days referred to in sub-rule (4) shall be construed as twenty-four hours.'

(26.) Having perused the aforesaid extract of Rule 63 of the BSF Rules, we find substance in the submission of the learned counsel for the Petitioner that copies of the charge sheet and ROE proceedings were not furnished to the Petitioner 24 hours before the commencement of the trial. No doubt, as per the record of the SSFC, the Petitioner was provided with a copy of the charge sheet and ROE on 18 January 2022, but no time is specified therein as to when the said documents were furnished to him on the said date. It is also not in dispute that the SSFC proceedings commenced on 19 January 2022 at 1200 hours, even though the Petitioner on 17 January 2022 itself had been informed that the SSFC shall commence at 10.30 hrs on 19 January 2022. The Respondent has not furnished any explanation as to why despite opportunity to provide the aforesaid documents to the Petitioner on 17 January 2022 itself, when he was informed that he would be tried by the SSFC, they waited till 18 January 2022. In any event, the Respondent has failed to show that they had furnished the copy of the charge sheet and ROE to the Petitioner more than 24 hours before the commencement of the SSFC. Even though, as per Rule 63, the said documents were mandatorily required to be provided to the Petitioner atleast 24 hours before commencement of the trial.

(27.) We also find merit in the Petitioner's plea that it would not have been possible for him, in such a short time, to prepare his defence after going through the statements of all the witnesses and the documents running into 29 pages but the Respondent seemed to be in a hurry to conclude the trial and pronounce the sentence thereby implying that holding of SSFC was merely an empty formality.

(28.) It is well settled that a disciplinary inquiry/trial by the Security Force Court is not meant to be conducted mechanically as a mere formality, but should be held in accordance with the principles of natural justice and the laid down procedure, so as to enable the disciplinary authority to take an informed decision. The entire purpose of issuance of a charge sheet is to enable the noticee to respond to the allegations on the basis of which, action against him is proposed. In these circumstances, we are of the considered view that the Respondent had acted in violation of the Rules by not providing copies of the charge sheet and the ROE to the Petitioner atleast 24 hours before the trial.

(29.) Coming to the next submission of the Petitioner that he was coerced by the commandant to plead 'guilty' to the charge, who without explaining him about the contents of the charge, had made him sign the 'plea of guilty'. Further, even his 'friend of accused' was not one of his choice.

(30.) We find that Rule 142 provides for recording of the plea of 'guilty' or 'not guilty' of an accused and lays down the elaborate procedure regarding the manner in which this plea has to be recorded. It provides that on the accused pleading guilty before a finding of guilt is recorded, the Court is essentially required to ascertain whether the accused understands the nature and meaning of the charge to which he has pleaded guilty; he must also be informed of the general effects of that plea and of the difference in procedure to be followed upon taking the plea of 'guilty'. Additionally, if it appears from the record or the abstract of evidence that the accused ought to have pleaded 'not guilty', the Court is required to advise the accused to withdraw that plea of 'guilty' and proceed with the trial after recording a plea of 'not guilty'.

(31.) In this regard, reference may be made to a recent decision of the Apex Court in the case of *Union of India and Ors. vs Jogeshwar Swain,* (2023) 9 SCC 720, wherein the Apex Court emphasised upon compliance of procedure as provided under Rule 142(2) before accepting the 'plea of guilty' of the accused. The relevant observations thereof read as under:-

> '42. Before acting on the plea of guilty, compliance of the procedural safeguards laid down in sub-rule (2) of Rule 142 is important as it serves a dual purpose. <u>First, it ensures that before pleading guilty the accused is aware of not only the nature and meaning of the charge which he has to face but also the broad consequences that he may have to suffer once he pleads guilty.</u> This not only obviates the possibility of an uninformed confession but also such confessions that are made under a false hope that one could escape punishment by pleading guilty. <u>The other purpose which it seeks to serve is that it ensures that confessions do not become an easy way out for deciding cases where marshalling of evidence to prove the charge becomes difficult.</u> It is for this reason that sub-rule (2) of Rule 142 requires an SSFC to advise the accused to withdraw the plea of guilty if it appears from the examination of the record or abstract of evidence that the accused ought to plead not guilty. Since, the procedure laid in sub-rule (2) of Rule 142 serves an important purpose and is for the benefit of an accused, in our view, its strict adherence is warranted before accepting a plea of guilty.'

(Emphasis supplied)

(32.) To sum up the legal position, we may note that Rule 142 is to be strictly adhered to, by the officer holding the SSFC. In the present case, it emerges from the record that the SSFC was convened on 18 January 2022 wherein the Commandant, 158th BN, BSF was the Presiding Officer of SSFC with Insp. Ram Khilari Yadav having been appointed as a 'friend of accused' of the Petitioner. The proceedings of SSFC commenced on 19 January 2022 in the presence of the Petitioner. The charge, after being translated, was explained to him and the presiding officer enquired from the Petitioner whether he pleads 'guilty' or 'not guilty' to the charge against him. The answer of the Petitioner is recorded in the proceedings as follows:-

'Ans. Guilty'

(33.) Further, we have also perused the original records of the SSFC proceedings that were produced before us from which it appears that the proceedings were conducted in a most slipshod manner with the Commandant, who was the Presiding Officer, having prepared the record of the SSFC proceedings in advance, which is evident as all the pages of the proceedings were pre-typed. Only some blanks were left to be filled for recording the answer of the Petitioner to plead guilty/not guilty which alone were during the proceedings filled in 'Pen'.

(34.) Interestingly, from the original record, it also emerges that the Commandant's signatures were placed on each page of the proceedings at the 'bottom right corner' reflecting a pattern. The said signatures are undated and appear uniformly on all the pages of the proceedings at the very same place on each page. Further, what is particularly unusual is that these signatures of the Commandant are also appearing on another set of the proceedings, which too were evidently prepared in advance, apparently to deal with a situation where the Petitioner would have pleaded 'not guilty'.

(35.) It is further surprising that even on the proceedings sheet on which the plea of 'guilty' of the Petitioner has been recorded, the undated signatures of the Commandant, like in the previous sheets, appear. However, the Commandant has again signed on the said sheet with the date after recording the purported plea of 'guilty' of the Petitioner, which also bears the signatures of the Petitioner and his next friend with date. Notably, on some proceeding sheets, the signatures of the Commandant are also not affixed immediately beneath the contents of the proceedings but are appearing at the same place i.e. bottom right corner.

(36.) From the aforesaid, it clearly emerges that the signatures of the Commandant were appended before the start of the SSFC proceedings, and the proceeding sheets were all pre-typed having been prepared in advance. Though, it is seriously disputed by the Petitioner, even if, we were to accept the Respondent's plea and assume that he had pleaded 'guilty' it is evident that the procedure as prescribed by Rule 142(2) was not followed in its true letter and spirit, thereby making the recording of the plea of 'guilty', a mere formality.

We seriously doubt that the Petitioner understood the contents of the charge and consequences thereof, as well as those of his pleading guilty to the same.

(37.) Thus, in view of the above, the SSFC proceedings/sheets, though claimed to be conducted in the presence of the Petitioner, had actually been prepared in advance and merely the plea of 'guilty' was recorded in the presence of the Petitioner on 19 January 2022. Moreso, as far as the award of sentence proceeding is concerned, the same is also pre-typed, leaving the blanks to be filled in the proceeding sheet.

(38.) It is further relevant to note that after recording the plea of 'guilty', the Commandant by borrowing the language contained in Rule 142(2) made a note at page no. 5 of the SSFC, which reads as under:-

> 'The accused having pleaded Guilty to the charge, the Court read and explains to the accused the meaning of the charge to which he has pleaded Guilty and ascertains that the accused understands the nature of the charge to which he has pleaded Guilty. The Court also inform the accused in the language he understands, the general effect of that plea and the difference in procedure which will be followed consequent to the said plea. The Court having satisfied itself that the accused understands the charge and the effect of his plea of guilty and satisfied from the record/abstract of evidence or otherwise that there is no need for the accused to withdraw his plea of guilty, accepts his plea and records the same.
>
> The provisions of Rule 142(2) are complied with.'

(39.) From what has been noted hereinabove, it is clear that the plea of 'guilty' was recorded first and thereafter the Petitioner, was perhaps informed about what was laid down in Rule 142(2). The manner in which the plea of 'guilty' was recorded in the trial, when examined in the light of other surrounding circumstances, we are constrained to hold that either the Petitioner never pleaded 'guilty' to the charge or his plea of 'guilty' as recorded by the Court was not voluntary. We are, therefore, of the considered view that the right of the Petitioner to have a fair trial before the SSFC has been violated and he has been condemned unheard without following the principles of natural justice.

(40.) In the light of the aforesaid, we have no hesitation in holding that the SSFC proceedings including the award of sentence of 'dismissal from service' awarded to the Petitioner are vitiated. At this stage, we may also note that the SSFC without indicating any reasons or referring to any evidence proceeded to conclude as under:-

'VERDICT OF COURT

I am of the opinion on the evidence before me that accused No. 124519398 CT/GD Rajneesh of 158 Bn BSF is guilty of the charge.'

'SENTENCE BY THE COURT

Taking all these matter into consideration. I, now sentence the accused No. 124519398 Rank CT/GB Name Rajneesh of 158 Bn BSF to "be dismissed from service"'

(41.) For the foregoing reasons, the SSFC, having been conducted in blatant violation of Rule 63(6) and Rule 142(2) of BSF Rules, is liable to be set aside. **We, accordingly, allow the writ petition and set aside the impugned orders dated 19 January 2022 and 5 April 2022.** We direct the Respondent to reinstate the Petitioner in service w.e.f. the date of his dismissal from service i.e. 19 January 2022 with all consequential benefits. However, taking into account the nature of charge leveled against the Petitioner, we grant the Respondent liberty to conduct a de novo trial and direct that the same be concluded within three months.

(42.) Having dealt with the claims raised in the present petition, we may also note that this Court has been coming across a number of cases where the SSFC proceedings are being conducted in a lackadaisical and perfunctory manner by disregarding the rules and procedures laid under the BSF Act and Rules. It is also being noticed that despite there being no urgency, SSFC proceedings are being conducted in almost every case as a matter of routine. The provisions providing for other kinds of Security Force Courts which lay down more elaborate procedure for trial are very rarely being resorted to. This raises a serious concern as any deviation from the Rules and the laid down procedure during the trial not only compromises the rights of the accused but also results in grave injustice especially in cases where the trials, pertaining to misconduct committed by the force personnel, ends with an award of a major penalty of dismissal from service. Such a harsh penalty can have a lifelong implications not only for the officer involved but for this entire family.

(43.) It, thus, becomes incumbent upon the Officers conducting the SSFC proceedings to be properly trained and sensitized of the manner in which the SSFC proceedings ought to be conducted, i.e. by giving due regard to the rules and procedures outlined in the BSF Act and Rules. The presiding officers holding the SSFC must understand that these trials are not just mere formalities but are a fundamental aspect of ensuring justice and maintaining discipline in the Force by following the prescribed procedure. The presiding officers have to be sensitised on these matters in order to safeguard the rights of the accused as well as the commitment of the Force in upholding the rule of law and maintaining the highest standards of discipline within its ranks. Failure thereof, will only result in miscarriage of justice, for both the individuals as well as the Force.

(44.) We, therefore, direct the Respondent that officers, who hold SSFCs, be provided mandatory regular trainings on the subject of conducting the SSFC proceedings in accordance with law. Copy of this order be sent to DG, BSF, BSF Hqr, CGO Complex, New Delhi.

Shalinder Kaur, J
Rekha Palli, J

28 August 2024

(2025) I FLR 309 (India)

Punjab and Haryana High Court

Civil Writ Petition 19116/2024

Union of India and Others vs Ex Naik Azad Singh and Anr

Composition of Court: Justice Sudhir Singh and Justice Karamjit Singh

Date of Decision: 20 August 2024

Counsel for the Petitioner: Ms. Bhavana Datta, Senior Panel Counsel for Government of India
Counsel for the Respondent: Navdeep Singh, Advocate

Summary

The writ petition was filed by the Union of India challenging the Armed Forces Tribunal's (AFT) order dated 24 January,2019, which granted Respondent No 1, a disabled solider, the benefit of rounding-off of his disability pension from 20% to 50% for file from the date of his discharge from which he was granted disability pension. As per the rounding-off policy, disability percentage was to be rounded off to 50% if the disability was less than 50% for the purposes of calculating the amount of disability pension following the Supreme Court's decision on the subject. The Union of India, citing another judgment of the Supreme Court argued that arrears of the rounding-off benefit should be limited to three years before the respondent's application since there was delay on part of the disabled soldier in approaching the Court.

Respondent No. 1 contended that the three-year limitation applied only to cases of disability pension filed after a considerable delay when the solider was not in receipt of disability pension but not to cases involving rounding-off, as the latter pertains to increasing an already granted disability pension. The court referred to prior Supreme Court judgments which clarified that the three-year restriction does not apply to rounding-off benefits and full arrears were to be released. The High Court also noted that the Supreme Court had previously upheld similar AFT decisions and expressed disapproval of repeated challenges by the Union of India. Finding no merit in the arguments raised by the Union of India, the High Court dismissed the writ petition, affirming the entitlement of the disabled soldier to full arrears without the three-year restriction.

Headnotes

<u>Facts:</u> On 24 January, 2019 the Armed Forces Tribunal's (AFT) passed an order disposing of the Original Application filed by respondent No.1 by holding respondent No.1 entitled to the benefit of rounding off by computing his disability to the extent of 50% as against 20% w.e.f. 01 August,1998 to 05 March, 2000, 14 March, 2000 to 13 March 2005 and thereafter 10 January, 2005 for life, in terms of Supreme Court's judgement in Union of India and others vs. Ram Avtar. Thereafter, the petitioners filed the present writ petition for issuance of a writ in the nature of Certiorari quashing the impugned order.

<u>Issue(s):</u> Whether the restriction of the payment of arrears to three years prior to the filing of the application is applicable to the cases of rounding off?

<u>Contentions of the parties:</u> Relying on Shiv Dass vs. Union of India, the petitioners contended that the benefit of arrears accruing to respondent No.1 on account of grant of rounding off benefit, should be restricted to three years prior to the filing of the Original Application filed by respondent No.1. However, the respondents contended that the said judgement is only applicable to the cases of disability pension, where a member approaches the AFT after a delay for grant of such pension and that in case of rounding off, the period of three years restriction will not be applicable as the member has

already been in receipt of the disability pension and the rounding off would only mean the increase in such pension.

Held: The learned Court cited the Supreme Court's observations in the cases of Union of India vs. Piyush Bahuguna, Union of India vs. Ram Avtar and Davinder Singh vs. Union of India. It was observed that the order passed by the learned AFT restricting the arrears of rounding off to three years prior to the filing of the application, was set aside by the Supreme Court in Davinder Singh and the applicant therein was held entitled to the arrears of rounding-off the disability pension from 01 Jan 1996. The Punjab & Haryana High Court thus held that the legal issue stood settled and that the restriction of the payment of arrears to three years prior to the filing of the application is not applicable to the cases of rounding-off. Due to the inability to find any merit in the writ petition filed by the Union of India, the same was dismissed.

Case Laws Cited

Union of India and Others vs. Ram Avtar [2014 SCC OnLine SC 1761]; Shiv Dass vs. Union of India [(2007)9 SCC 274]; Union of India vs. Piyush Bahuguna [Civil Appeal No.10713 of 2021]; Davinder Singh vs. Union of India and Others [Civil Appeal No.9946-2016]

JUDGEMENT

Sudhir Singh, J

The Petitioners have filed the present writ petition for issuance of a writ in the nature of Certiorari quashing the impugned order dated 24 January 2019, passed by the learned Armed Forces Tribunal (for short AFT), whereby the Original Application filed by Respondent No.1, has been disposed of by holding Respondent No. 1 entitled to the benefit of rounding off by computing his disability to the extent of 50% as against 20% w.e.f. 1 August 1998 to 5 March 2000, 14 March 2000 to 13 March 2005 and thereafter 10 January 2005 for life, in terms of judgment of the Hon'ble Supreme Court in Civil Appeal No. 418 of 2012 *Union of India and others vs Ram Avtar,* decided on 10 December 2014.

(2.) Learned counsel appearing for the Petitioners submits that the only challenge in the present writ petition is to grant of arrears of the rounding off benefit beyond three years. It is further contended that in terms of the judgment of Hon'ble Supreme Court in *Shiv Dass vs Union of India,* (2007) 9 SCC 274, the benefit of arrears accruing to Respondent No. 1 on account of grant of rounding off benefit, should be restricted to three years prior to the filing of the Original Application filed by Respondent No. 1.

(3.) On the other hand, Maj. Navdeep Singh, Advocate, who is present in Court on the service of advance notice, on behalf of Respondent No. 1, submits that the judgment of *Shiv Dass case* (supra), is only applicable to the cases of disability pension, where a member approaches the learned AFT after a delay for grant of such pension. However, in case of rounding off, the period of three years restriction will not be applicable as the member has already been in receipt of the disability pension and the rounding off would only mean the increase in such pension.

(4.) We have heard learned counsel for the parties and have also gone through the paper book, including the impugned order passed by the learned AFT.

(5.) It may be noticed that against an identical order dated 10 August 2018 passed in Original Application No. 3106 of 2018 by learned AFT, the Union of India had filed civil appeal No. 10713 of 2021 – Union of India vs Piyush Bahuguna. The said appeal was dismissed by the Hon'ble Supreme Court by passing the following order:-

> 'Leave to appeal under Section 31(1) of the Armed Forces Tribunal Act, 2007 is granted.
> Delay condoned.
>
> We are not inclined to interfere with the impugned order and hence, the appeal is dismissed.
>
> We must observe and express our displeasure at the manner in which the Appellants have been filing appeals against grant of disability pensions, even where the legal issue is settled.
>
> Pending application(s), if any, stand disposed of.'

(6.) The Hon'ble Supreme Court in *Union of India and Ors. vs Ram Avtar*, 2014 SCC OnLine SC 1761, while considering the issue of grant of rounding off of disability pension, has held as under:-

> '4. By the present set of appeals the Appellant(s) raise the question, whether or not, an individual, who has retired on attaining the age of superannuation or on completion of his tenure of engagement, if found to be suffering from some disability which is attributable to or aggravated by the military service, is entitled to be granted the benefit of rounding-off of disability pension. The Appellant(s) herein would contend that, on the basis of Circular No. 1(2)/97/D (Pen-C) issued by the Ministry of Defence, Government of India, dated 31 January 2001, the aforesaid benefit is made available only to an Armed Forces personnel who is invalidated out of service, and not to any other category of Armed Forces personnel mentioned hereinabove.
>
> 5. We have heard learned counsel for the parties to the *lis*.
>
> 6. We do not see any error in the impugned judgment(s) and order(s) and therefore all the appeals which pertain to the concept of rounding-off of the disability pension are dismissed, with no order as to costs.
>
> 7. The dismissal of these matters will be taken note of by the High Courts as well as by the tribunals in granting appropriate relief to the pensioners before them, if any, who are getting or are entitled to the disability pension.'

(7.) Still further a reference may also be made to a Three Judge Bench of the order of the Hon'ble Supreme Court in *Davinder Singh vs Union of India and Ors.* civil appeal No. 9946-2016 decided on 20 September 2016. In the said case, the order passed by the learned AFT restricting the arrears of rounding off to three years prior to the filing of the application, was set aside by the Hon'ble Supreme Court and the Applicant/Appellant therein was held entitled to the arrears of rounding off the disability pension w.e.f. 1 January 1996. The relevant extracts from the said order of the Hon'ble Apex Court, would read as under:-

> '......There was no reason for reducing the said period to three years only immediately prior to the filing of the petition in the case of the Appellant.

> It is submitted that this Court having already affirmed the view taken in *Jaisingh's* case, similar relief could be granted to the Appellant also. We find merit in that submission. From a perusal of the order passed in Jaisingh's case, it appears that while most of the cases disposed off in the said batch were transferred cases where writ Petitioners had been filed earlier than 2010, there were half a dozen fresh cases that were filed in the year 2010 and later. The Tribunal had notwithstanding the delay in the filing of the O.A.s granted redress to the Petitioners in the said batch of cases w.e.f. 1 January 1996 with interest @ 8% p.a. That being so and the order passed by the Tribunal in Jaisingh's case and batch of cases having been affirmed by this Court, we see no distinction between the cases dealt with by the Tribunal in that batch and the Appellant's case to warrant a differential treatment to him in the matter of grant of arrears. We accordingly allow this appeal and modify the order passed by the Tribunal to the extent that the Appellant shall also on the analogy of the order passed by the Tribunal in *Jaisingh's* case supra be entitled to arrears payable to him by reason of rounding off of disability pension w.e.f. 1 January 1996 with interest @ 8% p.a. subject to adjustment of any amount already received by him for the said period...'

(8.) Indisputably, the legal issue stands settled. As has been noticed above, the restriction of the payment of arrears to three years prior to the filing of the application is not applicable to the cases of rounding off as held by the Hon'ble Supreme Court in *Davinder Singh case* (supra).

(9.) In view of the above, we do not find any merit in the present writ petition, the same is hereby dismissed.

Sudhir Singh, J
Karamjit Singh, J

20 August 2024

(2025) I FLR 315 (India)

Punjab and Haryana High Court

Pushplata vs State of Haryana & Others

Composition of Court: Aman Chaudhary, J

Date of Decision: 27 July 2024

Counsel for Petitioner: Mr. Gurpreet Singh
Counsel for the State: Mr. Harish Rathee

Summary

The Petitioner, the wife of a deceased soldier, had requested the State of Haryana for the applicable ex-gratia compensation and compassionate appointment to members of late soldier's family. Ashok Kumar, the Petitioner's husband and a soldier in the Indian Army, died while on sentry duty due to the accidental discharge of his weapon. His death was classified as a "battle casualty" by the military authorities. The Petitioner's request was initially denied, citing that the terms and conditions for ex-gratia compensation were not met and that her husband's death did not occur during active operational duties.

However, the court ruled in favor of the Petitioner, distinguishing the life-threatening realities faced by soldiers in operational areas from the environment in a peace-time location where an accident could be perceived differently. Further, the court acknowledged that her husband's death was classified as a "battle casualty" by the competent authority. The court granted the Petitioner the ex-gratia amount and directed the Respondents to consider her request for a compassionate appointment.

Headnotes

<u>Facts:</u> Ashok Kumar, a soldier in the Indian Army, posted in an operational area of Jammu and Kashmir. While on Sentry duty at Sitni Firing Range on 24 April 2006, Kumar accidentally discharged his weapon, resulting in a fatal gunshot wound. Death classified as "Battle Casualty" by military authorities. The wife of the deceased soldier petitioned the High Court for ex-gratia compensation and compassionate appointment which had been denied to her by the State of Haryana.

<u>Issue:</u> Whether a claim for ex-gratia should be granted due to the accidental death of a soldier in an operational area?

<u>Contentions of the Parties:</u> Petitioner contended that she was fully entitled to relief as the death had occurred in an operational area and had been declared a "Battle Casualty". Respondents contended that the terms and conditions of receiving ex-gratia were not fulfilled. Further, that no application for compassionate appointment was submitted by the Petitioner, and even if it were submitted, the appointment was only given to family members of those whose death occurred during active operational duties. Respondent contended here that the death of Kumar was due to the accidental discharge of a weapon while on guard duty, which was different from the those who died during active operational duties.

<u>Held:</u> Petitioner entitled to grant of ex-gratia compensation and consideration for compassionate appointment since the death was in operational area. Observed that a beneficial provision must be construed meaningfully and liberally and not in a manner to restrict or deprive. Further observed that the harsh realities faced by soldiers posted at regions where there is lurking danger to life cannot be lost sight of. When the Courts find it unfathomable as to how while implementing the policy, logic was being stretched to illogical limits just to deny benefits to personnel in uniform, relief must be granted to them.

Case Law Cited

Smt Santosh vs Union of India, (2010) 1 SCT 518
Major Arvind Kumar Suhag (Retired) vs State of Haryana, (2010) 4 SCT 395

Smt Daljit Kaur vs Union of India, 2003 SCC Online P&H 513

JUDGMENT

Aman Chaudhary, J

(1.) The prayer made in the present petition is for directing the Respondents to grant ex-gratia amount of Rs. 10 lakh to the Petitioner in terms of policy dated 15 June 2001, Annexure P-9 on account of death of her husband, declared as 'battle casualty', as also to give compassionate appoint to any member of his family in terms of policy dated 28 September 2018, Annexure P-8.

(2.) The facts that remain undisputed as stated in para 2 of the petition and admitted being matter of record in the written statement, are that the husband of the Petitioner, late Cfn Ashok Kumar, enrolled in the Indian Army on 19 March 2001, was posted in Operation Area in Jammu and Kashmir ('Op Rakshak'). On 24 May 2006 at 09.15 hours, while on sentry duty at Sitni Firing Range, Nagotra (J&K), he died on account of a gunshot wound (GSW) abdomen, due to accidental discharge of his personal weapon.

(3.) The husband of the Petitioner was classified as a 'battle casualty' by the Integrated Headquarters of MOD (Army) vide order dated 16 November 2006, Annexure P-1. Consequently, the application filed by his wife – the Petitioner herein, before the Armed Forces Tribunal was allowed vide judgment dated 23 November 2017, Annexure P-2 and Liberalised Family Pension was granted, by referring to the finding of Court of Inquiry in the matter, whereby his death was declared as 'battle casualty'.

(4.) The request of the Petitioner made through serving a legal notice dated 8 September 2021, to grant the ex-gratia amount, was rejected by Welfare Officer, District Sainik and Ardh Sainik Welfare Department, Jind – Respondent No.

3 vide reply dated 12 October 2021, Annexure P-7, on the premise that the terms and conditions of the policies for ex-gratia were not fulfilled, as also no application for compassionate appointment was submitted. Further, the same was only given to the family members of those martyrs whose death occurred during active operational duties, whereas that of her husband was due to accidental discharge of weapon, while being on guard duty.

(5.) This Court in *Smt Santosh vs Union of India and Ors.*[1], wherein the Army personnel posted in State of Jammu & Kashmir as Havildar, died of a heart attack, held his wife entitled for ex-gratia compensation, relevant paras whereof read thus:

> '3. The sole question which needs to be considered is whether the death of the husband of the Petitioner falls in any of the categories notified by the Government whereunder the Petitioner is entitled to any other benefit. The Petitioner has relied upon three Government policies (Annexure P-3, P-4 and P-5). Annexure P-3 is the policy dated 30 September 1999 issued by the Government of Haryana. The relevant portion of the aforesaid policy reads as under:-
>
> > "...Haryana Government has decided that with effect from 1 April 1999 the ex-gratia grant/compensation to the families of the Defence Services Personnel and of Para Military Forces who lie in harness in the performance of their bonafide official duties while serving in operations like Kargil and other sectors shall be Rs. 10 lacks for all categories namely Officers, Junior Commissioned Officers and other ranks and to the disabled as explained under for all categories depending upon the percentage of disability as assessed by concerned authorities irrespective of the fact whether they are retained as welfare measure or boarded out..."
>
> 4. The aforesaid policy was followed by policy dated 15 June 2001 (Annexure P-4) which reads as under:-
>
> > "1. XX XXX XXX

1. (2010) 1 SCT 518.

(a) A reward money of Rs. Ten Lakhs in recognition of acts of bravery, gallantry and sacrifice would be paid to the families of those who die during an enemy action in International War or such war like engagements, which are specifically notified by the Ministry of Defence, Government of India. This would be in addition to whatever ex-gratia relief is admissible under Government of India instructions.

(b) Ex-gratia will be admissible to the families of those defence personnel who hail from Haryana and get killed in militant encounters and declare as battle casualties as per amounts given in Annexure-A and conditions of eligibility given in Annexure B..."

5. In the first policy, it is provided that ex-gratia compensation be paid to the families of the defence service personnel and para military forces who died in harness in performance of their bonafide official duties while serving in operations like Kargil and other sectors. In the subsequent policy letter, such benefits are payable to such of the officials who earned recognition of acts of bravery, gallantry and sacrifice and who died during an enemy action in International War or such war like engagements, which are specifically notified by the Ministry of Defence, Government of India. Such ex-gratia is also admissible to families of defence personnel who hail from Haryana and get killed in militant encounters and is declared as battle casualties. Similar instruction have been issued by the Government of India vide its letter dated 22 September 1998 wherein a different kind of compensation has been provided under following categories:-

"...a) Death occurring due to accidents in the course of

performance of duties: 5.00 Lakhs

b) Death occurring in the course of performance of duties attributable to acts of violence by terrorists, anti-social elements etc.: 5.00 Lakhs

c) Death occurring during (i) enemy action in International War or border skirmishes and (ii) action against militants, terrorists, extremists, etc.: 7.50 Lakhs"

6. I have heard learned counsel for the parties. No doubt, the Petitioner's husband was posted at Border in a remote area and was member of the Operation Karma, but he died on account of heart failure while discharging his duty in Gore Sector which is known as a coldest place. At the time of his death, the Petitioner was not engaged in any military action, though part of the Operation Karma and posted at the Morcha. The entire stand of the Respondents that he died of heart attack. The fact that he was part of the Operational Unit and was posted at the Line of Control in a Morcha is not disputed. Though he did not die in an encounter or in the battle, but he was in the battlefield. His case is, however, not covered by the Government instructions, issued by the Ministry of Defence (Annexure P-5) whereby the ex-gratia is attributable to acts of violence by the terrorists and anti-national elements and during enemy action in international war or border skirmishes and action against militants/terrorists/extremists. The case of the husband of the Petitioner also does not fall under the Government instructions dated 15 June 2001. However, the Government instructions dated 30 September 1999 provides for ex-gratia compensation to the families of defence personnel who died in harness in the performance of their bonafide official duties while serving in operations like Operation Karma and was posted at the Line of Control in a Morcha. He was performing a bona official duty and died in harness while performing such duty. It is also admitted position that he died due to severe cold in the area. Such a situation cannot be divorced from the performance of the bonafide duty. It is not necessary that he should die by a bullet of the enemy or on account of any injury or other factor. Another aspect of the matter which cannot be ignored is that the Government of India instructions even provides for payment of compensation where death occurs due to accident in course of performance of duty. The accident does not mean only vehicular accident but has wider connotation. It can be of any kind of accident. The Petitioner's husband suffered on account of severe cold while discharging his duty and thus his case falls within the put purview of Government instructions dated 30 September 1999.

7. In view of the above, this petition is disposed of with a direction to the Respondents that the Petitioner be paid ex-gratia compensation in terms

of the Government instructions dated 30 September 1999 (Annexure P-3) within a period of three months from the date of receipt of a certified copy of this order.'

(6.) In the case of *Major Arvind Kumar Suhag (retired) vs State of Haryana through the Secretary in-Charge, Defence Services Welfare Branch, and Ors.*[2], the Petitioner, who had suffered 100% disability in a motor transport accident while posted in Kargil area, was declared a battle casualty and this Court allowed the petition, despite the rejection to grant ex-gratia being negligence on his part. The observations in this regard read thus:

> '3. The learned counsel states that the casualty taking place inan operational area itself shall not enable a person to obtain the benefit. The clear expressions are that no type of casualty except the battle casualties or battle accidents are covered under the policy of the year 1999. If we must give the expression battle casualty any meaning, I would understand it to mean to a situation where a person while actively involved in the military service in an area, which is a battle zone suffers an injury, then it shall be a battle casualty. In fact, the certificate issued by the Additional Directorate General characteristic the injury suffered by the Petitioner as a battle casualty. If an entitlement to a benefit under ex-gratia policy has to be applied, the Government ought not to be looking for any certification more than how the army itself has treated the injury as having arisen. If there is, therefore, a certificate that the Petitioner has suffered a battle casualty (see para 1 above), to take a different view and stonewall the claim of the Petitioner from obtaining a benefit of the policy will make meaningless the beneficent and lofty objective which the policy prefers. A State cannot drive a person, who claims a benefit under the policy for a full-fledged adjudication in a Civil Court to ascertain the nature of injury, so long as the policy statement itself does not require any specific mode of proof. There could be no better proof than how the Army has itself perceived the injury as having resulted and that ought to be sufficient for the State to apply its Policy. The claim of the Petitioner is perfectly justified and the statement in defence refusing to extend the benefit on a specious plea that the Petitioner was negligent

2. 2010 (4) SCT 395.

in his conduct that led to his injuries and that again the injury was not a battle casualty, are meaningless defenses that have to be only discarded as unworthy of acceptance.

4. The writ petition is, therefore, allowed as prayed for. The amount which is granted under the policy shall be disbursed within six weeks from the date of receipt of copy of this order, failing which the amount shall bear interest @ 9% from the date of his claim.'

(7.) The Division Bench in *Smt Daljit Kaur vs Union of India*[3], wherein the son of the Petitioner had died due to accidental discharge of his rifle while he was on duty in Counter Insurgency Field and Operation area (Operation Rakshak), held her entitled to ex-gratia amount, relevant paras whereof read thus:

'13. Even otherwise, a perusal of the instructions clearly shows that the compensation is intended to provide an additional insurance and security to the employees who are required to function under trying circumstances and are exposed to different kinds of risk in the performance of their duties. The provisions being beneficent in nature, were required to be liberally construed by Respondent No. 2. Even if there was a default or contributory negligence on the part of the deceased, the same was required to be ignored as it is specifically so provided in the instructions in condition No. 3. The impugned order smacks of arbitrariness and total non-application of men. It is cryptic in nature. The quasi judicial authorities exercising powers with far reaching consequences, are required by law to pass well reasoned speaking orders in support of their decisions. We are constrained to observe that the order passed by Respondent No. 2 is woefully lacking any cogent reason in support thereof.

14. On facts, it deserves to be noticed that both the inquest report and the Court of inquiry, have held that the death has occurred due to accident. It has been held that the death has occurred whilst Amandeep was on duty. It has also been held Amandeep was performing duty in insurgency area popularly known as "Operation Rakshak". It has been categorically held

3. 2003 SCC Online P&H 513.

that his death is attributable to military service. These findings have been confirmed by the Competent Military Authority in the field, Brigadier Harendra Mohan. Such being the position, we are unable to comprehend how the grant of ex-gratia lump sum compensation could have been declined to the Petitioner.'

(8.) A beneficial provision must be meaningfully and liberally construed, so as to advance its object, being the intention of the rule making authority, to give its full effect and not to restrict or to deprive.

(9.) This Court in *Sharanjit Kaur (Dr) vs State of Punjab*[4], wherein the Petitioner was declined the benefits of the policy on the ground that her husband had died in a road accident on his way back from Mamun after attending a conference, thus his death was termed as 'physical casualty' and not 'battle casualty', held there being no distinction between the two as per Rules, granted her an amount of Rs. 5 lakhs or she would be allotted residential plot in a colony set up by PUDA at the reserved price and the said amount shall be paid towards the price of the plot out of the relief fund, along with an amount of Rs. 2 lakhs by way of ex-gratia as contemplated under the Rules.

(10.) The additional objection taken in the written statement filed to the present petition, that since her husband belonged to the State of Punjab at the time of recruitment, was not entitled to any benefit under the policies of Haryana Government, is not only in the teeth of law laid down in *Mohinder Singh Gill vs Chief Election Commr.*[5], but even if considered, is untenable in the wake of the averments made by the Petitioner in paras 12 to 14, having been duly admitted in corresponding paras of the written statement as a matter of record, that related to he hailing from State of Haryana, which stood substantiated by Annexures P-10 to P-12, being the communication from secretary, Haryana Vidhan Sabha conveying that his demise was condoled, as he belonged to District Jind and eligibility of his son for scholarship, etc.

(11.) The harsh realities faced by soldiers posted at regions not only of high-altitude but where there is lurking danger to life, being operational field infested with insurgency, cannot be lost sight of. When the Courts found

4. 2001 SCC Online P&H 621.

it unfathomable as to how while implementing the policy, logic was being stretched to illogical limits, just to deny benefits regarding men in uniform, it extended relief thereof to the families of soldiers who died in notified operations even though due to falls or accidents or cardiac arrests. Incidents of such a nature are not far and few but just a tip of the iceberg. In an intense atmosphere prevailing in these areas, a death that occurs even due to an accidental discharge of a weapon is way different than an incident of that kind that may have occurred in a peace location. The above coupled with the fact of the death of the husband of the Petitioner, having been classified as 'battle casualty', by the competent authority, tilts the scales of justice in her favour for due consideration of the claim.

(12.) On a conspectus evaluation of the matter, the present petition deserves to be and is hereby allowed. The Respondents are directed to grant the ex-gratia amount in terms of the policy dated 15 June 2001, Annexure P-9 to the Petitioner, with further directions to consider the case for compassionate appointment in terms of policy dated 28 September 2018, Annexure P-8. Needful be done within a period of two months from the date of receipt of a certified copy of this judgment.

(13.) Pending applications, if any, stand disposed of.

Aman Chaudhary, J

26 July 2024

(2025) I FLR 325 (Barbados)

2025 Forces Law Review __ (Barbados)

Citable as: 2025 FLR __ (Barbados)

CCJ Appeal No BBCR2023/002

BB Criminal Appeal No 12 of 2021

The Barbados Defence Force vs David Anthony Harewood and Regional Security System

Caribbean Court of Justice, Appellate Jurisdiction

Date of Decision: 26 July 2024

Composition of Court: Mr. Justice Saunders, President, Mr. Justice Anderson, Mme Justice Rajnauth-Lee, Mr. Justice Barrow, Mr. Justice Jamadar (Five Judge Bench)
Counsel for the Appellant: Mr. Leslie F. Haynes K.C., Mr. Noah M. Haynes and Mr. Kashawn K. Woods
Counsel for the Respondent: Mr. Vincent D. Watson
Counsel for Amicus Curiae: Mrs. Melissa Yearwood

Summary

This case involves an appeal by the Barbados Defence Force (BDF) against the Court of Appeal's decision to quash the conviction of a commissioned officer (the Respondent) under Section 75 of the Barbados Defence Act, Cap 159. The Respondent had been convicted by court-martial on 04 June, 2019 on two charges related to misconduct within the Barbados Coast Guard. The Respondent appealed to the Court of Appeal of Barbados, which, conceded the dismissal one charge and found insufficient legal and evidential support for the other, leading to the present BDF's appeal. In dismissing the appeal, the court considered whether Section 75, which penalizes conduct prejudicial to military discipline, violated the rule of law and due process. Jamadar J concluded that while the language of Section 75 was broad, it did not offend constitutional standards for clarity, foreseeability, or legality. However, the particulars of the charges lacked sufficient detail, which violated the Respondent's right to a fair trial. Similarly, Saunders P emphasized the importance of specificity in framing charges under Section 75. The CCJ affirmed that Section 75 was constitutional, but upheld the dismissal of the appeal because the charge was not adequately particularized, making it impossible for the Respondent to mount a proper defence.

Headnotes

<u>Facts:</u> The Respondent was a commissioned BDF officer serving under Barbados Coast Guard's (BCG) authority. The Respondent's duties constituted being in charge of 120 soldiers and15 assets and their management on behalf of the Commanding Officer of the BCG. In October 2018, in lieu of a Convening Order, an investigation into suspected criminal activity involving drug trafficking, money laundering, and gun trafficking within the Coast Guard raigned on four charges under Section 75 of the Defence Act. At the court-martial, Charges One and Two were di smissed because of a successful no case submission. On 04 June 2019, the court-martial panel unanimously ruled that the Respondent was guilty in respect of Charges Three and Four due to which the Respondent was sentenced to dismissal from the BDF and termination of his commission. He then appealed to the Court of Appeal. On appeal, Charge Three was conceded to be bad during the hearing by the BDF, and the Court of Appeal found no legal or evidential bases for Charge Four and quashed the decision of the court martial. The Court reasoned that Charges Three and Four were

not proven to be offences within the meaning and scope of s 75. The BDF appealed the decision of the Court of Appeal, Barbados to the Appellate Jurisdiction of the Caribbean Court of Justice, wherein Charge Four was abandoned in oral submissions. On 26 April 2024, the Caribbean Court of Justice dismissed the BDF's appeal.

Issue(s):

(a.) Whether s.75 of the Act offends the rule of law for legal uncertainty and vagueness (the vires of the section)?

(b.) Whether the particulars of the s.75 charge laid against the Respondent were sufficiently clear to have the specific misconduct alleged brought to his attention with adequate particularity and in compliance with due process and fair hearing standard?

Contentions of the Parties: With regard to s.75, the Appellant contended that the Act provides sufficient legal certainty and that the particulars of the misconduct charged against the Respondent were sufficient. Further, it was also contented that the Court of Appeal has too narrowly restricted the application of s.75 and that interpretation is detrimental to the effective running of the military. Another argument put forth was that s.75 was intended to also cover charges that were not specifically identified in the Act or the Military Manual even though there was no written law proscribing charged behaviours. Lastly, the appellant argued that what is required to constitute a legally vires but unspecified charge under s 75, is either the commission of a positive action or the omission or failure to discharge a duty imposed or reasonably to be assumed by military custom or convention or practice and that s.75 ought to be 'prejudicial to good order and military discipline.' The Respondent, on the other hand, contended that there was no or not sufficient evidence to support the s.75 charges. In relation to the third charge, it was argued that the words that were said to have constituted the threat did not in fact constitute a threat at all and that, in any event, the evidence adduced did not establish that the alleged threat had not been reported. Lastly, as to the second s.75 charge, it was submitted that the other party failed to provide a definition of what amounts to 'information gathering' or to prove that he had engaged in unauthorised information gathering.

<u>*Amicus Curiae's Contention:*</u> Contending on the legality of s.75, it was asserted that s.75 meets the sufficiency test requirements for its legality as the language is not, so hopelessly vague to offend due process, the protection of the law, and the rule of law. The purpose of the offence, as held in R v Brandt stating that the purpose of the offence goes to the core need to maintain a disciplined armed force, which is the underlying justification for the breadth of the s.75 offence was also brought to light.

<u>Held:</u> With regard to the principle of rule of law, Justice Jamadar reinstated the supremacy of the constitution and highlighted the 'fair hearing' protection for criminal offences which mandates that a person charged shall be informed in detail about the nature of the offence. The Court observed that the Court of Appeal's approach to s.75 was too strict and restrictive and that a law expressed in broad terms does not necessarily mean that it is vague and offends the rule of law requirements for clarity and legality. The Court established the test of 'sufficient clarity' which should be judged in terms of a reasonable foreseeability in relation to the consequences of a person's conduct. On the contention of the Criminal Manual, the Court clearly stated that the pre-existence of a written law, rule, regulation, standing order, precedent, or policy proscribing the charged behaviour(s) is not necessary for laying a charge under s 75 of the Act.

It was unanimously agreed by the Bench that the nature of conduct amounting to an offence under s.75 is limited to actions/ omissions which prejudice good order and military discipline. The Court has taken a view contrary to the Court of Appeal and reiterated that the conduct charged under Charges Three and Four need not have been contained in a pre-existing written law as the utility of s.75 is to censure conduct which is objectively contrary to military standards, and which ought to attract military disciplinary measures even if not expressly proscribed. With regard to the particulars of the charge and offence, the Court has laid down that a charge must inform an accused of the precise details of the alleged misconduct including time, place and manner and that an offence must be adequately described both in the statement of charge, and in the particulars of offence. Further linking the charge under s.75 with the constitutional ambit, the Court has remarked that in a s.75 charge, the constitutional requirements of due process, the protection of the law, and fundamental fairness will need to be satisfied in the statement of the particulars of the offence, given the broad and general wording of the statutory offence. Lastly, the Court directed the BDF to take the care and time to create such written guides, standing operation procedures, and manuals, that are regularly updated, and conduct periodic education and training on these codes of conduct. The Court then proceeded to dismiss the present appeal with no order as to costs.

<u>Concurring Opinion:</u> Saunders P, J, concurring, stated that the pre-existence of a written law, rule, regulation, standing order, precedent, or policy proscribing the charged behaviour is unnecessary for laying a charge under s 75 of the Act. He emphasized that the section is an essential catch- all provision targeting misconduct. An observation was made regarding courts-martial which was supported by Section 79 A of the Constitution which grants an exception to the same. the Judge has reasoned that courts-martial are not exempt from a duty to abide by overarching constitutional values and that soldiers do enjoy a basic right to the protection of the law. Saunders P, J, remarked that the prosecution must satisfy the court-martial that the accused person must have known or had reasonable cause to believe that the impugned conduct was prejudicial to good order when it was engaged in. He agreed with the Court of Appeal's decision on the need for s. 75 offences to be properly particularised however, he additionally emphasised expressly that s.75 is neither vague not constitutional. On the particularisation of charged, it was concluded that provided they are adequately particularised, charges laid under s.75 may be brought and are often conducive to maintaining discipline, unit cohesion and overall operational effectiveness.

Provisions Involved

S. 75 of the Defence Act

S. 18(2)(b) of the Constitution of Barbados, 1966

S. 36(2) of the Defence Act

Case Laws Cited

A-G of Belize v Zuniga [2014] CCJ 2 (AJ) (BZ) (2014) 84 WIR 101; A-G of Guyana v Thomas [2022] CCJ 15 (AJ) GY, (2022) 101 WIR 403; Ali v David [2020] CCJ 10 (AJ) GY, (2020) 99 WIR 363; Commissioner of Police v Alleyne [2022] CCJ 2 (AJ) BB, [2022] 2 LRC 590; Dottin's Academy Inc v Norville [2021] CCJ 08 (AJ) BB, BB 2021 CCJ 2 (CARILAW); Harewood v Barbados Defence Force (BB CA, 27 June 2023); Khan v The State [2003] UKPC 79, (2003) 64 WIR 319 (TT); Kolender v Lawson 461 US 352 (1983); Lassalle v A-G (1971) 18 WIR 379 (TT CA); Leung Kwok Hung v HKSAR [2005] 3 HKLRD 164; McEwan v A-G of Guyana [2018] CCJ 30 (AJ) (GY), (2019) 94 WIR 332; Nervais v R [2018] CCJ 19 (AJ) (BB), (2018) 92 WIR 178; Ontario v Canadian Pacific Ltd [1995] 2 SCR 1031; Parker v Levy 417 US 733 (1974); R v Addis (1965) 49 Cr App Rep 95; R v Armstrong [2012] EWCA Crim 83; R v Army Council ex p Ravenscroft [1917] 2 KB 504; R v Brandt 2022 CM 4006; R v Davies [1980] Crim LR 582; R v Dodman (1998) 2 Cr App R 338; R v France (1898) 1 CCC 321; R v Landy [1981] 1 All ER 1172; R v Lunn (1993) 5 CMAR 157; R v Quintner (1934) 25 Cr App Rep 32; R v Secretary of State for War, ex p Martyn [1949] 1 All ER 242; R v Spear [2002] UKHL 31, [2003] 1 AC 734; R v Tyler (1992) 96 Cr App Rep 332; R (Rybarczyk) v Military District Court of Poznan, Poland [2013] EWHC 180 (Admin); Sabapathee v State [1999] 4 LRC 403.

REASONS FOR DECISION

Reasons

Jamadar J (Saunders P and Anderson, Rajnauth-Lee and Barrow JJ concurring) [1] – [36]

Saunders P (Anderson, Rajnauth-Lee, Barrow and Jamadar JJ concurring) [37] – [54]

Disposition [55]

Jamadar J

Introduction

(1.) There can be no doubt that in the military, officers must conform to certain standards and codes of behaviour and must be held accountable for related shortcomings. It ought to be self-evident as a general proposition, and it has been held to be so for eons that behaviour that is inimical to Good Order and Military Discipline within the service may be properly the subject of inquiry, investigation, and, if necessary, disciplinary measures. Yet, in these proceedings, the statutory ambit of this notion is contested. Thus, resolving this issue has far-reaching consequences for how the military in Caribbean spheres will regulate its affairs and function in the future, the clarification of which the Appellant implored in this appeal.

(2.) There can also be no doubt that in Barbados, the Constitution is the supreme law and that all other laws are subject to its dictates, its standards, core values, and principles.1 Furthermore, in Barbados, the rule of law prevails[2] and the protected fundamental rights include the protection of the law (and the inherent and accompanying right to due process).[3] Moreover, in Barbados, in what is known as the 'fair hearing' protection, Section 18(2)(b) of the Constitution mandates that for criminal offences (as is apposite for disciplinary proceedings in court-martial proceedings[4]), a person charged 'shall be informed ... in detail, of the nature of the offence charged'. These constitutional values are the lenses through which the issues that were contested before this Court must also be viewed.[5]

---

1. Constitution of Barbados 1966, Section 1. See *A-G of Belize vs Zuniga [2014] CCJ 2 (AJ) (BZ), (2014) 84 WIR 101; Ali vs David [2020] CCJ 10 (AJ) GY, (2020) 99 WIR 363; Commissioner of Police vs Alleyne [2022] CCJ 2 (AJ) BB, [2022] 2 LRC 590.*

2. Preamble to the Constitution of Barbados 1966, cl (b). See *Dottin's Academy Inc vs Norville [2021] CCJ 08 (AJ) BB, BB 2021 CCJ 2 (CARILAW).*

3. Constitution of Barbados 1966, Section 11(c). See *Nervais vs R [2018] CCJ 19 (AJ) (BB), (2018) 92 WIR 178.*

4. *R vs Spear* [2002] UKHL 31, [2003] 1 AC 734; 'Justice Through Court Martials' (UK Legal News Analysis, LexisNexis, 24 October W2002).

5. *A-G of Guyana vs Thomas [2022] CCJ (AJ) GY, (2022) 101 WIR 403 at [135] and [147].*

(3.) This appeal specifically involves the Barbados Defence Act6 ('the Act') and the jurisprudence on ordinary courts-martial. It raises issues of military law with a specific focus on Section 75 of the Act and offences relating to conduct prejudicial to Good Order and Military Discipline,[7] for which there are no local precedents and is therefore of great importance for the Defence Forces in Barbados and the Caribbean. In particular, this appeal focuses on the constitutionality and *vires*, per se, of Section 75, as well as the legal sufficiency of the charges and evidence in this matter.

Background

(4.) The Respondent was at all material times a commissioned officer of the Barbados Defence Force ('BDF') serving under the authority of the Barbados Coast Guard.[8] The Respondent's duties entailed, among other things, being in charge of over one hundred and twenty (120) soldiers and fifteen (15) assets, including vessels and the management of same on behalf of the commanding officer of the Barbados Coast Guard.

(5.) In October 2018, pursuant to a Convening Order,[9] an investigation into suspected criminal activity involving drug trafficking, money laundering, and gun trafficking within the Coast Guard division of the BDF was commenced, and in furtherance of this, the Respondent was interviewed.[10] Arising out of disclosures which were made during his interview, the Respondent was charged and arraigned on 27 May 2019 on four (4) charges under the Act.[11]

6. Defence Act, Cap 159.

7. Ibid. Section 75 states: 'Any person who, being subject to military law under this Act, does, or omits to do, any act or thing that is prejudicial to Good Order and Military Discipline is guilty of an offence and liable on conviction by court-martial to 2 years imprisonment or any less punishment provided by this Act.'

8. *Harewood vs Barbados Defence Force (BB CA, 27 June 2023) at [21].*

9. See Defence Act (n 6), s 92.

10. *Harewood (n 8) at [21] – [23].*

11. Charge One: Communicated with the enemy contrary to Section 36(2) of the Defence Act, Chapter 159. In that he, on a date unknown in January 2018, without lawful authority communicated with a known drug trafficker.

(6.) At the court-martial, Charges One and Two were dismissed as a consequence of a successful no-case submission.[12] However, on 4 June 2019, the court-martial panel unanimously ruled that the Respondent was guilty in respect of Charges Three[13] and Four.[14] As a consequence, the Respondent was sentenced to dismissal from the BDF and termination of his commission.[15] He appealed to the Court of Appeal. On appeal, Charge Three was conceded to be bad during the hearing by the BDF,[16] and the Court of Appeal found no legal or evidential bases for Charge Four and quashed the decision of the court-martial.[17]

(7.) In the reasoning of the Court of Appeal, Charges Three and Four were not proven to be offences within the meaning and scope of Section 75.[18] In relation to Charge Four, the Court reasoned that: (i) there must

---

Charge Two: Communicated with the enemy contrary to Section 36(2) of the Defence Act, Chapter 159. In that he, between the 7th to 10th August 2018, without lawful authority, knowingly communicated with Akem Waithe also known as "Ellis" by cellular phone using Barbados cellular phone 836-3185.

Chapter Three: Neglect to the Prejudice of Good Order and Military Discipline, contrary to Section 75 of the Defence Act, Chapter 159. In that he, in the Island of Barbados on an unknown date in January 2018, being a commissioned officer in the Barbados Defence Force, having knowledge of a threat to the life of a junior member of the Barbados Defence Force, namely, Ordinary Seaman Marlon Scott, neglected to inform his superiors of such a threat.

Charge Four: Conduct to the prejudice of Good Order and Military Discipline contrary to Section 75 of the Defence Act, Chapter 159. In that he, without lawful authority between 1st January 2018, and 30th September 2018, at various places in Barbados conducted unauthorised information gathering operations, conduct unbecoming of a commissioned officer in the Barbados Defence Force.

12. *Harewood (n 8) at [27].*

13. Charge Three: neglect to the prejudice of Good Order and Military Discipline, contrary to Section 75 of the Act, by neglecting to report a threat on the life of a junior officer.

14. Charge Four: conduct to the prejudice of Good Order and Military Discipline contrary to Section 75 of the Act, by conducting an unauthorised investigation.

15. *Harewood (n 8) at [28].*

16. ibid at [60].

17. ibid at [103].

18. ibid at [101].

be some framework defining what constitutes 'unauthorised' information gathering operations, (ii) there must be legal certainty that informs soldiers what is prohibited so that they may regulate their conduct,[19] (iii) the prosecution failed to unequivocally show a formal or informal standard operating procedure regarding reporting guidelines in the chain of command,[20] and (iv) the prosecution failed to discharge the burden of proving that the offences charged exist expressly and/or impliedly.[21]

(8.) The BDF appealed the decision of the Court of Appeal to this Court. Before this Court, Charge Four was abandoned in oral submissions. As a consequence, on 26 April 2024, this Court dismissed the BDF's appeal with reasons to follow. In this Court's opinion, the jurisprudential importance of some of the issues that were aired calls for clarification, including this Court's views on the reasoning of the Court of Appeal, all of which are discussed in the reasons which follow.

The Issues

(9.) Before this Court, the two issues that engaged counsel and that this Court was urged to give its views on concerned Charge Four and whether (i) Section 75 of the Act offends the rule of law for legal uncertainty and vagueness (the vires of the section),[22] and (ii) the particulars of the Section 75 charge laid against the Respondent were sufficiently clear to have the specific misconduct alleged brought to his attention with adequate particularity and in compliance with due process and fair hearing standards.[23]

(10.) Section 75 of the Act states:

> Any person who, being subject to military law under this Act, does, or omits to do, any act or thing that is prejudicial to Good Order and Military

19. ibid at [100] 4 [sic].

20. ibid at [100] 5 [sic].

21. ibid at [100] 6 [sic].

22. See *McEwan vs A-G of Guyana [2018] CCJ 30 (AJ) (GY), (2019) 94 WIR 332 at [80] and following.*

23. *R vs Quinner (1934) 25 Cr App Rep 32. See also R vs Tyler (1992) 96 Cr App Rep 332.*

> Discipline is guilty of an offence and liable on conviction by court-martial to 2 years imprisonment or any less punishment provided by this Act.

Charge Four was stated as follows:

> Conduct to the prejudice of Good Order and Military Discipline Contrary to Section 75 of the Defence Act, Chapter 159. In that he, without lawful authority between 1st January 2018, and 30th September 2018, at various places in Barbados conducted unauthorized information gathering operations, conduct unbecoming of a commissioned officer in the Barbados Defence Force.

(11.) As explained, the Court of Appeal raised concerns regarding the lack of a clear pre-existing framework defining what constitutes 'unauthorised information gathering operations' and, additionally, the prosecution's failure to establish clear reporting guidelines within the chain of command, which in its opinion further complicated the matter. The Appellant contended that the Act provides sufficient legal certainty and that the particulars of the misconduct charged against the Respondent were sufficient.

(12.) This case underscores not only the intricacies of military law but also the importance of explaining the particulars of an offence in laying charges of a criminal nature. For the Appellant, what is at stake is a concern that if the reasoning of the Court of Appeal stands, then in order to prove an omission or act 'that is prejudicial to Good Order and Military Discipline' (a Section 75 offence), which it insists is a necessary regulatory provision in the military, proof of some pre-existing prohibition for alleged offending conduct will be necessary. A situation that, it is contended, is untenable because Section 75 is intended to be open-ended to facilitate matters that may arise from time to time that are prejudicial to Good Order and Military Discipline, but not necessarily anticipatorily proscribed. The Appellant contends that the Court of Appeal has too narrowly restricted the application of Section 75 and that interpretation is detrimental to the effective running of the military.

(13.) What these two issues address are, first, the *vires* of Section 75 per se, and second, how the particulars of a charge under Section 75 are integral to an offence under the Section (and, therefore, by implication, the sufficiency of Charge Four in this case). As will be discussed, these discrete issues are, in fact, two sides of a single coin.

(14.) In passing, it may also be important to note that before this Court no issue was taken with the jurisdiction of either the Court of Appeal or this Court to hear and determine this appeal, which is founded in the exercise of its criminal jurisdiction. The issue was dealt with at [45] to [48] of the judgment of the Court of Appeal. There is also agreement in relation to the burden and standard of proof in a court-martial; the burden lies on the prosecution on a criminal standard of proof of guilt beyond a reasonable doubt. This issue was also dealt with in the judgment of the Court of Appeal at [49] to [52].

The Vires of Section 75

(15.) The Court of Appeal, in its analysis of the issues noted in relation to Section 75:[24]

> It is impossible not to make the general observation here that Section 75 is drafted in vague and general terms that call for an interpretation of the term 'prejudicial to Good Order and Military Discipline'. Or alternatively, the lack of evidence of regulations, standing orders and an established practice or precedent that defines with some degree of legal certainty the meaning of the term 'Good Order and Military Discipline' and conduct liable to attract the criminal sanction of two years imprisonment or in this case dismissal from the BDF.

(16.) The Court of Appeal was sufficiently troubled by this issue, that it directed supplemental submissions be filed on whether, in light of the alleged vagueness of Section 75, Charges Three and Four 'are military ... offences within the meaning and scope of Section 75 of the Act.'[25] Ultimately the Appellant would concede before the Court of Appeal that

24. *Harewood (n 8) at [56].*

25. ibid at [57].

as a result of the sparseness of the particulars underpinning it, Charge Three was unsustainable but continued to argue that Charge Four was proper.[26]

(17.) At the heart of the Appellant's argument, which the Court of Appeal rejected, was the contention that Section 75 was intended to also cover charges that were not specifically identified in the Act or the Military Manual[27] (considered the two formal sources of military law), even if there was no written law, Rule, Regulation, standing order, precedent, or policy proscribing the charged behaviour(s). Before the Court of Appeal, it was agreed that there was no offence of 'unauthorised information gathering operations' to be found in the Act, the Military Manual, or contained in any written Rule, Regulation, or policy of the BDF.[28] However, and as the Court of Appeal summarised, the Appellant's contention is that not all duties imposed on members of the military are expressly stated ..., they can be necessarily implied[29] for the purposes of a charge under Section 75. And, to constitute a legitimate Charge Four under Section 75 what is essential is that the Respondent 'knew or ought to have known that he required specific orders to gather information in the way he admittedly did'.[30]

(18.) In more general terms, the Appellant argues that what is required to constitute a legally vires but unspecified charge under Section 75, is either the commission of a positive action or the omission or failure to discharge a duty imposed or reasonably to be assumed by military custom or convention or practice (as a species of implied military negligence),31 that, for the purposes of Section 75, was known or ought to have been known to be 'prejudicial to Good Order and Military Discipline.'

26. ibid at [60].

27. The Military Manual refers to the United Kingdom's Ministry of Defence, *Manual of Military Law Pt 1 (HMSO 1972), widely considered a Commonwealth authority on military law and treated as such by the parties to this appeal. See also Harewood (n 8) at [4] and [21].*

28. See discussion in *Harewood (n 8) at [68] to [81].*

29. ibid at [81].

30. ibid at [85].

31. ibid at [61] and [62].

(19.) The Court of Appeal was not persuaded by the Appellant's implied criminal offence construction of Section 75. It would opine:32

> In our view, in order to rely on an implied code of conduct it was incumbent on the prosecution to establish a policy and/or practice brought to the attention of members of the force or alternatively satisfy the court-martial on the criminal standard that the Appellant was fully aware that his conduct constituted a punishable offence under Section 75 of the Act.
>
> It appears to us that there may be cause for a distinction between matters engaging the Force's powers of disciplinary control (offences against discipline) and 'offences' (criminal) within the scope of Section 75 of the Act as having been established by Regulations, standing orders, or service precedent.

(20.) In our opinion the approach of the Court of Appeal to Section 75 was too strict and restrictive, though the concerns that informed it are well founded. This Court, in *McEwan vs Attorney General of Guyana,*[33] explained its general approach to vagueness in criminal laws, as follows:

> A penal statute must meet certain minimum objectives if it is to pass muster as a valid law. It must provide fair notice to citizens of the prohibited conduct.[34] It must not be vaguely worded. It must define the criminal offence with sufficient clarity that ordinary people can understand what conduct is prohibited.[35] It should not be stated in ways that allow law enforcement officials to use subjective moral or value judgments as the basis for its enforcement. A law should not encourage arbitrary and discriminatory enforcement.[36]
>
> ...
>
> It was suggested to us by the Solicitor General that any potential vagueness

---

32. ibid at [94] and [95].

33. *McEwan (n 22) at [80] and [82].*

34. ibid citing *Ontario vs Canadian Pacific Ltd [1995] 2 SCR 1031.*

35. *McEwan (n 22), citing Kolender vs Lawson 461 US 352 (1983) at 357.*

36. ibid.

> could be removed if, when a person is charged, details are given of the improper purpose that prompted the laying of the charge. This is not an effective solution to the problem. It seeks to cure the vagueness after the individual has been arrested for the offence. On the contrary, individuals require advance notice of any proscribed conduct so as to regulate their behaviour so as to avoid getting into trouble.

(21.) In *McEwan* this Court found that the law in question in that case was 'hopelessly vague' and was unconstitutional as offending the rule of law. It was struck down.[37] However, the issue of statutory vagueness is more nuanced in practice. And an important distinction must also be drawn between a law that is so vaguely stated per se that it offends the rule of law, and a charge brought on a valid (albeit broadly stated) law that is not sufficiently precise and particularised.

(22.) A law expressed in broad terms does not necessarily mean that it is vague and offends the rule of law requirements for clarity and legality.[38] Legislation creating criminal conduct may be intentionally and purposively open ended to avoid excessive rigidity and to cover emerging future circumstances. What is essential is that any criminal offence charged under that law is defined and described with sufficient clarity to enable a person to understand how their conduct violated the statute and rendered them liable to be prosecuted.

(23.) In Fundamentals of Caribbean Constitutional Law,[39] the authors explain the relationship between legal certainty, due process, and the rule of law, as follows: 'A criminal statute will violate the due process right and, likewise, the right to the protection of the law if it is so vague that a citizen cannot regulate his or her conduct.[40] ... The degree of certainty or precision expected depends on the circumstances.'[41]

---

37. *McEwan (n 22) at [85], citing Sabapathee vs State [1999] 4 LRC 403 at 412 (Lord Hope).*

38. See *Sabapathee vs State [1999] 4 LRC 403 at [17]-[19].*

39. Tracy Robinson, Arif Bulkan and Adrian Saunders, *Fundamentals of Caribbean Constitutional Law (2nd edn, Sweet and Maxwell 2021) para 6-014.*

40. ibid citing *Lassalle vs A-G (1971) 18 WIR 379 (TT CA) at 383 and Khan vs The State [2003] UKPC 79, (2003) 64 WIR 319 (TT) at [10].*

41. ibid citing *Sabapathee (n 38).*

(24.) These legality requirements for certainty and clarity are heightened with laws that interfere with fundamental rights and in such situations the need for precision is enhanced. The test is one of sufficiency and is often expressed as 'sufficient clarity'.[42] This is a contextual and not an absolute standard. What is often determinative of legality, is an objective assessment of whether a person can regulate their conduct knowing with a reasonable degree of confidence whether their conduct will be considered criminal or not. To this extent, legal certainty requires a measure of reasonable foreseeability in relation to the consequences of a person's conduct.[43]

(25.) Section 75 defines and describes as proscribed conduct 'any act or thing that is prejudicial to Good Order and Military Discipline'. This is its intention and purpose. In and of itself, this language is not, in our opinion, so hopelessly vague to offend due process, the protection of the law, and the rule of law. As explained in *R vs Brandt*,[44] the purpose of the offence goes to the core need to maintain a disciplined armed force, which is the underlying justification for the breadth of the Section 75 offence. A justification that the amicus appearing before this Court re-iterated. On the face of it, Section 75 meets the sufficiency test requirements for its legality.

(26.) In any event, the following four reasons prevail. First, similar provisions to Section 75 exist in numerous other jurisdictions and have been interpreted and applied without compromising the stated fundamental rights of military officers.[45] Second, the language is expressed with sufficient clarity to be capable

42. *McEwan (n 22).*

43. Robinson, Bulkan and Saunders (n 39) para 6-015. See also *Leung Kwok Hung vs HKSAR [2005] 3 HKLRD 164.*

44. 2022 CM 4006.

45. The Act is modelled after the Army Act 1955 (UK). Section 75 exists in similar form in many pieces of military legislation including the United Kingdom, Canada, United States, and Australia, among others. See for example in the *UK, R vs Davies* [1980] Crim LR 582: a variety of offensive behaviours may be prosecuted under the UK equivalent of Section 75 and these are not limited to an exhaustive list. Moreover, per *R vs Armstrong* [2012] EWCA Crim 83, it is irrelevant that the conduct does not have the potential to become known to others within the military or that it was not in fact known until it was discovered on investigation. And as stated in *R (Rybarczyk) vs Military District Court of Poznan, Poland* [2013] EWHC 180 (Admin), it is not a requirement of establishing an offence under the Section 75

of an objective assessment and a reasonable measure of self-regulation. The proscribed conduct must be prejudicial, in the context of the military, to Good Order and Discipline. Third, in the Military Manual there are examples given of what could constitute a Section 75 offence. These are clearly illustrative and not exhaustive and include conduct such as the improper use of a vehicle or service property, improper possession of leave passes, and the wearing of badges of rank that have not been awarded.[46] These, self-evidently, can be prejudicial to and undermine Good Order and Discipline in the military. No doubt there can be innumerable other examples and occurrences of conduct that can constitute an offence under Section 75.[47] Fourth, academic writers acknowledge the open-endedness of Section 75 and the difficulty for a person to know in advance whether their conduct falls within the Section, but nevertheless accept its utility in the context of the military.[48]

(27.) In our opinion, the pre-existence of a written law, rule, regulation, standing order, precedent, or policy proscribing the charged behaviour(s) is not necessary for laying a charge under Section 75 of the Act. In this case, the Appellant clearly identified that the alleged offence was contrary to Section 75 and purported to give particulars (a matter that will be considered presently). As such, the Respondent's constitutional right to notice of the charge, subject to the extent of the specificity of the particulars, has not been compromised. The essential elements of the charge are clear: the alleged conduct must be proven, beyond a reasonable doubt, to be prejudicial to Good Order and Military Discipline in the context of the BDF, and the burden of proof

---

equivalent that it should be proved that a soldier realised that acts which objectively were prejudicial to Good Order and Discipline amounted to conduct prejudicial to Good Order and Discipline. In Canada and the United States, similar approaches have been taken. In Canada, *R vs Lunn* (1993) 5 CMAR 157 at 166 essentially upheld that the equivalent to Section 75 is not constitutionally too vague. See also Martin L Friedland, 'Military Justice and the Somalia Affair' (1998) 40 Crim LQ 360. In the *United States, in Parker vs Levy* 417 US 733 (1974), the equivalent Section to Section 75 was held to be not unconstitutionally vague nor facially invalid because of overbreadth.

46. See *Harewood (n 8) at [72]*.

47. See (n 45).

48. Kate Grady, 'Disciplinary Offences at the Court Martial' [2016] Crim LR 714; Paul Camp, 'Section 69 of the Army Act 1955' (1999) 149 NLJ 1955. See also E J D McBrien, 'An Outline of British Military Law' (1983) 22 Mil L & L War Rev 9, 14.

is on the Appellant. To require, as a general rule, that a pre-condition for bringing a charge under Section 75 is the pre-existence of a written law, rule, regulation, standing order, precedent, or policy proscribing the specific charged behaviour(s),[49] would undermine the intention, purpose and utility of Section 75 in the scheme of the Act.

(28.) Accordingly, applying the requirements for legal certainty, Section 75, although drafted in broad and general terms, meets the constitutional standard of foreseeability which would allow members of the BDF to understand the consequences of and appropriately regulate their conduct to avoid censure. The nature of conduct amounting to an offence under Section 75, is limited to actions/omissions which prejudice (undermine) Good Order and Military Discipline. Whether an offence has occurred is determined on an objective test, irrespective of how an accused subjectively perceived their conduct. Thus, it does not matter whether an accused perceived their conduct as culpable. Therefore, the conduct charged under Charges Three and Four need not have been contained in a pre-existing written law, rule, regulation, standing order, precedent, or policy, as the utility of Section 75 is to censure conduct which is objectively contrary to military standards, and which ought to attract military disciplinary measures even if not expressly proscribed. Thus, the view of the Court of Appeal seemingly to the contrary is to be reconsidered in this light.[50]

The Particulars of Charge Four

(29.) The legitimate concerns of the Court of Appeal are adequately met in a Section 75 charge if the elements of the charge are satisfactorily enumerated with sufficient particularity and clarity. This is also a part of due process, and the protection of the law, whereby an accused must be informed of the nature and cause(s) of an accusation. A charge is sufficient if it contains all the elements of the offence charged and fairly informs an accused with sufficient particularity of what they must answer so as to enable them to plead

49. In this case, and in relation to Charge Four, conducting unauthorised information gathering operations.

50. *Harewood (n 8)* [99] – [100].

in response, and if not guilty, to properly prepare for and adequately defend the charge(s).

(30.) A charge must therefore inform an accused of the precise details, or particulars, of the alleged misconduct that support the charge. These particulars should provide a clear and concise description of the alleged criminal act including details, say, about the time, place, and manner in which the offence was committed. Particulars must give the accused adequate notice of the charge(s) they face, enabling them if necessary, to prepare a defence. Particulars also assist in focusing the trial on the relevant facts and legal issues. Hence, they go to due process and the protection of the law.

(31.) Indeed, in Barbados Section 18(2)(b) of the Constitution mandates that for criminal offences (and therefore for disciplinary proceedings in court-martial proceedings under the Act[51]), a person charged 'shall be informed ... *in detail*, of the nature of the offence charged.' (emphasis added). This provision encapsulates the constitutional mandates of fairness and due notification, that require a Section 75 charge to detail and make specific in the content of the particulars of the charge what is broadly stated (conduct that is prejudicial to Good Order and Military Discipline).

(32.) These constitutional standards required the Appellant to expressly allege every element and material detail of a charge with precise particularity. Thus, an offence must be adequately described both in the statement of charge, and in the particulars of offence.[52] The degree of detail depends on the nature of the offence and circumstances of the charge. For example, in cases involving, say, complicated conspiracies, the particulars of offence should contain sufficient details such as will enable an accused and the adjudicating judicial officer to clearly know the nature of the prosecution's case, and to ensure fairness, to prevent the prosecution from shifting its ground during a trial without first

---

51. *R vs France (1898) 1* CCC 321 at 328 (Wurtele J). See also Dana S Seetahal and Roger Ramgoolam, Commonwealth Caribbean Criminal Practice and Procedure (5th edn, Routledge 2019).

52. *R vs Quintner (1934)* 25 Cr App Rep 32. See also R vs Tyler (1992) 96 Cr App Rep 332 (indictment, the particulars of which disclose a correct offence but widen the ambit of the offence, capable of amendment and not a nullity).

applying for leave to amend the indictment.[53] A reviewing Court is therefore entitled to narrowly interpret the language and specifications of the charge so as to protect the fundamental rights of an accused and to ensure a fair trial.

(33.) In this matter, it is precisely a deficiency in the particulars of Charge Four that led the Appellant to withdraw its appeal, and rightly so, agreeing that Charge Four lacked sufficient particularity. The charge and particulars stated, were as follows:

> Conduct to the prejudice of Good Order and Military Discipline Contrary to Section 75 of the Defence Act, Chapter 159. In that he, without lawful authority between 1 January 2018, and 30 September 2018, at various places in Barbados conducted unauthorised information gathering operations, conduct unbecoming of a commissioned fficer in the Barbados Defence Force.
>
> (Footnote omitted)

(34.) What was the nature and what were the details of the unauthorised information gathering operations that were allegedly conducted by the Respondent? How could the Respondent fairly and properly prepare to plead to or defend such an accusation? These are but two questions that demonstrate the conceded deficiency in particulars of Charge Four. It cannot be overstated, that in a Section 75 charge, the constitutional requirements of due process, the protection of the law, and fundamental fairness will need to be satisfied in the statement of the particulars of the offence, given the broad and general wording of the statutory offence.

Conclusion

(35.) Though we have held that Section 75 satisfies the requirements of legal certainty, and that there is no need for the pre-existence of a written law, rule, regulation, standing order, precedent, or policy proscribing charged behaviour(s) as a pre-condition for laying a charge under Section 75 of the Act (provided there is sufficiency of detail in the statement of the particulars of the

53. See *R vs Addis (1965) 49 Cr App Rep 95; R vs Landy [1981] 1 All ER 1172.*

offence), this is by no means to suggest that the BDF should not be strongly encouraged to provide cogent guidance in relation to proscribed conduct that could result in a Section 75 offence.[54] As a responsible military organisation we urge the BDF to take the care and time to create such written guides, standing operation procedures, and manuals, that are regularly updated, and conduct periodic education and training on these codes of conduct.

(36.) It is our hope that the BDF will learn from this experience and will endeavour to ensure that their processes and procedures are clear and accessible and where any gaps are discovered they are remedied, for the guidance and benefit of their officers and the organisation as a whole.

Saunders P

(37.) The accused, a Barbados Defence Force ('BDF') officer, was tried by court-martial for breaches of the Defence Act[55] ('the Act'). Two of the four offences charged were stated to be contrary to Section 36(2) of the Act which criminalises 'Communicating with the enemy'. The other two offences, Charges Three and Four allegedly contravened Section 75 of the Act. Section 75 speaks to 'Conduct to [the] prejudice of Military Discipline'. The four offences are specifically laid out at [5] footnote 11 of the judgment of Jamadar J.

(38.) The first of the two Section 75 offences charged the accused with neglect. The charge alleged that, having knowledge of a threat to the life of a junior member of the Defence Force, the accused had neglected to inform his superiors of the threat. The second of the Section 75 offences alleged that, without lawful authority, the accused had conducted unauthorised information gathering operations and that this constituted conduct unbecoming of a commissioned officer in the BDF.

(39.) The court-martial, ably presided over by Lieutenant Colonel Rohan

54. Ideally this should be done in the form of written Rules, Regulations, standing orders, and policies.

55. Cap 159 (n 6).

Johnson of the Jamaica Defence Force, heard evidence and submissions in relation to all four charges. The tribunal properly upheld a no-case submission in relation to the Section 36 charges. The court-martial accepted that an alleged drug trafficker, with whom it was claimed the accused had been in communication, did not fall within the compass of 'the enemy' as referenced in Section 36. The court-martial, however, did find the accused guilty of both Section 75 charges relating to conduct to the prejudice of Military Discipline. The sentence imposed on him was dismissal from the BDF.

(40.) The accused appealed to the Court of Appeal against his conviction. His grounds of appeal revolved around three broad areas. First, he claimed that there was no or no sufficient evidence to support the Section 75 charges. Indeed, he argued that the court-martial had wrongly refused to uphold his no-case submission made at the end of the case for the prosecution. Secondly, he argued, in relation to the third charge, that the words that were said to have constituted the threat did not in fact constitute a threat at all and that, in any event, the evidence adduced did not establish that the threat (if indeed it was such) had not been reported. Thirdly, as to the second Section 75 charge, it was submitted that the prosecution failed to provide a definition of what amounts to 'information gathering' or to prove that he had engaged in unauthorised information gathering. The accused also appealed against the sentence imposed on him.

(41.) In treating with the appeal, the Court of Appeal effectively put to one side the grounds of appeal formally set out by counsel for the accused. The Court decided to concern itself with what it regarded to be 'the more foundational or in limine issue of the offences charged themselves'. The Court of Appeal felt that this issue had to be settled before it could go on to consider a) the elements of the offences charged and b) whether there was a sufficiency of evidence to prove the commission of the offences beyond reasonable doubt.

(42.) In looking at 'the offences charges themselves' the Court of Appeal reasoned that Section 75 was 'vague' and that a consideration of this vagueness and of the charges laid under that Section was potentially dispositive of the appeal. The Court of Appeal was so concerned with the question of whether the accused was properly or appropriately charged that it invited the parties to file supplementary submissions on this issue. As a consequence of these further submissions, the prosecution accepted that the first of the Section 75 charges (Charge 3) must be dismissed. The prosecution persisted in defending the conviction for unauthorised information gathering (Charge 4) but the prosecution's arguments on Charge 4 did not prevail.

(43.) The Court of Appeal concluded that the prosecution had failed to establish that the Section 75 offences 'exist in law or by implication'. Accordingly, the appeal of the accused was upheld. Both Charges, 3 and 4, were dismissed. The Court therefore found it unnecessary to address either the grounds of appeal relating to the sufficiency of the evidence to support Charge 4 or the excessiveness or the disproportionality of the sentence.

(44.) The prosecution appealed to this Court, the Court of Appeal's dismissal of the fourth charge. In the course of the proceedings before us, it was evident that the appeal had no prospects of success and counsel for the prosecution rightly agreed to withdraw the appeal. Counsel was however of the opinion that, given the broad views of the Court of Appeal on Section 75 of the Act and charges laid under Section 75, it was important that this Court should express itself on those matters.

(45.) The Court of Appeal had indicated that because of the alleged 'vagueness' of Section 75 it entertained grave doubts that a charge under that Section could be maintained where there was no relevant law, regulation made pursuant to the Act, or stated military policy or practice against which unbecoming conduct of an accused could be assessed. According to the Court:[56]

> [56] It is impossible not to make the general observation here that Section 75 is drafted in vague and general terms that call for an interpretation of the term 'prejudicial to Good Order and Military Discipline'. Or alternatively, the lack of evidence of Regulations, standing orders and an established practice or precedent that defines with some degree of legal certainty the meaning of the term 'Good Order and Military Discipline' and conduct liable to attract the criminal sanction of two years imprisonment or in this case dismissal from the BDF.

56. *Harewood (n 8) at [56].*

(46.) Regrettably, I cannot associate myself with these observations and the main purpose of this concurring judgment is to make clear some views on this matter. I start where all law and legality can usefully begin; with the Constitution.

(47.) The Constitution of Barbados recognises as a distinct specie of criminal proceedings, even if only inferentially so, the uniqueness of courts-martial. Section 79A of the Constitution grants wide powers to the Director of Public Prosecutions to institute and undertake criminal proceedings against any person before any court, but the Section carefully excepts courts-martial from this sweeping remit.

(48.) Why does the Constitution make this exception for courts-martial? The Constitution does so because it recognises and accepts the peculiar nature of military service and the resulting specialised procedures and rules that must exist for the prosecution of service members for derelictions committed in the course of that service. The ordinary civil courts should be wary of trespassing the jurisdiction of a court-martial unless a person's fundamental rights are affected. See for example R vs Army Council, ex p Ravenscroft57 and *R vs Secretary of State* for *War, ex p Martyn*[58].

(49.) What distinguishes the military is that it is an institution that absolutely requires enforcement of the strictest discipline. The service has therefore had to develop a distinct culture, set of rules, standards and procedures geared at maintaining order and operational efficiency. Courts-martial are specifically designed to ensure that breaches of Military Discipline and the unique requirements of military life and service are appropriately addressed, not by civilian Magistrates or Judges but by military personnel. By excluding them from the remit of the normal criminal trial Courts the Constitution recognises that courts-martial are best equipped to fulfil this objective.

(50.) Of course, courts-martial are not exempt from a duty to abide by overarching constitutional values. Soldiers do enjoy a basic right to the protection of the law; and this is why I agreed that the appeal here could not

57. [1917] 2 KB 504 at 508.

58. [1949] 1 All ER 242 at 243 (Goddard CJ).

succeed. The problem in this case was not that Section 75 was vague or that charges laid under it are inherently deficient in substance. The problem here was that the charge, as laid, lacked the specificity, the particulars, necessary to allow the accused to properly defend himself. This defect implicated the constitutional right of the accused to the protection of the law. Merely to accuse an officer that, without lawful authority, between 1 January 2018 and 30 September 2018, at various places in Barbados, the officer conducted unauthorised information gathering operations, was insufficient. Where were these 'various places'? In St Lucy? In Christ Church? In what manner did the accused conduct the alleged unauthorised information gathering operations? What exactly did the accused do and with whom and how?

(51.) When a person is charged, even before a court-martial, it is important that they are told precisely what they are accused of, including the time, place, and manner of commission of the alleged offence. This clarity ensures that the defendant understands the nature of the charges and is able to prepare an appropriate defence. A well-particularised charge also guides the tribunal in the presentation and evaluation of evidence, making it easier for all to focus on relevant facts and determine whether the alleged conduct matches the elements of the charged offence. From that standpoint, the charge laid here was not appropriately framed.

(52.) I emphatically agree with Jamadar J, however, that the pre-existence of a written law, rule, regulation, standing order, precedent, or policy proscribing the charged behaviour is unnecessary for laying a charge under Section 75 of the Act. That Section is an essential catch-all provision targeting misconduct that undermines the maintenance of strict discipline. As pointed out by Jamadar J, variants of Section 75 are to be found in military codes almost everywhere.

(53.) Service women and men, steeped in the culture of the military, would or ought readily to appreciate (even if civilian trial and appellate Judges might struggle with the concept) what conduct would disrupt the efficient operation or morale of the armed forces. Certainly, the prosecution must satisfy the court-martial that the accused person must have known or had reasonable cause to believe that the impugned conduct was prejudicial to Good Order when it was engaged in. And the court-martial must ultimately decide whether the conduct was objectively prejudicial (in other words, whether a reasonable service person would have contemplated that the conduct alleged was prejudicial) and whether it was engaged in intentionally or recklessly[59].

(54.) While the military is encouraged to and will undoubtedly provide general guidance in the form of rules, written policies and protocols, it is impossible to specify beforehand every conceivable infraction that will undermine authority. The Court of Appeal was right to draw attention to the need for these Section 75 offences to be properly particularised. On this basis the Court of Appeal was also right to dismiss those charges. But it must be emphasised that Section 75 is not vague nor unconstitutional. A similar conclusion was reached by the Office of the Judge Advocate General in London when that Office offered the opinion that a similar provision is not incompatible with Article 7 of the European Convention on Human Rights[60]. Provided they are adequately particularised, charges laid under Section 75 may be brought and are often conducive to maintaining discipline, unit cohesion and overall operational effectiveness.

Disposition

(55.) The following are the orders of the Court:

(1.) The appeal is dismissed.

(2.) No order as to costs:

/s/ A. Saunders
Mr. Justice Saunders (President) /s/ /W. Anderson/s/ M. Rajnauth-Lee

Mr. Justice Anderson Mme Justice Rajnauth-Lee/s/ D. Barrow /s/ P. Jamadar

Mr. Justice Barrow Mr. Justice Jamadar

59. See *R vs Dodman (1998) 2 Cr App R 338.*

60. See Office of the Judge Advocate General, 'Practice in the Service Courts Collected Memoranda'(Military Court Service,1 September 2016) para 1.3 < https://www.judiciary.uk/wp-content/uploads/2020/08/practice-memo-ver-6-1Sep16.pdf> accessed 10 July 2024.

(2025) I FLR 351 (India)

Supreme Court of India

Union of India & Others vs Naresh Kumar Yadav

Composition of Court: Hima Kohli and Rajesh Bindal, JJ

Date of Decision: 15 June 2024

Counsel for the Appellants: Mr. Ashok Panigrahi, Mr. Ishaan Sharma, Mr. Annirudh Sharma II, Mr. Rajan Kumar Chourasia, Ms. Sweksha, Mr. Arvind Kumar Sharma

Counsel for the Respondent: Mr. Ankur Chibber, Mr. Anil Kumar Gautam

Summary

In this case, the Supreme Court of India reached the conclusion that one's ignorance of criminal allegations against him and failing to disclose them did not warrant removal from service in the Central Reserve Police Force (CRPF). In this case, the Respondent enlisted in CRPF in 2003, declaring no criminal convictions or pending cases. Four years later, a complaint surfaced alleging Respondent's involvement in a pre-enlistment criminal case, which authorities verified. Once Respondent learned of this, he approached the trial court for bail. For this, the Appellants-Union of India initiated a departmental enquiry and the Respondent received a punishment of three increments' stoppage for three years in the CRPF.

Subsequently, the trial court convicted the Respondent but released him on probation. The magistrate clarified that the judgment would not affect Respondent's service. However, the next year, Appellants issued a Show Cause Notice asking him as to why should the punishment not be enhanced and why should he not be dismissed or removed from service. Respondent argued that the initial punishment sufficed. Nonetheless, Appellants ordered his removal from service.

The Respondent challenged the removal from service before the Delhi High Court which set-aside the order of removal by holding that the powers were not correctly exercised by the authorities, and after allowing the first penalty to run its course, it would be improper to impose another penalty, that too, after a long period of more than three years. The High Court also held that this amounted to double penalty on the employee.

The Appellants challenged the judgment of the Delhi High Court before the Supreme Court of India. The Supreme Court agreed with the High Court of Delhi and also observed that the criminal offence, of which the Respondent was accused of and regarding which he had pleaded ignorance, was trivial in nature and a dispute between neighbours and was liable to be ignored. The Supreme Court also held that it did not appear that the Respondent was aware of the pendency of the case against him and dismissed the appeal filed by the Appellants-Union of India against the Respondent.

Headnotes

Facts: Respondent enlisted in the CRPF on 21 May 2003. During enlistment, he stated that he had no criminal convictions or pending criminal cases against him. Appellants also took steps to verify Respondent's disclosure. Four years later, Appellant received a complaint alleging Respondent was involved in a criminal case prior to his enlistment. Respondent learned of this the year prior and approached the trial court for bail. The Assistant Public Prosecutor verified the complaint. Appellants imposed a punishment of stoppage of three increments for three years without cumulative effect on Respondent. The Chief Judicial Magistrate convicted the Respondent of the alleged offences, however, released him on probation of good conduct. The magistrate also gave him the benefit of Section 12 of the Probation of Offenders Act clarifying the judgment would not affect Respondent's service. The next year the Appellants issued a Show Cause Notice to the Respondent as to why he should not be dismissed or removed from service. Respondent argued that he should not be dismissed because Appellants had already imposed a stoppage of three increments for three years. Appellants nonetheless ordered his removal from service which was challenged by the Respondent before the Delhi High Court which set-aside the order of removal from service and ordered his reinstatement.

Issue: Respondent, a Central Reserve Police Force member, denied any criminal history during enlistment. Four years later, a pre-enlistment criminal complaint surfaced. Respondent received received a punishment of three increments' stoppage for three years in the CRPF. Later, the Appellants removed him from service. The issue that arose in the case was whether the removal from service reasonable given the circumstances, especially considering the time lapse and the initial penalty?

Contentions of the Parties: Appellant contended that the Respondent had suppressed the criminal complaint against him and this warranted Respondent's dismissal. Appellants cited *Daya Shankar Yadav vs Union of India & Anr.*, (2010) 14 SCC 103 and *Avtar Singh vs Union of India and others*, (2016) 8 SCC 471 in support of their argument. Respondent argued his ignorance of the criminal complaint at the time of enlistment. He also submitted that he could not be punished twice and that too after a lapse of a long time after the first punishment had already been given effect to.

Held: The Supreme Court held that the Delhi High Court was right in allowing the petition in favour of the Respondent. Judgment of the Delhi High Court upheld, appeal filed by the Appellants-Union of India dismissed as meritless and Respondent was directed to be reinstated in service.

ORDER

(1.) The present appeal is directed against the judgment and order dated 27 January 2015 passed by the Division Bench of the High Court of Delhi in WP(C) No. 7607 of 2014 filed by the Respondent challenging the order dated 1 July 2013 passed by the Appellant No.4 – Deputy Inspector General of Police, CRPF, Hyderabad Range, Hyderabad imposing a punishment of removal from service on him and order dated 2 July 2014 passed by the Appellant No.5 – Additional Director General, Southern Zone, Hyderabad, rejecting the Revision Petition filed by the Respondent against the order of his removal from service.

[2.] Facts of the Case

[2.1] The brief facts of the case are that the Respondent was enlisted in the Central Reserve Police Force[1] as a Constable on 21 May 2003 and posted in the 5th Battalion. While filling up the verification form furnished by the Appellants, on 28 December 2003, he stated that he was not involved in any criminal case and nor was any criminal case pending against him. On 31 March 2004, the Appellants initiated steps to verify the character and antecedents of the Respondent through the District Magistrate, Alwar. After four years, on 8 March 2008, a complaint was received from one Balraj Singh, a neighbour of the Respondent at his native place alleging that the latter was involved in a criminal case prior to his being enlisted in the CRPF, which fact had been suppressed by him. The Appellants took steps to seek relevant information from the District Magistrate, Ajmer and the civil authorities so as to verify the contents of the complaint received.

[2.2] In the course of the aforesaid verification, the Assistant Public Prosecutor wrote letters dated 17 February 2009 and 20 February 2009 to the Appellants informing them that the Respondent was involved in a criminal case arising from FIR No. 311 of 2002 registered under Sections 323, 452 and 435 of the Indian Penal Code[2] at Police Station Alwar Gate, Ajmer. The said letters also stated that the Respondent had approached the trial Court seeking for bail[3] on 26 May 2006. The said case was stated to be pending before the learned Civil Judge [Junior Division] and Judicial Magistrate, Ajmer.

---

1. For short 'CRPF'.

2. For short 'IPC'.

3. Case No. 297 of 2003, arising from FIR No. 311 of 2002.

[2.3] On the basis of the aforesaid information gathered by the Appellants, a departmental enquiry was ordered against the Respondent under Section 11(1) of the Central Reserve Police Force Act, 1949[4] read with Rule 27 of the CRPF Rules, 1959 and Memorandum of Articles was served on the Respondent. On conclusion of the enquiry, the disciplinary authority imposed a penalty of stoppage of three increments for three years without cumulative effect on the Respondent, reckoned from the next date when the increment would be due. The Respondent was further directed to keep the Appellants apprised of the status of Case No. 297 of 2003[5].

[2.4] On 27 February 2012 a judgment was delivered by the learned Chief Judicial Magistrate, Ajmer in the captioned Criminal Case[6] holding the Respondent guilty of offences under Sections 451 and 435 IPC and the co-accused[7] was found guilty for the offence under Section 435 IPC. On the point of sentence, having regard to the submission made by the parties that they had arrived at a settlement, being neighbours and the said settlement has taken place between them in the cross cases, the learned trial Court observed that having regard to the compromise deed entered into between the parties for the offence under Section 323 IPC, and noting that the offences under Section 452 and 435 IPC are not capable of being compromised, the Court indicted the Respondent for the offence under Section 451 IPC but gave him the benefit of Section 4[8] of the Probation of Offenders Act, 1958. As a result,

---

4. For short 'the CRPF Act'.

5. Criminal Case arising out of FIR 311 of 2002.

6. Subsequently re-numbered as Criminal Case No. 44 of 2009.

7. Mother of the Respondent.

8. 4. Power of Court to release certain offenders on probation of good conduct.—

> (1) When any person is found guilty of having committed an offence not punishable with death or imprisonment for life and the Court by which the person is found guilty is of opinion that, having regard to the circumstances of the case including the nature of the offence and the character of the offender, it is expedient to release him on probation of good conduct, then, notwithstanding anything contained in any other law for the time being in force, the Court may, instead of sentencing him at once to any punishment direct that he be released on his entering into a bond, with or without sureties, to appear and receive sentence when called upon during such period, not exceeding three years, as the Court may direct, and in the meantime to

the order of sentence imposed on the Respondent was suspended and he and the co-accused were released. It was also clarified that the Respondent will not be affected by any disqualification in his Government service in terms of Section 12 of the Probation of Offenders Act, 1958[9].

[2.5] On 7 May 2013 during the course of annual inspection, the Appellant No. 3 reviewed the case of the Respondent and the Appellant No. 4 issued a notice to Show Cause to the Respondent calling upon him to show cause as to why the penalty of stoppage of increment for three years imposed on him, ought not to be enhanced to dismissal/removal from service. The Respondent submitted a reply to the captioned Show Cause Notice on 24 May 2013 stating *inter alia* that he had already been awarded a punishment of stoppage of increment for three years which punishment had by then worked itself out. Not satisfied with the said reply, the Appellant No. 4 – DIG, CRPF, Hyderabad passed an order on 1 July 2013 in exercise of the powers vested under Rule 29(d) of the CRPF Rules, 1955 read with the relevant Government instructions, imposing a punishment of removal from service on the Respondent. Aggrieved by the said order, the Respondent preferred an appeal which was rejected vide order dated 23 December 2013. The Revision Petition preferred by the Respondent was also dismissed by the Appellant No. 5 vide order dated 2 July 2014.

[2.6] The aforesaid orders were assailed by the Respondent by preferring a Writ Petition before the High Court of Delhi which was allowed by the impugned order with the following observations:

> keep the peace and be of good behaviour: Provided that the Court shall not direct such release of an offender unless it is satisfied that the offender or his surety, if any, has a fixed place of abode or regular occupation in the place over which the Court exercises jurisdiction or in which the offender is likely to live during the period for which he enters into the bond.

9. 12. Removal of disqualification attaching to conviction.— Notwithstanding anything contained in any other law, a person found guilty of an offence and dealt with under the provisions of Section 3 or Section 4 shall not suffer disqualification, if any, attaching to a conviction of an offence under such law:

> Provided that nothing in this Section shall apply to a person who, after his release under Section 4 is subsequently sentenced for the original offence.

'11. As a thumb rule, the reasonable time would be within the period of the earlier penalty being in force. The reason being, if a penalty which is levied is allowed to run its period, awarding a higher penalty for the same wrong would amount to levying two penalties.

12. The Respondents have not explained as to why it took the Competent Authority over three years and five months to issue a show cause notice to enhance the penalty.

13. In our opinion, the facts of the instant case require us to hold that the Competent Authority was wrongly exercised the power under Rule 29(d) ignoring that for the wrong in question the Petitioner had been levied a penalty, duration whereof was three years. The Petitioner had suffered the said penalty for three years.

14. We dispose of the writ petition quashing the impugned order dated 1 July 2013 as also the order dated 2 July 2014. The Petitioner is reinstated in service with all consequential benefits which would include arrears of pay and continuity in service for purposes of pension and other benefits. Seniority shall also be retained. No costs.'

Dissatisfied by the aforesaid judgment, the present appeal has been filed.

[3.] submissions of the counsel for the Parties

[3.1] Mr Ashok Panigrahi, learned counsel for the Appellant submits that the High Court has erred in passing the impugned order, inasmuch as it has ignored the fact that the Respondent has concealed material information from his employer at the time of being enlisted in service. He submits that there are several decisions of this Court where it has been held that where a declarant has answered questions posed in the verification form in the negative, which specifically turned out to be false, the employer is well entitled to refuse employment to the declarant, even though he may have been cleared of the charges or been finally acquitted. It is submitted that in the instant case, the Respondent had suppressed material information from the Appellants which was sufficient reason for the employer to have dismissed him from service. In support of the said submission, learned counsel relies on a decision of a Division Bench of this Court *Daya Shankar Yadav vs Union of India and Anr.*[10] and a decision by a three-Judge Bench in the case of *Avtar Singh vs Union of India and Ors.*[11].

[3.2] *Per contra,* Mr Ankur Chibber, learned counsel appearing for the Respondent supports the impugned judgment and asserts that the High Court did not err in passing the impugned order quashing the orders dated 1 July 2013 and 2 July 2014 passed by the Appellants particularly when he was not even aware of registration of any FIR against him at the time of enlistment. To substantiate this submission, he points out that the Respondent had approached the trial Court only in May 2006 for seeking bail in Case No. 297 of 2003, arising from FIR No. 311 of 2002. He further states that the subject matter of the FIR was a dispute that had arisen between neighbours which was finally compromised as is borne out from a perusal of the judgment dated 27 February 2012 passed by the trial Court.

[4.] Observations and Analysis

[4.1] Having heard learned counsel for the parties, we find that reliance placed by learned counsel for the Appellants on the decisions in the cases of Daya Shankar Yadav (supra) and Avtar Singh (supra) is misplaced, particularly in the light of the observations made in Avtar Singh (supra) to the effect that in a case of trivial in nature in which conviction has been recorded, the employer may ignore such suppression of fact. In the instant case, admittedly the dispute was between neighbours and there were cross FIRs filed by them against each other, which finally culminated in a settlement arrived at between the parties and it was the very same neighbour who had earlier on made the complaint against the Respondent herein. Even if the Respondent would have been aware of the registration of the FIR against him, which in the present case does not appear to be the position, there were good reasons for the Appellants to have ignored such suppression of fact, more so, when the punishment of stoppage of three increments had already been imposed upon him vide order dated 7 November 2009 and the said order had been duly implemented.

---

10. (2010) 14 SCC 103.

11. (2016) 8 SCC 471.

[4.2] We are, therefore, of the opinion that the impugned judgment does not deserve any interference, inasmuch as the penalty of stoppage of increments for three years imposed on the Respondent had already worked itself out by the time the Appellants had issued a fresh notice to show cause to the Respondent on 7 May 2013 proposing imposition of higher penalty. The onus would lie on the Appellants to demonstrate that the Respondent was all along aware of the registration of the aforesaid FIR against him, in particular, at the time of his selection and when he had submitted the verification Form No. 25 to the Appellants, on 28 December 2003. From a perusal of the documents placed on record, it does not emerge that the Respondent was aware of the subject FIR. Therefore, there is substance in the submission made by the learned counsel for the Respondent that as soon as the Respondent had gained knowledge of the aforesaid FIR and registration of a case against him, he had approached the concerned Court for seeking bail which was in May 2006, much after his selection and enlistment.

[4.3] Even otherwise, the judgment dated 27 February 2012 rendered in Criminal Case No. 44/200912 itself records that the parties had arrived at a compromise and that the Respondent and the co-accused were being released under Section 4 of the Probation of Offenders Act. Furthermore, the trial Court had given the benefit of the provisions of Section 12 of the said Act to the Respondent, specifically noting that the decision in the said case will not adversely affect him or disqualify him from his Government service.

[5.] Conclusion/Result

[5.1] In view of the aforesaid discussion, the present appeal is dismissed as meritless and the impugned judgment and order dated 27 January 2015 is upheld. The Respondent shall report to the Appellants for rejoining his duty at the earliest. It is, however, clarified that the Respondent will not be entitled to any back wages for the period during which he has not rendered service, but he shall be entitled to notional fixation of his pay and allowances.

[6.] There shall be no orders as to costs.

Hima Kohli, J
Rajesh Bindal, J

New Delhi
15 June 2023

(2025) I FLR 360 (Australia)

Supreme Court of the Australian Capital Territory

Original Case Citation: (2024) ACTSC 147

R vs McBride (The King vs David McBride)

Composition of Court: Mossop, J

Date of Decision: 14 May 2024

Counsel for the Crown: P. McDonald SC and C. Tran

Counsel for the Offender: S. Odgers SC and E. Kerkyasharian

Counsel for the Attorney General and Commonwealth: A. Berger KC and L. Johnston

Summary

David McBride, a former Major and legal advisor in the Australian Defence Force (ADF), was sentenced to five years and eight months' imprisonment for theft and unauthorized disclosure of military information. In 2018, police seized 235 stolen Commonwealth documents from his property, 207 classified as "SECRET." McBride disclosed these documents to journalists and also published some on his personal website, motivated by dissatisfaction with ADF management and the handling of Special Forces' actions in Afghanistan, including civilian deaths. McBride's charges included:Theft under s 131.1(1) of the *Criminal Code,* Two counts of unauthorized disclosure of military information under s 73A(1) of the DefenceAct One of the disclosure charges also considered a breach of s 70(1) of the *Crimes Act* relating to unauthorized online publications.

The primary legal issue in this case was the interpretation of the maximum punishment under s 73A (1) of the *Defence Act*, which provides for imprisonment "for any term" or an unlimited fine. The court had to determine whether this allowed for the imposition of a proportionate sentence despite the broad statutory language. The court emphasized the need for a balanced approach to statutory construction, ensuring that the sentence reflected the seriousness of the offence without imposing excessive punishment.

The court concluded that while the provision permits flexibility, sentencing should still adhere to the principles of proportionality, fairness, and deterrence, as established in earlier precedents. McBride's significant breach of trust and the potential national security impact warranted imprisonment, but not the maximum possible term. This construction of the statute provided valuable guidance for future cases involving military disclosures.

Acknowledging McBride's guilty plea and cooperation, the court imposed a non-parole period of two years and three months. His aggregate sentence will end in January 2030, with eligibility for parole in August 2026. A request for a community-based sentence was denied, given the gravity of his offences.

Headnotes

Facts: David McBride, a senior legal advisor in the Australian Defence Force (ADF), was convicted on three charges related to theft and unauthorized disclosure of classified military documents. McBride stole 235 documents from ADF premises, 207 of which were classified as "SECRET," and disclosed them to journalists, alleging mismanagement within the ADF. His disclosures, including those published as "The Afghan Files," revealed allegations of civilian killings by Special Forces in Afghanistan. The unauthorized release caused serious harm to national security, defence operations, and Australia's diplomatic relations.

Issues: The central issue was the interpretation of the statutory language in s 73A(1) of the *Defence Act 1903 (Cth)*, which allows for imprisonment "for any term." The court had to determine whether this provision permitted discretion for a proportionate sentence or mandated an indefinite term. Another issue involved weighing McBride's motives of whistleblowing against the substantial breach of trust and the national security impact of his actions.

Contentions of the Parties

- **Prosecution:** Argued that McBride's actions were a gross betrayal of his duties as both a soldier and lawyer, with severe consequences for national security, warranting a harsh custodial sentence. They contended that the sentencing under s 73A(1) should reflect the legislative goal of deterring such disclosures.

- **Defence:** Claimed that McBride acted in the public interest to expose misconduct within the ADF and sought leniency through a non-custodial sentence. They further argued that the indefinite nature of the punishment under s 73A(1) should be narrowly construed.

Held: The court emphasized McBride's lack of remorse, gross breach of trust, and the need for general deterrence. It upheld the broad discretion provided by s 73A(1), determining that sentences should be proportionate and aligned with public law principles.

Case Law Cited

Chia vs The Queen [2018] WASCA 103

Della-Vedova vs R [2009] NSWCCA 107

DPP vs Vincent (No 2) [2023] ACTSC 379

Grant vs Headland (1977) 17 ACTR 29

Markarian vs The Queen [2005] HCA 25; 228 CLR 357

McBride vs R [2023] ACTCA 42

Nguyen vs The Queen [2016] HCA 17; 256 CLR 656

Peterson vs R (District Court (NSW), Hanley DCJ, 30 November 2020, unrep)

R vs Campbell [2010] ACTCA 20

R vs Crowley (District Court (WA), Voil DCJ, 17 March 1997, unrep)

R vs Jafari [2017] NSWCCA 152

R vs Johns (a pseudonym) [2019] ACTSC 399

R vs Kessing (District Court (NSW), Bennet DCJ, 22 June 2007, unrep)

R vs Lappas [2003] ACTCA 21; 152 ACTR 7

R vs McBride [2023] ACTSC 328; 20 ACTLR 272

R vs McBride (No 2) [2023] ACTSC 330

R vs Seivers and O'Ryan (Supreme Court (ACT), Gray J, 10 June 2009, unrep)

R vs Scerba (No 2) [2015] ACTSC 359

Seivers vs The Queen [2010] ACTCA 9

Mossop, J

Introduction

(1.) On 17 November 2023, David McBride pleaded guilty to three offences:

(a.) Count 1, theft, contrary to Section 131.1(1) of the Criminal Code (Cth) (CAN 41388/2018). The particulars of the charge are that, between about 1 December 2013 and about 26 February 2018, in Griffith and other places in the Australian Capital Territory (ACT) and New South Wales, Mr McBride dishonestly appropriated property belonging to a Commonwealth entity with the intention of permanently depriving the entity of the property. The maximum penalty is 10 years' imprisonment or a fine of 600 penalty units, or both.

(b.) Two counts of unlawfully communicating naval, military or air force information, contrary to Section 73A(1) of the Defence Act 1903

(Cth) (CAN 2897/2019 and CAN 2899/2019). The particulars of the charges are as follows:

(i.) Count 2: Between about 1 August 2014 and about 31 December 2015, in New Acton and Forrest and other places in the ACT, Mr McBride, being a member of the Defence Force, communicated documents relating to naval, military or air force information to other persons, namely Chris Masters and Andrew Clark, and that communication was not in the course of his official duty.

(ii.) Count 3: Between about 2 May 2016 and about 11 July 2017, in Griffith and other places in the ACT, Mr McBride, being a member of the Defence Force, communicated documents relating to naval, military or air force information to another person, namely Daniel Oakes, and that communication was not in the course of his official duty.

(2.) The maximum penalty for an offence against Section 73A is set out in Section 73F. Where the offence is prosecuted upon indictment, the maximum penalty is 'a fine of any amount or imprisonment for any term, or both'. If the offence is prosecuted summarily, the maximum fine for an individual is two penalty units and the maximum period of imprisonment is six months.

(3.) There is also a charge of contravening Section 70(1) of the Crimes Act 1914 (Cth). This is included in a schedule pursuant to Section 16BA of the Crimes Act in relation to count 3. Section 16BA permits an offender to admit his guilt in respect of offences specified in the list and then have them taken into account by the Court in passing sentence on him for the offence or offences for which he has been convicted. The particulars of the charge are that, between about 4 April 2016 and about 31 May 2016, in Deakin and other places in the ACT, Mr McBride, being a Commonwealth officer, published a fact or document, except to some person to whom he was authorised to publish it, which came to his knowledge or into his possession by virtue of him being a Commonwealth officer and which it was his duty not to disclose. This relates to disclosures on a website known as 'The Ops Room'.

(4.) In summary, the chronology of the offending is as follows:

- (a.) about 1 December 2013 to about 26 February 2018 – theft;
- (b.) about 1 August 2014 to about 31 December 2015 – disclosure to Mr Masters and Mr Clark;
- (c.) about 4 April 2016 to about 31 May 2016 – disclosure on The Ops Room; and
- (d.) about 2 May 2016 to about 11 July 2017 – disclosure to Mr Oakes.

Maximum Penalty

(5.) It is necessary to say something more about the maximum penalty for counts 2 and 3, the offences under Section 73A. Permitting an offence to be punishable by 'a fine of any amount or imprisonment for any term, or both' is a rare formulation. It has only been included in three Commonwealth Acts and the Defence Act is the only one of those Acts where such a provision remains in force.

(6.) The formulation was first included in the War Precautions Act 1914 (Cth) as amended by the War Precautions Act 1915 (Cth). The Act introduced a scheme for punishing contraventions of regulations or orders made pursuant to the Act, which distinguished between offences prosecuted summarily and offences prosecuted upon indictment. Where an offence was prosecuted upon indictment, the Act permitted 'a fine of any amount or imprisonment for any term, or both'. If it was proved that the offence was committed with the intention of assisting the enemy, the penalty was death. The 1915 amending Act followed changes made to the Defence of the Realm Act 1914 (UK) when it was superseded by the Defence of the Realm Consolidation Act 1914 (UK). The War Precautions Act 1914 (Cth) was repealed in 1920.

(7.) In September 1939, shortly after the commencement of the Second World War, the National Security Act 1939 (Cth) was passed. It was intended to operate until six months after the end of the war, but no longer. Like the earlier War Precautions Act, it included a broad regulation making power to be exercised by the Governor-General. Section 10 provided that a person who contravened or failed to comply with a regulation made under the Act was guilty of an offence against the Act. Section 10(3) provided different penalties depending upon whether or not the offence was prosecuted summarily or upon indictment. A modest penalty was imposed if prosecuted summarily, but if prosecuted upon indictment, the maximum penalty was 'a fine of any amount or imprisonment for any term, or both'. The consent of the Attorney General or the Minister for Defence was required if an offence was to be prosecuted summarily. The second reading speech by the Prime Minister, Mr Menzies, made it clear that the legislation followed the model in the War Precautions Act 'with which most honourable members are already familiar': Commonwealth, Parliamentary Debates, House of Representatives, 7 September 1939, 163 (Robert Menzies, Prime Minister).

(8.) In 1941, the Defence Act was amended so as to insert Section 73F. This was a penalty provision that related to offences against Sections 73, 73A, 73B, 73C, 73D and 73E of the Act. Prior to the amendments, the offence under Section 73A (as well as those against Sections 73, 73B and 73C), if prosecuted upon indictment, had a maximum penalty of three years' imprisonment. Following the amendment, Section 73F provided for a modest penalty if the offence was prosecuted summarily and, if prosecuted upon indictment, 'a fine of any amount or imprisonment for any term, or both'.

(9.) While counsel for Mr McBride correctly pointed out that the National Security Act provision was designed to accommodate breaches of a wide variety of regulations, it is not correct to say that this fact should be used to qualify the significance of the unlimited sentence available under the Defence Act. Section 73F of the Defence Act related to six particular offences in the Act. Most of those involved fraud affecting matters relating to the war effort and it was to those provisions that the Minister for the Army referred in his second reading speech as 'serious frauds'. For example, Section 73C made it an offence to provide food of a quality inferior to that specified in a contract to supply such food to the Commonwealth for use by the Defence Force. Section 73(3) related to obtaining pay belonging to another member of the Defence

Force. Section 73A, while not involving what would be characterised as a 'serious fraud' in the same way that the other offences might, is an offence provision which, by its terms, can obviously be very serious.

(10.) The amendments made in 1941 involved a clear choice to dramatically increase the penalties for particular types of offending, including that under Section 73A. Those penalties are to be contrasted with the penalties in other provisions, such as the penalties for resisting the draft (Section 75) or refusing to take the required oath (Section 76), which remained modest.

(11.) Finally, it must be noted that each of the other offence provisions in relation to which the penalty provision, Section 73F, applied (Sections 73, 73B, 73C, 73D and 73E) were repealed in 2001. Section 73A was repealed and substituted so as to accommodate drafting more suitable for the application of the Criminal Code (Cth). This was done by the Defence Legislation Amendment (Application of Criminal Code) Act 2001 (Cth). The decision to maintain Section 73A as the only one of the original provisions the subject of the unlimited term of imprisonment represents a recent legislative decision recognising the ongoing significance of the offence and its penalty, and precludes characterisation of Sections 73A and 73F as being relics of the Second World War.

(12.) In that context, it is not possible to accept the submission made on behalf of Mr McBride that the unlimited penalty was only imposed to accommodate a smorgasbord of possible offences available under the National Security Act and that there was no intention to increase the maximum penalty for Section 73A at all when the Defence Act was amended in 1941. Further, it is not possible to accept the submission that 'it certainly would not be appropriate to treat the penalty as indicating a maximum penalty of life imprisonment' or that 'it is inconceivable that it was intended that even serious frauds might be the subject of very lengthy terms of imprisonment'. When understood in its proper context, the parliamentary intention to dramatically increase the penalty for offences including Section 73A is clear. Further, given the repeal and substitution of Section 73A in 2001 when the surrounding Sections were repealed, there can be no doubt that Section 73F applies to Section 73A in accordance with its terms.

(13.) Given the legislative history, it is also not possible to accept the submission made on behalf of Mr McBride that guidance as to the appropriate sentence should be obtained not by the terms of Section 73F itself, but instead by reference to the penalties provided in other provisions, such as Section 58 of the Defence Force Discipline Act 1982 (Cth) (two years) and Section 70(1) of the Crimes Act (two years). Section 73F must be applied in accordance with its terms and not subject to qualification by the penalties provided in other legislation. While that means that the 'yardstick' (in the sense described in Markarian vs The Queen [2005] HCA 25; 228 CLR 357 at [30]–[31]) provided by a fixed maximum penalty or by a maximum penalty of imprisonment for life are not available, an appropriate sentence that meets the requirements of Section 16A of the Crimes Act must be worked out. Such a sentence must necessarily be determined in the context of general expectations as to how long people live, even in the absence of a more specific numerical yardstick provided by the legislature.

Facts

(14.) The facts are set out in an Agreed Statement of Facts. The Agreed Statement of Facts contains 138 paragraphs and has four annexures totalling 108 pages. The Agreed Statement of Facts sets out in substantial detail what happened. The annexures shed light on Mr McBride's motivations for doing what he did. The following description of the events giving rise to the charges largely reflects the facts upon which the parties have expressly agreed.

Mr McBride

(15.) Mr McBride is a lawyer. On 15 December 2005, he joined the Australian Defence Force (ADF) as a Reserve Legal Officer with the rank of Captain. At that time, he signed two acknowledgements relating to his duty to keep information confidential.

(16.) One was an 'Acknowledgement of the Requirements of Service in the Australian Defence Force (ADF)' dated 15 December 2005, in which he acknowledged that:

(a.) he had been informed of the provisions of the laws of the Commonwealth relating to official secrecy, including Section 73A of the Defence Act 1903 (Cth) and Section 70 of the Crimes Act 1914 (Cth); and

(b.) as a member of the ADF he must comply with directions and orders given to him by persons in the ADF who have the legal authority to issue such directions and orders.

(17.) The other was an 'Official Secrecy Acknowledgment' dated 15 December 2005, in which he:

(a.) acknowledged that laws of the Commonwealth relating to official secrecy may apply to him, including Section 70 of the Crimes Act and Section 73A of the Defence Act;

(b.) stated that he understood that all official information acquired by him in the course of his duties was to be regarded as the property of the Commonwealth and any such information which it was his duty not to disclose was not to be published or communicated to another person in any form either during or after his service in, or in association with, the Commonwealth; and

(c.) stated that he understood that any breach of laws in relation to the safeguarding of official information was an offence, and may render him liable to prosecution.

(18.) On 1 January 2009, Mr McBride was promoted to the rank of Major and transferred from the Army Reserve to the Regular Army.

(19.) In 2010, he was posted to an Army base in Townsville, Queensland. Prior to this, he had been stationed at various locations in New South Wales.

(20.) In April 2011, Mr McBride was deployed to his first tour in Afghanistan with the Combined Team Uruzgan (CTU). CTU was a brigade level organisation numbering around 5000 troops with a US commander. He was the senior Legal Advisor for that commander. His job was to advise on the Rules of Engagement, the use of force and charging or defending soldiers.

He was based at the Tarin Kowt base in Uruzgan Province. Mr McBride was deployed in Afghanistan with CTU until February 2012.

(21.) On 16 January 2012, he was posted to the position of Special Operations Legal Officer at the rank of Major at Special Forces Command, at an ADF facility near Bungendore. In this role, he was responsible for the legal issues that arose during overseas deployments as well as domestic anti-terrorism operations. His principal responsibility was oversight of legal matters in Afghanistan.

(22.) Between August and December 2013, Mr McBride was the Special Operations Task Group (SOTG) Legal Officer and was deployed in that role to the Special Forces base in Tarin Kowt, Urzugan Province, Afghanistan.

(23.) In December 2013, Mr McBride returned to Australia from overseas deployment and was based at Special Operation Headquarters at the Bungendore facility as a Special Operations Legal Officer. During that time, his private residence was in the ACT.

(24.) On 19 January 2015, Mr McBride was posted to the Military Law Centre in Canberra.

(25.) On 18 January 2016, Mr McBride was posted to the Directorate of Administrative Law and Advisings in Canberra as a Staff Officer Grade 2.

(26.) From 7 September 2016, Mr McBride moved between various temporary positions at different locations.

(27.) From 25 January 2017, Mr McBride was no longer part of the ADF. He was discharged for medical reasons, including due to suffering from Major/Agitated Depression, Attention-Deficit/ Hyperactivity Disorder and Substance Abuse Disorder. In late 2016, he was also diagnosed with Post-Traumatic Stress Disorder (PTSD).

(28.) On 1 July 2012, 1 July 2013, 1 July 2014 and 30 June 2015, Mr McBride was issued a Legal Officer Practising Certificate under ACT law.

(29.) Mr McBride has not been previously charged with or convicted of any criminal offence.

Background – Security

(30.) The Commonwealth Government applies the Australian Government Security Classification System (AGSCS) to Commonwealth records. The four levels of national security classification are PROTECTED, CONFIDENTIAL, SECRET and TOP SECRET. Significantly for present purposes, the SECRET classification indicates that a compromise of the confidentiality of the information could be expected to cause 'serious damage' to the national interest, organisations or individuals. That damage may include loss of life. Compromise of the confidentiality of TOP SECRET material could be expected to cause 'exceptionally grave damage' to the national interest, organisations or individuals. The purpose of the policy is to require that agencies take all reasonable and appropriate precautions to ensure that only people with a proven need-to-know and correct security clearance gain access to sensitive and security classified information.

(31.) In addition to the security classifications, there are other classifications referred to as 'caveats' which further restrict the access to Commonwealth information. The caveat AUSTEO, meaning Australian Eyes Only, indicates that information should only be viewed by Australian citizens with an appropriate security clearance. The caveat LIMDIST, meaning Limited Distribution, limits access to an identified list of persons or classes of persons. There are other caveats known as codewords which provide that an individual needs further security briefings before they can access the information.

(32.) Mr McBride held a level of security clearance known as 'Positive Vetting', which allowed him to access information at all classification levels, including TOP SECRET, as well as certain types of caveated information.

(33.) Mr McBride had completed security awareness training on five occasions during his career with the ADF, in 2008, 2009, 2010, 2011 and 2014, which reinforced the rules relating to the handling of classified material.

McBride's Concerns

(34.) Rules of Engagement (ROE) are directives issued to the ADF in consultation with the Australian Government, which regulate the use of force and activities connected to the use of force. On 21 December 2012, members of the Special Forces Command were involved in drafting a ROE amplification (ROEAMP). This was a clarification of the meaning of the existing ROE.

(35.) In late 2012 and early 2013, prior to his deployment on his second tour of Afghanistan, Mr McBride prepared a working paper on the ROE. As a result of Mr McBride's work, his supervisor sought the legal advices that had been prepared during the course of formulating the ROEAMP. Mr McBride's concern was that the ADF was overcomplicating things and thereby misdirecting its efforts. He was provided with the legal advices and prepared a minute outlining his concerns. The minute was addressed to the Chief of Joint Operations (CJOPS). This was the appropriate way to raise such concerns.

(36.) In around April 2013, Mr McBride expressed concern to his supervisor about whether the military police had jurisdiction to commence investigations into matters in theatre in the absence of a reasonable suspicion that a crime had been committed. His supervisor did not regard it as necessary or appropriate to pursue the matter further because she was aware, from a discussion with the CJOPS and another officer, that they were aware of a disagreement between deployed forces and military police regarding the circumstances under which military police had a right to ask questions about operational incidents.

(37.) In late 2013, while deployed in Afghanistan, Mr McBride advised four ADF members of an issue that he was having with another more senior ADF officer. His concern related to search warrants obtained by military police of the Australian Defence Force Investigative Service (ADFIS) in relation to the SOTG. Mr McBride believed that the SOTG should not be subject to such action.

(38.) Upon his return from deployment in late 2013, Mr McBride advised his supervisor that he held concerns that there were soldiers doing their operational duties on behalf of the Commonwealth who were being held to account for actions on operations that were appropriate in the operational context, but that were being misconstrued, misinterpreted or recast as contrary to the ROE by persons in the chain of command who were outside

Afghanistan. Mr McBride advised his supervisor that he intended to raise a complaint with the Inspector General of the Australian Defence Force (IGADF). Mr McBride's supervisor believed that this was the appropriate avenue available for Mr McBride to resolve the matters that concerned him.

(39.) In the middle of 2014, Mr McBride met with two senior ADF officers and advised them that he was working on an IGADF complaint about ADFIS' conduct in Afghanistan. One of the senior officers was frustrated by what he perceived to be Mr McBride's work performance and asked Mr McBride, 'why are you persisting with the complaint to the detriment of your work'. Further, this senior officer said, forcefully, 'what are you trying to achieve?' and 'how will it benefit you, command and the army?' The officer was one who often spoke in a forceful manner. That senior officer did not say that Mr McBride should not make a complaint.

Misappropriation of Documents

(40.) In early 2014, when Mr McBride resolved to make a formal complaint, he did so because he was dissatisfied with certain practices in the ADF which he considered to be corrupt.

(41.) As part of his employment, he had access to ADF records on a record management system which ran on a secure ADF network. That system could hold information up to and including the SECRET classification.

(42.) In May 2014, Mr McBride began accessing documents on the record management system and storing them in a personal folder on his ADF computer at the Bungendore headquarters after his ordinary work day had ended. He printed several documents and removed them from the headquarters by putting them in his backpack and exiting the facility. He took them to his private residence in the ACT. This was the commencement of his offending which is charged as count 1, the rolled up count of theft.

(43.) He engaged in similar conduct of printing and removing documents from other ADF facilities where he was based from time to time. This included the Victoria Barracks in Sydney. He took these documents to his private residence in the ACT. Between May 2014 and December 2015, he removed

235 documents from ADF facilities. He did not have permission to do so. 207 of the documents held the national security classification SECRET.

(44.) On 3 November 2016, he moved into a new residence in Griffith in the ACT. He stored the documents in four large plastic storage tubs in a cupboard in the lounge room. Unsurprisingly, this did not comply with the Commonwealth Government's policy on storage of information bearing the protective marking SECRET.

(45.) On 1 February 2018, Mr McBride engaged a real estate agent to sell the property. It was open for inspection by prospective buyers on a number of occasions. Members of the public walked through the property to inspect it. Mr McBride was not in attendance during these inspections. During the public inspections, the documents remained in the plastic tubs in the cupboard of the lounge room.

(46.) On 26 February 2018, the Australian Federal Police (AFP) executed a search warrant at the Griffith property, where they located and seized the documents from the tubs in the cupboard in the lounge room.

(47.) **It is the theft of the 235 documents between May 2014 and February 2018 that gives rise to count 1, the count of theft.**

Complaint to AFP

(48.) On 14 May 2014 (the day after his initial submission to the IGADF – see [51] below), Mr McBride accessed the AFP website to report a crime. He submitted a document entitled 'Notification of Potential Improper Conduct by Senior Defence Officers, and the Defence Force Investigation Service'. In the document (which was not tendered for the purposes of the sentencing hearing), Mr McBride outlined that the following offences may have occurred:

(a.) conspiracy to pervert the course of justice;

(b.) misuse of Commonwealth resources;

(c.) interference with a legal officer performing their duty;

(d.) failure to comply with a general order; and

(e.) improperly prejudicing ADF members' careers.

(49.) On 16 May 2014, Mr McBride met with two AFP officers to discuss his complaint. He told them that he was concerned that ADFIS was investigating matters in which no criminal offence had occurred. He made reference to four incidents in which the deaths of civilians had occurred and contended that there were insufficient grounds to suspect that a criminal offence had been committed by an Australian soldier. He also complained that even if the investigators had formed the view that the investigations were warranted, proper processes were not followed. Mr McBride stated that certain investigations by ADFIS into Australian soldiers were a waste of time and were having a severely adverse effect on the soldiers being investigated.

(50.) At the conclusion of this meeting, the AFP advised Mr McBride that the information provided by him did not disclose evidence of a criminal offence and related to internal ADF matters. The AFP indicated that the IGADF would be best placed to investigate his concerns.

Mr McBride's Complaint to the IGADF

(51.) Mr McBride used the documents he removed from ADF facilities to prepare various complaints about practices within the ADF. On 13 May 2014 (the day before he used the AFP website to report a crime), he sent a submission to the IGADF enclosing 'two individual submissions relating to Military Justice'.

(52.) The first submission was entitled 'Individual Submission for IGADF on the Investigation of Serious Incident Occurring On Operations'. It was one page long and contained four numbered paragraphs. It asserted that the 'current ADF policy resulted in the commencement of discipline investigations in contravention of Australian law and ADF policy'. It indicated that he would supply detailed reasoning and evidence upon request. It indicated that his superiors were aware of him having made the individual submission and had neither discouraged nor endorsed it.

(53.) The second submission was entitled 'Individual submission for IGADF on Improper Discrimination in the ADF'. It was also one page long. The submission asserted that 'Army (through DOCM) are using illegal/and or improper process to select officers for promotion and ACSC'.

(54.) The same day that he sent the submission to the IGADF, an officer responsible for investigations within the Office of the IGADF asked Mr McBride to provide the relevant evidentiary materials so as to enable a proper preliminary assessment of the matters raised.

(55.) In July 2014, Mr McBride corresponded with the officer, indicating that he had completed his submission and that it included three lever arch files of supporting documents, most of which were classified SECRET.

(56.) On 15 August 2014, he personally delivered his submission and its supporting documents to the office of the IGADF. In these reasons, the submission made on 15 August 2014 will be referred to as the IGADF Submission.

(57.) There were 86 supporting documents. They were in two lever arch folders. Two versions of the IGADF Submission were also in the folders. The documents in the two folders of documents will be referred to as the Supporting Documents. Most of the Supporting Documents were the same as documents that Mr McBride had removed from the ADF facilities.

(58.) The IGADF Submission contained information derived from the SECRET documents that Mr McBride had removed from ADF facilities. It also included other SECRET information that Mr McBride knew by virtue of his employment at the ADF. Because of the SECRET information within the IGADF Submission, that submission was also classified SECRET. Mr McBride was aware of the classification of the IGADF Submission. Most of the Supporting Documents were classified SECRET. The IGADF Submission and the Supporting Documents contained substantial amounts of naval, military or air force information as defined in Section 73A(1) of the Defence Act.

(59.) A redacted and unclassified version of the IGADF Submission was admitted into evidence as part of the Crown Tender Bundle.

The IGADF Submission

(60.) The IGADF Submission was entitled 'Detailed Information Relating to the Allegations of Illegal Investigations of Special Operations Task Group in 2013'. The summary at the commencement of the submission was as follows:

> 'In the following five cases, revealed under the protections provided by ref A, I believe there was an absence of the "reasonable suspicion" necessary to commence a criminal investigation IAW ref B:
>
> (a.) 3 October 2010 (Shooting death of detainee)
>
> (b.) 28 February 2013 (Helicopter fire support CIVCAS)
>
> (c.) 28 April 2013 (SSE Incident)
>
> (d.) 23 September 2013 (Shooting death of PRC detainee)
>
> (e.) 26 September 2013 (CIVCAS)'
>
> (Citations omitted)

(61.) The reference to 'ref A' was to the Public Interest Disclosure Act 2013 (Cth) (PID Act). The reference to 'ref B' was to a Defence Instruction entitled 'Management and Reporting of Notifiable Incidents'.

(62.) Although this summary suggested that the submission was a narrowly focused legal contention, the terms of the balance of the document suggest that it reflected broader concerns.

(63.) In addition to the summary, the submission contained eight parts (A to H) and a conclusion. They were headed as follows:

(a.) The gradual growth of bias against SOTG by HQJOC Legal;

(b.) The commencement of illegal/vexatious investigations;

(c.) The incident of 28 February 2013;

(d.) The CIVCAS of 26 September 2013;

(e.) The incident of 28 April 2013;

(f.) The deaths of 'detainees' of 3 October 2010 and 23 September 2013;

(g.) The investigation into the incident of 3 October 2010;

(h.) The investigation of the incident of 23 September 2013; and

(i.) Conclusion.

(64.) Section A dealt with the ROEAMP. This was characterised as taking the ADF backwards and reinforcing unrealistic expectations of ADF soldiers during the course of a firefight. The justification for the ROEAMP was characterised as 'spurious'. The criticism was that the ADF was placing unnecessary risk on the lives of their own soldiers in order to avoid any public embarrassment. The ROEAMP was promulgated on 29 April 2013 and the submission indicated that there could have been better training on the existing ROE.

(65.) Section B asserted that, in early 2013, a change occurred, so that where civilians were killed, the deaths were automatically investigated as possible murders even if there was no suspicion that a crime had been committed.

(66.) Section C related to an incident on 28 February 2013, when a number of civilians were killed by mistake. There were two groups which matched the description of 'two boys with donkeys/farm animals'. The wrong group was targeted and civilians were killed. The submission contended that there was no basis for an investigation of the war crime of murder because there was nothing to suggest that the boys were deliberately targeted with the knowledge that they were not insurgents. Despite this, the submission records that a decision was made to conduct an investigation into the war crime of murder.

(67.) Section D related to an incident on 26 September 2013. A child was killed when a bullet went through the body of an armed individual and into an unseen sleeping child behind him during a night engagement. The submission contended that the circumstances did not give rise to a suspicion of a crime that would warrant an investigation. A sensitive incident was not synonymous with a suspicious one. The submission contended that the appropriate method to investigate the incident was an Administrative Inquiry, until some suspicious piece of evidence emerged. The submission pointed out that, ultimately, the experienced inquiry team cleared the soldiers.

(68.) Section E related to an incident on 28 April 2013. This was an incident where one or more (the submission was ambiguous) dead insurgents' hands were removed in order to identify whether any one of them was a key bomb maker. The submission indicated that this involved a failure to distinguish between an incident which was sensitive and one which was suspicious. The Section on this incident was lengthy. It contended that the soldier's actions were justified by military necessity and that the soldier had received a lecture from an ADFIS member who had given him the impression that removing the whole hand was best practice to ensure accurate identification. The submission criticised the commencement of a disciplinary investigation in circumstances where the action had been investigated and no administrative action had been recommended. It criticised the finding of the Administrative Inquiry that the officer in question had exercised 'poor judgment' by failing to appreciate potential responses from 'the Australian public and media'. The submission criticised the lack of support from the Minister for Defence and the Chief of the Defence Force when, on 30 August 2013, the Australian Broadcasting Corporation (ABC) reported on the incident. It criticised the proposition that Special Forces should have to consider what the 'Australian media' might think of their actions during combat. Finally, the submission contended that if there was a failure, it was a failure by the Army to train the officer properly if the practice was so abhorrent. It noted that there was no criticism of the Army at all in the documentation.

(69.) Section F introduced the investigations of incidents that occurred on 3 October 2010 and 23 September 2013. These were both cases in which an ADF member was momentarily alone in a room with a suspected insurgent. In both cases, the ADF member said that the suspected insurgent made an attempt to attack him, the first by grabbing a sickle-like blade from the door and the second by trying to wrestle control of the member's slung weapon while his handcuffs were removed. In both cases, the suspected insurgent was shot and killed. In neither case was there a motive for the member to shoot the insurgent in cold blood. In both cases, their commanders were said not to have doubted the soldiers' version of events.

(70.) Section G was a brief section relating to the incident on 3 October 2010. It referred to a brief from the CJOPS to the Chief of the Defence

Force which recorded his satisfaction that the Special Forces soldier acted in accordance with his ROE and that the lethal force was applied in a lawful exercise of self-defence. Notwithstanding that, the head of ADFIS directed an investigation. The investigators were said to have interviewed 97 members and two commanding officers over 14 months and produced a five-page report that came to the same conclusion as the CJOPS.

(71.) Section H dealt with the investigation of the incident on 23 September 2013. It is another long section and arose out of events with which Mr McBride was personally involved. It related to the shooting of an Afghan detainee who was shot while apparently trying to wrestle the control of a weapon from a Special Forces member who was removing the detainee's handcuffs from behind his back with the intention of reapplying them in front to prepare the detainee for a helicopter flight. The submission criticised the decision of the ADFIS to investigate the incident on the basis of a suspicion that a murder had occurred. It criticised the murder investigation as being of an 'ill-conceived "political" nature' despite all the known facts supporting the soldier's story. It then criticised in detail the conduct of the ADFIS investigators in attempting to secure the weapon involved in the incident, notwithstanding that it had been subsequently used and cleaned and, the submission contended, would be of no forensic value. It criticised the process adopted by the investigators and the legal basis for the warrants for the weapon and equipment. It then referred to abusive and threatening telephone calls that were made to Mr McBride in relation to his questioning of the validity of the warrants. It suggested that the threats may constitute an 'offence against Section 122B of the Defence Act'. (Section 122B provides: 'A legal officer acting in that capacity is entitled to exercise his or her professional rights, and discharge his or her professional duties and obligations, in accordance with the generally accepted rights, duties and obligations applying to legal practitioners.')

(72.) The conclusion of the IGADF Submission provided:

> 'Ever since the "Jedi Council" investigations begun, all Army units have been under extreme scrutiny. Unpalatable as those allegations were, they involved a hand-full [sic] of people, and any similar sized organisation would have had similar in recent years. Our existing systems are quite capable of dealing with such incidents.

> The challenge for the ADF is to maintain a sense of balance and proportion. Appearance is important, but it is not the only thing. If one reads "Pathways to Change" (I wonder how many have), it's [sic] seems to focus on two things, only: our appearance to government and our appearance to the public. I wonder if they have missed anything.
>
> I believe the over-zealous investigations of the Special Forces in 2013 were driven by appearances rather than suspicion of a crime. However, as I stated in the covering minute, they come at a cost. It is acceptable for the ADF to be uncompromising on [breaches] of policy and the law. But it works both ways.'

The Consideration of the IGADF Submission

(73.) The officer responsible for investigations at the IGADF undertook a preliminary assessment of the IGADF Submission and distilled 65 concerns from it.

(74.) On 25 August 2014, Mr McBride attended a meeting with the IGADF himself. He then had a meeting with the investigating officer and the Deputy IGADF. While the IGADF does not remember whether he briefed the Chief of the Defence Force with an outline of Mr McBride's complaint, it would have been usual practice to have done so.

(75.) In the meeting with the investigating officer and the deputy IGADF, Mr McBride confirmed that the investigating officer had accurately identified the concerns raised in the IGADF Submission. The investigating officer discussed the operation of the PID Act. At that time, disclosures about alleged ADF misconduct could not be made under the PID Act to the IGADF. The investigating officer explained to Mr McBride the process that could be followed to allow the IGADF Submission to be treated as a disclosure under the PID Act, but Mr McBride declined that opportunity, saying that he preferred the IGADF to investigate his disclosure.

(76.) The IGADF determined to hold an inquiry into the matters identified in the IGADF Submission. Two assistant IGADFs were appointed for that task. One was a former judge of the County Court of Victoria and one was a captain in the Royal Australian Navy. Mr McBride was interviewed by them on 2 December 2014.

(77.) On 21 August 2015, Mr McBride was advised of the outcome of the inquiry. In summary, the assistant IGADFs found that:

(a.) many of the complaints made by Mr McBride could not be substantiated; and

(b.) some warrants issued by ADFIS were invalid because they identified the wrong service offence, and they made adverse findings in relation to the issuing of those warrants.

(78.) Nothing in the Agreed Statement of Facts indicates that the conclusions reached by the inquiry were incorrect.

(79.) In late 2015, Mr McBride was given, and took up, the opportunity to read the report that had been prepared by the officers of the IGADF. He did not raise any concerns about the report with anyone at the IGADF.

The Disclosure to Chris Masters

(80.) In late 2014 (or early 2015), after he had submitted the IGADF Submission but before he was advised of the outcome of the inquiry, Mr McBride obtained the phone number of Chris Masters, an Australian journalist. He sought out Mr Masters because he knew that Mr Masters had written about the ADF. He phoned him and left a message. Mr Masters returned his call and they had a lengthy conversation in which Mr McBride outlined some of his complaints about the ADF.

(81.) Subsequently, at Mr Masters' request, they met at a hotel named 'Hotel Hotel' in New Acton, ACT, and discussed Mr McBride's complaints. Mr McBride took a plastic bag to the meeting containing two lever arch folders, being the IGADF Submission and the Supporting Documents. He gave Mr Masters the two folders of documents. At the time of doing so, he was aware that his conduct gave rise to the risk of him being prosecuted and punished by being subject to a sentence of imprisonment.

(82.) Mr McBride met with Mr Masters on two subsequent occasions, but they did not discuss the documents or complaints in great detail. The IGADF Submission and the Supporting Documents provided to Mr Masters contained a significant amount of 'military information' within the meaning of Section 73A of the Defence Act. Mr McBride did not have authority or permission to provide the documents and the provision was not in the course of his official duties. Mr McBride was aware that ADF Instructions, which had the force of law, prohibited the provision of the documents to Mr Masters. **It is the giving of the IGADF Submission and the Supporting Documents to Mr Masters that is one component of count 2.**

(83.) Mr Masters did not publish any of the material provided to him by Mr McBride.

Disclosure to Andrew Clark

(84.) In late 2014 (or early 2015), after he had provided the documents to Mr Masters, Mr McBride contacted another Australian journalist named Andrew Clark. He knew Mr Clark through a family member. He arranged to meet Mr Clark at a property in Forrest in the ACT.

(85.) Mr McBride took two lever arch folders with him to the meeting. These contained the IGADF Submission and the Supporting Documents. He gave these folders to Mr Clark as he believed Mr Clark could help him advance his complaints. Mr McBride knew that what he was doing was inconsistent with the ADF Instructions on handling classified information.

(86.) Mr McBride and Mr Clark subsequently met at a café in Manuka in the ACT to discuss the complaint and the documents. During this meeting, Mr Clark expressed interest in publishing a story based on the material that he had been given. Mr Clark asked Mr McBride whether he was prepared for the repercussions of publishing a story based on the material, including whether he was prepared to go to jail. Mr McBride responded by saying words to the effect of, 'Look, I don't really want to go to jail, obviously, but I'm prepared to be named if you need to.'

(87.) As with Mr Masters, the documents provided by Mr McBride to Mr Clark contained a significant amount of 'military information' within the meaning of Section 73A of the Defence Act. Mr McBride did not have authority or permission to provide the documents to Mr Clark. He was aware that ADF Instructions, having the force of law, prohibited the provision of the documents to Mr Clark. It is this disclosure to **Mr Clark which, along with the earlier disclosure to Mr Masters, constitutes count 2.**

(88.) Mr Clark did not publish any of the material provided by Mr McBride. In 2015, Mr Clark told Mr McBride that he had destroyed the documents that had been provided to him and thereafter ceased contacting him.

Mr McBride's awareness of the PID Act scheme

(89.) Mr McBride was aware of the PID Act scheme. He made reference to it in his IGADF Submission and, on 2 April 2015, he made use of it in relation to a recruitment matter unrelated to these proceedings. Following correspondence in April 2015, that complaint did not proceed further under the PID Act.

The Ops Room

(90.) On or about 4 April 2016 (that is, approximately eight months after he was told of the outcome of the IGADF inquiry and several months after he had read the report), Mr McBride created a website called 'The Ops Room'. It was publicly accessible at www.THEOPSROOM.com. This will be referred to as 'the Website'. Between April and May 2016, Mr McBride wrote and posted a number of blog posts on the Website which detailed his concerns about how the ADF was managed. Some of the facts contained in some of the blog posts came to Mr McBride's knowledge or into his possession by virtue of him being a Commonwealth officer. He also uploaded a number of documents to the Website in order to substantiate his concerns. These included:

(a.) an unsigned version of the IGADF Submission, which was 20 pages long and dated July 2014;

(b.) pages 74 and 75 of a 2014 ADF report titled 'Review into the Treatment of Women in the Australian Defence Force';

(c.) a report commissioned by the ADF and authored by the consultancy firm Deloitte titled 'Chief of Army's Women's Workshop' (9 May 2012);

(d.) a document titled 'Chief of Service Committee Outcomes' which was marked 'Committee in Confidence';

(e.) a document titled 'Decision Brief for SOCAUST: CASAC Prebrief Submission – Enhancing Capability through Diversity – Gender Plan' (9 March 2012) marked 'Committee in Confidence'; and

(f.) a two page report authored by Mr McBride titled 'Illegal Investigations of Special Operations Task Group in 2013'.

(91.) The unsigned version of the IGADF Submission was the only document on the Website which contained information classified SECRET, but the document itself was not marked SECRET. The two documents which were marked 'Committee in Confidence' contained information classified PROTECTED. The remaining documents were not marked with national security classifications, but were not otherwise publicly available.

(92.) Mr McBride was not authorised to publish or communicate much of the information contained in the blog posts or the documents available on the Website. It is the conduct of publishing the material on the Website which gives rise to the offence on the schedule under Section 16BA of the Crimes Act.

(93.) On 31 May 2016, an officer of ADF Legal Services wrote to Mr McBride in relation to the publication of documents and information on the Website. He reminded Mr McBride of his duties as a member of the ADF not to disclose information obtained by virtue of his employment as a Commonwealth officer. He noted in the correspondence that he was 'very cognisant of the need to support [Mr McBride in his] current state of health'. The officer said that, as a result of the disclosure of the material on the Website, Mr McBride's Positive Vetting security clearance had been suspended and, as a result, his access to ADF systems and secure buildings was also suspended.

(94.) By the time of the officer's correspondence, Mr McBride had already removed some of the materials from the Website. He removed the remainder of the materials after receiving the correspondence.

Disclosure to Daniel Oakes

(95.) On 2 May 2016, that is, while the Website was still up and prior to the letter from the officer at ADF Legal Services, another Australian journalist, Daniel Oakes, contacted Mr McBride after reading material on the Website. He asked Mr McBride whether he wanted to discuss the complaints and material on the Website. Mr McBride said that he did, and Mr Oakes told Mr McBride that he wanted to communicate using the encrypted app 'Signal', as he was concerned about security.

(96.) On about 17 May 2016, Mr Oakes and his colleague, Neil Mercer, travelled to Canberra and met Mr McBride at his home in Deakin. During the meeting, Mr McBride showed Mr Oakes and Mr Mercer a number of documents to substantiate his complaints. Mr Oakes asked Mr McBride for copies of these documents and suggested that they meet later that day at the Kingston Hotel in Griffith in the ACT.

(97.) Later that day, Mr McBride met Mr Oakes and Mr Mercer at the Kingston Hotel. Mr McBride provided Mr Oakes with a plastic bag containing two lever arch folders of documents. Those documents included the IGADF Submission and Supporting Documents. They also included some additional documents that Mr McBride had collected since he first made his complaint to the IGADF. Mr McBride knew that what he was doing was inconsistent with the ADF Instructions on handling classified information.

(98.) In relation to the additional documents that Mr McBride provided to Mr Oakes, the following facts are known.

- (a.) In June 2019, when the AFP executed a search warrant at the ABC, they located seven spreadsheets which detailed a number of individual documents. The AFP made a comparison of the documents seized at Mr McBride's Griffith property and the documents listed on the ABC spreadsheets. In addition to the

Supporting Documents, 139 additional documents were listed on the ABC spreadsheets that correlated with documents seized at the Griffith property. Of those 139 additional documents, 120 were classified SECRET. The 139 additional documents contained naval, military or air force information as defined in Section 73A(1) of the Defence Act. In relation to 10 of the documents referred to in the ABC spreadsheets, the AFP could not identify a correlating document from the Griffith property.

(b.) In court proceedings between the ABC and members of the AFP which followed the execution of the search warrant, it was an agreed fact that Mr Oakes and another journalist relied on information provided to Mr Oakes by informants in circumstances where Mr Oakes had promised the informants not to disclose their identity. The stories ultimately run by the ABC, referred to as 'The Afghan Files', stated that they were based upon information provided by such sources. The AFP has not identified any other person apart from Mr McBride known or suspected to have passed information or material to the ABC that resulted in the publication of those stories.

(99.) The IGADF Submission, most of the Supporting Documents and most of the additional documents which Mr McBride provided to Mr Oakes contained 'military information' within the meaning of Section 73A. Mr McBride did not have authority or permission to provide the documents to Mr Oakes. He was aware that ADF Instructions, having the force of law, prohibited the provision of the documents to Mr Oakes. It is the disclosure of documents to Mr Oakes by Mr McBride that gives rise to count 3.

(100.) Mr McBride and Mr Oakes had one subsequent meeting in person. After that, they communicated via the Signal app. Mr McBride later deleted most of his communications with Mr Oakes.

(101.) Later, Mr Oakes contacted Mr McBride via Signal to discuss the contents of the stories that Mr Oakes intended to publish. In his interview with police, Mr McBride said:

> 'But I met Dan Oakes, and I gave him all the materials. So again he was very enthusiastic and again he seemed to get it. And again, he was going to do a story. And he did do a story on it, but a totally different story to the one, um, that I was pushing.
>
> ...
>
> He calls me and he says, "I'm going to run a story, it's going to be very damning, it's going to say the SAS kill people unnecessarily. I'm going to use this other witness[.] A total opposite to what you've said. I'm just warning you." And I was like, "Never call me again." '

(102.) On 10 and 11 July 2017, Mr Oakes published a series of articles which were collectively titled The Afghan Files. The information contained in the documents provided to Mr Oakes by Mr McBride was contained in this series of articles.

(103.) On 11 July 2017, the AFP received a referral from the Chief of the Defence Force and the Secretary of the Department of Defence to investigate the unlawful communication of information.

(104.) The Commonwealth Director of Public Prosecutions subsequently decided that, notwithstanding that there was a reasonable prospect of conviction, it was not in the public interest to prosecute Mr Oakes.

Departure, Return, Arrest and Interviews

(105.) Mr McBride departed Australia for Spain on 22 September 2017. He had no immediate intention of returning to Australia. Almost a year later, on 1 September 2018, he returned to Australia to attend a family event. He was arrested on 5 September 2018 at Sydney International Airport as he attempted to board a plane to return to Spain.

(106.) On 13 October 2018, he participated in a recorded interview with the AFP. On 22 January 2019, he participated in another interview with the police.

The Police Interviews

(107.) Mr McBride participated in two interviews with police, the first on 13 October 2018 and the second on 22 January 2019. The first interview largely involved Mr McBride saying what he wanted about what had occurred. It extended over 33 pages of transcript. This interview is of significance because, in parts of it, Mr McBride gives his explanation for why he did what he did. The second interview involved the police asking specific questions relevant to the offence provisions. Mr McBride gave his answers over 49 pages of transcript. This interview is of significance because it allowed the police to obtain admissions relating to particular aspects of the offences with which Mr McBride had been, or would be, charged. On both occasions, his ex-wife attended as a support person.

Procedural History

(108.) Prior to 31 May 2016, when the officer at ADF Legal Services wrote to Mr McBride in relation to the publication of documents on the Website, the ADF was aware that he had created the Website. No disciplinary action or prosecution was brought in relation to this conduct.

(109.) On 5 September 2018, when Mr McBride was arrested, he was charged with one count of an offence of theft under Section 131.1 of the Criminal Code. He was granted bail.

(110.) On 7 March 2019, three charges were laid under Section 73A(1) of the Defence Act and one charge of an offence under Section 70 of the Crimes Act.

(111.) On 30 May 2019, he was committed for trial. At that stage, Mr McBride was unrepresented. He indicated that he wished to formally make admissions of certain matters by way of agreed facts. The Crown drafted a document reflecting, in large part, the admissions made by Mr McBride in the course of his interviews with the AFP. The agreed facts reflected almost all of the factual matters (as distinct from the conclusions to be drawn from those facts) alleged in the Crown Case Statement prepared for trial. The agreed facts were approved by Elkaim J for the purposes of Section 184(2)(b) of the Evidence Act 2011 (ACT) on 25 October 2019.

(112.) Mr McBride was arraigned on 11 November 2019. The trial was listed to commence on 2 March 2020. However, on 5 February 2020, Mr McBride sought immunity from prosecution under the PID Act. The claim was listed for a pre-trial hearing to commence on 2 March 2020. However, on 14 February 2020, the trial listed to commence on 2 March 2020 was vacated because Mr McBride had obtained legal representation.

(113.) The PID Act claim was listed for hearing to commence on 29 September 2020. Because of the COVID-19 pandemic, the date was subsequently vacated and relisted for 3 May 2021. On 2 March 2021, the hearing to commence on 3 May 2021 was vacated on the application of the Commonwealth Director of Public Prosecutions. The hearing was relisted for 20 September 2021. That listing was subsequently vacated at Mr McBride's request and relisted for 24 October 2022. However, when it came to the hearing of the claim, Mr McBride discontinued his claim under the PID Act.

(114.) On 13 April 2023, the criminal proceedings were again listed for trial commencing on 6 November 2023 with an estimate of three weeks.

(115.) At the commencement of the trial, the Court made a ruling as to the directions that would be given to the jury: *R vs McBride* [2023] ACTSC 328; 20 ACTLR 272; *R vs McBride* (No 2) [2023] ACTSC 330. An application for leave to appeal to the Court of Appeal was refused on 16 November 2023: *McBride vs R* [2023] ACTCA 42. On 17 November 2023, Mr McBride pleaded guilty to the three counts for which he is to be sentenced.

The Documents

(116.) It is agreed in the Agreed Statement of Facts that the public disclosure of information in many of the documents taken by Mr McBride would, or would have been likely to, have prejudiced the defence, national security or international relations of Australia at the time. The information in a number of the documents is still capable of causing such prejudice as at the date when the Statement of Facts was agreed. The potential risks from disclosure of the documents will continue to decrease over time. However, some documents, in particular the ROE, have enduring intelligence value. The harm or potential harm to Australia's defence, national security or international relations from disclosure of the ROE still exists.

(117.) It is agreed in the Agreed Statement of Facts that risk should not be assessed by reference only to a particular piece of information, because pieces of information can be combined to reveal more information than each piece of information considered individually. It is also agreed that the risk of prejudice is incapable of precise quantification and that any prejudice may not be immediately realised or apparent. Information in some of the documents has been declassified and publicly released. In their declassified format, those documents are incapable of prejudicing the defence, national security or international relations of Australia.

(118.) In August 2016, Major General Paul Brereton contacted Mr McBride via his ADF email address, which was still current. He advised Mr McBride that he had been appointed to conduct the IGADF's Afghanistan Inquiry and invited Mr McBride to speak to him. Mr McBride did not respond to this email and has no recollection of receiving an email from Major General Brereton. Major General Brereton used some information from Mr McBride's IGADF Submission to identify some issues for inquiry. The Afghanistan Inquiry was initiated by the ADF more than 12 months prior to the ADF becoming aware of Mr McBride's disclosures.

(119.) A small number of the documents that Mr McBride took contained within them confidential cabinet communications.

(120.) The harm or potential harm to the defence, national security or international relations of Australia is agreed to have arisen in the following ways:

- (a.) the removal of the documents from ADF facilities, including the subsequent multiple movements of the documents and storage of the documents at Mr McBride's Griffith property;
- (b.) the unauthorised disclosure of the documents to three journalists, including the copying of the documents and multiple movements of the documents; and
- (c.) the publication of materials on the Website.

(121.) These three aspects of the harm or potential harm are elaborated in the Agreed Statement of Facts as follows.

Removal of the Documents from ADF Facilities

(122.) Mr McBride's removal of the documents from ADF facilities and their subsequent movements gave rise to the possibility that an unauthorised person had access to them. No investigation has been conducted into whether any such access occurred.

(123.) Because of the potential that a person had read or copied the materials found in Mr McBride's Griffith property, Australia's foreign partners had to be, and were, notified of that potential. The public disclosure of information obtained confidentially from allies and partners may damage Australia's relationship with those allies and partners. Such disclosure may reduce their willingness to share information with Australia and Australia may not be informed of that change in attitude. If that occurred, it would disadvantage ADF operations and, more broadly, would be to the detriment of Australia's international relations and national security interests.

(124.) Further, the public disclosure of identities of any Special Operations Command or Special Forces personnel may have exposed those personnel and their families to an increased risk of attack and harassment and may have exposed them to exploitation by foreign intelligence services. While there is no evidence that this has occurred, it is an ongoing concern to the ADF.

(125.) The ADF has taken steps in respect of future operations because of the possibility that an unauthorised person has accessed the material. Those steps are outlined in a confidential annexure to the Agreed Statement of Facts, which was admitted into evidence and which I have read but which it is not necessary to say any more about.

(126.) If a person had read or copied the documents found at Mr McBride's Griffith property, the information contained in those documents may have given rise to certain risks:

> (a.) The public disclosure of information which would likely prejudice future collection and analysis of intelligence, risk of damage to critical international relationships and risk prejudicing the security of future ADF operations.

(b.) The public disclosure of information relating to ROE risks informing Australia's adversaries of the limits of the ADF's use of force. This would give adversaries tactical advantages, including by employing methods that took advantage of the limitations imposed by the ROE. That would give rise to an increased risk of harm to ADF personnel and compromise the effectiveness of current and future military operations.

(c.) Some documents reveal sensitive information such as policies, capabilities and response times, the public disclosure of which would prejudice their ongoing effectiveness and which could be employed to the detriment of Australia or its partners by domestic or overseas adversaries.

Unauthorised Disclosure to Journalists

(127.) Although the three journalists to whom disclosures were made were professional journalists, they were not authorised to receive the classified documents. The risks relating to identification of Special Operations Command or Special Forces personnel and the need for the ADF to take precautions or countermeasures ([123] and [125] above) arise from the possibility of disclosure of the material by the journalists and any work-related use of the material. Further, the need to notify Australian foreign partners ([123] above) and the potential damage arising from the risks ([126] above) also exists. However, the ADF has taken no steps to ascertain whether or not the documents were accessed by any person other than the named journalists. There is no evidence that they were.

Publication on the Website

(128.) As a result of Mr McBride's publication of materials on the Website, there is the possibility that an unauthorised person accessed the materials. However, the information in the materials published on the Website was such that it gave rise to very little risk of any prejudice to the defence, national security or international relations of Australia.

Subjective Circumstances

(129.) Some facts relevant to the subjective circumstances of Mr McBride are outlined earlier as part of the Agreed Statement of Facts. Other evidence of his subjective circumstances is contained in the intensive correction order assessment report dated 15 March 2024, two reports by Sam Borenstein, a clinical psychologist, dated 31 January 2024 and 23 February 2024, 15 character references, four performance appraisal reports prepared between August 2012 and September 2014 and his interviews with police.

(130.) Mr McBride is 60 years old. His parents were both doctors. His father was famous for alerting the world to the negative impacts of thalidomide and subsequently being deregistered for scientific fraud.

(131.) He was sent to boarding school at the age of seven and then boarded at high school until Year 12. He studied law at the University of Sydney. He had a good relationship with his parents. He went to the United Kingdom to complete a Masters degree in law at Oxford University. He joined the British Army in 1988. He was deployed to Northern Ireland in 1994. He served until 1998, leaving with the rank of Captain.

(132.) He returned to Australia to work as a solicitor at a big firm. He left the firm and worked in a security-related role with a TV documentary team for about two years, travelling through Afghanistan, the Sahara and South Africa. He then returned to Australia and worked as a political staffer for a federal politician. He stood as a candidate at an election for the New South Wales seat of Coogee in the 2003 state election but was unsuccessful. After that, he practised as a barrister in New South Wales for five years.

(133.) He married his wife in 2005. They have two children, born in about 2006 and 2008.

(134.) As a barrister, he took on some legal work with the Army Reserve and eventually joined the Army on a full-time basis as a lawyer in 2009.

(135.) In 2011, he was deployed to Afghanistan where he remained for nine and a half months as a legal officer.

(136.) The performance appraisals from the Army show that, during the period from August 2012 until September 2014, he was receiving very positive assessments of his performance and conduct. These are discussed in more detail later in these reasons (see [153]–[157] below).

(137.) He returned to Afghanistan in 2013 as a Legal Officer for the Special Operations Task Group.

(138.) In December 2013, he again received a positive performance assessment.

(139.) In a performance assessment in September 2014, he was recorded as having prioritised a personal representation to the IGADF (the IGADF Submission) between May and September of that year, which impacted upon his capacity to perform his assigned duties.

(140.) He separated from his wife in 2016. The couple were divorced in 2018.

(141.) He was diagnosed in 2016 as suffering from Major Depressive Disorder. He was medically discharged from the Army in early 2017. He was diagnosed to be suffering from PTSD. Dr Adesanya, a psychiatrist, identified the primary diagnosis as being PTSD, which explained the development of the symptoms of Major Depressive Disorder, anxiety, Alcohol and Substance Use Disorders and associated symptoms.

(142.) After being medically discharged, and after Mr Oakes published 'The Afghan Files', Mr McBride went to Spain. He lived off his superannuation. He was arrested after returning to Australia in September 2018.

(143.) Mr Borenstein records the conclusion that Mr McBride's 'sensitivity to diversions from moral and ethical standards made him vulnerable to developing symptoms of Major Depressive Disorder and PTSD against which he relied on alcohol and prescription medication (Dexamphetamine), as a form of self-medication, which was the case prior to and during the offending period'.

(144.) Mr Borenstein also records that Mr McBride's current presentation is improved because of daily exercise, attendance at Alcoholics Anonymous meetings and combined psychiatric and psychological treatment. In a supplementary report, he records that Mr McBride's symptoms would worsen if subject to a custodial sentence, 'possibly requiring intensive psychiatric and psychological treatment, and inpatient care'.

(145.) The personal references recorded that Mr McBride has 'a rare combination of humility and at the same time a passion for justice'. Another reference relates to his participation in Alcoholics Anonymous and suggests that a non-custodial sentence would make a 'huge and positive difference' both to Mr McBride and to other members of Alcoholics Anonymous who he helps to stay sober. It also records that separation from his therapy dog would be 'extremely damaging'.

(146.) Amongst the additional bundle of references that were tendered are a mix of references from members of his family, long-time friends of his as well as those that have known him through his work as a reserve legal officer or a full-time member of the ADF. A common theme of the references relating to his time in the military is his sense of duty, his sense of professional responsibility, his intelligence and hard work. The long-time friends talk of his empathy, kindness and compassion. One of the references, which recognises the significant emotional toll taken on him by his tours of active service, attempts to address the offending conduct and describes it as 'an appalling lack of judgment'.

(147.) The intensive correction order assessment report does not record any remorse in relation to the offending. It records the following:

> 'He minimised the offending, attributing it to a difference in legal interpretation. Mr McBride expressed the belief that, if prosecuted, his conduct would be protected under a the [sic] defence of acting in the public interest. However, he recognised a Judge had now determined this defence was not available to him and therefore conviction and punishment were to follow.
>
> Despite this, he emphasised his differing interpretation of the legislation and stated he was likely to appeal the decision, regardless of whether this would impact his sentence. Mr McBride justified his decision to offend, claiming he believed the Department of Defence (the Department) had been acting outside the bounds of the law, due to political interference, in a manner which was dangerous to the community. He positioned himself as acting in a completely lawful manner due to a belief he had a responsibility, as a lawyer, to rectify this issue. Mr McBride expressed the belief the theft

of the documents was justified to prove the above claims. He also stated the provision of these documents to the media felt necessary, as he was unsatisfied with the result of his internal complaint and felt he had no other available options.

(148.) Mr McBride has no criminal history.

(149.) Some further aspects of Mr McBride's subjective circumstances are addressed in the next section of these reasons which relate to specific submissions on factual matters made on behalf of Mr McBride.

Defendant's Submissions on Issues of Fact

(150.) At the sentencing hearing, counsel for Mr McBride submitted that five findings of fact, favourable to Mr McBride, should be made for the purposes of determining the appropriate sentence. They were as follows:

(a.) prior to the offending, during the period of conduct constituting the offending and to this day, Mr McBride was and is a man of exemplary character;

(b.) Mr McBride's motivation in engaging in the offending conduct was honourable in that he honestly believed that there was misconduct within the ADF with respect to the conduct of the Defence Force investigations of Special Forces soldiers in 2013;

(c.) Mr McBride honestly believed at the time he did all of the conduct that was the subject of the offences, that he was not committing any criminal offence;

(d.) prior to and during the period that he engaged in the conduct of taking the copies of the documents home and then passing some of them on to journalists, he suffered from a number of mental disorders which materially contributed to his offending; and

(e.) the level of harm or the risk of harm from Mr McBride's offending was low.

(151.) These matters include matters going to the objective seriousness of the offending, as well as the subjective circumstances of the offender. They will be considered in the manner and order that the arguments were presented.

Exemplary Good Character

(152.) Counsel for Mr McBride submitted that the Court should find that, prior to the offending, during the period of conduct constituting the offending and to this day, Mr McBride was and is a man of exemplary character. He went as far as to say that Mr McBride's character was unusual insofar as it involved 'adherence to the highest ethical and moral standards of honesty, duty, courage, honour and passion for justice'.

(153.) He relied upon the terms of performance appraisals relating to the period of his service as a full-time Army officer between March 2012 and September 2014.

(154.) In August 2012, Mr McBride was recorded as being 'a well respected specialist officer' and a strong contender for advancement to Lieutenant Colonel in 2013.

(155.) In February 2013, his assessor was 'thoroughly impressed with his performance' as acting Command Legal Officer at the Special Operations Command. He continued to be a strong contender for promotion to Lieutenant Colonel.

(156.) In December 2013, he was assessed as having been 'a very effective Legal Advisor' for the SOTG rotation 20. He was identified as being of 'superior intellect' and 'a very articulate and convincing speaker'. Some indications of the tensions that were developing are shown by the comments that he could improve 'by continuing to develop a more detailed understanding of the [nuances] involved in providing legal advice when there are competing priorities between command responsibilities and policy/legality' and the need to find common ground 'when there are competing priorities between command responsibilities and policy/legality'. However, he continued to be recommended for higher rank.

(157.) By September 2014, the performance appraisal noted that he had 'prioritised his development of a personal representation to [the] IGADF, impacting on the time and resources he was able to commit to the legal Section'. It indicated that working on the IGADF Submission had 'caused him stress and fatigue, impacting on his performance'. It noted that he 'works relentlessly – sometimes to his personal detriment'. It noted that he 'stands firm to his convictions' and takes 'a deep personal responsibility and interest in the professional wellbeing of the Command and its members'. He was identified as 'a highly confident lawyer with a strong belief in himself, his abilities and capacity to effect change'. Although at that stage, the assessors anticipated him re-establishing his usual work capacity, no subsequent assessments were put into evidence.

(158.) The report of Mr Borenstein summarises Mr McBride as placing 'significant emphasis on honesty and adherence to morals and ethics' and notes his 'sensitivity to diversions from moral and ethical standards'.

(159.) A personal reference from a former lawyer and friend of Mr McBride refers to him as having 'a rare combination of humility and at the same time a passion for justice'. The other personal references to which I have briefly referred earlier support the proposition that, in his personal and professional life, except during the period of the offending, he was a person of good character.

(160.) I accept that Mr McBride was a person of good character. More than that, he demonstrated a strong devotion to his duty and performed well in the roles that he was assigned, at least up until his return from his second tour of Afghanistan. He was consistently identified as a person who was a strong candidate for further promotion within the ADF. There were signs, however, even within the performance appraisals upon which he relied, that he came to lack the ability to moderate his own opinions and the conviction of the correctness of his own opinions in a way which would allow him to continue to function at the level that he had within the Army.

(161.) As a result of his experiences when posted to Afghanistan in 2013, he appears to have, over time, become obsessed with the correctness of his own opinions as to the conduct of the organisation for which he worked. He came to be unable to accept that his views may not be correct. It was this misguided self-belief that led him to disregard the institutional methods for addressing his grievances and pursue them through the criminal conduct for which he is now charged.

(162.) It is therefore not possible to make the finding contended for by counsel for Mr McBride. He was a person of good character and committed to his service within the ADF until he became so convinced of the correctness of his own opinions that he was unable to operate within the legal framework that his duty required him to.

Motivation

(163.) Counsel for Mr McBride submitted that his motivation in engaging in the offending conduct was honourable in that he honestly believed that there was misconduct within the ADF with respect to the conduct of the Defence Force investigations of Special Forces soldiers in 2013. It was submitted that this was relevant both to the objective seriousness of the offending, as well as to subjective considerations.

(164.) It is significant to note that no attempt was made to prove as a fact, for the purposes of sentencing, that the claims made by Mr McBride were justified, that they were inappropriately addressed by the IGADF or that the mechanisms for complaint or redress available under the law were not adequate. Rather, the contention put on behalf of Mr McBride was merely that he had an honest belief in the matters that he put forward.

(165.) It is clear that Mr McBride had formed the opinion that the extent of the investigation of soldiers involved in the killing of civilians in Afghanistan had changed in 2012, and that this reflected the desires of the senior commanders of the ADF, but was improper because it involved investigation of soldiers even in circumstances where there was no prospect that they had committed the war crime of murder.

(166.) It appears that his experiences during his second Afghanistan posting, during which he was personally involved in conflict with investigators sent by the ADFIS, had a very profound impact upon him. He had specific issues with the threshold for the commencement of investigations, the conduct of investigators and their use of warrants in one particular case. His experience caused him to lose faith in the leadership of the ADF in relation to the approach adopted to the investigation of killings of civilians in Afghanistan. He came to believe that the approach involved what he described as 'cynical window dressing' in order to satisfy political concerns as to the death of civilians.

(167.) His motivation was therefore to remedy what he perceived to be an injustice occurring within the ADF, even if it involved him committing very serious criminal offences. It is clear that he did not commit the offences in order to achieve any financial gain for himself or in order to assist Australia's adversaries. Rather, the offending was motivated by his opinion that there was an injustice occurring to individuals and to the institution of the Army because of political pressures upon its senior management. Characterising the conduct as 'honourable' is apt to mislead, unless that word is simply used to indicate that there were not base motivations of financial gain or other personal advantage or a desire to assist Australia's adversaries.

(168.) It is therefore more appropriate to simply identify that the offending was not motivated by financial gain, personal advantage or a desire to assist Australia's adversaries. It may be accepted that the conduct reflected strongly held beliefs on his part. As I have indicated, no attempt was made to establish the correctness of those beliefs in these proceedings or to undermine the validity of the conclusions reached by the IGADF as a result of the inquiry arising from the IGADF Submission. Insofar as counsel submitted that Mr McBride was of the view that 'the IGADF was biased and controlled by the Chief of the Defence Force', there was no attempt to establish that this was true or was a reasonable belief. To the extent that Mr McBride held that belief, it is only of relevance insofar as it precludes more reprehensible motivations such as a desire to assist foreign powers.

Honest Belief Not Committing an Offence

(169.) Counsel for Mr McBride submitted that the Court should find that Mr McBride honestly believed, 'at the time he did all of the conduct that was the subject of these offences', that he was not committing any criminal offence. This was said to be on the basis that, although he knew that what he was doing breached disciplinary regulations and orders, he believed that he would ultimately be vindicated and a court would conclude that he acted in the public interest and thereby committed no criminal offence.

(170.) Principal reliance is placed upon what is said in his recorded interviews with police in October 2018 and January 2019. However, the statements made during these interviews, when taken as a whole, do not permit a finding that Mr McBride honestly believed that he was not committing any criminal offence. Rather, they indicate that, in a non-specific way, he hoped that his conduct would ultimately be somehow vindicated. That is very different from an honest belief that no offence was occurring.

(171.) Amongst the passages from the transcript of the police interviews which were relied upon were the following. At page 74 of the Crown Tender Bundle:

> 'You know, of course the Department of Defence lie, of course it's all a big sham, of course, you know, what did you think it was. I mean I don't accept that and I never did, you know, maybe I am strung too tight, maybe I do have to – to a higher sense of public duty, but it's genuine and I, um, I can't see that it – it means I'm guilty of an offence because, um, I take truth in public life or in the ADF seriously. I think it matters when generals lie. I think it matters when they sacrifice [the] lives of their own troops in order for their own careers to go ahead. I think it matters, um, when Australian officers turn the other way. Um, and I am happy to go to court and have the judge or the jury decide whether I am a criminal, a mad man or a soldier.'

(172.) At page 78:

> '... but a bit of a spoiler alert, I'll say now, that the reason why I'm making all these points is because I'm going to admit, um, that I took the documents from the base, I won't say illegally, because I don't, um, admit that it was illegally, because I believe that was in pursuit of, um, a legal duty. But I did take them ...'

(173.) At page 86:

> 'I'm firmly of the opinion that it was my legal obligation to expose criminal activity, I believe I was doing what I was meant to do as a soldier.'

(174.) At page 87:

> '... my justification is – it was an obligation to – no law, no matter how, you know, no matter what, the Official Secrets Act or the equivalent says, it can never over-ride the reporting of a serious crime, you know, no government can say, um, to the police, for example, "Oh, if you see a murder, you're not allowed to tell anybody, and if you tell anybody, we're going to put you in jail." ... And I'm happy for – you know, that may go to the High Court, the High Court may decide differently, but I am convinced that that must be the case. Ah, that it must be interpreted, I believe that's what the Act actually says, the Protected Disclosure Act, I believe I'm within that, but I believe that even if I'm not within that, there must be some sort of common law – it would be an illegal abusive government that could say, "You're not allowed, as a public servant, you're not allowed to reveal, um, criminal activity within the government, on penalty of jail, um, at any cost." Especially, if you're a legal officer and your job is exactly that to make sure the law is enforced. [He then made reference to the holding of a practising certificate and continued] But it comes with responsibilities, you can't lie, you have to report crime, you have to abide by the law. And I had a legal obligation to report – I believe anyway. That's – of course, that's going to be the question that comes up in court.'

(175.) At page 102, when discussing whether he should have destroyed the stolen documents, he said:

> 'And, um, ah, you know, I – because afterwards, when I'd heard you came and done the, um – and – and taken the documents with the warrant, I was thinking, well, I actually wished I had destroyed the documents. But even then, something – something inside me was kind of glad that I didn't, because it was – it was always, as I said to you, or I said to Paul, your colleague, I always thought that I was going to be vindicated at some point. I always thought eventually there would be an investigation into my allegations, and eventually people – someone would say, "You've done well here, you've stuck to your guns and you've exposed corruption." ... So I was

> glad that I kept them in some ways, even though I could see that it was - I was possibly facing prison, because I felt - as I said, I felt that they, um, that they would vindicate me.'

(176.) At page 107, when asked about the obligations of a person who holds a Positive Vetting top secret clearance, he said:

> '... I don't think I did the wrong thing. I think the Positive Vetting is a – must lie under overarching national security obligations ... And while I deserved my – I didn't tell any lies to get my PV, I deserved it, I did a good job, but I'd never said during my PV that I will cover up crime by the government or the organisation I work for in order not to breach my PV. I mean, that's – that goes without saying.'

(177.) Counsel submitted that the crimes to which Mr McBride referred in his interview with police were those which were recorded in the Agreed Statement of Facts as having been disclosed to the AFP in May 2014, namely:

(a) conspiracy to pervert the course of justice;

(b) misuse of Commonwealth resources;

(c) interference with a legal officer performing their duties;

(d) failure to comply with a general order; and

(e) improperly prejudicing ADF members' careers.

(178.) No particulars were provided of any such offences. The AFP reached the conclusion that, based upon the information that Mr McBride had provided, no criminal offence was disclosed. That conclusion on the part of the AFP has not been shown to be wrong.

(179.) I do not accept that the passages in the interviews with police demonstrate, on the balance of probabilities, that Mr McBride genuinely believed that he was not committing a crime. The statements do not reflect any coherent argument as to how his conduct may have been rendered lawful. They involve vague and unparticularised claims of criminal activity. They involve complaints of lies and 'window dressing' by the senior leadership of the ADF. His statements also involve vague and unparticularised claims of a legal entitlement to breach the law in order to expose such (vague and unparticularised) criminal activity. This may be seen from other passages in his interview with police.

(180.) At page 66 of the Crown Tender Bundle, he said:

> 'I'm pleading not guilty, the whole – well, there's a lot of central tenets of my [d]efence, but one of the – the core of my defence is that, um, the senior officers of the Australian Defence Force were not truthful and did things that were underhand, unethical and half-truths – and actually broke the law.'

(181.) At page 67:

> '... but there's no point, um, beating around the bush in that regard. By that I mean the law was being habitually broken. And I don't mean, um, I mean the law, yeah, but it definitely comes down to it wasn't things I didn't like or things that were unethically, it was certainly – it's suspicious anyway as I said. I can't make that judgment but there were things that I believed needed to be looked at by either judges or, um, the High Court would be a good thing ... I imagined, one of the things the prosecution will claim is, "Oh, well, you just weren't happy about the way your internal complaints went." But I – I refute that completely, in that I will intend to prove that the complaints that I made were never properly dealt with, never legally dealt with, forcing me, um, to consider further options, because they were either side-stepped or they were ignored or they were, a smoke screen was used. Anyway that's obviously a matter for the court.'

(182.) He described at pages 78–79 having prepared the IGADF Submission between May and August 2014:

> '... it took me till the end of two thousand and fourteen to write a detailed – so that – another August, so May, June, July, August, three – three or four months after I first saw the police in May, two thousand and fourteen, ah, that I finished, um, a very long document detailing all the – what I would call relatively small breaches of the law, because I'd written this to the Special Operations Command. But the point I was clearly trying to make was not about the illegal searches and the illegal investigations or that. But

> there was something very wrong in the Defence Force that, um, as I said, the first complaint was to ... the AFP ... it was about spending. So even from a spending point of view, doing investigations which had no – had no – had no genuine purpose but were just being done to window dress in order to make the minister or the press happy, I believe is illegal, because it's a waste of tax payers money and you couldn't – you couldn't get away with it – I'm sure you wouldn't get away with it as police officers. ... And that was just a symptom of a – of a complete lack of leadership, because not only these investigations cost money, they cost lives, they cost people – as I was later to find out, in the JEDI [council] case, which was another symptom of a sick, a sick management policy where anything – anything would be done, and I mean that, you know, anything would be done by Defence in order to make themselves look good or the senior management look good and sacrifice the soldiers ... but the documents which I saw with my own eyes, the documents which I took and the documents which I spent hours and hours of downloading purposely to show that the Defence Force habitually lied to the Australian public, which I believe is an offence, habitually lied to their own people. Habitually, um, destroyed the lives of their own soldiers, betrayed their own Special Forces operatives ... the ADF knew they committed no crime, they were still sacrificed to the god of public relations and it just sickened me.'

(183.) Even taking into account the decline in Mr McBride's mental state following his return from Afghanistan, I do not accept that he held a belief that what he was doing was not a criminal offence. He was not such a bad lawyer as to have genuinely reached a legal conclusion along the lines expressed in his interview. Rather, he had a hope at the time that his actions would ultimately be vindicated in some way other than by being found to be legally correct. I consider that the statements he made to police at the time were reflective of a desire to justify his conduct in the context of having been charged and that they expressed a hope that there may be some legally plausible defence, but did not reflect any actual belief that the conduct did not involve criminal offending at the time that it occurred.

Mental Disorders

(184.) Counsel for Mr McBride submitted that the Court should find that, prior to and during the period that he engaged in the conduct of taking the copies of the ADF documents home and then passing some of them on to journalists, he suffered from a number of mental disorders which materially contributed to his offending. It was submitted that the Court should find that he developed PTSD during his deployment in Afghanistan in 2011 and particularly in the latter half of 2013.

(185.) Counsel for Mr McBride principally relied upon the evidence in Mr Borenstein's report, which records the first diagnosis of Major Depressive Disorder in 2013 and Mr McBride's medical discharge from the army in 2017 following a diagnosis of PTSD. Mr Borenstein expressed the opinion that, during the offending, Mr McBride was suffering from symptoms of Major Depressive Disorder and combined Alcohol and Substance Use Disorders as well as PTSD. He also expressed the opinion that the level of disturbance to his thought, mood, volition, perception and memory impaired Mr McBride's emotional wellbeing, judgment and behavioural choices.

(186.) The foundation for the opinion of Mr Borenstein is undermined by what Mr McBride told the author of the intensive correction order assessment report:

> 'Mr McBride acknowledged his consumption of alcohol had escalated prior to and during the commission of the offences. He also recognised his diagnosis of PTSD had come shortly after the offending occurred. Despite this, he denied that alcohol or his mental health played a role in his decision to offend. He stated he was currently [abstinent] from alcohol and still believed he made the correct choice. Mr McBride also advised he believed his PTSD was, in part, caused by the offences.'

(187.) Notwithstanding Mr McBride's denial, there is no basis upon which to reject the statement in Mr Borenstein's report that 'in 2013, following return from deployment to Afghanistan, he was diagnosed to be suffering with Major Depressive Disorder and PTSD'. It is not clear whether it was his underlying personality or his declining mental health which led to him becoming obsessed with the conduct of senior management of the ADF. Both propositions appear to be consistent with Mr Borenstein's opinion.

However, it is likely that the stress caused by the years of offending conduct after his return from deployment contributed to the decline in his mental health. It is in that context that it is possible to accept the opinion of Mr Borenstein that during the offending period Mr McBride was suffering with symptoms of Major Depressive Disorder, combined Alcohol and Substance Use Disorders and PTSD. It is also possible to accept that his mental health condition made a material, if only minor, contribution to his offending conduct.

Harm from Actions

(188.) Counsel for Mr McBride submitted that an inference should be drawn from the agreed facts that the level of harm or the risk of harm caused by his conduct was low.

(189.) In relation to count 1, while accepting that the documents were and remain highly sensitive and could have presented serious risks to Australia's interests, counsel submitted there is no evidence of actual harm and it could not be inferred that significant harm was in fact caused. He also submitted that the risk of actual disclosure was low, given that the documents were kept in tubs at Mr McBride's home. While the possibility of disclosure cannot be excluded, he emphasised that there has been no investigation to try to find out whether there has been any unauthorised access to the documents other than the access the subject of the other charges.

(190.) In relation to counts 2 and 3, counsel submitted that the disclosures were to reputable journalists. As a consequence, the risk that the documents would find their way to some adversary country or entity was low.

(191.) In my view, it is not appropriate to go beyond the detailed and nuanced description of the level of harm and risk of harm which is articulated in the Agreed Statement of Facts. There are multiple types of harm and risks of harm which are there described and it would not be consistent with those agreed facts to subject them to a uniform gloss by characterising the harm or risk as being 'low'. Rather, the harm and risk of harm is accurately described in the Agreed Statement of Facts.

(192.) In the written submissions made on behalf of Mr McBride, it was submitted that the disclosure of some of the information has advanced the public interest. First, this was said to be because it was 'used by Major General Brereton to identify issues for inquiry in the course of the [IGADF] Afghanistan inquiry'. I do not accept this submission. The agreed facts referred to the use by Major General Brereton of some information from the IGADF Submission, a lawful disclosure which Mr McBride was allowed time at work to prepare. Major General Brereton did not use any information from the unlawful disclosures the subject of the charges. Second, the advancement of the public interest was said to have arisen through raising awareness of the conduct of Australian Special Forces through the publication of The Afghan Files. I do not accept the thrust of this submission. There is no doubt that the subject matter of The Afghan Files was a matter of significant public interest. However, the agreed facts indicate that the IGADF inquiry into the conduct of Special Forces in Afghanistan was initiated by the ADF more than 12 months prior to the ADF becoming aware of Mr McBride's disclosures. Further, the articles published by Mr Oakes were the exact opposite of what Mr McBride had intended when making the disclosures. In those circumstances, it is not appropriate to treat any raising of awareness by reason of Mr Oakes' journalistic activities as being a matter reducing the seriousness of Mr McBride's conduct.

Objective Seriousness

(193.) The following points can be made about the objective seriousness of count 1, the count of theft.

(a.) The removal of documents occurred over a substantial period, between May 2014 and December 2015 (one year and seven months) and their retention continued over years.

(b.) The taking of the documents involved multiple occasions on which the offender surreptitiously removed documents from ADF facilities.

(c.) The course of conduct that Mr McBride engaged in involved a gross breach of the trust reposed in him as a senior legal advisor in a sensitive position within the ADF.

(d.) It involved a breach of obligations in relation to which Mr McBride had received specific training on multiple occasions.

(e.) The course of conduct also involved grave breaches of his duty as a lawyer.

(f.) Having regard to the evidence that Mr McBride was working on his IGADF Submission during work hours and at the expense of his other duties, his culpability is not reduced by any need that might have existed to refer to the documents for the purposes of preparing a submission.

(g.) Although the motivation for the thefts may have varied somewhat over time, the motivation for the thefts was to give the offender the potential to use and disclose the documents other than for the purpose of his official duties.

(h.) It is a rolled up charge involving a large number of documents, a significant proportion of which held the SECRET classification. Of the 235 documents removed, 207 were classified SECRET.

(i.) There have been specific consequences that flowed from the theft, arising from the need to make disclosures to Australia's foreign partners, the concern arising from the disclosure of identities of Special Operations Command and Special Forces personnel and operational consequences disclosed in the confidential annexure to the Agreed Statement of Facts.

(j.) Although it was an agreed fact that, at the time he commenced the misappropriation of the documents, he considered certain practices in the ADF to be 'corrupt', no attempt was made for the purposes of sentencing to establish the correctness of that belief or, indeed, its reasonableness.

(194.) It is necessary to address some of the specific submissions made on behalf of Mr McBride in relation to the objective seriousness of this offence:

(a.) Counsel for Mr McBride submitted that it was relevant that the theft of the documents did not deprive the Commonwealth of the original documents. That the Commonwealth was not deprived of the original documents is not of great significance in the present case because the value of the documents arose from their confidential nature.

(b.) Counsel for Mr McBride submitted that, although the taking of the documents was dishonest, it did not involve 'actually telling lies or actively misleading any person'. That the taking of the documents did not involve actually telling lies or misleading any person is only a feature of the present case because of the very trusted position which Mr McBride held and which was abused in order to complete the theft.

(c.) Counsel for Mr McBride submitted that the property was not obtained in order to obtain a financial advantage. This is not of great significance because financial advantage is not the sole nor necessarily the most culpable motivation for an offence of theft.

(d.) Counsel for Mr McBride submitted that the dishonestly appropriated property was initially taken in order to prepare the IGADF Submission. If that was the case, his conduct was unnecessary as the evidence indicates that Mr McBride was able to prepare his submission during work hours and, as a result, his performance of his usual duties was affected (see [157] above).

(e.) I have earlier rejected the submission that Mr McBride believed that he was not committing any offence (see [183] above).

(195.) Although the offending in the present case is not a traditional example of theft because the financial value of that which was stolen is not a significant factor in assessing its objective seriousness, the above features of the offending put it above the mid-range of objective seriousness for this offence.

(196.) Count 2, the charge of disclosing information to Mr Masters and Mr Clark, is a rolled up charge because it involves disclosures to two separate journalists on two distinct occasions and each such disclosure involved multiple documents. It involved disclosures of substantial volumes of documents, many of which bore the SECRET classification. The disclosures occurred at a time when legitimate processes for addressing Mr McBride's concerns were still on foot and after he had been told by the AFP that no criminal offences were disclosed by his complaints. It did not involve any subsequent publications by the journalists because, for undisclosed reasons, they did not see fit to publish stories based upon the material. The harm and risk of harm are as described at [122]–[126] above.

(197.) I do not accept the submission made on behalf of Mr McBride that breach of trust cannot be an aggravating feature of the offence because this feature of the offending is necessarily engaged by the fact that it is an element of the offence that the person be a member of the Defence Force or engaged under the Public Service Act 1999 (Cth). While the requirement to be a member of the ADF or a public servant means that the relationship of any charged person to the Commonwealth will necessarily involve duties of loyalty and confidentiality, there is a difference between someone in a junior position with limited access to information and someone in a more senior and trusted position with access to more sensitive information. Mr McBride was plainly in the latter category, having trusted access to very sensitive information. That is clearly an aggravating feature of his offending.

(198.) I assess count 2 as being in the mid-range of objective seriousness for an offence against Section 73A.

(199.) Count 3 relates to the disclosure to Mr Oakes. Once again it involved disclosures of substantial volumes of documents, many of which bore the SECRET classification. It involved disclosure of more documents than had been disclosed to Mr Masters or Mr Clark. The documents disclosed included the Supporting Documents and some additional documents that Mr McBride had collected since he first made the complaint to the IGADF. The correlation between the documents in Mr McBride's possession and those listed in Mr Oakes' spreadsheets is described at [98(a)] above. It is not possible to determine beyond reasonable doubt the number of additional documents because of the possibility that Mr Oakes obtained them from another source. There were 86 Supporting Documents, most of which were classified SECRET. The disclosure occurred after Mr McBride knew the outcome of the IGADF process, of which there was no criticism by Mr

McBride at the time or in these proceedings. Publication did occur as a result of the disclosure. The intent of those stories was the opposite of that which the Mr McBride had hoped to be published. The harm and risk of harm is described at [122]–[126] above.

(200.) It too is an offence in the mid-range of objective seriousness, even though it involved publication to only one person.

(201.) The charge to be taken into account at sentence in relation to count 3 involves the disclosure of documents on the Website. The provision creating the offence is slightly broader than Section 73A of the Defence Act because it extends to any document coming into his possession which it was his duty not to disclose and is not limited to documents relating to naval, military or air force information. Nevertheless, the nature of the conduct involved is essentially the same as that for count 3, namely, disclosure of documents that should not have been disclosed. Having said that, the material that was in fact disclosed was such that it gave rise to very little risk of any prejudice to the defence, national security or international relations of Australia. It is connected with count 3 because it was this disclosure which Mr Oakes came across and that then prompted him to get in contact with Mr McBride, leading to the offence the subject of count 3.

Plea of Guilty and Assistance to Authorities

(202.) Mr McBride provided substantial assistance to authorities by making admissions about his conduct in the two interviews that he did with the AFP. His claim relating to the possible application of the PID Act, which was ultimately not pursued, had the effect of delaying the proceedings. The assistance to authorities is to be taken into account pursuant to Section 16A(2)(h) of the Crimes Act.

(203.) Following the rejection of the legal argument that he put forward at the commencement of his trial and the refusal of leave to appeal from that decision, he entered a plea of guilty. There is substantial utilitarian value in the plea of guilty having been entered, even though it was late. This is to be taken into account pursuant to Section 16A(2)(g). A reduction on account of the plea of guilty of 10 percent appropriately reflects its utilitarian value. It is also appropriate to take his guilty plea into account in determining the manner in which any sentence of imprisonment should be served.

(204.) I do not accept that this is a case where it was not reasonably possible for Mr McBride to have pleaded guilty at an earlier stage. I accept that the ruling in relation to the directions that would ultimately be given to the jury proved decisive in causing him to change his plea. The absence of a definitive ruling upon that legal issue did not preclude him from entering his plea earlier. There is no evidence that he only chose not to enter an early plea because of legal advice as to the merits of the argument to be put on that issue.

Time in Custody

(205.) Mr McBride has spent no time in custody prior to sentence. Therefore, no issue of backdating his sentence arises.

Comparative Cases

(206.) The Crown provided a schedule of cases said to be comparable. The schedule included cases involving Section 131.1(1) of the Criminal Code as well as those said to be of comparative value for the purposes of Section 73A. Counsel for Mr McBride identified an additional comparable case.

Section 131.1(1)

(207.) So far as the offence of theft contrary to Section 131.1(1) of the Criminal Code is concerned, the cases provided were not very comparable at all. That may simply be a product of the fact that the present circumstances were unusual.

(208.) *Chia vs The Queen* [2018] WASCA 103 related to misappropriation of Centrelink payments. It is not usefully comparable.

(209.) *R vs Jafari* [2017] NSWCCA 152 involved a solicitor responsible for managing a trust for a disabled person. The solicitor misappropriated $220,000. There was limited evidence of remorse or contrition and the offender had a gambling addiction. He was given a sentence of three years' imprisonment, to be released after 18 months upon entry into a recognisance to be of good behaviour.

(210.) *Della-Vedova vs R* [2009] NSWCCA 107 involved a long-serving member of the ADF who misappropriated 10 rocket launchers. The offender had no criminal record and his ADF service record was impressive. He was given a six-year sentence with a non-parole period of four years on the theft charge.

(211.) *Peterson vs R* (District Court (NSW), Hanley DCJ, 30 November 2020, unrep) was a charge which proceeded summarily involving theft of tools and equipment from Air Services Australia. It was not usefully comparable.

(212.) Generally speaking, because of the different circumstances of these cases, they do not have much value as comparable cases. Although the circumstances in *Jafari* are very different to the present case, they did involve a gross breach of trust by a lawyer and, in that respect, *Jafari* is comparable to some extent.

Section 73A

(213.) The schedule of cases provided by the Crown indicates that there have been no previous prosecutions for an offence against Section 73A(1) of the Defence Act. The schedule did identify some cases involving the disclosure of material contrary to laws of the Commonwealth.

(214.) *R vs Scerba* (No 2) [2015] ACTSC 359 involved a contravention of Section 70 of the Crimes Act, which carried a maximum penalty of two years' imprisonment. It involved uploading two pages of a Defence Intelligence Report to the 4chan website. The pages contained a summary of key intelligence assessments and identified the intelligence sources used to develop the report. It was not possible to determine whether the publication had caused actual damage to Australia's national security. The offender was suffering from Major Depressive Disorder, had a low risk of reoffending and there was evidence of contrition. The offender was sentenced to 12 months' imprisonment, to be released after three months subject to a good behaviour order.

(215.) *R vs Crowley* (District Court (WA), Voil DCJ, 17 March 1997, unrep) involved another breach of Section 70 of the Crimes Act. A junior legal officer at the Commonwealth Director of Public Prosecutions published documents concerning the Attorney-General's consent to the institution of proceedings against Alan Bond to Alan Bond's son, John. This conduct involved a gross breach of the officer's obligations as a prosecutor. The offender was of prior good character, had a record of public service and a sentence of imprisonment would have had an adverse effect on his family. There was the prospect of disciplinary proceedings. He received a sentence of 15 months' imprisonment to be released after six months on a recognisance to be of good behaviour.

(216.) *Grant vs Headland* (1977) 17 ACTR 29 involved a charge of attempting to communicate prescribed information to a person not authorised to receive it, contrary to Section 79(3) of the Crimes Act. The maximum penalty was two years' imprisonment. The offender was a 19-year-old probationary trainee at the Australian Security Intelligence Organisation (ASIO) who had undertaken a misguided personal practical experiment to ascertain whether a response could be obtained to an overture to a foreign agency. He was stopped before the communication could be sent. He was not motivated by disloyalty, but by a desire to outperform other trainees. He was of very good character. He was sentenced to three months' imprisonment to serve one month and enter into a recognisance to be of good behaviour.

(217.) *R vs Lappas* [2003] ACTCA 21; 152 ACTR 7 involved an intelligence analyst who befriended a sex worker. He gave the sex worker a TOP SECRET report so that she could sell it to a particular foreign power. Annotations made by Mr Lappas on the document 'tended to reveal sources of ongoing intelligence'. He then initiated contact with representatives of foreign countries to attempt to sell it. He also photocopied two even more sensitive documents and gave them to the sex worker to sell. He was found guilty of espionage contrary to Section 78(1)(b) of the Crimes Act, which carried a maximum penalty of seven years' imprisonment, and Section 79(3), unauthorised communication of a prescribed document, which carried a maximum penalty of two years' imprisonment.

(218.) The espionage offence required that the offender be acting 'for a purpose intended to be prejudicial to the safety or defence of the Commonwealth or a part of the Queen's dominions'. He was about 25 years old at the time of the offences. He was found to be suffering from significant mental illness at the time of the offending. He was sentenced to two years' imprisonment for the espionage count and six months' imprisonment for disclosing a prescribed document. The total sentence was 27 months' imprisonment, to serve six months prior to release on a recognisance to be of good behaviour.

(219.) *R vs Kessing* (District Court (NSW), Bennet DCJ, 22 June 2007, unrep) involved a former Australian Customs Service Officer who provided two documents about Sydney Airport to journalists. The charge was under Section 70 of the Crimes Act and carried a maximum penalty of two years' imprisonment. The documents related to drug offences and breaches of airport security that had not been reported or otherwise addressed. The documents were sensitive and confidential and could compromise law enforcement operations and methodology. As a result of the disclosure, the Commonwealth Government appointed a committee which recommended increased airport security. The offender was motivated by a sense of injustice and frustration at the lack of security. He had no contrition. He had no prospects of rehabilitation from the current type of offending. He was otherwise of good character and was 59 years old. He was given a suspended sentence of nine months' imprisonment.

(220.) *R vs Seivers and O'Ryan* (Supreme Court (ACT), Gray J, 10 June 2009, unrep) involved a contravention of Section 18(2) of the Australian Security Intelligence Organisation Act 1979 (Cth) which carried a maximum penalty of two years' imprisonment. It involved disclosure of documents marked 'confidential' or not marked at all. Mr Seivers brought the documents home to prepare for a Senate inquiry. Mr O'Ryan, on his own initiative, copied them and sent them to four different news organisations. The documents had the capacity to prejudice Australia's national security as well as the functions of ASIO. Mr Seivers demonstrated no contrition but was of good character. Mr O'Ryan showed contrition and had been motivated by a desire to make public certain matters related to the Bali Bombings. Both received a sentence of imprisonment of 12 months, with six months to be served by periodic detention and the balance suspended. Mr Seivers' conviction was set aside on appeal: *Seivers vs The Queen* [2010] ACTCA 9.

(221.) *R vs Johns* (a pseudonym) [2019] ACTSC 399 was a case in which the offender entered pleas of guilty to a number of offences which bear some similarity to those in the present case. The difficulty is that the judgment has been so heavily redacted it is not possible to say what offences were committed or to describe the circumstances of the offending. It is therefore not possible to determine the maximum penalties for the offences which were committed and hence how the seriousness of the offences was assessed against that yardstick. The aggregate sentence of imprisonment was two years and seven months. The motivation for the offending was anger over what the offender considered to be unfair treatment. The risk of harm arising from the conduct involved the possibility of 'critical harm to Australia's national security' and 'quite grave' risks to individuals.

(222.) The most obvious point to be made about these cases is that all except for Lappas and possibly Johns involve a maximum penalty of two years' imprisonment, and this has clear consequences for the length of the sentences ultimately imposed. Lappas did involve the espionage offence, which carried a maximum penalty of seven years' imprisonment and contained within it a purposive element not required as part of the present charges. Even the maximum penalty that applied in Lappas is very different from the unlimited maximum penalty available in the present case. Kessing involved an offender who was motivated by a sense of injustice and frustration in relation to the issue which he disclosed, but there appears to have been some evidence that his concerns were ultimately found to have substance as evidenced by the subsequent recommendations for increased security. None of the cases involved such substantial volumes of SECRET material as involved in the present case.

Consideration

(223.) In sentencing Mr McBride, it must be recognised that the unlimited term of imprisonment that may be imposed for offending against Section 73A has to accommodate circumstances much more extreme than those that exist in the present case. It must accommodate offending which involves the disclosure of extremely damaging naval, military or air force information in circumstances, such as war, where Australia is under immediate military threat. Recognition of that fact means that, notwithstanding that the objective seriousness of the offending can be characterised as in the mid-range, any sentence imposed on Mr McBride must accommodate the need for much more severe sentences in other cases committed in more extreme circumstances.

(224.) The nature and circumstances of the offences (Section 16A(2)(a)) and the manner in which it involved a course of conduct (Section 16A(2)(c)) have been described above.

(225.) I will take into account the charge on the Section 16BA schedule in relation to count 3, in accordance with the principles outlined in *R vs Campbell* [2010] ACTCA 20 at [47]–[48] (Section 16A(2)(b)).

(226.) The extent to which there has been harm arising from the offences (Section 16A(2)(e)) is also described above.

(227.) As pointed out earlier, the offender has shown no contrition for his offending (Section 16A(2)(f)).

(228.) I have taken into account the fact of his guilty plea, its timing and the degree to which that has resulted in benefit to the community through the avoidance of the need for a trial (Section 16A(2)(g)). I have also addressed above the extent of his cooperation with law enforcement agencies through his participation in the two interviews with police (Section 16A(2)(h)).

(229.) It is necessary to give consideration to the need for both specific and general deterrence (Sections 16A(2)(j) and (ja)). General deterrence is clearly of very significant importance in the circumstances of this case. The system for security classification and the protection of material from disclosure is fundamental to the operation of government institutions. That is even more the case when dealing with military information. It is of greater significance when that information involves active conflicts such as that with which the Special Forces were concerned in Afghanistan.

(230.) Undoubtedly, a large organisation has the capacity to generate tensions and frustrations for those operating within it. That is particularly so when it is a disciplined force and that force is involved in life or death military conflicts. However, the Army was the institution that Mr McBride chose to serve. That comes with it both privileges and constraints, particularly when he was not only a soldier but also a lawyer. Mr McBride was not prepared to operate within the constraints of the organisation which he had taken an oath to serve. I do not accept his statements that somehow, either as a lawyer or a soldier, he had an obligation or duty to do what he did. He very clearly breached his duty as both. His statements to the contrary made to police did not reflect reality.

(231.) Notwithstanding the availability of other legitimate means by which he could raise his concerns, he decided that he knew best and that he should disregard his legal obligations in order to pursue his own view of how the ADF should be managed. It is very important to deter others from such conduct. Self-confident people with strong opinions who are subject to legal duties not to disclose information must be deterred from making disclosures in order to advance their own opinions. They must know that breaching their legal obligations to maintain the confidentiality which they have undertaken to protect will be met by significant punishment. That is particularly so when that information is secret and its disclosure has the potential to harm Australia's national security.

(232.) Recognising the importance of general deterrence, its significance (and the significance of some of the other purposes of sentencing) may be lessened where a disclosure is made that is recognised as in the public interest or in circumstances where legitimate means of addressing the matters of concern were not available. It is important to note that no attempt was made in the sentencing proceedings either to establish that Mr McBride's thefts or disclosures were somehow in the public interest or that the legitimate and lawful means by which Mr McBride could have raised his concerns were inadequate.

(233.) The need for specific deterrence is somewhat less than that for general deterrence. It is, however, significant that the offender has no remorse and still considers that he did the right thing. Mr McBride needs to be deterred from any further disclosures of military information which he learned during his service as a soldier.

(234.) Two factors qualify the need for specific deterrence. First, it is unlikely that he will be placed in any position of equivalent trust in government or the military in the future. Despite that, the intensive correction order assessment report makes reference to him continuing to practice as a solicitor, a situation in which compliance with obligations of confidentiality remains fundamental. Second, it is clear that the process of being subject to criminal charges has had a substantial impact upon him (and thereby his family) and this will tend to have a deterrent effect upon him which reduces the significance of specific deterrence in the sentence.

(235.) The sentence must ensure that he is adequately punished for his offending (Section 16A(2)(k)). Punishment must adequately reflect the importance of the obligations which were breached. In relation to count 3, the sentence must take into account that there will be no punishment for the conduct the subject of the Section 16BA schedule offence.

(236.) The relevant aspects of his character, antecedents, age, means and physical or mental condition have been described earlier in these reasons (Section 16A(2)(m)). So far as his mental condition at the time of the offending and today are concerned, I have accepted Mr Borenstein's conclusion that during the offending Mr McBride suffered from a number of mental health conditions. I also accept Mr Borenstein's evidence that his present condition has improved with psychiatric and psychological treatment as well as exercise. I have concluded, despite Mr McBride's statement to the contrary, that his mental health conditions made a material, albeit minor and indirect, contribution to his offending conduct. That is relevant to his moral culpability but only in a minor way. I do not consider that his mental health conditions have any significant consequence for the suitability of his sentence as a vehicle for general deterrence or the need for specific deterrence. I also accept Mr Borenstein's evidence that there is a risk of deterioration of his condition if incarcerated and that includes a risk of a significant deterioration. It is not possible to quantify the extent of that risk. Having regard to the possibility of deterioration of his condition if he is incarcerated, I have taken into account the potential that, by reason of his mental health conditions, particularly the PTSD, a sentence of imprisonment may be more burdensome than it would otherwise be for a person without that condition.

(237.) Section 16A(2)(ma) requires consideration of whether the person's standing in the community was used by the person to aid in the commission of the offence. This was the subject of competing submissions by the parties. I do not think that this is the sort of case in which that specific consideration has effect. It was the position of trust in which he was placed as a result of being an officer in the Army that made it possible for him to commit the offences. The grave breach of trust involved in the offending must be taken into account. However, that is a different consideration to the specific consideration in paragraph (ma), which refers to 'standing in the community' as a means of engaging in other offending.

(238.) So far as his prospects of rehabilitation are concerned (Section 16A(2)(n)), that is difficult to assess in circumstances where Mr McBride has demonstrated no remorse and, as a consequence, has not recognised the wrongfulness of his own conduct. So far as this type of offending is concerned, his prospects of rehabilitation must be considered to be guarded because of his apparently unwavering belief in his own correctness and his willingness to commit serious breaches of the criminal law.

(239.) The imposition of a custodial sentence would have an adverse effect upon his family (Section 16A(2)(p)), most particularly his two daughters, although they are beyond an age where they would be most seriously affected by incarceration of their father. The imposition of an intensive correction order would require him to live in the ACT, away from his ex-wife and daughters. Such a disposition would be likely to have a lesser impact upon him and his family.

(240.) The sentences must also recognise the state of uncertainty in which the offender has lived since the charges were laid in September 2018 and March 2019. The delay in bringing the matter to trial was a product of the complexities of dealing with confidential information, the COVID-19 pandemic and the making, by Mr McBride, of the application under the PID Act which he subsequently abandoned.

(241.) Having regard to the fact that no maximum penalty is specified for an offence under Section 73A, it is necessary for the court to formulate a sentence in relation to each of counts 2 and 3 which appropriately reflects the purposes of sentencing and is of a severity appropriate in all the circumstances of the offence. As pointed out earlier in these reasons, the unlimited term of imprisonment available for a contravention of Section 73A cannot be characterised as a relic of the past (cf the quote in Markarian at [30]). On the other hand, it must be recognised that the very high penalties available under the Section must accommodate extremely serious disclosures in grave circumstances of a threat to the Australian nation.

(242.) The contention on behalf of Mr McBride was that, if a custodial penalty was to be imposed, it should be of a length which could be served by an intensive correction order. On the other hand, the submission put by the Crown was that a custodial sentence requiring full-time imprisonment should be imposed along with a non-parole period.

(243.) The starting point must be consideration of whether or not the threshold in Section 17A of the Crimes Act has been passed. I am satisfied that the seriousness of the offending is such that, having considered the other available alternatives, no sentence other than a sentence of imprisonment is appropriate. I do not consider that a sentence other than imprisonment would appropriately satisfy the purposes of sentencing.

(244.) So far as individual sentences are concerned, having incorporated a 10 percent reduction on account of the plea of guilty (referred to at [203] above) the appropriate sentences are as follows:

(a) Count 2: a sentence of 34 months' imprisonment;

(b) Count 3: a sentence of 34 months' imprisonment (having taken into account the Section 16BA offence); and

(c) Count 1: a sentence of 27 months' imprisonment.

(245.) The sentences on count 2 and count 3 are the same, notwithstanding that count 2 involved disclosure to two different journalists, because the disclosure to Mr Oakes involved the disclosure of additional documents.

(246.) It is next necessary to consider the structure of the sentence, which includes consideration of the issue of totality. Notwithstanding the submissions made on behalf of Mr McBride, I do not consider that this is a case in which wholly concurrent sentences would be appropriate. It is not a case where the criminality of one offence was sufficiently comprised within the criminality of another offence so as to warrant making them wholly concurrent: cf *Nguyen vs The Queen* [2016] HCA 17; 256 CLR 656 at [62]. Rather, while the offences were related to some extent, each involved additional criminality beyond the others. Therefore, while there is room for a significant degree of concurrency, there must also be some cumulation. Count 2 will be imposed first. Count 3 will be cumulative as to 17 months, but otherwise concurrent. Count 1 will be cumulative as to 17 months upon count 3, but otherwise concurrent. This gives an aggregate sentence of imprisonment of 68 months, or five years and eight months.

(247.) The next question is how that sentence should be served. In considering this issue, I have had specific regard to the evidence of Mr Borenstein as to the possible consequences of a sentence of imprisonment for Mr McBride's mental health.

(248.) If the availability of an intensive correction order is to be assessed by reference to the aggregate sentence imposed then, clearly, one is not available because the aggregate sentence exceeds four years. However, I have previously held that the availability of an intensive correction order is to be assessed in relation to each individual sentence that is imposed, rather than the aggregate sentence: *DPP vs Vincent* (No 2) [2023] ACTSC 379 at [71]–[75]. Each of the sentences which I have imposed is below the four-year threshold. It is therefore necessary to consider the matters in Section 11(3) of the Crimes (Sentencing) Act 2005 (ACT) and determine whether the imposition of an intensive correction order is appropriate in the circumstances of the case. In my view, the level of harm done to the community caused by the offending is significant. Further, the offender's culpability for the offending having regard to all the circumstances is high. Given the nature of the offending and the aggregate sentence, I do not consider that it is appropriate that it be served by intensive correction. I consider that an intensive correction order would not adequately reflect the need for general deterrence, specific deterrence and punishment of the offender.

(249.) Given that the aggregate sentence exceeds three years, the appropriate means of serving the sentences is by full-time detention with a single non-parole period: Crimes Act, Section 19AB. The non-parole period will be a period of 27 months. Although representing a smaller than usual proportion of the head sentence, it nevertheless reflects the minimum period of full-time detention necessary to fulfil the purposes of sentencing. The lengthy period on parole will continue to provide a deterrent for any further offending.

Orders

(250.) For those reasons, the orders of the Court are:

1 On the charge of contravening Section 73A(1) of the Defence Act 1903 (Cth) (CAN 2897/2019), the offender is convicted and sentenced to imprisonment for 34 months, commencing on 14 May 2024 and ending on 13 March 2027.

2 On the charge of contravening Section 73A(1) of the Defence Act 1903 (Cth) (CAN 2899/2019), and having taken into account the charge of contravening Section 70(1) of the Crimes Act on the Section 16BA schedule (CAN 2900/2019), the offender is convicted and sentenced to imprisonment for 34 months, commencing on 14 October 2025 and ending on 13 August 2028.

3 On the charge of contravening Section 131.1(1) of the Criminal Code (Cth) (CAN 41388/2018), the offender is convicted and sentenced to imprisonment for 27 months, commencing on 14 October 2027 and ending on 13 January 2030.

4 The non-parole period commences on 14 May 2024 and ends on 13 August 2026.

I certify that the preceding two hundred and fifty [250] numbered paragraphs are a true copy of the Reasons for Sentence of his Honour Justice Mossop.

Associate:
Date: 31 May 2024

****

Amendments

31 May 2024 Orders 2 and 3 amended pursuant to Rule 6906 of the Court Procedures Rules 2006 (ACT)

(2025) I FLR 427 (Canada)

The Supreme Court of Canada

R vs Edwards

Case Numbers: 39820, 39822, 40046, 40065, 40103

Neutral Citation: 2024 SCC 15

Composition of Court: Wagner, CJ and Karakatsanis, Côté, Rowe, Kasirer, Jamal and O'Bonsawin, JJ (Seven Judge Bench)

Date of Decision: 26 April 2024

Counsel for the Appellants: Defence Counsel Services, Gatineau

Counsel for the Respondent: Canadian Military Prosecution Service, Ottawa

Summary

In *Edwards,* the issue is whether the National Defence Act's (NDA) requirement that military judges be military officers infringes on the right to a hearing by an independent and impartial tribunal. The appeals in this case were brought by nine members of the Canadian Armed Forces who were accused of various service offences under the Code of Service Discipline. Their cases were tried before a court-martial with a military judge presiding. The appellants argued that "military judges who are part of a chain of command cannot be truly independent," and there is no absolute independence within such a military tribunal like the civilian criminal court system. Writing for the majority, Justice Kasirer analyses judicial independence for military judges with the conditions of security of tenure, financial security, and administrative independence. The Court concludes that Canada's system of military justice ensures judicial independence for military judges in a way that takes account for concerns of the judge simultaneously being an officer.

Headnotes

Facts: Nine members of the Canadian Armed Forces were charged with various service offences under the Code of Service Discipline (CSD). Before the court-martial, they challenged the statutory requirement under the NDA that judges presiding over courts-martial be military officers, alleging that it violates their right to trial by an independent and impartial tribunal. Some judges of the courts-martial ruled in favour of the accused by holding that the statutory requirement of military judges presiding over court-martials violates the right to trial by an independent and impartial tribunal. On appeal, the Court Martial Appeal Court reversed the decision of the court-martial. Aggrieved by the order of the Appeal Court, the accused approached the Supreme Court of Canada.

Issue: Whether the statutory requirement under the NDA that courts-martial be presided-over by military judges violates the right to trial by an independent and impartial tribunal under section 11(d) of the Canadian Charter of Rights and Freedoms?

Contentions of the Parties: The appellants contended that the statutory requirement of military judges presiding over courts-martial violates the right to trial by an independent and impartial tribunal because: i) military judges being part of the chain of command are prone to interference/influence by their hierarchical superiors and to prosecution and subsequent removal under the CSD; ii) the dual status of military judges as judicial officers as well as military officers raises a reasonable apprehension of bias in the mind of "an informed person, viewing the matter realistically and practically" as it violates the constitutional imperative of separation of powers and; iii) the scheme under the NDA fails to ensure sufficient independence of military judges and hence, should be declared to be of no effect.

The respondent argued that the independence of military judges is sufficiently protected under the NDA as: i) the status of military judges as officers does not, in itself, violate s. 11(d); ii) the military judicial system conforms to the hallmarks of judicial independence as military judges have security of tenure, financial security and administrative independence under the NDA and; iii) military judges being subject to prosecution under the CSD does not adversely impact their judicial independence.

Held:

Majority Opinion

A. Court-martial proceedings – Independence thereof – Whether statutory requirement of appointment of military officers as judges violates the right to trial before an independent and impartial forum

- Held, a reasonable and informed person would not conclude that the officer status of military judges amounts to a lack of sufficient independence such that there is a breach of the right to a trial by an independent and impartial forum – Military justice system fulfils the grounds necessary for independence of a judicial forum: i) security of tenure, ii) financial security and, iii) administrative independence – The first ground of security of tenure is guaranteed as the NDA provides that military judges are appointed by Governor-in-Council and they hold office till the age of 60 years except in cases of voluntary resignation or removal for cause by the Governor-In-Council upon recommendation of the Military Judges Inquiry Committee (MJIC) – The second ground of financial security is fulfilled as a remuneration scheme and compensation for military judges is fixed through a process centred on an independent committee – The final ground of administrative independence is also fulfilled as matters relating to assignment of military judges to preside at court martials or establishing rules of procedure are in the hands of military judges, including the Chief Military Officer and are insulated from non-judicial interference by the chain of command.

B. Court-martial proceedings – Independence thereof – Military judges being members of the executive while acting in their capacity of military officers if results in a conflict of interest with their judicial role

- Held, military judges as members of the executive while acting in their capacity of military officers are not in an irretrievable conflict of interest with their judicial role – Duties so assigned to military judges by the Chief Military Officer are of such nature that they are not incompatible with their judicial duties – A reasonable and informed person would expect military judges to act impartially and recuse themselves in case of apprehension of influence – Military judges, similar to judges under the civilian criminal justice system, take an oath of office to act impartially – Moreover, they are required to have adequate legal training (requirement of standing as a barrister for at least 10 years) in addition to military training (requirement of having served as a military officer for at least 10 years).

C. Court-martial proceedings – Independence thereof – Military judges being prone to prosecution under the CSD if creates apprehension of interference/influence by superior officers

- Held, reasonable and informed person would not be concerned that military judges being prone to prosecution under the CSD while acting in their role as military officers undermines their independence – Though military judges liable to prosecution under CSD for acts of dereliction of duty in their capacity of a member of armed forces, it does not create an apprehension that they are prone to interference by their superiors – Statutory safeguards present: the person who seeks to initiate prosecution against a presiding military judge must receive legal advice concerning the appropriate charge – Also, the Director of Military Prosecutions (DMP), which makes the decision of proceeding with the charges, has an obligation to act independently of partisan concerns.

Dissenting Opinion by Karakatsanis, J

<u>Held:</u>

A. Court-martial proceedings – Independence thereof – Military judges as part of the chain of command whether prone to influence/interference by their superiors while imparting their judicial duties

- Observed, military judges are subjected to pressure and influence as part of chain of command and hence, the legislative scheme under the NDA should be declared of no force or effect insofar as it subjects military judges to the disciplinary process administered by military authorities - Prosecution under the CSD can be initiated by hierarchical superiors to disrupt their judicial functions – Disciplinary process administered by military authorities undermines judicial independence of military judges - Not enough institutional separation or independence between the executive and the legislature - Military judges face a unique disciplinary regime that is launched and prosecuted by the executive, which has no equivalent in the civilian world - Independent reports, which provide material insight on the concerns of a reasonable and informed member of the public, have long insisted that military judges, who currently keep the rank they held before their judicial appointment, should be awarded their own distinct rank, or civilianized.

B. Court-martial proceedings – Independence thereof – Apprehension of bias by a reasonable and informed person

- Observed, the safeguards said to alleviate the risk that military judges would feel pressure to be loyal towards the chain of command are insufficient – A reasonable and informed observer would therefore be concerned about institutional bias because military judges could face disciplinary action from their superiors aimed at interfering with their judicial functions - Firstly, the statutory requirement of taking an oath of office, though an important foundation for an individual judge's independence, does little to guard against an apprehension of institutional bias – Secondly, military judges do not enjoy security of tenure as upon conviction for a disciplinary offence (the prosecution for which may be initiated by their superiors), the demolition or dismissal from the Armed Forces follows – Thirdly, the presumption that the DMP will carry out its functions independently is insufficient to ensure judicial independence; the DMP is not independent of the chain of command as it works under the supervision of the Judge Advocate General and hence, it may be influenced by partisan concerns.

Case laws cited

By Kasirer J.:

Applied: R. vs Généreux, [1992] 1 S.C.R. 259; *Valente vs The Queen,* [1985] 2 S.C.R. 673; *Committee for Justice and Liberty vs National Energy Board,* [1978] 1 S.C.R. 369;

Considered: *MacKay vs The Queen*, [1980] 2 S.C.R. 370; *R. vs Stillman*, 2019 SCC 40, [2019] 3 S.C.R. 144; R. vs *Pett*, 2020 CM 4002; *R. vs D'Amico*, 2020 CM 2002;

Referred to: *R. vs Lippé*, [1991] 2 S.C.R. 114; *R. vs Kirkpatrick*, 2022 SCC 33; *R. vs Chouhan*, 2021 SCC 26, [2021] 2 S.C.R. 136; Reference re Public Service Employee Relations Act (Alta.), [1987] 1 S.C.R. 313; *Re B.C. Motor Vehicle Act*, [1985] 2 S.C.R. 486; *Wewaykum Indian Band vs Canada*, 2003 SCC 45, [2003] 2S.C.R. 259; *Miglin vs Miglin*, 2003 SCC 24, [2003] 1 S.C.R. 303; *Yukon Francophone School Board, Education Area #23 vs Yukon (Attorney General)*, 2015 SCC 25, [2015] 2 S.C.R. 282; *Cojocaru vs British Columbia Women's Hospital and Health Centre*, 2013 SCC 30, [2013] 2 S.C.R. 357; *Canada (Minister of Citizenship and Immigration) vs Tobiass*, [1997] 3 S.C.R. 391; *British Columbia (Attorney General) vs Provincial Court Judges' Association of British Columbia*, 2020 SCC 20, [2020] 2 S.C.R. 506; *Conférence des juges de paix magistrats du Québec vs Quebec* (Attorney General), 2016 SCC 39, [2016] 2 S.C.R. 116; Reference re Remuneration of Judges of the Provincial Court of Prince Edward Island, [1997] 3 S.C.R. 3; *R. vs Wigglesworth*, [1987] 2 S.C.R. 541; 2747-3174 *Québec Inc. vs Quebec* (Régie des permis d'alcool), [1996] 3 S.C.R. 919; *Ell vs Alberta*, 2003 SCC 35, [2003] 1 S.C.R. 857; *Application under s.* 83.28 of the Criminal Code (Re), 2004 SCC 42, [2004] 2 S.C.R. 248; *R. vs Leblanc*, 2011 CMAC 2, 7 C.M.A.R. 559; *Moreau-Bérubé vs New Brunswick (Judicial Council)*, 2002 SCC 11, [2002] 1 S.C.R. 249; Therrien (Re), 2001 SCC 35, [2001] 2 S.C.R. 3; *Canada (Director of Military Prosecutions) vs Canada (Office of the Chief Military Judge)*, 2020 FC 330, [2020] 3 F.C.R. 411; *Nova Scotia (Attorney General) vs Judges of the Provincial Court and Family Court of Nova Scotia*, 2020 SCC 21, [2020] 2 S.C.R. 556; R. vs Kokopenace, 2015 SCC 28, [2015] 2 S.C.R. 398; R. vs Teskey, 2007 SCC 25, [2007] 2 S.C.R. 267; *President of the Republic of South Africa vs South African Rugby Football Union*, [1999] ZACC 9, 1999 (7) B.C.L.R. 725; *R. vs Moriarity*, 2015 SCC 55, [2015] 3 S.C.R. 485; *R. vs Billard*, 2008 CMAC 4, 7 C.M.A.R. 238; *R. vs Finta*, [1994] 1 S.C.R. 701; *R. vs Lalande*, 2011 CM 2005; *R. vs Liwyj*, 2010 CMAC 6, 7 *C.M.A.R.* 481; *R. vs Edmunds*, 2018 *CMAC* 2, 8 *C.M.A.R.* 260; *R. vs Cawthorne*,2016 SCC 32, [2016] 1 S.C.R. 983; *Boucher vs The Queen*, [1955] S.C.R. 16; *R. vs Nur*, 2015 SCC 15, [2015] 1 S.C.R. 773.

By Karakatsanis J. (dissenting):

R. vs Généreux, [1992] 1 S.C.R. 259; *Valente vs The Queen*, [1985] 2 S.C.R. 673; *R. vs Pett*, 2020 CM 4002; *R. vs D'Amico*, 2020 CM 2002; R. *vs Bourque*, 2020 CM 2008; *R. vs MacPherson and Chauhan and J.L.*, 2020 CM 2012; *R. vs Cogswell*, 2020 CM 2014; *R. vs Jacques*, 2020 CM 3010; *R. vs Pépin*, 2021 CM 3005; *Ocean Port Hotel Ltd. vs British Columbia (General Manager, Liquor Control and Licensing Branch)*, 2001 SCC 52, [2001] 2 S.C.R. 781; Beauregard *vs Canada*, [1986] 2 S.C.R. 56; 2747-3174 *Québec Inc. vs Quebec (Régie des permis d'alcool)*, [1996] 3 S.C.R. 919; *IWA vs Consolidated-Bathurst Packaging Ltd., [1990] 1 S.C.R. 282; Reference re Remuneration of Judges of the Provincial Court of Prince Edward Island*, [1997] 3 S.C.R. 3; *References re Greenhouse Gas Pollution Pricing Act*, 2021 SCC 11, [2021] 1 S.C.R. 175; *Mackin vs New Brunswick (Minister of Finance)*, 2002 SCC 13, [2002] 1 S.C.R. 405; *MacKeigan vs Hickman*, [1989] 2 S.C.R. 796; *R. vs Lippé*, [1991] 2 S.C.R. 114; *British Columbia vs Imperial Tobacco Canada Ltd.*, 2005 SCC 49, [2005] 2 S.C.R. 473; *Application under s. 83.28 of the Criminal Code* (Re), 2004 SCC 42, [2004] 2 S.C.R. 248; *Moreau-Bérubé vs New Brunswick (Judicial Council)*, 2002 SCC 11, [2002] 1 S.C.R. 249; Therrien (Re), 2001 SCC 35, [2001] 2 S.C.R. 3; *R. vs Golzari*, 2017 CMAC 3, 8 C.M.A.R. 106; *MacKay vs The Queen*, [1980] 2 S.C.R. 370; *R. vs Stillman*, 2019 SCC 40, [2019] 3 S.C.R. 144; *Canada (Director of Military Prosecutions) vs Canada (Office of the Chief Military Judge)*, 2020 FC 330, [2020] 3 F.C.R. 411; *R. vs Cawthorne*, 2016 SCC 32, [2016] 1 S.C.R. 983; *R. vs Nur*, 2015 SCC 15, [2015] 1 S.C.R. 773; *R. vs Anderson*, 2014 SCC 41, [2014] 2 S.C.R. 167; *R. vs Appulonappa*, 2015 SCC 59, [2015] 3 S.C.R. 754; *R. vs Bain*, [1992] 1 S.C.R. 91; *R. vs Oakes*, [1986] 1 S.C.R. 103.

JUDGMENT

The judgment can be accessed at this link: https://decisions.scc-csc.ca/scc-csc/scc-csc/en/item/20408/index.do

The text of the judgment is not being reproduced in FLR since the Supreme Court of Canada does not permit reproduction of its judgments except on its own website/official publication"

(2025) I FLR 434 (New Zealand)

The High Court of New Zealand

CIV-2022-485-551

The General Manager of Veterans' Affairs New Zealand vs The Estate of Lieutenant Colonel Tā Harawira Gardiner KNZM

Composition of Court: McQueen J.

Date of Decision: 20 July 2023

Counsel for the Appellant: Mr. A.B. Goosen and T.L. Lamb

Counsel Assisting: R.L. Roff and S.W.H. Fletcher

Summary

The late Lieutenant Colonel Tā Harawira Gardiner was a member of the New Zealand Army who was deployed in Vietnam during the Vietnam War between 1969 and 1970. In 2021, he approached the Veterans' Affairs New Zealand (VANZ) to claim for disablement pension under the Veterans' Support Act, 2014 (the Act) on the ground that he had contracted glioblastoma, a disease of the brain, while he was in service in Vietnam. He was granted relief by the Veterans' Entitlements Appeal Board (Appeal Board), whose decision was challenged by the VANZ before the High Court. The Court refrained from making any substantial comments on the merits of Tā Harawira's claim and instead, settled the questions of law raised in the appeal to the effect that the procedure prescribed under section 14 of the Act was held as not being exhaustive, and a benevolent approach while considering any claims under the Act was encouraged. Also, the *Kenyon* decision rendered under the now-repealed War Pensions Act, 1954 was held to be relevant to claims raised under the 2014 Act as the latter is broadly based on the same principles as the former. The matter was remanded back to the Appeal Board for a reconsideration of the claim, in accordance with the questions of law settled by the Court.

Headnotes

Facts: Lieutenant Colonel Tā Harawira Gardiner served in the New Zealand Army from 11 January, 1963 to 12 July, 1983. From 4 June 1969 to 8 May 1970, he was deployed in Vietnam under "qualifying operational service" (service in a war or emergency). In 2021, he was diagnosed with glioblastoma, a disease of the brain. This disease was contracted by several veterans who had served in the Vietnam War suspected as due to being exposed to Agent Orange, a chemical herbicide. Subsequently, Tā Harawira applied for disablement pension before the VANZ under the Act. The Decision Officer and the Review Officer did not consider his condition of glioblastoma to be service-related, and his claim for disablement pension was dismissed. On appeal against the decision of the Review Officer, the Appeal Board reversed the decision and held that Tā Harawira's condition is service-related, which entitles him to disablement pension under the Act. The present matter before the High Court arose through an appeal against the Appeal Board's decision.

Issues: 1. Does section 14 of the Act exhaustively state the process that must be followed by the Appeal Board in considering an appeal under the Act?

2. Whether the *Kenyon* decision can be considered as an 'equal claim' while adjudicating upon a claim under the Act?

3. Whether the Appeal Board erred in law in concluding that Tā Harawira Gardiner's claim for glioblastoma must be treated as a service-related condition under the Act?

Contentions of parties: The arguments put forth by the Appellant were: *firstly*, that the Appeal Board failed to follow the procedure prescribed for deciding claims for disablement pensions under section 14 of the Act as it wrongfully gave overriding effect to the principles governing the conduct of any person acting under the Act (like fair entitlements to veterans, equal treatment of equal claims, benevolent approach towards claims etc.) laid down under section 10(b) of the Act; secondly, that as glioblastoma is not mentioned in the list of illnesses/diseases for which the veterans who served in the Vietnam War are entitled to under the Veterans' Support Regulations, 2014 (the Regulations), the Appeal Board erred in presuming that the applicant was entitled to disablement pension; *thirdly*, that in light of the *Keelan vs General Manager, VANZ* ruling, the Appeal Board could not have relied upon the *Kenyon* decision rendered under the War Pensions Act, 1954 (which was repealed by the Veterans' Support Act, 2014), in which the applicant was held entitled to disablement pension for service-related glioblastoma.

The proceedings in this case were not adversarial in nature as the respondent did not wish to defend the decision on the basis of an argument they did not raise. Therefore, a counsel assisting was appointed by the court to contradict the statements put forth by the Appellant. The arguments put forth by the counsel assisting were: *firstly*, that the procedure prescribed under section 14 of the Act is not exhaustive. It must be interpreted in light of the broad scheme of the Act and the appeal must be decided on its merits, rather than on some technicality; while on the other hand the principles prescribed under section 10 are mandatory to be followed; *secondly*, that the *Kenyon* decision can be relied upon and considered as an 'equal claim' to the present case because the applicant in that case was also granted pension for glioblastoma, irrespective of the fact that it was rendered when the War Pensions Act, 1954 was in force. *Thirdly*, that the Appeal Board did not err in reaching the conclusion that Tā Harawira's disease of glioblastoma was service-related.

<u>Held:</u>

A. Procedure to be followed by the Appeal Board under the Veterans' Support Act, 2014 not exhaustive – Mandatory adherence to the principles prescribed under section 10

Held, that the procedure laid down under section 14 of the Act is not exhaustive. The legislative intent was not to let genuine claims for service-related diseases contracted by veterans to be defeated by mechanical adherence to section 14, but instead to ensure that each claim is decided on substantive grounds. The principle of benevolence entails that even if the factors laid down in the Statements of Principles (SOP) are not being fulfilled in a case, the primary question to be decided should still be whether there is a "reasonable hypothesis" that the condition is service-related. Merits and substantial justice, and not technicalities or legal rules hold precedence.

B. Precedential value of decisions rendered under the War Pensions Act, 1954 with respect to claims under the Veterans' Support Act, 2014 – What constitutes 'equal claim' – Keelan, differentiated

Held, that the *Kenyon* decision can be considered as an 'equal claim' to the present case. As the Veterans' Support Act, 2014 is essentially a continuation of the now-repealed War Pensions Act, 1954 and is broadly governed by the same principles, a decision rendered under the latter can be considered as an 'equal claim' for the purposes of a claim under the former. However, what constitutes an 'equal claim' must be decided upon a full consideration of the two claims and the surrounding circumstances, which would vary from case-to-case. Also, the *Keelan* decision cannot be interpreted as propounding a strict rule of law that a decision under the 1954 Act is not relevant while adjudicating a claim under the 2014 Act, as the main question in this case was that whether an interpretation of the 1954 Act could be superimposed on the 2014 Act; no specific claim was in question before the court. Holding that Keelan bars reliance upon decisions rendered under the 1954 Act would entail granting preference to legal technicalities over substantial justice, which would defeat the objective of the 2014 Act.

C. Matter remanded back to the Appeal Board for adjudication of the claim

Held, that the Appeal Board should reconsider Tā Harawira claim in light of the questions of law so settled by the Court. Though as a matter of law, it was open in principle to the Appeal Board to reach the verdict that Tā Harawira's condition of glioblastoma was service-related, their decision needs a reconsideration as it was not supported by clear reasons. Also, the Appeal Board being a specialist body, must be afforded an opportunity to reconsider the claim in light of the medical information by the Appellant, the Kenyon decision and other relevant information.

Case-laws cited

Keelan vs The General Manager of Veterans' Affairs New Zealand, [2016] NZHC 1869; Kenyon War Appeal 7, 19 December 2013.

JUDGMENT OF MCQUEEN J

(1.) This is an appeal on a question of law pursuant to Section 239 of the Veterans' Support Act 2014 (the Act), against a decision of the Veterans' Entitlements Appeal Board (the Appeal Board).

(2.) The General Manager of Veterans' Affairs New Zealand (the GMVA) appeals on the ground that the majority of the Appeal Board erred in law in concluding that the late Lt Col Tā Harawira Gardiner's claim for glioblastoma must be treated as a service-related condition under the Act.

(3.) I acknowledge the passing of Tā Harawira, a rangatira who gave a lifetime of service to Aotearoa New Zealand.[1]

(4.) This is an appeal that is effectively unopposed. Major Ross Himona, a long-time friend and colleague of Tā Harawira, and the Hon Hekia Parata, Tā Harawira's widow, as representative and executor respectively of Tā Harawira's estate, advised the Court that the estate did not wish to defend a decision made on the basis of an argument the estate did not raise, in a claim that was intended to be representative of all veterans. Accordingly, Ms Roff has been appointed as counsel assisting, to act as contradictor to the arguments of the GMVA.2 Ms Roff has provided submissions which contradict the GMVA's position on the law, but only to the extent appropriate to assist the Court. I thank Ms Roff for her assistance in this matter.

---

1. See Eulogy for Sir Harawira Tiri Gardiner – Tā Wira – (Te Kawa Mataaho | Public Service Commission dated 16 November 2022) < Eulogy for Sir Harawira Tiri Gardiner – Tā Wira - Te Kawa Mataaho Public Service Commission>.

2. Minute of Palmer J dated 10 October 2022.

(5.) For the reasons below, I consider that the appeal should be allowed, although not on the grounds advanced by the GMVA. In light of my findings, I direct the Appeal Board to consider again Tā Harawira's application for a disablement pension.

Background

Factual Background

(6.) The late Lieutenant Colonel Tā Harawira Gardiner served in the New Zealand Army between 11 January 1963 and 12 July 1983. Tā Harawira had 'qualifying routine service' from 11 January 1963 to 3 June 1969 and from 9 May 1970 to 31 March 1974 and 'qualifying operational service' in Vietnam from 4 June 1969 to 8 May 1970.[3]

(7.) Tā Harawira was diagnosed with glioblastoma on 28 July 2021. That is a condition that has been previously experienced by veterans who served in Vietnam, and were exposed to Agent Orange, a chemical herbicide used during the Vietnam War. On 3 September 2021, Tā Harawira applied for a disablement pension pursuant to Section 47(1) of the Act, which provides that a veteran who suffers disablement as a consequence of a service-related injury or illness is entitled to a disablement pension.

(8.) On 20 September 2021, Veterans' Affairs New Zealand (VANZ), through its Decision Officer, declined to accept the claim for glioblastoma as a service-related condition. On 5 January 2022, Tā Harawira sought a review of that decision.

(9.) On 4 February 2022, the Review Officer upheld the Decision Officer's decision and declined to accept glioblastoma as a service-related condition on the grounds that:

(a.) Tā Harawira was not diagnosed during his operational service;

(b.) glioblastoma is not a presumptive condition for Vietnam; and

3. The terms 'qualifying routine service' and 'qualifying operational service' are defined in Section 8 of the Act.

(c.) no factor in the relevant Statement of Principles 'Malignant Neoplasm of the Brain (Reasonable Hypothesis) No. 85 of 2016' (SOP 85/2016) was met.

(10.) The estate of Tā Harawira filed an appeal against that decision dated 23 February 2023.

(11.) On 11 April 2022, the Appeal Board conducted a preliminary hearing to determine:

(a.) whether or not the review was properly conducted;

(b.) whether or not the review was in breach of Section 220(2) of the Act; and

(c.) whether or not the Review Officer's decision should be revoked.

(12.) On 27 April 2022, the Appeal Board:

(a.) found that the Review Officer breached Section 220(2) of the Act because he had previous involvement with the claim before being appointed Review Officer, and therefore lacked jurisdiction to conduct the review;

(b.) found the effect of the breach was the Review Officer's decision was a nullity;

(c.) revoked the decision under Section 237(1)(c) of the Act; and

(d.) directed that the appeal be set down for a substantive hearing before the Appeal Board.

(13.) That hearing took place on 17 June 2022, with the Appeal Board's decision issued on 14 July 2022. It is this decision that the GMVA appeals against.

The Relevant Law

The Act's Legislative History

(14.) The Act was enacted in 2014. It replaced the War Pensions Act 1954. The Act's purpose is to provide for:4

(a.) the rehabilitation of and support for veterans who, as a result of being placed in harm's way in the service of New Zealand, have been injured or become ill; and

(b.) entitlements for eligible veterans who suffer service-related injuries or illnesses; and

(c.) entitlements and support for eligible spouses, partners, children, and dependants of veterans with service-related injuries or illnesses and for other persons who provide non-professional support to those veterans.

(15.) The main impetus for the Act's passage was the need to replace the War Pensions Act, which was designed for the needs of veterans of the Second World War.[5] The War Pensions Act did not reflect modern understandings of psychological and environmental trauma. Nor had it been amended to reflect the introduction of the accident compensation scheme in 1974. The Act was intended to give effect to the recommendations of Te Aka Matua o te Ture o Aotearoa | Law Commission (the Law Commission) in its report *A New Support Scheme for Veterans: A Report on the Review of the War Pensions Act 1954*.[6]

(16.) The principles and decision-making presumptions of the War Pensions Act were not to be different in the Act.[7] This was emphasised by the responsible

---

4. Veterans' Support Act 2014, Section 3(1). Section 3(2) goes on to specify that the purpose of pt 2 of the Act is to promote positive veteran and claimant interaction with Veterans' Affairs New Zealand through the development and operation of a Code of Veterans' and Other Claimants' Rights.

5. Veteran's Support Bill 2013 (158–1) (explanatory note) at 1.

6. Te Aka Matua o te Ture o Aotearoa | Law Commission *A New Support Scheme for Veterans: A Report on the Review of the War Pensions Act 1954 (NZLC R115, 2010).*

7. Veteran's Support Bill 2013 (158–1) (explanatory note) at 2.

Minister when the Veterans' Support Bill was introduced.[8] This thread was also present in the Law Commission's report. That report provided that the legislation replacing the War Pensions Act should be guided by the following principles:[9]

'**Community responsibility** – Veterans put themselves in harm's way during service on behalf of the nation. The community therefore has a reciprocal responsibility to look after veterans and their families if they are injured or killed. This is an enduring obligation.

Fair entitlements – A fair entitlement scheme should provide for greater entitlements than are available to other New Zealanders, and include:

- Compensatory payments for the effects on a veteran's quality of life caused by injury or disease attributable to service;
- Income support or replacement where a veteran's injury or disease affects his or her ability to earn money by working;
- Rehabilitation services, including medical support and services and support based on a veteran's needs; and
- Compensation and income support payments to eligible family members upon the death or serious impairment of a veteran.

Equality – There should be equal treatment of equal claims.

Decision-making criteria should be clear.

Benevolent approach to claims – In considering veterans' claims for entitlements, beneficial evidential provisions should be applied to veterans.

Administrative efficiency – The scheme should be as simple as possible and should aim to minimise delays. It should not replicate existing structures.

Affordability – The scheme should be affordable in terms of the community's expectations and priorities. This concept should encompass sustainability and resource efficiency.'

---

8. (22 October 2013) 694 NZPD 14102.

9. See Law Commission, above n 6, at [1.3].

Claims, Reviews and Appeals under the Act

(17.) Section 47 of the Act provides that a veteran who suffers a disablement as a consequence of a service-related injury or illness is entitled to a disablement pension. This is one of the entitlements available under the Act. Section 7 of the Act provides a definition of 'veteran'. There is no dispute in this case that Tā Harawira was a veteran as defined. Section 48 of the Act provides for veterans to apply to VANZ for a disablement pension. 'Service-related' is defined in Section 7 as 'in relation to an injury, an illness, a condition, or a whole-person impairment, means an injury, an illness, or a whole-person impairment caused by, contributed to by, or aggravated by qualifying service'.10

(18.) The entitlements for which a veteran may be eligible depends on their service. 'Qualifying operational service' means service on any deployment treated as a war or emergency for the purposes of the War Pensions Act, or service on any deployment declared to be operational service under Section 9 of the Act.[11] 'Qualifying routine service' means service in the armed forces before 1 April 1974 that is not qualifying operational service.[12] 'Qualifying service' means qualifying operational service or qualifying routine service.[13]

(19.) Operational service relates to a deployment which the Minister is satisfied poses a significant risk of harm to the members deployed, and is declared as such by the Minister.14 The Chief of Defence Force advises the Minister for the purpose of making such decisions.[15]

(20.) Section 215 of the Act permits a veteran or other claimant to apply for a review of a decision by VANZ. A review officer may conduct such a review.16 A review officer must decide the review on the basis of

10. See Veterans' Support Act 2014, Section 7, which also defines 'service-related death'.

11. Section 8(2).

12. Section 8(2).

13. Section 8(2).

14. Section 9(3).

15. Section 9(1).

16. Veterans' Support Act 2014, Section 219.

the substantive merits under the Act.17 Section 220(2) prohibits a review officer from conducting a review if they have had any previous involvement with the claim. Section 228 permits a review decision to be appealed to the Appeal Board. Such an appeal is 'a *de novo* appeal'.18 Section 229(5) requires the Appeal Board to comply with the principles of natural justice, the principles specified in Section 10(b), any other relevant provisions of the Act, and any Regulations made under Section 265 of the Act. A determination of the Appeal Board may be appealed to the High Court only on a question of law, pursuant to Section 239.

Approach to Deciding Claims under the Act

(21.) Section 10 of the Act provides principles for how functions are to be performed and how powers are to be exercised under the Act. It is a provision that accords with the principles preferred by the Law Commission, as noted above, by providing:[19]

> 'Every person who performs any function or exercises any power under this Act must do so—
>
> (a.) in acknowledgement, on behalf of the community, of the reponsibility for the injury, illness, or death of veterans as a result of them being placed in harm's way in the service of New Zealand; and
>
> (b.) in accordance with the following principles:
>
> (i.) the principle of providing fair entitlements to veterans and other claimants;
>
> (ii.) the principle of promoting equal treatment of equal claims;
>
> (iii.) the principle of taking a benevolent approach to claims;
>
> (iv.) the principle of determining claims—

17. Section 220(3)(a).

18. Section 229(1).

19. Section 10.

A. in accordance with substantial justice and the merits of the claim; and

B. not in accordance with any technicalities, legal forms, or legal rules of evidence.'

(22.) Section 12 provides that VANZ must perform its functions and exercise its powers on reasonable grounds and in a timely manner, having regard to the requirements of the Act, the nature of the function or power and all the circumstances.

(23.) Sections 14 and 15 set out a sequential process for how claims to entitlements are to be decided under the Act. This may be summarised as follows:

(a.) The first step is to consider all of the relevant available material and decide whether the material is consistent with a hypothesis that the veteran's injury, illness, or death was service-related.[20]

(b.) If the relevant available material is consistent with such a hypothesis, the second step is to decide whether there is a 'statement of principles'[21] that applies.[22] If there is no applicable statement of principles, then Section 15 applies.[23]

(c.) If there is a statement of principles that applies, the third step is to decide whether the hypothesis is consistent with the statement of principles.[24]

(d.) If the hypothesis is consistent with the statement of principles, the fourth step is to accept the claim, unless there are reasonable grounds for believing that the veteran's injury, illness, or death was

20. Veterans' Support Act 2014, Section 14(2).

21. Section 14(7). In Sections 14 and 15, a 'Statement of Principles' means a Statement of Principles that, under Sections 22(6) and Regulations made under Section 265, applies for the purpose of the Act.

22. Section 14(3).

23. Section 14(4).

24. Section 14(5).

not service-related.[25]

(e.) In circumstances where there is no applicable statement of principles, the person deciding whether to accept the claim must decide whether the claim is consistent with a hypothesis that is reasonable.[26] A hypothesis is reasonable if it is more than a possibility, consistent with known facts, and not inconsistent with proved or known scientific facts.[27]

(f.) If the claim is consistent with a hypothesis that is reasonable, then the claim must be accepted, unless there are reasonable grounds for believing that the veteran's injury, illness, or death was not service-related.[28]

(24.) Section 16 provides that the process set out in Sections 14 and 15 applies to the extent that it is not modified or overtaken by the presumptions contained in Sections 17 to 21, or the provisions of Section 28. For present purposes, only Section 21 is relevant. Section 21 provides that regulations made on the recommendation of the Minister under Section 265 may specify injuries, illnesses, and conditions that must be treated as service-related if a veteran has been exposed to specific events, served in a specific place, or served over a particular time period, during qualifying operational service.

(25.) Relevant to the present case, therefore, is regulation 13 of the Veterans' Support Regulations 2014 (the Regulations), which applies to a veteran who served in Vietnam:[29]

(a.) at any time during the period beginning on 29 May 1964 and

(b.) with 41 Squadron RNZAF at any time during the period beginning on 1 January 1973 and ending on the close of 21 April 1975; or

25. Section 14(6).

26. Section 15(2).

27. Section 15(4).

28. Veterans' Support Act 2014, Section 15(3).

29. Veterans' Support Regulations 2014, Regulation 13(1).

(c.) as a member of the civilian surgical team at Qui Nhon Provincial State Hospital, Binh Dinh province at any time during the period beginning on 1 December 1963 and ending on the close of 31 March 1975.

(26.) Tā Harawira was a veteran to whom Regulation 13 applied, as he had qualifying operational service in Vietnam from 4 June 1969 to 8 May 1970. Regulation 13(2) provides that if a veteran to whom Regulation 13 applies suffers from an illness or condition described in Regulation 13(3), the illness or condition must be treated as service-related. However, glioblastoma does not appear in the list of illnesses and conditions contained in Regulation 13(3).

Statements of Principles under the Act

(27.) Statements of Principle (SOPs) are an important part of decision-making under the Act. SOPs are used in the assessment of whether a claimed condition can be attributed to a person's qualifying service. The Act expressly draws on SOPs already made by the Australian Repatriation Medical Authority, under the Veterans' Entitlements Act 1986 (Cth).

(28.) The application of these SOPs in New Zealand is determined by the Minister through the making of regulations pursuant to Section 265.[30] The scheme relating to SOPs envisages the Minister adopting the approach taken by the Australian Repatriation Medical Authority in most circumstances, emphasised by the direction that 'as soon as practicable', a new or revoked SOP should be reviewed and a report provided to the Minister so they may decide whether to apply or revoke a SOP.31

(29.) The Regulations also provide for the applicable statement of principles. Regulation 15 states that the SOPs contained in Schedule 1 of the Regulations apply for the purposes of the Act. Regulation 15(2) requires that the version of the SOP referred to in Schedule 1 in the column headed 'Reasonable hypothesis' is to be applied if a veteran's service-related injury,

30. Veterans' Support Act 2014, Section 22(6).

31. Sections 22 and 23.

illness, condition, whole-person impairment, or death relates to 'qualifying operational service'.

(30.) The relevant SOP in the present case is SOP 85/2016. Clause 9 of SOP 85/2016 states:

> **'9 Factors that must exist**
>
> At least one of the following factors must as a minimum exist before it can be said that a reasonable hypothesis has been raised connecting malignant neoplasm of the brain or death from malignant neoplasm of the brain with the circumstances of a person's relevant service:
>
> (1) having received a cumulative equivalent dose of at least 0.1 sievert of ionising radiation to the brain at least two years before the clinical onset of malignant neoplasm of the brain;
>
> (2) being infected with human immunodeficiency virus before the clinical onset of malignant neoplasm of the brain;
>
> (3) inability to obtain appropriate clinical management for malignant neoplasm of the brain.'

(31.) It is common ground that Tā Harawira's medical condition, glioblastoma, is a form of malignant neoplasm of the brain, but that none of the factors specified in Clause 9 applied to Tā Harawira.

The Kenyon Decision

(32.) Of some importance in the present case is the effect of a decision of the War Pensions Appeal Board (the WPAB), the Appeal Board's equivalent under the War Pensions Act.32 It is convenient to discuss it at this point.

(33.) This decision concerned William Kenyon, who appealed against a decision of the National Review Officer dated 9 September 2013 on the ground that his disabilities of glioblastoma and pulmonary embolism were attributable to or aggravated by his service. Mr Kenyon was a veteran who,

32. *Kenyon War Appeal 7, 19 December 2013.*

like Tā Harawira, had served in Vietnam and had experienced exposure to Agent Orange. Mr Kenyon's claim was initially denied for want of evidence that his illnesses were attributable to his service.

(34.) Section 17(3) of the War Pensions Act entitled an applicant to produce any evidence (whether strictly legal or not) to show that the condition that resulted in their disablement was possibly or probably attributable to or aggravated by their service with the forces in connection with any war or emergency. Section 17(3) further provided that if any reasonable evidence to that effect is produced by that applicant, a presumption that that condition was in fact attributable to or aggravated by their service was established. Thereafter, that presumption could be rebutted only by evidence that satisfied the WPAB that the condition was not so attributable or aggravated but was due entirely to other causes. This is a similar analysis to the procedure established by Section 15 of the Act.

(35.) The issue before the WPAB was whether there was reasonable evidence to show that Mr Kenyon's conditions were possibly or probably attributable to his service. The WPAB concluded that there was such reasonable evidence, and therefore allowed Mr Kenyon's appeal, notwithstanding that the presumptive lists for service in Vietnam (the equivalent of Regulation 13) did not include glioblastoma or pulmonary embolism. The evidence relied upon by the WPAB included that:

(a.) Mr Kenyon had never smoked, and there was no family history of his condition;

(b.) he had been exposed to Agent Orange during his service in Vietnam, and to the best of his knowledge had never been exposed to any other radiation or toxins, other than for his treatment;

(c.) his service was in connection with a war or emergency; and

(d.) medical evidence provided that Mr Kenyon's condition was the same as that suffered by American veterans who had served in Vietnam, as referred to in two United States cases cited to the WPAB.

The Appeal Board Decision under Appeal

(36.)The Appeal Board for the hearing of Tā Harawira's appeal comprised three members.[33] Ms Anderson was the chairperson, while Mr Griggs and Dr Holdaway were the other two members. The Appeal Board reached its decision by majority, with Ms Anderson dissenting. All three members approached the appeal differently. I summarise their reasoning below.

(37.) The submissions presented in support of the appeal raised several arguments. The first was that Tā Harawira's claim was lodged through Section 35 of the Legislation Act 2019 rather than under the Act. Reliance was also placed on the *Kenyon* decision, the United States and Australian contexts, the application of the reasonable hypothesis approach, and the principle of benevolence.

(38.) VANZ opposed the appeal on all grounds.

Ms Anderson's Reasons

(39.) Ms Anderson considered that Tā Harawira's claim had been made under the Act and that the claim was to be determined under the Act, stating:

> 'While Section 35 of the Legislation Act provides that powers exercised under repealed or amended legislation have continuing effect, that provision does not allow for new claims to bypass the VSA [the Act] statutory scheme for determining claims. The effect of Section 35 of the Legislation Act is to preserve any decision made under the WPA [War Pensions Act] as if that decision had been made under the VSA, provided that it could have been made under the VSA.'

(40.) Ms Anderson did not accept the argument that Tā Harawira's claim was required to receive equal treatment to claims made under the War Pensions Act in accordance with Section 10(b)(ii) of the Act. She accepted

33. The Appeal Board is established pursuant to Section 240 of the Act. Section 241 provides for the membership of the Appeal Board. Section 230(1) requires that every appeal must be heard by not fewer than three members, one of whom must be a medical practitioner and one the chairperson. Section 230(2) requires every appeal to be determined by a majority of the votes of the members hearing the appeal, and the chairperson has a casting vote if voting is equal.

that Section 10(b)(ii) of the Act provides for equal treatment of equal claims but considered that Section must be read in a manner which is consistent with Section 14, to mean equal treatment of equal claims made under the Act rather than equal treatment with claims made and determined under the War Pensions Act. Ms Anderson went on to say:

> 'Section 10 of the VSA does not allow the Appeal Board to judicially review the Minister's decision not to include glioblastoma in the list of conclusively presumed conditions for service in Vietnam between 1964 and 1972 as set out in Regulation 13(3) of the Veterans' Support Regulations 2014 (VSR). Neither can the Appeal Board rely on Section 10 to find that a Minister was bound to adopt and carry forward decisions such as Kenyon made under the WPA (prior legislation) when they drafted the presumptive list, as that would not be consistent with the prescribed process for deciding claims provided for in the VSA.
>
> ...In this appeal there is no doubt about the interpretation of Section 14 and the proper application of the law to the facts. While the Appeal Board acknowledges the Appellant's service, it is not open to us to step around Section 14 and simply decide the appeal in accordance with a broader assessment of the substantial justice and merits of the claim than is provided for in the Regulations.'

(41.) Ms Anderson therefore considered that she could not refuse to apply the Act and the regulations made under it. She considered that neither could she determine what ought to have been specified in the regulations prescribing the presumptive list of illnesses and conditions for Vietnam veterans.

(42.) Ms Anderson accepted that there is a reasonable hypothesis that Tā Harawira's glioblastoma was service-related, and that SOP 85/2016 applied. Ms Anderson referred to a US National Academies of Sciences, Engineering and Medicine's systemic review of scientific literature concerning glioblastoma in Vietnam, recording that it shows there is an absence of evidence connecting glioblastoma and exposure to herbicides in Vietnam. She went on to say:

> 'On the other hand, I accept that the condition of glioblastoma is such a rare cancer tumour that no one can say definitively that it is not related

to Agent Orange exposure. I also understand there is literature suggesting that there may be an association between exposure to Agent Orange and other agents used in the Vietnam War and the carcinogenic changes this has long term on DNZ and cellular metabolism. I also accept that Courts in the United States have accepted veterans' claims for glioblastoma where the evidence is equivocal.'

(43.) Ms Anderson then concluded that the hypothesis was not consistent with SOP 85/2016 because there was no evidence that Tā Harawira met any of the three factors listed in Clause 9. She also considered that Section 15 of the Act was inapplicable as there is a relevant SOP.

(44.) Ms Anderson concluded that it was not open to her to find that Tā Harawira's glioblastoma was service-related.

Mr Griggs' Reasons

(45.) Mr Griggs agreed with Ms Anderson that the claims should be considered under the Act, and that Section 35 of the Legislation Act did not have the effect contended for on behalf of Tā Harawira. However, he saw the core issue in the appeal as 'what the Appeal Board should do if there is a conflict between one or more of the principles specified in Section 10(b) and a Regulation made under Section 265'.[34]

(46.) Mr Griggs observed that Section 10 is unique and deserves careful reading. He accepted that the operative provisions of the Act must be interpreted consistently with the principles specified in Section 10(b), and said that if a provision of the Act cannot reasonably be given a meaning consistent with those principles, it must be given effect on its terms. However, he considered that the same considerations do not apply where regulations rather than the operative provisions of the Act are concerned. Mr Griggs was of the view that Section 10 applies to any person who performs any function or exercises any power under the Act, including the making of Orders-in-Council by the Governor-General on the advice of the Minister, and imposes mandatory duties.

34. Mr Griggs noted that this was not directly addressed by the parties.

(47.) Mr Griggs therefore concluded that:

> 'When the Governor-General made the VSR [the Regulations] on 1 December 2014, His Excellency had a duty under Section 10(b)(ii) of the VSA [the Act] to give effect to the principle of promoting equal treatment of equal claims. Equally, when the Minister provided his recommendation for the purposes of Section 21, he had a duty to give effect to that principle.'

(48.) And:

> '...when the Minister provided his recommendation in 2014 as to which conditions ought to be specified in the presumptive list for Vietnam veterans in Regulation 13(3) of the VSR [the Regulations], the Kenyon case was an "equal claim". It established a precedent that glioblastoma in Vietnam veterans might be related to their service, due to their exposure to Agent Orange. In my view it was the Minister's duty to make his recommendation in accordance with the principle of promoting equal treatment of equal claims, namely by including glioblastoma in the presumptive list. When the GovernorGeneral made the Order-in-Council, His Excellency similarly had a duty to ensure that the presumptive list promoted equal treatment of equal claims, by including glioblastoma.'

(49.) Mr Griggs considered that it could not have been Parliament's intent that equal claims should be confined to claims made under the Act, and if that had been intended, Parliament would have made that clear. He said that:

> 'As a matter of ordinary usage, it seems to me that a previous claim by a New Zealand veteran of the same operational theatre in respect of the same condition is, absent any other distinguishing characteristics, an "equal claim", whether or not it has been considered under the VSA [Act].'

(50.) He did not 'entirely agree' with Ms Anderson's view that the Appeal Board does not have jurisdiction to review the Regulations and must apply them on their terms. He considered that the Appeal Board may consider collateral challenges to the Regulations if it is alleged they are invalid.[35] Mr

35. Mr Griggs relied on *Attorney General vs PF Sugre Ltd [2004] 1 NZLR 207 (CA) [48]; and Conley vs Hamilton City Council [2008] 1 NZLR 789 (CA) at [45].*

Griggs did not however consider it necessary to take this approach in the present case.

(51.) Rather, Mr Griggs considered that Section 10(b)(iv), read together with Section 229(5) of the Act, obliged the Appeal Board to determine the claim in accordance with the substantial justice and merits of the claim, given his view that the Governor-General had a duty to include glioblastoma in the relevant presumptive list. He said that while Section 229(5) requires the Appeal Board to comply with the Regulations, it does not require the Appeal Board to give effect to an omission from the Regulations which contravenes Section 10(b) or any other provision of the Act. On that basis, Mr Griggs was of the view that Tā Harawira's claim for glioblastoma must be treated as a service-related condition under the Act.

Dr Holdaway's Reasons

(52.) The remaining member of the Appeal Board, Dr Holdaway agreed that the claim should be determined under the Act. He considered that the Appeal Board does not have the authority to change or add conditions to the presumptive list. However, he agreed with Mr Griggs that exercising benevolence required that Tā Harawira's claim for glioblastoma should be treated as a service-related condition under the Act. Dr Holdaway did not set out reasons for these conclusions.

The Appeal Board's Decision

(53.) Therefore, in accordance with the votes of the majority (being Mr Griggs and Dr Holdaway), the Appeal Board decided that Tā Harawira's claim for glioblastoma should be treated as a service-related condition under the Act.

Approach to Appeal

(54.) An appeal to the High Court against a determination of the Appeal Board may only be on a question of law, and is to be made in accordance with the High Court Rules 2016.[36] Rule 20.18 of the High Court Rules provides that an appeal is by way of rehearing.

---

36. Veterans' Support Act 2014, Section 239.

(55.) On the hearing of an appeal, the court may:37

(a.) make any decision it thinks should have been made:

(b.) direct the decision-maker—

(i.) to rehear the proceedings concerned; or

(ii.) to consider or determine (whether for the first time or again) any matters the court directs; or

(iii.) to enter judgment for any party to the proceedings the court directs:

(c.) make any order the court thinks just, including any order as to costs.

(56.) I note also that when a general right of appeal is exercised, the persons exercising those rights are:38

> '...entitled to judgment in accordance with the opinion of the appellate court, even where that opinion is an assessment of fact and degree and entails a value judgment. If the appellate court's opinion is different from the conclusion of the tribunal appealed from, then the decision under appeal is wrong in the only sense that matters, even if it was a conclusion on which minds might reasonably differ. In such circumstances it is an error for the High Court to defer to the lower court's assessment of the acceptability and weight to be accorded to the evidence, rather than forming its own opinion.'
>
> (Footnotes omitted)

Grounds of Appeal

(57.) The main ground of appeal advanced by the GMVA against the Appeal Board's decision is that the majority erred in law by not deciding the claim under the prescriptive process set out in Section 14 of the Act. The GMVA

---

37. High Court Rules 2016, Rule 20.19.

38. *Austin, Nichols & Co Inc vs Stichting Lodestar [2007] NZSC 103, [2008] 2 NZLR 141 at [16].*

says that the approach of the majority contained the following specific errors of law:

(a.) The majority erred in treating Section 10(b) of the Act as a substantive overriding provision under which a claim can be considered and ruled on, despite the prescriptive process for deciding claims in Section 14 of the Act. Rather, the role of Section 10(b) is to provide guiding interpretation principles for persons performing functions or exercising powers under the Act.

(b.) Mr Griggs erred in proceeding on the basis that the Board had the jurisdiction to review regulations made under the Act and determining the appeal as if the Regulations had been drafted differently to include glioblastoma in the presumptive list. Rather, he should have applied the Regulations as they are.

(c.) Mr Griggs erred in finding the Governor-General (when the Regulations were made on 1 December 2014) and the Minister (when he provided his recommendation for the purposes of Section 21) had a duty under Section 10(b)(ii) to give effect to the principle of promoting equal treatment of equal claims. Neither Section 10 nor Section 21 were in force when the Regulations were made.

(d.) Mr Griggs erred in finding that when the Minister provided his recommendation as to which conditions ought to be specified in the presumptive list for Vietnam veterans in Regulation 13(3) of the Regulations, the Kenyon claim was an equal claim giving rise to a duty to include glioblastoma in the presumptive list.

(e.) Mr Griggs erred in finding that the principle of promoting equal treatment of equal claims in Section 10(b)(ii) does not confine the enquiry to claims made under the Act.

(58.) Ms Roff submitted that in light of the GMVA's grounds of appeal and submissions, the following four issues require determination:

(a.) Does Section 14 of the Act exhaustively state the process that must be followed by the Appeal Board in considering an appeal under Section 229 of the Act?

(b.) Is the Appeal Board bound by regulations issued under Section 265 of the Act, such that, if a regulation is or may be unlawful, the Appeal Board must apply that regulation notwithstanding any issues of illegality?

(c.) Will a regulation be intra vires, if at the time it is promulgated, a provision that renders it unlawful has not yet come into effect?

(d.) Can a claim be an 'equal claim' for the purposes of the Act if it was decided under the War Pensions Act?

(59.) I address the appeal broadly in accordance with those issues.

The Effect of Section 10(b) on the Process Envisaged by Section 14

Submissions for the GMVA

(60.) Counsel for the GMVA, Mr Goosen, submits that Ms Anderson correctly interpreted and applied Section 14 to Tā Harawira's claim. He contends that Tā Harawira's claim that his illness was service-related is unable to succeed because there was no evidence of the three factors in SOP 85/2016 applying to him, and therefore the hypothesis that his illness was service-related was not consistent with the SOP. Mr Goosen says that the majority of the Board erred by failing to apply that analysis.

(61.) Mr Goosen submits that Section 14 provides an exhaustive process unless a presumption under Section 16 applies (which it does not, in this case). He argues that the Law Commission report supports his position, emphasising particularly its comments about the need for change because of cumbersome administrative and decision-making processes, which led to its recommendations about the use of SOPs and presumptions.[39] Mr Goosen notes that the Law Commission recommended that SOPs be introduced and said:[40]

39. See Law Commission, above n 6 at [iv], [5.46]–[5.48], [5.78]–[5.79] and [5.85].

40. At [5.98].

> 'The SOPs should be exhaustive, in that they would provide a complete list of the service-factors that link a condition with service. If not, it would defeat the purpose of these decision-making instruments, which is to overcome the difficulty of making consistent, legally correct decisions using the beneficial evidential provisions.'

(62.) Mr Goosen says that the SOPs reflect decisions favourable to veterans. He also emphasises that the Act contemplates a process whereby SOPs are adopted and revoked as necessary, and this is the appropriate way in which the grounds for claims are kept up to date.

Submissions from Counsel Assisting

(63.) Ms Roff promotes a broader approach to understanding Section 14, which necessarily takes longer to outline here. She submits that Section 14 'should not be seen as a procedural straitjacket prohibiting decision makers from adopting procedures in particular cases not provided for'. She says that Sections 10 to 12 are mandatory provisions, which must be complied with when exercising powers or performing functions under the Act. She submits that the principle of benevolence (Section 10(b)(iii)) underpins the scheme and purpose of the Act, as seen in the way the usual rules of evidence are 'jettisoned' (Section 10(b)(iv)) and the 'presumptions' contained in Sections 17 to 21 and 28 are intended to displace the need for a claimant to prove that their condition was caused by their service.[41] Ms Roff submits that when determining what a 'reasonable' decision is, the facts must be viewed through this benevolent lens, as too high a standard of reasonableness undermines the necessary focus on the substantial merits of a claim.[42]

(64.) Ms Roff highlights that these principles were established under the War Pensions Act and were reintroduced in the Act, as intended by Parliament. She says this was acknowledged in *Edwards vs Attorney General* when Williams J said that '...the spirit of the 1954 presumption remains although the structure and application of that spirit is rendered with the greater clarity characteristic of modern drafting practice'.[43]

---

41. See *Te Ua vs Secretary for War Pensions [2014] NZHC 1050 at [114]–[116].*

42. At [115].

43. *Edwards vs Attorney General [2017] NZHC 3180 at [68].*

(65.) Ms Roff submits that as the Appeal Board was required to reach a new and fresh decision on the evidence of Tā Harawira's claim, it was operating subject to a mandatory obligation to ensure that its decision was compatible with Section 10. She says:

> 'That the Appellant does not agree Section 10 required this of the Board on the facts is not a basis for an appeal on a question of law. As with any other decision-maker, it was a matter for the Board what Section 10 required in this particular case, and the majority held that it required a different approach to that set out in Section 14. The only issue could be, as discussed below, whether the Board had any residual discretion outside Section 14 to reach that conclusion.'

(66.) Ms Roff emphasises that Section 12 requires that all decisions made by VANZ must be made on 'reasonable grounds' and have regard to 'all the circumstances'. She suggests that when read consistently with Section 12, the Section 14 process must result in a decision that is consistent with VANZ reaching a decision on reasonable grounds with the effect that the 'reasonable grounds' standard operates as a final check to ensure a claim is not unreasonably rejected.[44] Ms Roff also argues that while Section 12 on its face applies only to VANZ, it would be absurd if VANZ was required to ensure its decisions were made on reasonable grounds but other decision-makers under the Act were not. Given that reviewers and appeal boards are required to reach decisions afresh on the same claims first considered by VANZ, it would be expected the same standard applies. Ms Roff submits that the entire Act is characterised by a different, lower, standard of causation that exists in ordinary and adversarial civil litigation, which is essentially the principle of benevolence rendered into practice.[45] She also notes that, as a general principle, regulation cannot exhaust decision-making discretion as a matter of public law.[46]

---

44. 'Reasonable grounds' requirements are found throughout the Act, see Sections 12, 14(6), 15(3), 27(5), 28(1A), 28(2), and 63(3).

45. This is apparent in the definitions of 'service-related' and 'service-related death' in Section 7 of the Act which include the notions of 'contributed to' and 'aggravated by' as opposed to simply 'caused by'.

46. See *Westhaven Shellfish Ltd vs Chief Executive of Ministry of Fisheries [2002] 2 NZLR 158*

(67.) Ms Roff says that the application of Section 14 therefore requires the principle of benevolence to be given effect, and that Section 14 can be informed by what occurs under Section 15 when there is no applicable SOP—being an assessment of whether the hypothesis determined under Section 14(2) is a reasonable hypothesis. If a reasonable hypothesis is then established, the claim must be accepted unless there are reasonable grounds for believing that the injury was not service-related. The overarching question under the Act is still whether there is a reasonable hypothesis that the injury is service-related.

Analysis

(68.) As is apparent from the summary of submissions, Mr Goosen contends for a straightforward interpretation of the plain words of Section 14, while Ms Roff contends that the correct interpretation is reached following a broader consideration of the Act and its legislative history.

(69.) Section 10 of the Legislation Act 2019 requires me to ascertain the meaning of legislation from its text and in light of its purpose and its context. I have already set out the legislative background, but it is helpful here to consider specifically how Sections 10 and 14 of the Act evolved.

(70.) Sections 10 and 14 were introduced at the Select Committee stage because of the substantial amendments proposed by the Select Committee to Clause 15 of the Bill, which set out the central decision-making provision of the Bill.[47] In effect, the proposal was to shift the elements of Clause 15 that the Select Committee considered relevant to the overarching decision-making principles to be applied in determining veterans' claims, away from the specific procedural steps to be taken by VANZ in reaching decisions.[48] The Select Committee explained that the clause was 'necessary to make the claim decision process, and the establishment of entitlements under the

---

(CA) at [47]–[50]; and Graham Taylor Judicial Review: A New Zealand Perspective (4th ed, LexisNexis, Wellington, 2018) at [15.70] and [15.74]–[15.76].

47. Veterans' Support Bill 2013 (158–2) (select committee report) at 5.

48. At 5. This was recommended by officials in New Zealand Defence Force 'Veterans' Support Bill – Departmental Report' (February 2014) at [92]–[96].

proposed legislation, as clear as possible for both VANZ as decision-makers, and veterans.'[49]

(71.) In the Departmental Report on the Bill, officials also addressed how veterans were to establish their entitlements under the Act. They recommended that Clause 15 be amended to clearly reflect how the Bill is intended to operate using commonly understood language.[50] The officials observed that the Bill was intended to 'apply conclusive decision-making tools to aid the establishment of entitlements, largely removing the decision-making discretion ...'.[51] They went on to recommend that the hierarchy of decision-making tools be amended to make the SOPs the primary tool to apply, noting that when a more generous presumptive decision-making condition applied, the benefit of benevolence must be accorded to a veteran despite any SOP that may apply.[52] When the Bill was introduced into Parliament, the then acting responsible Minister, Hon'ble Nathan Guy, noted that the decision-making provisions and the points of reference for deciding claims were an area of change. He said that:[53]

> 'Underlying the rewrite of the 1954 Act was a desire not only to modernise the legislation but to make it more accessible for both veterans and administrators to understand and use. ...There was very broad support for the use of the Australian statements of principle as the main reference point for deciding claims. The statements of principle are comprehensive, soundly based in medical terms, and introduce a much needed element of certainty to the process.
>
> The bill also needed to modernise the legal and evidential tests for establishing entitlement ... [I]t became clear that more work was needed to reduce legal jargon and ensure the provisions are clearer, easier to

49. At 6.

50. New Zealand Defence Force 'Veterans' Support Bill – Departmental Report' (February 2014) at [87].

51. At [89].

52. At [91].

53. (10 April 2017) 697 NZPD 17188.

understand, and fully aligned with the benevolence principle in decision-making.'

(72.) The explanatory note to the Bill records that it 'enables the adoption of decision-making tools to assist the decision maker in determining whether a condition is linked to a veteran's service'.[54] The explanatory note goes on to say that presumptive lists will continue to be used and SOPs will be introduced. It describes the introduction and use of the SOPs as greatly benefiting the decision-making process as it will 'reduce the amount of discretion applied by the decision-maker'.[55] Thus, although the Law Commission may have recommended that SOPs be exhaustive, it does not appear that this was carried through into the Act.[56]

(73.) The separation out of the overarching principles from the claim process is significant. Section 10 may, as Mr Griggs commented, be unique in the statute book. In it, Parliament has not indicated matters for decision-makers under the Act to have regard to, rather it has imposed duties that are mandatory. When a person is performing a function or exercising a power under the Act, they must do so in accordance with the principles set out in Section 10(b). In my view, these principles must be taken into account in ascertaining the proper meaning of Section 14.

(74.) Having carefully reviewed the Act overall, and its legislative history, I consider that Section 14 is properly understood as establishing a default process by which claims would be determined—but not an exhaustive process. In my view, the creation of both presumptive conditions (as, for example, in Regulation 13) and SOPs were intended to benefit veterans making claims by providing, as far as possible, clear bases on which claims might be made out. I do not consider that Parliament intended the effect of introducing the default process to be to exclude possible claims, to the disadvantage of veterans. Rather, I am satisfied that Parliament intended that claims made for a service-related condition should be considered and determined on

54. Veterans' Support Bill (158-1) (explanatory note) at 5.

55. At 5.

56. See Law Commission, above n 6 at [5.98].

substantive grounds. This is clearly contemplated in the Act, as the process in Section 15 provides.

(75.) In my view, it would not be taking a benevolent approach, as required by Section 10(b), to conclude that where a veteran is not assisted by a relevant SOP, they are not entitled to the benefit of Section 15, whereas a veteran in respect of whom there is no relevant SOP, is entitled to the benefit of Section 15. This can also be compared with effect of the presumptive conditions in Regulation 13(2). These assist a potential claimant if their condition appears in the Regulation—but does not preclude them from arguing a further reasonable hypothesis, if it does not.

(76.) I accept that on its face the Act is silent on what is to occur, as a matter of process, when there is a relevant SOP, but it is not applicable to the claimant's circumstances. The effect of the GMVA's submissions is that this must be understood as Parliament deliberately choosing that such a claim could never succeed. The further effect of this approach is that a veteran would be better off if there was no relevant SOP. I find such a conclusion unattractive, and inconsistent with the purpose and scheme of the Act, its legislative history, and a proper reading of Sections 10 to 12, 229(5)(b), and 229(5)(c).

(77.) I consider that in such circumstances, a claimant should be treated as if there is no applicable SOP, and the process in Section 15 should apply. This approach accords with the requirements in Section 10(b) that a benevolent approach is taken, and that claims are not determined in accordance with any technicalities, legal forms, or legal rules of evidence, but rather in accordance with substantial justice and the merits of the claim.

(78.) Thus, even when a SOP is apparently applicable, but no factors relate to the claimant, the overarching question should still be whether there is a reasonable hypothesis that the condition or injury is service-related. If it is, the claim should be accepted unless there are reasonable grounds for believing that the veteran's injury, illness or death was not service-related.

(79.) This approach is consistent with the requirement in Section 12, which mandates that decisions must be made on reasonable grounds and in light of all the circumstances.

(80.) This approach also takes into account Ms Roff's concern that the discretion under the Act cannot be exhausted after the fact by the issuing of SOPs. I accept that the Act's requirements of 'consistency' with a SOP or a reasonable hypothesis contemplates a claim that does not fit strictly with that SOP or reasonable hypothesis. This accords with Section 12 and its mandate that decisions must be made on reasonable grounds and in light of all the circumstances. It also allows the decision maker to consider the application of the principles in Section 10(b). This is important in the present case, as it allows the decision maker to consider whether an 'equal claim' exists, as required under Section 10(b)(ii).

(81.) In my view, then, the majority of the Appeal Board did not err by adopting a broader approach than the process described in Section 14 in the determination of Tā Harawira's claim. Nonetheless, I do not entirely agree with the reasoning set out by Mr Griggs, and of course Dr Holdaway did not explain in any detail why he thought exercising benevolence required that Tā Harawira's claim for glioblastoma should be treated as a service-related condition under the Act. I return to this matter when I consider the appropriate relief to be given in this case.

The Board's Jurisdiction in Relation to the Regulations

Submissions

(82.) Mr Goosen submits that the Appeal Board did not have the jurisdiction to address the question of 'what the Appeal Board should do if there is a conflict between one or more of the principles specified in Section 10(b) and a Regulation made under Section 265'. This was the question posited by Mr Griggs in his reasons as the core issue in the appeal.

(83.) Mr Goosen says instead that Sections 229(5)(b) and 229(5)(c) require an Appeal Board to apply the general principles in Section 10(b) when deciding appeals under any relevant provisions of the Act and any Regulations made under Section 265. He submits that an Appeal Board is not empowered or authorised to determine appeals on the basis of what it considers should have been included in Regulations made under the Act, and that the interpretation principles in Sections 10(b) cannot override Regulations made under the Act. Rather, any Regulations must be taken as they are and interpreted and applied in light of the Section 10(b) principles.

(84.) Ms Roff does not consider that the Appeal Board reached a view as to whether the Regulations were ultra vires and so the error of law raised by the GMVA is academic and not properly subject to appeal. She also submits that in any event, the Appeal Board would have been justified in embarking on a 'collateral challenge' analysis.[57] Regulations are only lawful to the extent that they comply with the empowering legislation, which is assessed against the Act's wording, and also the purpose for which regulation-making power is conferred.[58] Ms Roff argues that s 10 would be important in determining that purpose and that a regulation incompatible with s 10 is likely ultra vires as involving an improper purpose. Ms Roff contends that the Appeal Board need not apply regulations it considers to be unlawful when making its decisions.

Analysis

(85.) While Mr Griggs did express a view that a 'collateral challenge' could be contemplated in principle, he said that it was not necessary for him to consider whether the omission of glioblastoma from Regulation 13(3) was 'in breach of the duty in Section 10(b)(ii) [and] could be viewed through the lens of invalidity' because:

> '... Section 10(b)(iv), read together with Section 229(5), obliges the Appeal Board to determine the Appellant's claim in accordance with substantial justice and the merits of the claim. If, as I do, the majority of the Appeal Board considers that the GovernorGeneral had a duty to include glioblastoma in the relevant presumptive list, then in my view it is the duty of the Appeal Board to determine the claim as if that had in fact been done. While Section 229(5)(c) of the VSA does require the Appeal Board to comply with the VSR, it does not oblige the Appeal Board to give effect to an omission from the VSR which contravenes Section 10(b) or any other

57. *Brady vs Northland Regional Council [2008]* NZAR 505 (HC).

58. *Unison Networks Limited vs Commerce Commission [2007]* NZSC 74, [2008] 1 NZLR 42 at [53].

provision of the Act. That would contravene the VSA, with which the Appeal Board is also required to comply.'

(86.) I find Mr Grigg's reasoning problematic. I accept that he made no findings explicitly 'through the lens of invalidity', but there seems to be little difference between doing that, and his ultimate conclusion, being that the inconsistency of Regulation 13(3) with Section 10(b) required the reading in of glioblastoma. The pre-eminent ground under which a Regulation might be considered invalid is that it is inconsistent with its empowering provision.

(87.)While Dr Holdaway agreed with Mr Griggs that exercising benevolence required that Tā Harawira's claim for glioblastoma be treated as a service-related condition under the Act, he also said that the Appeal Board must apply the Act 'as intended' and had no authority to change or add conditions to the presumptive list. In this respect (despite some residual uncertainty as to what Dr Holdaway meant by applying the Act 'as intended'), this suggests he and Ms Anderson were in agreement as to the latter point.

(88.) For these reasons, I do not consider that a majority of the Appeal Board reached a view that the Regulations were unlawful, or purported to judicially review them. There is simply no basis for such a conclusion, having regard to the reasons of the three members of the Appeal Board. On this basis, I conclude that a majority of the Appeal Board did not take an approach which could establish the grounds for asserting an error in law in its decision, in this respect. Accordingly, I do not need to address the further question of the availability of a 'collateral challenge' to the regulations as a matter of law, although I note that such a challenge may indeed be available in principle.[59]

The Alleged Duty of both the Governor General and Minister to Give Effect to Section 10(b)

Submissions

(89.) Mr Goosen submits that neither the Governor-General nor the Minister

59. See *Attorney General vs PF Sugre Ltd [2004] 1* NZLR 207 (CA) at [48]. *See also Judicial Review: A New Zealand Perspective* (4th ed, LexisNexis, Wellington, 2018) at [6.11].

could have been subject to the duty pursuant to Section 10(b)(ii) to give effect to the principle of promoting equal treatment for equal claims, described by Mr Griggs, at the time the Regulations were made, and could therefore not have breached such a duty. Mr Goosen submits when the minister recommended the Regulations be made, and when the GovernorGeneral made the Regulations on 1 December 2014, they were not subject to Section 10, as the Act was not yet in force. He says:

'(a.) the Act received royal assent on 7 August 2014;

(b.) pursuant to Section 2(1), the Act came into force four months after the date of royal assent, being 7 December 2014, except the provisions specified in Sections 2(2), and 2(3), which came into force on 8 August 2014;

(c.) Sections 10 and 21 are not in any of the provisions that came into force on 8 August 2014, and accordingly came into force on 7 December 2014;

(d.) Section 265, which provides the power for the Governor-General to make regulations, came into force on 8 August 2014;

(e.) the Regulations were made on 1 December 2014; and therefore

(f.) Section 10 was not in force at the time the Regulations were made, and could not have applied to the Minister recommending, or the Governor-General making, those Regulations.'

(90.) Mr Goosen says that, as a result, it is unnecessary to address Mr Griggs' conclusion that the Governor-General could have a duty of care under Section 10 to consider whether proposed regulations are lawful as against the requirements of Section 10.

(91.) Ms Roff submits that a regulation must always be lawful. She says that if the empowering legislation is changed such that the regulation is no longer lawful, then it is unlawful. She submits that in this case the Regulations cannot be preserved merely by 'fortuity of timing'.

Analysis

(92.) I agree that secondary legislation must always be lawful, and that amendment to empowering legislation that necessarily makes secondary legislation unlawful would have the effect of invalidating that secondary legislation. Secondary legislation must align with its empowering provisions, and the principles which apply to the exercise of discretion to promulgate secondary legislation. Whether regulations comply with the empowering legislation is assessed against an Act's wording, and also the purpose for which regulation-making power is conferred.

(93.) However, I consider that this issue is moot, as a majority of the Appeal Board in the present case did not make, nor purport to make, explicit findings as to the validity or legality of the Regulations as made under the Act. While I consider that the Regulations are indeed required to comply with Section 10 and all other relevant provisions in the Act, it is therefore not necessary for me to reach a conclusion about this for the determination of the present appeal and I do not do so.

The Impact of the *Kenyon* Decision and the Principle of Equal Treatment

Submissions for the GMVA

(94.) Mr Goosen submits that as Section 10(b)(ii) was not in force at the time the Regulations were made, Mr Griggs erred in law in concluding that the *Kenyon* decision was required to be considered an 'equal claim' at the time the minister provided his recommendation in 2014 as to which conditions ought to be specified in the presumptive list for Vietnam veterans.

(95.) Mr Goosen also says that the Kenyon case cannot be an equal claim under the Act. He relies both on the fact that it was decided under the War Pensions Act and on comments made by Simon France J in *Keelan vs The General Manager of Veterans' Affairs New Zealand*.[60] In that case, Simon France J considered whether principles espoused by Whata J in a decision

60. *Keelan vs The General Manager of Veterans' Affairs New Zealand [2016] NZHC 1869.*

pursuant to the War Pensions Act could be considered to be applicable in full to decisions made under the Act.[61] His Honour stated:[62]

> 'Sections 14 and 15 prescribe a process for deciding claims that is both prescriptive and different from that which existed under the War Pensions Act 1954. A central feature of the new scheme is the adoption of what are called statements of principles which govern the consideration of claims for different conditions. These statements of principles are extensive documents that identify a list of criteria applicable to almost every condition. For example, in relation to osteoarthritis (for which there is a standalone Standard) 40 different circumstances are identified, any one of which, if applicable to the veteran, will see the claim presumptively accepted. In adopting this methodology the Act expressly at Section 22 draws on the statements of principle already established by the Australian Reparation Medical Authority. The fact that the existence of one such situation will trigger the presumption is an example of the benevolence principle being built in.
>
> ...
>
> ...it would be inappropriate to declare that Whata J's analysis of a very different scheme applies here. I am unaware of any principle of interpretation that would support such an approach. It would be rather unexpected that, Parliament having updated a statutory scheme that is itself the product of significant Law Commission work, the Court would then immediately read back various provisions from the old Act that have not been carried over.
>
> There is no good policy reason to make a declaration like the one sought. The new Act can stand for itself, and be interpreted as required. It would also be a declaration that is far too vague to be of benefit – in order to be effective, one would have to identify in the declaration what the Te Ua principles are (the plaintiffs provide a list of them) and then give some sort of detailed explanation as to how they apply to Sections 14 and 15 of the new Act.'

---

61. See *Te Ua vs Secretary for War Pensions, above n 41.*

62. Above n 59, at [33], [35] and [36].

(96.) His Honour considered that it would be an incorrect approach to interpretation to seek to in effect transfer repealed provisions from a repealed Act into a new statute with its own scheme.[63] Having declined to make any of the declarations sought, his Honour concluded:[64]

> 'The proposition that the language and presumptions contained in the previous Act should be overlaid on the text of the present Act is rejected. It is a new Act with its own purposes and principles. It establishes a different methodology for assessing claims. There is no interpretation approach or principle that would support what the plaintiffs propose.'

(97.) Mr Goosen says that Keelan is authority for the principle that the test for deciding claims under the Act and the War Pensions Act is different. He submits that the claim in *Kenyon* was successful because the veteran concerned was entitled to the benefit of the presumptions contained in the War Pensions Act, and that the principle of equal treatment for equal claims under the Act must mean equal treatment of equal claims under the Act, not the War Pensions Act. Parliament cannot have intended that the Act require claims to be decided by reference to claims decided under a different (and now repealed) Act. Mr Goosen submits that this accords with the requirement in Section 199 of the Act that it is a function of VANZ to provide entitlements to veterans and other claimants 'in accordance with the Act'.

Submissions from Counsel Assisting

(98.) Ms Roff says instead that *Keelan* is not authority for the proposition that an 'equal claim' in terms of Section 10 cannot be found by relying on a successful claim under the War Pensions Act. She submits the correct approach is that a claim under the War Pensions Act may amount to an equal claim in terms of Section 10 and whether it does will depend on the circumstances. She relies on the intention of Parliament noted above that the foundational provisions and principles of the War Pensions Act were to be carried through into the new legislation. She submits that it therefore cannot

63. Above n 58, at [42].

64. At [72].

be that Parliament intended for successful claims under the War Pensions Act to be entirely irrelevant to the scheme established by the Act.

(99.) Ms Roff submits that whether any two claims are 'equal' depends on those claims themselves factually, and where they arise under different legislation, the particular legal implications. A case-by-case analysis is required, with decisions under the Act to be made on the basis of substantial justice, rather than technicalities or legal forms.[65] Ms Roff submits that merely stating that the War Pensions Act is different to the Act is to invite reasoning based on form, rather than substance.

(100.) Ms Roff also says that in *Keelan*, Simon France J properly notes that Section 14 is procedurally more prescriptive, but submits that his Honour did not discuss Sections 10 to 12 or the history of the Act in any detail, and notes that the issue of 'equal claims' does not appear to have been directly in issue in that case. Rather, Simon France J observed that decisions were required to be 'context-specific', necessarily turning on the particular facts before the decision-maker, and that is not consistent with the suggestion that his Honour was deciding that claims under the War Pensions Act could never be equal claims under the Act.

(101.) Ms Roff also observes that the Appeal Board did not deal with the argument before it about the relevance of case law from the United States, where claims relating to glioblastoma have been accepted.

Analysis

(102.) I do not consider that Keelan is authority for the position that no successful claim made under the War Pensions Act can be relevant to the assessment of a claim under the Act. Keelan involved a group of veterans alleging that what they described as the 'Te Ua principles' had always to be applied by VANZ under the Act. The 'Te Ua principles' were matters discussed by Whata J in an earlier judgment under the War Pensions Act.[66] The Applicants in *Keelan* sought declarations that these principles apply to

---

65. Veterans' Support Act 2014, Section 10(b)(iv).

66. *Te Ua vs Secretary for War Pensions, above n 41.*

decisions to be made under the Act when no such decisions had yet been made. The central issue in the case was whether an interpretation of the War Pensions Act could be superimposed upon the Act, notwithstanding the differences between the two. No specific claim, or even factual context relating to a specific claim, was before the Court, and this was noted by Simon France J, who went to great lengths to describe why it would be inappropriate to make the declarations sought by the Applicants.[67] His Honour's conclusion was instead to reject the argument that any principle or claim under the War Pensions Act must automatically apply in the same way under the Act.

(103.) Further, as a matter of interpretation of the Act, particularly Section 10, I consider that Mr Goosen's interpretation of the effect of *Keelan* also prioritises form over substance, or legal technicalities over substantial justice. In my view, it is entirely clear that, despite the differences between the previous and current legislation, the broader principles that apply to the determination of claims are the same.

(104.) I consider that it would be inappropriate for the legal position to be that the Kenyon claim is unable to be regarded as equal to Tā Harawira's claim simply because the claims arose under different legislation, given the clear Parliamentary intention that the Act was, in important purposive senses, a continuation of the earlier legislation. Mr Kenyon's claim appears to be similar to Tā Harawira's claim and as stated by Mr Griggs, 'a previous claim by a New Zealand veteran of the same operational theatre in respect of the same condition is, absent any other distinguishing characteristics, an equal claim'. However, I make no finding about this as I consider that is a matter that is for the Appeal Board to further address.

(105.) Any other view is one that favours legal technicalities over substantial justice. When broadly the same principles apply to the determination of a claim under each statute, and the claim is sufficiently similar, that must be relevant to the determination of whether there is a reasonable hypothesis that an illness, injury, or death was service-related, both as a matter of fact and a matter of law. There can be no hard and fast exclusion of successful

67. *Keelan, above n 60, at [18]–[27].*

claims under the War Pensions Act; it must instead be a consideration of all of the circumstances as they present themselves before the decision-maker. I consider the principles in Section 10(b) prohibit an analysis that regards successful claims made under the War Pensions Act as automatically irrelevant, merely on the basis that there is now a different statute.

(106.) The argument advanced by Tā Harawira before the Appeal Board relied not only on Kenyon but also successful claims made for glioblastoma in the United States. As noted earlier, Ms Anderson accepted that there was a reasonable hypothesis that Tā Harawira's glioblastoma was service-related, based on scientific literature from the United States. Given the references in Sections 14 and 15 to reasonable hypotheses in relation to a finding that an injury is service-related, I consider that it remains open to a decision-maker to find such information, and overseas case law, of assistance. It is clear from the use of SOPs made in reliance on the work of the Australian Repatriation Medical Authority, that overseas approaches have been considered relevant to the New Zealand approach.

(107.) For the avoidance of doubt, I confirm that it must also be correct that where a claim was accepted under the War Pensions Act, it must not necessarily be accepted under the Act as an equal claim. Again, a full consideration of the two claims must be undertaken by the decision-maker.

(108.) Given these views, it will be apparent that I do not see any merit in the argument that as Section 10(b) was not enacted at the time the Regulations were made, the *Kenyon* case could not be an equal claim at the time the Minister provided his recommendation about Regulation 13 in 2014.

Conclusion

(109.) My conclusions as to the questions of law raised in this appeal are that:

'(a.) Section 14 is not an exhaustive code for considering a claim under the Act;

(b.) in circumstances where a SOP appears to be applicable to a claim but the claimant cannot establish any of the factors contemplated by the SOP, the correct interpretation of the Act requires VANZ to treat the claim in accordance with the process in Section 15, addressing whether the claim is consistent with a reasonable hypothesis, and accepting that claim unless there are reasonable grounds for believing that the veteran's injury, illness or death is not service-related;

(c.) in applying the principle of equal treatment for equal claims found in Section 10(b)(ii), a claim determined under the War Pensions Act may be considered an equal claim to a claim under the Act; and

(d.) in determining a claim under the Act, VANZ may take into account scientific literature and overseas caselaw if VANZ considers it will assist, consistent with Section 10(b).

(110.) It will therefore be apparent that there are aspects of the reasoning of both Ms Anderson and Mr Griggs with which I do not agree. I am also concerned about the absence of reasons from Dr Holdaway.

(111.) Nonetheless, I conclude that as a matter of law, it was open in principle to the majority of the Appeal Board to reach the outcome that Tā Harawira's claim for glioblastoma must be treated as a service-related condition under the Act. In my view, the appropriate approach to Tā Harawira's claim, in circumstances where there was a relevant SOP but none of the factors in the SOP applied to Tā Harawira, was for the Appeal Board to adopt the process set out in Section 15 of the Act. In undertaking that process, the Appeal Board should have also considered the principles in Section 10(b), especially that of equal treatment of equal claims. The Appeal Board may not refuse to take account of the decision in *Kenyon* solely because it was a decision under the War Pensions Act.

(112.) I have concluded that it would not be appropriate for me to use the power available to me make my own decision in relation to Tā Harawira's claim. Rather I find that, in the circumstances, the Appeal Board should consider the claim again, given my conclusions as to the questions of law. This is for two reasons. First, the nature of the Appeal Board decision is such that while there is a majority decision that Tā Harawira's claim for glioblastoma must be treated as a service-related condition under the Act, there is no clear shared reasoning for that outcome. In my view, the Appeal Board should have a further opportunity to consider the claim and provide reasoning that supports the outcome reached (or another outcome, once the claim is considered in light of my conclusions as to matters of law, above). Second, in undertaking this task, the Appeal Board will be required to assess Tā Harawira's medical information and other relevant information, such as *Kenyon*, and possibly other decisions or material. I am not confident that all such information is before me, and nor have I heard argument in relation to it. These reasons are enhanced by the fact the Appeal Board is a specialist body of which one member must be a medical practitioner.

Relief

(113.) I direct the Appeal Board to consider again Tā Harawira's application for a disablement pension. I direct the Appeal Board to take account of my conclusions as to the questions of law, in so doing. I also direct each member of the Appeal Board to provide reasons for their conclusions, which, as a matter of principle, they must do.[68]

Result

(114.) The appeal is allowed.

Costs

(115.) Costs were not addressed by counsel at the hearing. My preliminary view is that in the circumstances, costs should lie where they fall, particularly as Ms Roff's costs will be paid by the Court and the estate took no part in the appeal. If the GMVA or Ms Roff have a different view, they are to file a memorandum of no longer than five pages within 15 working days of the date of this judgment. Any memorandum in reply is to be filed within a further five working days. Costs will then be decided on the papers.

McQueen, J

---

68. A failure to give reasons or an inadequate statement of reasons is a reviewable error. See for example *Bell vs Victoria University of Wellington HC Wellington* CIV-2009-485-2634, 8 December 2010 at [76]; and *Graham Taylor Judicial Review: A New Zealand Perspective* (4th ed, LexisNexis, Wellington, 2018) at [9.05]–[9.06].

PART III

Notable Events

Notable Events

(With special thanks to Mr Eugene R. Fidell and the Global Military Justice Reform Blog: https://globalmjreform.blogspot.com)

January

Court Martial Sentences Civilians for Heinous Offences

The UPDF Mountain Division Court Martial's 30-year sentences for civilians, Peter Basara and Gideon Mugisa, convicted of robbery, illegal firearm possession, and attempted murder, sparked criticism for violating human rights by trying civilians in military courts.
https://www.monitor.co.ug/uganda/news/national/court-martial-sentences-civilians-overrobbery-murder-4502830

Swiss Air Traffic Controller Appeals Conviction for Negligent Homicide in Fatal Crash

A Skyguide air traffic controller appealed his negligent homicide conviction for a fatal 2016 military aircraft crash caused by a mistaken altitude instruction. Sentenced to a conditional fine, while the lead pilot was acquitted, his case came under military court review.
https://www.swissinfo.ch/eng/science/swiss-air-traffic-controller-appeals-military-crashconviction/49141314

Egypt Expands Military Jurisdiction, Further Cementing Martial Law Amid Growing Economic Crisis

The Egyptian parliament passed a new law granting the military expanded powers to arrest civilians and try them in military courts. The law significantly broadened the military's role in internal security, fuelling concerns of further repression as the country faced mounting social unrest. Additionally, new amendments added a *Military Court for Appellate Crimes*, expanding the scope of military judicial powers.
https://thearabweekly.com/egypt-expands-powers-military-judiciary-amid-mounting-public-anger

Supreme Court of Canada Upholds Acquittal in Military Sexual Assault Case

In a landmark ruling, the Supreme Court of Canada upheld Corporal Vu's acquittal in a military sexual assault case, citing the prosecution's failure to prove the complainant's incapacity to consent due to intoxication. The decision underscored challenges in prosecuting such cases and affirmed deference to trial judges' factual assessments. Vu's acquittal may influence future military and civilian cases involving consent and intoxication.
https://roryfowlerlaw.com/r-v-vu-redux/

February

New Legislation Empowers Egypt's Military Courtsin Civil Matters

Egypt's House of Representatives passed a law expanding military courts' jurisdiction to crimes affecting public food security and markets. It grants authority over any utility deemed a public good and allows the president, with the National Defence Council, to define threats to essential resources and national security.
https://www.hrw.org/news/2024/03/05/egypt-new-laws-entrench-military-power-overcivilians

VAdm Edmundson Faces Charges in a Sexual Assault Case

The trial of retired Vice Admiral Haydn Edmundson, resumed on February 16, 2024, highlighted the ongoing scrutiny of military misconduct cases. It marked the final trial of accused General/Flag Officers, with only one conviction to date.
https://www.cbc.ca/news/canada/haydn-edmundson-sexual-assault-trial-1.7110920

Supreme Court Pushes for Equality: Nari Shakti in the Coast Guard

The Supreme Court of India criticized the Centre and the Indian Coast Guard for the existing gender divide in the offering commissions to women eligible

for the same, emphasizing the need for a fair treatment and gender equality in policy making. The concern arose from a plea raised by Priyanka Tyagi, a short service commission (SSC) officer, seeking permanent commission for eligible officers in the ICG.
https://indianexpress.com/article/india/women-permanent-commission-indian-coast-guardsupreme-court-chandrachud-9181965/

Supreme Court Dismisses Vote-Rigging Petition, Imposes Rs. 500,000 Fine

The Supreme Court of Pakistan has dismissed a petition alleging vote-rigging in the recent election, stressing that individuals convicted by a court-martial should not use military titles. The court fined the petitioner, a retired Brigadier, Rs. 500,000 for using his former military title despite his court-martial conviction years earlier.
https://www.hindustantimes.com/world-news/pak-polls-imran-khan-s-party-moves-tosupreme-court-against-alleged-results-rigging-101708701011094.html

March

Civilian Courts to take up Sexual Assault Cases in South Korea

Civilian Courts took up cases related to sex crimes and homicides in South Korea, owing to the revised Military Court Act. Also, the military courts were streamlined and the police and prosecutors reported directly to the Defence Minister and Service Chiefs, rather than being under the command of individual military leaders.
https://www.jurist.org/news/2021/09/south-korea-passes-legislation-to-hear-military-sexcrime-and-homicide-cases-in-civilian-courts/

New Initiatives take shape in Canada's legislative sphere

The power of Military Courts in Canada to investigate sexual offences was addressed with the tabling of a new bill, C-66 which sought to amend the National Defence Act, brought by Canada's Minister of National Defence,

Bill Blair. Though the bill was an initiative in the right direction, it also raised several pertinent questions regarding the core issue of the Canadian Forces' (CF) failure to respond effectively to sexual misconduct. https://www.cbc.ca/news/politics/canadian-armed-forces-sexual-misconduct-assault-1.7151080

April

Russian Court Sentences Meta Spokesman Andy Stone to Six Years in Prison

Meta spokesman, Andy Stone wa sentenced to six years in prison in absentia on terrorism charges by Moscow's Second Western Military Garrison Court. The decision came from Stone's March 2022 announcement that Meta would temporarily lift its ban on violent speech targeting "Russian invaders" in Ukraine. https://www.hindustantimes.com/world-news/us-news/who-is-metas-andy-stone-jailed-for-6years-in-absentia-by-russia-for-terrorism-101713844438525.html

May

Calls for Reform in Military Administrative Separation Processes

Concerns over the fairness of U.S. military administrative separations (AdSeps) persisted, with critics like Gen. James Mattis citing a lack of transparency and due process, especially for Other Than Honorable (OTH) cases. Used to bypass courts-martial, AdSeps impacted service members' futures. Proposals for reform included better training, stricter evidence rules, and limiting OTH discharges to courts-martial to ensure a fairer system. https://scholarship.law.tamu.edu/cgi/viewcontent.cgi?article=1327&context=lawreview

ADF Whistleblower David McBride Sentenced to Prison

Former Australian Defence Force legal officer David McBride was sentenced

to 5 years and 8 months for leaking secret documents on alleged war crimes in Afghanistan. Eligible for parole in 27 months, his case sparked criticism of Australia's whistleblowing laws. With international attention from BBC and CNN, his legal team planned to appeal, which was funded via social media campaigns.
https://globalmjreform.blogspot.com/2024/05/david-mcbride-adf-whistle-blower-pleads.html

Russia Faces Criticism for Violating the Law of War

Russia undermined international humanitarian law by prosecuting Ukrainian prisoners of war for lawful acts of combat. Recent trials, such as an 18-year sentence for a Ukrainian Azov Battalion member, drew criticism for lacking fair trial guarantees. Critics argued that these proceedings violate global norms amid Russia's ongoing aggression against Ukraine.
https://globalmjreform.blogspot.com/2024/05/russias-continued-assault-against-law.html

Inter-Services Organisations Act Implemented in India

The Government of India implemented the Inter-Services Organisations (Command, Control & Discipline) Act, 2023, which took effect on 10 May 2024. The Act addressed the need for streamlined discipline in units where Army, Navy, and Air Force personnel had served together. It clarified command and disciplinary powers for officers who had led mixed-service troops, overcoming the limitations of separate service Acts.

June

Chilean Military Justice Faces Scrutiny for Human Rights Violations

Rachel Blair's *Military Justice in Chile* (2023) exposed how military courts retain jurisdiction over cases of military harm to civilians, undermining fair trials, and urged for a stronger judicial collaboration to address impunity and human rights abuses in Latin America.

https://jsis.washington.edu/jsjournal/wp-content/uploads/sites/25/2023/11/Military-Justice-in-Chile-Exploring-its-Ongoing-Violation-of-the-American-Convention-on-Human-RightsBlair.pdf

July

Amnesty International Highlights Concerns Over Lebanon's Military Court

Amnesty International's Sahar Mandour reported on Lebanon's military court and the trial of Syrian refugee Bashar Abed Saud, who died in custody after alleged torture by State Security Agency members. She observed that the military court acts more as an internal disciplinary body than a platform for justice, especially as Bashar's family reportedly dropped charges under pressure., Mandour stressed the need to transfer torture cases to civilian courts to ensure impartiality and accountability.
https://www.amnesty.org/en/latest/campaigns/2024/07/inside-lebanons-military-court-noplace-for-civilians/

Iraqi Military Court Appeals: Legal Framework Explored

A study in the *Tikrit University Journal* for Rights by Dr. Baraa Munther Kamal and Yasser Raad Abdullah explored Iraq's military court appeal mechanisms, and distinguished between ordinary and extraordinary appeals, and highlighted how the Military Code of Criminal Procedure differs from general criminal procedure by addressing absentia judgments under trial rules rather than appeals.
https://www.iraqoaj.net/iasj/article/318141

Chile's Supreme Court Raises Concerns Over Military Justice Reform Bill

The Supreme Court of Chile raised concerns about a proposed amendment to the Code of Military Justice, questioning its consistency with efforts to restrict military court jurisdiction, and highlighted contradictions in the

status of conscripts, and further identified systemic inconsistencies that could delay military justice reform.
https://www.diarioconstitucional.cl/2024/07/22/corte-suprema-emite-informe-sobre-proyectode-ley-que-modifica-el-codigo-de-justicia-militar-para-excluir-del-conocimiento-de-lostribunales-militares-aquellas-causas-que-involucren-a-soldados-conscr/#goog_rewarded

August

CCJ Upholds Military Justice in Barbados, Criticizes Vagueness of Defence Act in Harewood Case

In *Barbados Defence vs Harewood*, the Caribbean Court of Justice ruled on July 26, 2024, that while Section 75 of the Barbados Defence Act is broad yet sufficiently clear in a military context, the charge against David Anthony Harewood lacked necessary details, emphasizing the need for clarity to meet constitutional standards of fairness and due process.
https://ccj.org/wp-content/uploads/2024/08/Media-Release-BDF-v-Harewood2.pdf

September

Delhi High Court Overturns BSF Trooper's Dismissal, Criticizes Summary Court Process

The Delhi High Court set aside the dismissal of a BSF trooper, ruling that the Summary Security Force Court's actions were illegal due to procedural lapses, and emphasized the need for proper training and adherence to legal guidelines to prevent miscarriages of justice in SSFC trials.
https://indianexpress.com/article/cities/chandigarh/delhi-hc-reinstates-jawan-bsf-fair-trials-9541381/

Controversy as Majority of Irish Soldiers with Criminal Convictions Remain in Service Despite Calls for Accountability

A *Sunday Times* article from September 8, 2024, revealed that despite calls for accountability, 54 of 79 Irish Defence Forces personnel with criminal convictions remain in service, including three soldiers convicted of assault, sparking renewed criticism despite
https://www.independent.ie/irish-news/fifty-four-soldiers-still-serving-despite-criminal-convictions/a911386123.html

October

Guyana's Lt. Col. Lloyd Souvenir Presides Over Barbados Court Martial

Lieutenant Colonel Lloyd Souvenir, Commandant of the Guyana National Reserve, presided over an Ordinary Court Martial in Barbados to try Sub Lieutenant Nakeida Gibson of the Barbados Defence Force on multiple charges, highlighting regional cooperation in military justice.
https://www.stabroeknews.com/2024/10/13/news/guyana/national-reserve-lt-col-headed-barbados-court-martial/

Mary J. L. Gleason Appointed Chief Justice of Court Martial Appeal Court of Canada

On October 15, 2024, the Canadian Prime Minister appointed the Honourable Mary J. L. Gleason as Chief Justice of the Court Martial Appeal Court of Canada, succeeding Acting Chief Justice Elizabeth A. Bennett, with her extensive experience in military justice appeals that marked a new chapter for the system.
https://www.pm.gc.ca/en/news/news-releases/2024/10/15/prime-minister-announces-appointment-new-chief-justice-court

November

Rare Russian Prosecution of Soldiers for War Crimes

In a rare move, Russia prosecuted two soldiers in a military court for murdering nine family members in occupied Ukraine, but under domestic criminal

charges rather than war crimes, raising concerns about judicial fairness and the broader impunity for war crimes in the conflict.
https://www.reuters.com/world/europe/russian-accused-war-crimes-ukraine-goes-trial-finland-2024-12-05/

Conscientious Objection in Wartime Ukraine

The Ukrainian Constitutional Court is considering limiting conscientious objection during wartime to balance constitutional rights with military needs, potentially restricting alternative service and recommending legislative amendments to address tensions between Article 35 and existing laws amid troop shortages.
https://wri-irg.org/en/story/2024/ukraine-about-300-criminal-cases-against-conscientious-objectors

December

Court Martial Appeal Court Rules Military Justice System Incompatible with Youth Criminal Justice Act in R vs J.L. Case

The Court Martial Appeal Court of Canada (CMAC) in R v J.L., 2024 CMAC 10, ruled that prosecuting young military members under the Code of Service Discipline (CSD) conflicts with the Youth Criminal Justice Act (YCJA), affirming their right to civilian youth justice protections and rejecting the notion that enlistment waives these rights.
https://www.law360.ca/ca/articles/2277598/military-court-explores-use-of-youth-justice-laws-for-young-service-members

R vs Kohlsmith, 2024 CMAC 8 and R vs Meeks, 2024 CMAC 9

In R vs Kohlsmith and *R vs Meeks,* the Court Martial Appeal Court of Canada upheld judicial consistency in military justice by ruling that exceptional circumstances justified trial delays beyond the *Jordan* ceiling in *Kohlsmith,* while in *Meeks,* it admitted new evidence of administrative release but maintained that detention could still be appropriate, ultimately suspending the sentence due to changed circumstances.

https://roryfowlerlaw.com/recent-activity-in-the-court-martial-appeal-court-of-canada/

Former Suriname President Dési Bouterse Reported Dead

Dési Bouterse, Suriname's controversial former president and fugitive from justice, has reportedly died, leaving behind a legacy marked by his unserved 20-year prison sentence for the 1982 "December murders," his two-term presidency (2010–2020), and ongoing legal controversies documented by *The New York Times* and Brig. Gen. (ret.) Jan Peter Spijk.
https://www.reuters.com/world/americas/suriname-ex-president-desi-bouterse-dead-79-foreign-minister-says-2024-12-25/

January 2025

Court Granted Stay in 9/11 Pretrial Agreements Case

The U.S. Court of Appeals for the D.C. Circuit granted an administrative stay in the *In re United States case.* The stay halted military commission proceedings on pretrial agreements for 9/11 defendants. The court allowed time for briefing and oral argument on the government's mandamus petition. A decision on the petition and stay motion remained pending.
https://indianexpress.com/article/world/biden-administration-temporarily-blocks-9-11-guilty-plea-for-khalid-sheikh-9770627/

Delhi High Court Ensured Parity in Punishment

In *Vikesh Kumar Singh & Anr. vs Director General, Central Industrial Security Force & Ors.*, the Delhi High Court ruled that Central Armed Police Forces (CAPF) members could not receive unequal punishments for the same offence. An Indo-Tibetan Border Police (ITBP) member was reprimanded, while Central Industrial Security Force (CISF) personnel were dismissed. The court emphasized proportionality in sentencing for those involved in the same incident.

https://www.livelaw.in/labour-service/doctrine-of-equality-punishments-different-forces-same-administrative-framework-delhi-hc-279380

The Military Jurisdiction Dispute

The Supreme Court of the Philippines addressed whether an officer could end military jurisdiction by resigning. The government argued that Senator Trillanes remained under court-martial jurisdiction despite his resignation. Officials claimed his amnesty was void, reverting his status to pre-amnesty conditions. The case tested the principle of continuing military jurisdiction.
https://lawphil.net/executive/proc/proc2018/pdf/proc_572_2018.pdf

The Supreme Court of Uganda Barred Court-Martial Trials for Civilians

The Supreme Court of Uganda ruled that civilians could not be tried by court-martial in *Attorney General vs Kabaziguruka* (2021). Chief Justice Owiny-Dollo recommended reforms, including limiting military court powers, integrating them with the High Court, and ensuring fair trials. The decision urged constitutional amendments and judicial oversight to uphold democratic standards.
https://www.hrw.org/news/2025/01/31/uganda-supreme-court-bans-military-trials-civilians

February 2025

Military Justice Reforms in Colombia

In 2025, Colombia's military justice system transitioned to an accusatory model, ensuring military personnel were tried with the same guarantees as in ordinary courts. This reform aligned with broader judicial changes, including the ongoing trial of Colonel Hernán Mejía Gutiérrez in the Special Jurisdiction for Peace (JEP) for his alleged role in 72 extrajudicial executions in the "false positives" scandal.
https://www.dcaf.ch/sites/default/files/publications/documents/MJ%2520Colombia%252011-01-11.pdf

Trial of Civilians in Egypt

Egyptian authorities tried five civilian fishermen in a military court for fishing in Lake Bardawil, a site placed under military jurisdiction in 2019. Amnesty International and the Sinai Foundation for Human Rights condemned the trial as a violation of international human rights obligations. Rights groups called for the charges to be dropped and for the men to be tried in an independent civilian court.
https://www.amnesty.org/en/latest/news/2025/02/egypt-military-trials-of-fishermen-an-affront-to-justice/

Manner of Discharge from Service Irrelevant in Considering Benefits to War Disabled Soldiers: Punjab & Haryana High Court (India)

The Punjab & Haryana High Court ruled that the manner of a war-disabled soldier's exit from service cannot determine eligibility for disability-related benefits. The court upheld a soldier's son's right to compassionate employment under Punjab's "honour and gratitude" scheme, rejecting the state's refusal based on technical grounds. Citing case law, the court deemed such denial discriminatory and ordered the benefits to be granted.
https://www.verdictum.in/court-updates/high-courts/punjab-and-haryana-high-court/surinder-pal-and-another-vs-state-of-punjab-and-others-2025phhc011643-claim-for-job-in-category-of-son-of-a-war-herobattle-casualty-personnel-allowed-1567701